2.–

The Prehistory of the Mind

Steven Mithen

The Prehistory of the Mind

The cognitive origins of art, religion and science

with 70 illustrations

 THAMES AND HUDSON

For my children Hannah, Nicholas and Heather

© 1996 Thames and Hudson Ltd, London

First published in hardcover in the United States of
America in 1996 by Thames and Hudson Inc.,
500 Fifth Avenue, New York, New York 10110

First paperback edition 1999

Library of Congress Catalog Card Number 96-60367
ISBN 0-500-28100-9

Printed and bound in Slovenia

Contents

Preface   7

1 Why ask an archaeologist about the human mind?   9

2 The drama of our past   17

3 The architecture of the modern mind   33

4 A new proposal for the mind's evolution   61

5 Apes, monkeys and the mind of the missing link   73

6 The mind of the first stone toolmaker   95

7 The multiple intelligences of the Early Human mind   115

8 Trying to think like a Neanderthal   147

9 The big bang of human culture: the origins of art and religion   151

10 So how did it happen?   185

11 The evolution of the mind   195

Epilogue: the origins of agriculture   217

Notes and further reading   227
Bibliography   267
Illustration credits   284
Index   285

Preface

IT TOOK MILLIONS of years for the human mind to evolve. It is the product of a long, gradual process with no predestined goal or direction. During the final 2.5 million years of this process, our ancestors left traces of their behaviour such as their stone tools, food debris and paintings on cave walls. They only left written records towards the very end of this period, starting a mere 5,000 years ago. Consequently to understand the evolution of the mind we must look at our *prehistory*, for it was during that time that the distinguishing features of the human mind arose, features such as language and an advanced intelligence. To gain an understanding of the mind leads on to an appreciation of what it means to be human. I hope, therefore, that *The Prehistory of the Mind* will be of interest not just to archaeologists and psychologists, but to any moderately inquisitive and reflective reader.

I have tried to write a book that makes the evidence from prehistory accessible to readers who may never previously have heard of an australopithecine or a handaxe. But this book also tries to put forward a new theory for the evolution of the mind. The academic audience who must judge this theory will need to see it supported at a level of detail that is perhaps tedious for the general reader. I cater for those scholars with extensive notes to provide additional support for claims made within the text. These will also be of value to students trying to get to grips with the complexities of the archaeological record and human evolution.

Although the evolution of the mind was a slow, gradual process, there were nevertheless key events which acted as turning points for how the mind evolved. Similarly the evolution of this book has been a gradual process, but one for which I can see three defining events. Without these it would either not have been written, or, like the mind, have remained in a rather primitive state. After having my initial interest in prehistoric cognition stimulated by reading the work of the American archaeologist Thomas Wynn, the first of these defining events was in 1988 while I was a Research Fellow at Trinity Hall in Cambridge. At lunch one day the Master of the college, Sir John Lyons, casually asked me whether I had ever read *The Modularity of Mind* by Jerry Fodor. I hadn't, but did so immediately. And thus an idea about the prehistory of the mind was sown within my mind, although it remained there with little growth for the following six years. Then – the second event – one evening in April 1994, after having left Cambridge and joined the staff at Reading University, I had dinner with Leda Cosmides, John Tooby and Michael Jochim in a beach restaurant in Santa Barbara, California. Leda and John bombarded me with their ideas about an evolutionary psychology, and gave me a list of books to read, each of which became critical to the development of my work. Finally, a few months later, I chatted with a colleague of mine, Mark Lake, as we ate at a motorway service station somewhere on the M6 in the middle of the night while driving to my excavations in Scotland. We talked about archaeology, the mind and computers and I realized that it was time to get the prehistory of the mind out of my mind and on to paper.

The opportunity to do so was granted by my colleagues in the Department of Archaeology at Reading University who allowed me to take a period of research leave, between January and March 1995, during which the first draft of this book was written. I am grateful to my Reading colleagues not only for this period of leave but for having provided such a pleasant and stimulating environment for developing my version of cognitive archaeology since joining them in 1992. Richard Bradley, Dick Byrne and Clive Gamble kindly read that draft and provided many perceptive criticisms and words of encouragement.

While re-writing the book many people provided me with new references, their unpublished papers and simply their time – often no more than a few words in conversation which, unknown to them, were of such value to me. Others have been most helpful in my research on ancient minds during my time in Cambridge and Reading. I would particularly like to thank: Leslie Aiello, Ofer Bar-Yosef, Pascal Boyer, Bob Chapman, Michael Corballis, Leda Cosmides, Nyree Finlay, Bill Finlayson, Robert Foley, Chris Knight, Alexander Marshack, Gilbert Marshall, Paul Mellars, Richard Mithen, Steven Pinker, Camilla Powers, Colin Renfrew, Chris Scarre, Rick Schulting, John Shea, Stephen Shennan, James Steele, Chris Stringer and Thomas Wynn. Throughout that time, Mark Lake has been a sounding board for my ideas and to him I am particularly grateful. I also owe a debt to the editorial staff at Thames and Hudson for their help during the final stages of writing. And I would like to thank Margaret Mathews and Aaron Watson for the line drawings.

Most of the writing for this book was undertaken on the dining room table at home in the midst of the hurly-burly of my family life. Consequently my biggest thanks must go to my wife, Sue, and to my children for suffering the piles of books and my constant tapping at the wordprocessor. It is indeed to my children, Hannah, Nicholas and Heather, that I dedicate this book as thanks for having such lively and thoroughly modern young minds.

1 Why ask an archaeologist about the human mind?

THE HUMAN MIND is intangible, an abstraction. In spite of more than a century of systematic study by psychologists and philosophers, it eludes definition and adequate description, let alone explanation. Stone tools, pieces of broken bone and carved figurines – the stuff of archaeology – have other qualities. They can be weighed and measured, illustrated in books and put on display. They are nothing at all like the mind – except for the profound sense of mystery that surrounds them. So why ask an archaeologist about the human mind?

People are intrigued by various aspects of the mind. What is intelligence? What is consciousness? How can the human mind create art, undertake science and believe in religious ideologies when not a trace of these are found in the chimpanzee, our closest living relative?[1] Again one might wonder: how can archaeologists with their ancient artifacts help answer such questions?

Rather than approach an archaeologist, one is likely to turn to a psychologist: it is the psychologist who studies the mind, often by using ingenious laboratory experiments. Psychologists explore the mental development of children, malfunctions of the brain and whether chimpanzees can acquire language. From this research they may offer answers to the types of questions posed above.

Or perhaps one would try a philosopher. The nature of the mind and its relation to the brain – the mind-body problem – has been a persistent issue in philosophy for over a century. Some philosophers have looked for empirical evidence, others have simply brought their considerable intellects to bear on the subject.

There are other specialists one might approach. Perhaps a neurologist who can look at what actually goes on in the brain; perhaps a primatologist with specialized knowledge of chimpanzees in natural, rather than laboratory, settings; perhaps a biological anthropologist who examines fossils to study how the brain has changed in size and shape during the course of human evolution, or a social anthropologist who studies the nature of thought in non-Western societies; perhaps a computer scientist who creates artificial intelligence?

The list of whom we might turn to for answers about the human mind is indeed long. Maybe it should be longer still with the addition of artists, athletes and actors – those who use their minds for particularly impressive feats of concentration and imagination. Of course the sensible answer is that we should ask all of these: almost all disciplines can contribute towards an understanding of the human mind.

But what has archaeology got to offer? More specifically, the archaeology to be considered in this book, that of prehistoric hunter-gatherers? This stretches from the first appearance of stone tools 2.5 million years ago to the appearance of agriculture after 10,000 years ago. The answer is quite simple: we can only ever understand the present by knowing the past. Archaeology may therefore not only be able to contribute, it may hold the key to an understanding of the modern mind.

Creationists believe that the mind sprang suddenly into existence fully formed. In their view it is a product of divine creation.[2] They are wrong: the mind has a long evolutionary history and can be explained without recourse to supernatural powers. The importance of understanding the evolutionary history of the mind is one reason why many psychologists study the chimpanzee, our closest living relative. Numerous studies have compared the chimpanzee and human mind, notably with regard to linguistic capacities. Yet such studies have ultimately proved unsatisfactory, because while the chimpanzee is indeed our closest living relative, it is not very close at all. We shared a common ancestor about 6 million years ago. After that date the evolutionary lineages leading to modern apes and humans diverged. A full 6 million years of evolution therefore separates the minds of modern humans and chimpanzees.

It is that period of 6 million years which holds the key to an understanding of the modern mind. We need to look at the minds of our many ancestors[3] during that time, including the 4.5-million-year-old ancestor known as *Australopithecus ramidus*; the 2-million-year-old *Homo habilis*, among the first of our ancestors to make stone tools; *Homo erectus*, the first to leave Africa 1.8 million years ago; *Homo neanderthalensis* (the Neanderthals), who survived in Europe until less than 30,000 years ago; and finally our own species, *Homo sapiens sapiens*, appearing 100,000 years ago. Such ancestors are known only through their fossil remains and the material residues of their behaviour – those stone tools, broken bones and carved figurines.

The most ambitious attempt so far to reconstruct the minds of these ancestors has been by the psychologist Merlin Donald. In his book *The Origins of the Modern Mind* (1991), he drew substantially on archaeological data to propose a scenario for the evolution of the mind. I want to follow in Donald's footsteps, although I believe he made some fundamental errors in his work – otherwise there would be no need for this book.[4] But I want to turn the tables on Donald's approach. Rather than being a psychologist drawing on archaeological data, I am writing as an archaeologist who wishes to draw on ideas from psychology. Rather than having archaeology play the supporting role, I want it to set the agenda for understanding the modern mind. So here I provide *The Prehistory of the Mind*.

The last two decades have seen a remarkable advance in our understanding of the behaviour and evolutionary relationships of our ancestors. Indeed many archaeologists now feel confident that the time is ripe to move beyond asking questions about how these ancestors looked and behaved, to asking what was going on within their minds. It is time for a 'cognitive archaeology'.[5]

The need for this is particularly evident from the pattern of brain expansion during the course of human evolution and its relationship – or the lack of one – to changes in past behaviour. It becomes clear that there is no simple relationship between brain size, 'intelligence' and behaviour. In Figure 1 I depict the increase in brain size during the last 4 million years of evolution across a succession of human ancestors and relatives whom I will introduce more fully in the next chapter. But here just consider the manner in which brain size increased. We can see that there were two major spurts of brain enlargement, one between 2.0 and 1.5 million years ago, which seems to be related to the appearance of *Homo habilis*, and a less pronounced one between 500,000 and 200,000 years ago. Archaeologists tentatively link the first spurt to the development of toolmaking, but can find no major change in the nature of the archaeological record correlating with the second period of rapid brain expansion. Our ancestors continued the same basic hunting and gathering lifestyle, with the same limited range of stone and wooden tools.

The two really dramatic transformations in human behaviour occurred long after the modern size of the brain had evolved. They are both associated exclusively with *Homo sapiens sapiens*. The first was a cultural explosion between 60,000 and 30,000 years ago, when the first art, complex technology and religion appeared. The second was the rise of farming 10,000 years ago, when people for the first time began to plant crops and domesticate animals. Although the Neanderthals (200,000–30,000 years ago) had brains as large as ours today, their culture remained extremely limited – no art, no complex technology and most probably no religious behaviour. Now big brains are expensive organs, requiring a lot of energy to maintain – 22 times as much as an equivalent amount of muscle requires when at rest.[6] So here we find a dilemma – what was all the new brain processing power before the 'cultural explosion' being used for? What was happening to the mind as brain size

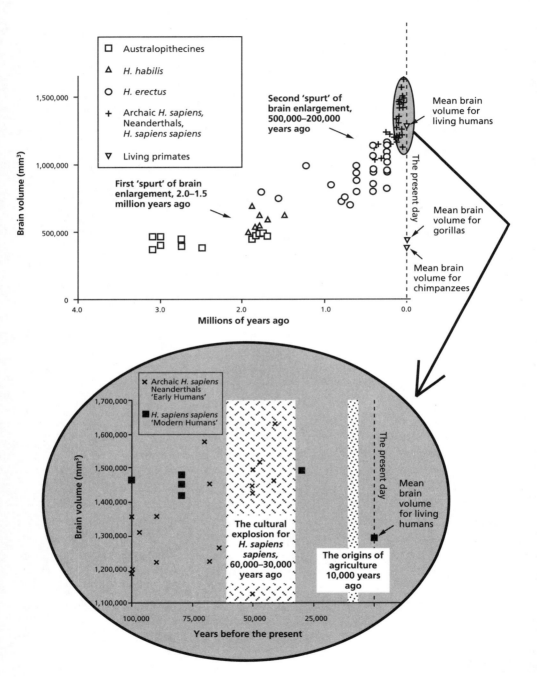

1 The increase in brain volume during the last 4 million years of human evolution. Each symbol denotes a specific skull from which brain volume has been estimated by Aiello & Dunbar (1993). Upper graph based on figure in Aiello (1996a) who discusses the evidence for the two bursts of brain enlargement separated by over a million years of stasis.

expanded in the two major spurts during human evolution? And what happened to it between these spurts, and to the mind of *Homo sapiens sapiens* to cause the cultural explosion of 60,000–30,000 years ago? When did language and consciousness first arise? When did a modern form of intelligence arise – what indeed *is* this intelligence and the nature of the intelligence that preceded it? What are the relationships of these, if any, to the size of the brain? To answer such questions we must reconstruct prehistoric minds from the evidence I introduce in Chapter 2.

We will only be able to make sense of the evidence, however, if we have some expectations about the types of minds that our ancestors may have possessed. Otherwise we will simply be faced with a bewildering mass of data, not knowing which aspects of it may be significant for our study. It is the task of Chapter 3 to begin to set up these expectations. I am able to do so because psychologists have realized that we can understand the modern mind only by understanding the process of evolution. Consequently while archaeologists have been developing a 'cognitive archaeology', psychologists have been developing an 'evolutionary psychology'. These two new sub-disciplines are in great need of each other. Cognitive archaeology cannot develop unless archaeologists take note of current thinking within psychology; evolutionary psychologists will not succeed unless they pay attention to the behaviour of our human ancestors as reconstructed by archaeologists. It is my task within this book to perform a union, the offspring of which will be a more profound understanding of the mind than either archaeology or psychology alone can achieve.

Chapter 3 will be concerned with outlining the developments in psychology that need to be brought into contact with the knowledge we have of past behaviour. One of the fundamental arguments of the new evolutionary psychology is that it is wrong to view the mind as a general-purpose learning mechanism, like some sort of powerful computer. This idea is dominant within the social sciences, and is indeed a 'common-sense' view of the mind. The evolutionary psychologists argue that we should replace it with a view of the mind as a series of specialized 'modules', or 'cognitive domains' or 'intelligences', each of which is dedicated to some specific type of behaviour[7] (see Box p. 14) – such as modules for acquiring language, or tool-using abilities, or engaging in social interaction. As I will explain in the following chapters, this new view of the mind does indeed hold a key to unlocking the nature of both the prehistoric and modern mind – although in a very different way from that in which the evolutionary psychologists currently believe. The contrast between a 'generalized' and 'specialized' mentality will emerge as a critical theme throughout this book.

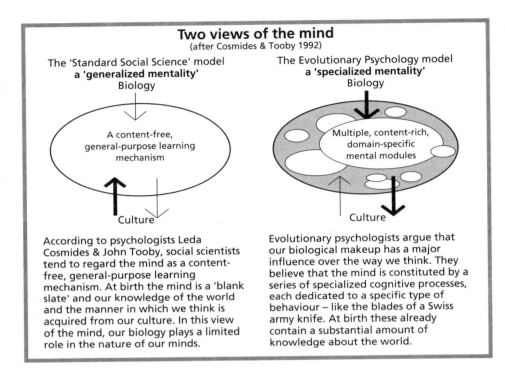

Two views of the mind
(after Cosmides & Tooby 1992)

The 'Standard Social Science' model
a 'generalized mentality'
Biology

A content-free, general-purpose learning mechanism

Culture

The Evolutionary Psychology model
a 'specialized mentality'
Biology

Multiple, content-rich, domain-specific mental modules

Culture

According to psychologists Leda Cosmides & John Tooby, social scientists tend to regard the mind as a content-free, general-purpose learning mechanism. At birth the mind is a 'blank slate' and our knowledge of the world and the manner in which we think is acquired from our culture. In this view of the mind, our biology plays a limited role in the nature of our minds.

Evolutionary psychologists argue that our biological makeup has a major influence over the way we think. They believe that the mind is constituted by a series of specialized cognitive processes, each dedicated to a specific type of behaviour – like the blades of a Swiss army knife. At birth these already contain a substantial amount of knowledge about the world.

As we look at the new ideas of evolutionary psychology, we will find another dilemma that requires resolution. If the mind is indeed constituted by numerous specialized processes each dedicated to a specific type of behaviour, how can we possibly account for one of the most remarkable features of the modern mind: a capacity for an almost unlimited imagination? How can this arise from a series of isolated cognitive processes each dedicated to a specific type of behaviour? The answer to this dilemma can only be found by exposing the prehistory of the mind.

In Chapter 4 I will draw upon the ideas of evolutionary psychology, supplemented by ideas from other fields, such as child development and social anthropology, to suggest an evolutionary scenario for the mind. This will provide the template for the reconstruction of prehistoric minds in the following chapters. In Chapter 5 we will begin that task by tackling the mind of the common ancestor to apes and humans who lived 6 million years ago. We have no fossil traces or archaeological remains of that ancestor and will consequently make an assumption that the mind of this ancestor was not fundamentally different from that of the chimpanzee today. We will ask questions such as what do the tool-using and foraging abilities of chimpanzees tell us about the chimpanzee mind – and hopefully that of the 6-million-year-old common ancestor?

In the next two chapters we will reconstruct the minds of our human ancestors prior to the appearance of *Homo sapiens sapiens* – our own species – in the fossil record 100,000 years ago. In Chapter 6 we will focus on the first member of the *Homo* lineage, *Homo habilis*. As well as being the first identifiable ancestor to make stone tools, *Homo habilis* was also the first to have a diet with a relatively large quantity of meat. What do these new types of behaviour tell us about the *Homo habilis* mind? Did *Homo habilis* have a capacity for language? Did this species possess a conscious awareness about the world similar to ours today?

In Chapter 7 we will look at a group of human ancestors and relatives whom I will refer to as the 'Early Humans'. The best known of these are *Homo erectus* and the Neanderthals. The Early Humans existed between 1.8 million years ago and a mere 30,000 years ago. It will be when reconstructing the Early Human mind that we face the problem of explaining what the new brain processing power that appeared after 500,000 years ago was doing, given that we see limited change in Early Human behaviour during this period – which is why we can group all these ancestors together as Early Humans.

The Neanderthals provide us with our greatest challenge, a challenge I take up when I ask in Chapter 8 what it may have been like to have the mind of a Neanderthal. Popularly thought to be rather lacking in intelligence, we will see how in many ways Neanderthals were very similar to us, such as in terms of their brain size and their level of technical skill as evident from their stone tools. Yet in other ways they were very different, such as in their lack of art, ritual and tools made from anything but stone and wood. This apparent contradiction in Neanderthal behaviour – so modern in some ways, so primitive in others – provides vital evidence for reconstructing the nature of the Neanderthal mind. By doing so we will gain a clue as to the fundamental feature of the modern mind – a clue that remains hidden from psychologists, philosophers and indeed any scientist who ignores the evidence from prehistory.

The climax of our enquiry then comes with Chapter 9, 'The big bang of human culture'. We will see that when the first modern humans, *Homo sapiens sapiens*, appeared 100,000 years ago they seem to have behaved in essentially the same manner as Early Humans, such as Neanderthals. And then, between 60,000 and 30,000 years ago – with no apparent change in brain size, shape or anatomy in general – the cultural explosion occurred. This resulted in such a fundamental change in lifestyles that there can be little doubt that it derived from a major change in the nature of the mind. I will argue that this change was nothing less than the emergence of the modern mind – the same mentality that you and I possess today. Chapter 9 will be concerned with describing the new mentality, while Chapter 10 will then suggest how it arose.

In Chapter 11, my final chapter, I will move from considering the pre-history of the mind, to the evolution of the mind. Whereas the course of the book tracks how the mind has changed during the last 6 million years, in that final chapter I will adopt a truly long-term perspective by beginning 65 million years ago with the very first primates. By doing so we will be able to appreciate how the modern mind is the product of a long, slow evolutionary process – although a process that has a remarkable and hitherto unrecognized pattern.

I complete my book with an epilogue which addresses the origins of agriculture 10,000 years ago. This event transformed human lifestyles and created new developmental contexts for young minds – contexts within sedentary farming societies rather than a mobile hunting and gathering existence. Yet I will show in the course of this book that the most fundamental events which defined the nature of the modern mind occurred much earlier in prehistory. The origins of agriculture are indeed no more than an epilogue to the prehistory of the mind.

In this book I intend to specify the 'whats', 'whens' and 'whys' for the evolution of the mind. While following its course I will be searching for – and will find – the cognitive foundations of art, religion and science. By exposing these foundations it will become clear how we share common roots with other species – even though the mind of our closest living relative, the chimpanzee, is indeed so fundamentally different from our own. I will thus provide the hard evidence to reject the creationist claim that the mind is a product of supernatural intervention. At the end of this prehistory I hope I will have furthered an understanding of how the mind works. And I also hope to have demonstrated why one should ask an archaeologist about the human mind.

2 The drama of our past

TO FIND THE ORIGINS of the modern mind we must look into the darkness of prehistory. We must go back to a time before the first civilizations, which began a mere 5,000 years ago. We must go back further than the first domestication of plants and animals 10,000 years ago. We must flash past the first appearance of art 30,000 years ago and even that of our own species, *Homo sapiens sapiens*, in the fossil record 100,000 years ago. Not even 2.5 million years ago, the time when the very first stone tools appear, is adequate. Our starting point for the prehistory of the mind can be no less than 6 million years ago. For at that time there lived an ape whose descendants evolved in two separate directions. One path led to the modern apes, the chimpanzees and gorillas, and the other to modern humans. And consequently, this ancient ape is referred to as the common ancestor.

Not only the common ancestor but also the missing link. It is this species that links us to the living apes, and it remains missing from the fossil record. We have not a single fossil fragment. But we cannot doubt that the 'missing link' existed. Scientists are hard on its heels. By measuring the differences in the genetic makeup of modern apes and humans, and by estimating the rate at which genetic mutations arise, they have tracked it down to living about 6 million years ago. And we can be confident that it lived in Africa, for – just as Darwin declared – Africa does indeed seem to have been the cradle of humankind. No other continent has yielded the requisite ancestral human fossils.

Six million years is a vast span of time. In order to begin to comprehend it, to grasp its salient pattern of events, it helps to think of those events as constituting a play, the drama of our past. A very special play, for no one wrote the script: 6 million years of improvisation. Our ancestors are the actors, their tools are the props and the incessant changes of environment through which they lived the changes of scenery. But as a play do not think of it as a 'whodunit', in which action and ending are all. For we already know the ending – we are living it. The Neanderthals and the other Stone Age actors all died out leaving just one single survivor, *Homo sapiens sapiens*.

Think of our past not as a novel by Agatha Christie or Jeffrey Archer but as a Shakespearean drama. Think of it as a story in which prior knowledge of the dénouement enriches enjoyment and understanding. For we need not worry about *what* is going to happen. Instead we can be concerned with *why* things happen – the mental states of the actors. We don't watch Macbeth to find out whether or not he will murder Duncan, nor do we have a sweepstake on whether Hamlet will live or die. Similarly, in this book our interest is not so much with what our Stone Age ancestors did or did not do, as with what their actions tell us about their mentality.

So look upon this short chapter as the play's programme notes. Different producers – the writers of archaeological textbooks – stress different versions even of the main events, which is why a few comments on the alternative versions have been added. I have divided the drama into four acts, and provide below a brief summary of the action, as well as 'biographical details' for the actors, and notes about the props and scene changes. These may be read either now or used as a source of reference later in the book. The changes of lighting I refer to reflect the variable quality and quantity of our knowledge about each of these acts of prehistory. And when I refer to 'he' or 'his', and 'she' or 'her' I am adopting these on an arbitrary basis simply to avoid the inelegant he/she and his/her. There is no implication that either of the sexes was necessarily more important than the other at any time in our past.

Act 1
6–4.5 million years ago
A long scene of little action.
To be watched virtually in total darkness.

Our play opens somewhere in Africa around 6 million years ago and has a single actor, the ancestral ape. This actor has not one but two stage names, common ancestor and missing link. Until some fossil traces are found, its true identity – a scientific name – must remain a blank. As we know nothing about the environment in which this ancestral ape lived, and as it appears to have left no stone tools, the stage for this whole act remains bare and silent. Some producers would be inclined to add trees and provide a set of simple tools, much like the termite sticks used by chimpanzees today. But this risks over-interpretation. We must leave the stage bare and have no action throughout this act. We are indeed virtually in total darkness.

Act 2
4.5–1.8 million years ago
This has two scenes which together last just over 2.5 million years.
They should be lit only by a flickering candle.

Act 2 takes place in Africa, initially just in regions such as Chad, Kenya, Ethiopia and Tanzania, and then the stage enlarges to encompass South Africa for the second scene. The act begins 4.5 million years ago with the appearance of *Australopithecus ramidus*, an actor only made known to the world in 1994. He is the first of the so-called australopithecines (literally 'southern apes'). After about 300,000 years a second player appears, *A. anamensis* – an even more recent arrival, having been found in 1995. Both of these actors are living in wooded environments and are principally vegetarian. By 3.5 million years they have both departed stage left and been replaced by a performer so famous that she has been given a stage name, Lucy (because her discoverer happened to be listening at the time to the Beatles' song, 'Lucy in the Sky with Diamonds'). Her true identity is *Australopithecus afarensis*. It seems most likely that she is descended from *A. ramidus*, but she may well have evolved from *A. anamensis*, or someone else altogether. Lucy is such an impressive character, adept at both walking upright on two legs and climbing trees, that the lack of props – tools – is hardly noticeable. She leaves the stage after just 0.5 million years and the play enters another period of silence until the second scene begins at 2.5 million years ago. But right at the very end of the first scene, we see some pieces of stone scattered on the stage. These seem little different from naturally cracked pieces of rock, but in fact they are the first props of the play. Unfortunately we cannot see the actor who made them.

Scene 2 opens at 2.5 million years ago with a rush of actors on to the stage. Most of these look similar to those of Scene 1, although they come in a variety of shapes and sizes. These are more australopithecines: they are Lucy's children. In fact one of these, which has a noticeably light build and is referred to as a gracile australopithecine, is very similar to Lucy, although we see him in South rather than East Africa. This is *A. africanus*, who behaves rather like a modern baboon, although he spends more time on two legs. The other australopithecines are physically much more robust, with representatives in both East and South Africa. These remind us of gorillas rather than baboons.

By 2 million years ago, after *A. africanus* has disappeared, a new group of actors appear who are big headed and seem rather precocious. Indeed they are the first members of the *Homo* lineage, and have brains 1.5 times larger than the australopithecines. But, as with the australopithecines, they show considerable variability in size and shape. Some commentators discern just a single actor, *Homo habilis*, but it is likely that three are present – *Homo habilis*, *Homo rudolfensis* and *Homo ergaster*. Nevertheless, because they are so difficult to differentiate, we will simply refer to them collectively as *Homo habilis*.

Homo habilis is definitely carrying tools, stone artifacts described as the Oldowan industry. Perhaps the robust australopithecines are as well, it is hard to tell. The anatomy of their hands would certainly allow them to do so. We can see *Homo habilis* butchering animals with his tools, but we cannot be confident as to whether the carcasses had been hunted or just scavenged from the kills of lions and leopards. As the scene comes to an end, the behaviour of *Homo habilis* and his robust australopithecine cousins appears to be diverging markedly, with the first becoming more proficient in making tools and including more meat in his diet, while the australopithecines seem to be chewing their way to an even more robust morphology.

Act 3
1.8 million–100,000 years ago
Two scenes, which have an exciting start at around 1.8–1.5 million years ago, but which lapse into utter tedium. The lighting is still poor, although it improves slightly for the second scene.

Act 3 opens with a grand announcement: 'The Pleistocene begins'. The ice sheets start to form in high latitudes. On to our stage at 1.8 million years ago strides a new figure, *Homo erectus*. She is descended from *Homo habilis* (or maybe one of the other types of *Homo*), who now leaves the action, and is taller and larger-brained. The robust australopithecines hang around in the shadows until 1 million years ago, but take no part in the events of this act. The astonishing thing about the appearance of *Homo erectus* is that her arrival seems to be practically simultaneous in three parts of the world, East Africa, China and Java – and consequently the stage has now had to expand to include the Near East, Eastern and Southeast Asia. Gradually we see *Homo erectus*, or her discarded tools, in all these areas. But it is difficult to tell exactly when she arrived in particular places and quite what she is doing.

After more than a million years of *Homo erectus* – during which there appears to have been no further expansion of the brain – we begin to see some new performers on the stage. As with the earliest *Homo*, it is unclear how many species we actually have. *Homo erectus* continues living in East Asia until a mere 300,000 years ago, but elsewhere in Asia and in Africa we see actors with more rounded skulls who are rather awkwardly referred to as archaic *Homo sapiens*. These are likely to be descended from *Homo erectus* in their respective continents and mark a return to a period of increasing brain size. By 500,000 years ago, the stage has become further enlarged to include Europe. The actor here is called *Homo heidelbergensis*, another descendent of *Homo erectus* who seems to have a particularly large physique.

While the props of Act 2 continue to be used throughout this act, some rather more impressive ones appear. Most notable are symmetrical pear-shaped stone tools called handaxes. Soon after these have first appeared in East Africa, at around 1.4 million years ago, they become pervasive in almost all parts of the world except for Southeast Asia, where no tools are discernible at all – some commentators think that they are made here from perishable bamboo.

The second scene of this act, beginning around 200,000 years ago, is traditionally referred to by archaeologists as the 'Middle Palaeolithic', distinguishing it from the 'Lower Palaeolithic' of the preceding scene. But the boundary between these is so blurred that this distinction is gradually being phased out. Yet it is clear that by this date there have been some significant changes in the props being used by the actors. These have become rather more diverse, and handaxes have become less prominent. New tools include those made with a new technique called the Levallois method which produces carefully shaped flakes and points of stone. Indeed, for the first time it looks as though performers in different parts of the stage are each carrying a different range of tools. In Africa alone we see a predominance of Levallois flakes in the north, heavy-duty stone 'picks' in sub-Saharan regions, and long thin flakes of stone in the south.

By 150,000 years ago a new actor has appeared in Europe and the Near East, *Homo neanderthalensis*, popularly known as Neanderthal man. He has a propensity to use tools made from the Levallois technique and can be seen to hunt large game. Like the other characters of this act, the Neanderthals are having to cope with frequent and dramatic changes of scenery: this is the period of the ice ages, and we watch ice sheets repeatedly advance and then retreat across Europe, and with them a change in vegetation from tundra to forest. Yet even with such changes, the action seems rather monotonous. Indeed one distinguished commentator on Acts 2 and 3, the archaeologist Glynn Isaac, described how 'for almost a million years, toolkits tended to involve the same essential ingredients seemingly being shuffled in restless, minor, directionless changes'. While some of these tools seem to be very finely crafted, they are all made of either stone or wood. Although unmodified pieces of bone and antler are used, no carving of these materials takes place.

The curtain falls on another long act. It has lasted more than 1.5 million years, and although much of the Old World has now become the stage, the props have become more diverse, brain size has reached its modern dimensions and a range of new actors have appeared, one has nevertheless to describe it as tedious stuff. We have now been watching this play for a fraction under 6 million years, but there is still nothing that we can call art, religion or science.

Act 4
100,000 years ago–present day
A much shorter act, into which are squeezed three scenes packed with more dramatic action than in all the rest of the play.

Scene 1 of Act 4 covers the period from 100,000 to around 60,000 years ago, although as we will see the boundary between Scenes 1 and 2 is rather blurred. But the start is clear cut: a new figure enters – our own species, *Homo sapiens sapiens*. He is first seen in South Africa and the Near East and joins a cast that continues to include the Neanderthals and archaic *Homo sapiens*. Perhaps surprisingly there is no major change in the props as a whole at this time: our new actor continues making the same range of stone tools as his forebears of the final scene of Act 3. Indeed in practically all respects his behaviour is no different from theirs. But there are hints of something new. In the Near East we see *Homo sapiens sapiens* not only burying their dead within pits – as indeed are the Neanderthals – but they are placing parts of animal carcasses on to the bodies seemingly as grave goods. In South Africa they are using lumps of red ochre, although it is unclear what they are doing with these, and are grinding pieces of bone to make harpoons. These are the very first tools made from materials other than wood or stone.

Scene 2 of this final act begins at around 60,000 years ago with a remarkable event: in Southeast Asia *Homo sapiens sapiens* builds boats and then makes the very first crossing to Australia. Quite soon we see new things happening in the Near East. Instead of flakes being produced using the Levallois method, long thin slivers of flint are removed that look like, and indeed are called, blades. And then quite suddenly – at around 40,000 years ago – the play becomes transformed in Europe, and in Africa. The props have come to dominate the action. To mark such dramatic behavioural change archaeologists use these props to define the start of a new period of our past, known as the Upper Palaeolithic in Europe and Late Stone Age in Africa. A similar transformation also occurs in Asia, but as we can only dimly make out that region, it is unclear whether this occurs at the same time as in Europe and Africa, or later, perhaps around 20,000 years ago.

In place of the small range of stone tools, the props are now diverse and made from a whole host of new materials, including bone and ivory. The actors are building the scenery themselves – constructing dwellings and painting the walls. Some sit carving animal and human figures from stone and ivory, others are sewing clothes with bone needles. And on their bodies they wear beads and pendants – whether those bodies are living or deceased. Who are the actors? Well, *Homo sapiens sapiens* is clearly setting the pace. We saw how she makes the sea crossing to Australia in the very first few moments of this scene, and then enters Europe 40,000 years ago. For about 10,000 years after that the Neanderthals of Europe may be trying to mimic the new types of blade tools that *Homo sapiens sapiens* is making and the necklaces of beads she is wearing. But the Neanderthals soon fade away, as have done all the other actors in the play. *Homo sapiens sapiens* is now left alone on the world stage.

The pace of the action slowly accelerates. Europe is ablaze with the colour of cave art between 30,000 and 12,000 years ago, even though the landscapes have become deeply frozen in the midst of the last ice age. As the ice sheets begin to retreat the stage becomes yet larger, with the addition of North and South America. The scenery shows dramatic fluctuations from periods of warm/wet climate to cold/dry climate as the ice age comes to an end, signing off with a period of rapid global warming at 10,000 years ago. This marks the end of the Pleistocene, when the actor is ushered into the warm world of the Holocene and the final scene of the play.

As soon as the third scene of Act 4 begins, we see people in the Near East planting crops, and then domesticating animals. Events now flash past at bewildering speed. People create towns, and then cities. A succession of empires rise and fall and the props become ever more dominant, diverse and complex: in no more than an instant carts have become cars and writing tablets word processors. After almost 6 million years of relative inaction, we find it difficult to make sense of this final, hectic scene.

The actors...

A. ramidus and
A. anamensis

A. ramidus is the oldest known human ancestor, dating to 4.5 million years ago. It is defined by 17 fossil specimens found in the Middle Awash area of Ethiopia in 1994, which display more ape-like features than any other human ancestor. The body of *A. ramidus* may have been similar to that of a chimpanzee. It has been suggested that these fossils should in fact be placed within a new genus, *Ardipithecus*. The abundance of fossil wood, seeds and monkeys from the sediments in which the fossils were found suggests that *A. ramidus* lived in a forested environment.

A. anamensis is defined by nine fossil specimens from Kanapoi, Kenya, which were discovered in 1995. This species appears to have lived between 4.2 and 3.9 million years ago and is also thought to have occupied wooded or bushland habitats. It appears to have been rather larger than *A. ramidus*, but the absence of postcranial skeletal fragments makes a comparison between the two species difficult. They are likely to have overlapped in date and their relationship with *A. afarensis* remains unclear.

ACT 2

Gracile australopithecines
A. afarensis and
A. africanus

These two species are jointly referred to as the 'gracile australopithecines' and lived between 4 and 2.5 million years ago. *A. afarensis* is best known from the nearly half complete fossil skeleton nicknamed 'Lucy'. This was found in the Hadar area of Ethiopia, where numerous other specimens of *A. afarensis* have also been recovered. *A. afarensis* is likely to have been 1–1.5 m (3ft 3 in–5 ft) tall and weighed 30–75 kg (66–165 lb), with a brain size of 400–500 cc. It had a light build with long arms relative to its legs and curved fingers and toes. These features suggest that *A. afarensis* may have been neither fully bipedal, nor fully arboreal. A trail of footprints dating to 3.5 million years ago found at Laetoli, Tanzania, are likely to have been made by *A. afarensis*.

The fossils of *A. africanus* are found in southern Africa. This species was about the same size as *A. afarensis* and had the same brain capacity. It appears to have been adapted for bipedal locomotion. Contrasts are found in the shape of the skull, with that of *A. africanus* having a higher forehead and less prominent brow ridges. With regard to dentition, *A. africanus* had smaller incisor-like canines and larger molars than *A. afarensis*.

ACT 2

Robust australopithecines
P. boisei and **P. robustus**

The australopithecines which evolved particularly robust features have been placed into a separate genus named *Paranthropus*. In southern Africa these are referred to as *P. robustus* and weighed between 40 and 80 kg (90 and 175 lb). This suggests that like modern gorillas the males were considerably larger than the females. The East African form, *P. boisei,* had an even greater range of size, and may have been a little taller at 1.4 m (4 ft 6 in).

The anatomical features of the robust australopithecines indicate a diet involving the processing of much plant food and the generation of considerable force between the teeth. The most notable features are the thick lower jaws, the very large molars and the sagittal crest of bone on the cranium which provided the attachment for powerful chewing muscles. After having appeared in the fossil record 2.5 million years ago, *Paranthropus* species survived until 1 million years ago.

ACT 2

The earliest *Homo*
H. habilis, H. rudolfensis
and **H. ergaster**

At around 2 million years ago, new types of fossils appear which have been assigned to the genus *Homo*. These show considerable variation in size and form and consequently are likely to represent several species. They are all characterized by a larger brain size than the australopithecines, reaching between 500 and 800 cc. The most important localities for these finds are Olduvai Gorge, Tanzania, and Koobi Fora, Kenya, where the best-preserved specimen of *H. habilis,* KNM-ER 1470, was recovered. *H. habilis* appears to have had a body that was more australopithecine in character but a human-like face and dentition, while *H. rudolfensis* had a human-like body but retained facial and dental features of the australopithecines. By 1.6 million years ago the fossils of these early *Homo* species are no longer found, appearing to have been replaced by *H. erectus,* which probably evolved from a further type of early *Homo*, *H. ergaster*.

ACT 2

H. erectus

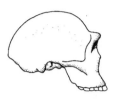

The first fossils of *H. erectus* are found in the Koobi Fora region of Africa and in Java at 1.8 million years ago. *H. erectus* is thought to have evolved from early *Homo* in Africa and to have then rapidly dispersed into Asia. A mandible of *H. erectus* has also been recovered from Dmanisi in Georgia, where it is thought to date to *c.* 1.4 million years old. *H. erectus* had a larger brain size than the earliest *Homo*, 750–1250 cc, with prominent brow ridges and a robust skeleton. The skulls of Asian *H. erectus,* such as those from the cave of Zhoukoudian which were once known as 'Peking man', are more heavily buttressed with ridges of bone than those of Africa. The most spectacular *H. erectus* fossil is that of an almost complete skeleton of a 12-year-old boy dated to 1.6 million years old from Nariokotome, Kenya, which provides evidence for a rapid rate of child development. This appears characteristic of early humans. He has the physique characteristic of humans living in tropical environments. *H. erectus* survived until around 300,000 years ago.

ACT 3

Archaic *H. sapiens/ H. heidelbergensis*

Specimens of archaic *H. sapiens* are found in Africa and Asia from between *c.* 400,000 and 100,000 years ago. Important specimens come from the sites of Broken Hill, Florisbad and Omo in Africa, and Dali and Maba in East Asia. This is an ill-defined species but is distinguished from *H. erectus* by a larger brain size, 1100–1400 cc, and a cranium which is higher and more rounded. Little is known about the rest of the skeleton, but it is thought to have been as robust and muscular as that of *H. erectus*.

H. heidelbergensis is the name used for the first humans in Europe and is a descendant of *H. erectus*. Very few remains are known, just a jawbone from Mauer in Germany and part of a leg bone from Boxgrove in England, both dating to around 500,000 years ago. Both of these specimens suggest that *H. heidelbergensis* was a large and robust species. Human fossils from Atapuerca in Spain, recently dated to at least 780,000 years old, may also belong to *H. heidelbergensis*.

ACT 3

ACT 4

The Neanderthals *H. neanderthalensis*

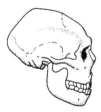

H. neanderthalensis is believed to have evolved from *H. heidelbergensis* by 150,000 years ago. Well-defined Neanderthal features are present on specimens from Pontnewydd Cave, North Wales, dating to 220,000 years ago. The 'classic' Neanderthals are found at sites in Europe and the Near East between 115,000 and 30,000 years ago, notably Saint Césaire in France (33,000), and Tabūn (110,000) and Kebara (63,000) in the Near East. *H. neanderthalensis* is distinguished from *H. erectus* by a larger brain size of 1200–1750 cc, larger noses and reduced brow ridges. Their bodies were very strongly built, being stout and muscular with short legs and large barrel-like chests. Many of their anatomical features are adaptations to living in glacial environments. Neanderthal bodies seem to have suffered a high degree of physical injuries and degenerative diseases that are likely to reflect a physically demanding lifestyle.

ACT 3

ACT 4

Anatomically modern humans *H. sapiens sapiens*

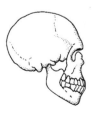

The earliest anatomically modern humans (AMHs) are found in the Near East, in the caves of Qafzeh and Skhūl, and in South Africa at Border Cave and Klasies River Mouth at about 100,000 years ago. Fossil specimens from Jebel Irhoud in North Africa are also likely to be *H. sapiens sapiens*. AMHs are believed to be descended from archaic *H. sapiens* in Africa. The fragmentary specimens from Klasies River Mouth show some archaic features and may represent a transitional form. AMHs are distinguished from both archaic *H. sapiens* and *H. neanderthalensis* by a less robust physique, the reduction and often absence of brow ridges, a more rounded skull, and smaller teeth. The brain size at between 1200 and 1700 cc is the same as, or slightly smaller, than that of *H. neanderthalensis*.

Soon after, 100,000 years ago AMHs are likely to have dispersed throughout Africa and into East Asia. They colonized Australia soon after 60,000 years ago, and first entered Europe 40,000 years ago. After 30,000 *H. sapiens sapiens* is the only surviving member of the *Homo* lineage.

ACT 4

The props...

The first stone tools

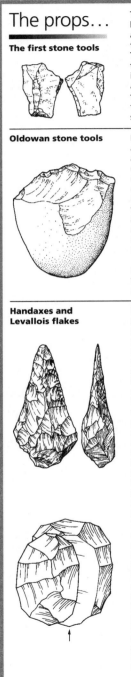

Oldowan stone tools

Handaxes and Levallois flakes

The very first stone tools date to between 3 and 2 million years ago and are often difficult to distinguish from naturally occurring rocks. These artifacts have been grouped together and termed the Omo industrial complex, after the Omo area of Ethiopia. The artifacts from this area come from the Shungura formation which has sediments spanning the period between 3 and 1 million years ago. The earliest of these tools consist of flaked and smashed up quartz pebbles. Similar artifacts thought to date to 2.7 million years ago have been found at Kada Gona, Ethiopia. A further early site is that of Lokalalei (GaJh 5) found near the base of the Kalochoro member of the Nachukui formation of West Turkana, Kenya, where the artifacts are dated to 2.36 million years ago.

Between 2 and 1.5 million years ago, the stone tools found in East and South Africa consist of flakes removed from pebbles, and the remaining 'core'. These are referred to as the Oldowan industry, named after the artifacts from Bed I at Olduvai Gorge. These artifacts come in various shapes and sizes and are characterized as heavy duty tools, light duty tools, utilized pieces and débitage.

Olduvai Gorge remains the most important site for Oldowan stone tools. This is a 100-m-deep (330-ft) gash stretching for 50 km (30 miles) in the Serengeti Plain, Tanzania, created by a river cutting through sediments laid down during the last 1.8 million years. It has an extensive series of archaeological sites found in four main beds containing artifacts and fossils, numerous of which were excavated by Mary Leakey. There are several other locations in East Africa of similar importance to Olduvai Gorge. Most notable is the area of Koobi Fora, Kenya, where extensive fieldwork by Glynn Isaac yielded many early sites.

Handaxes are a type of artifact made by the bifacial flaking of a stone nodule or a large flake. This means that flakes are alternately removed from either side of the artifact. Handaxes are typically pear shaped, while similar tools with a straight edge, rather than a pointed or curved tip, are called cleavers. When handaxes/cleavers are found at relatively high frequencies within stone artifact assemblages, those assemblages are referred to as Acheulian. The bifacial technique is first found in Bed II at Olduvai Gorge, and when present the stone industry is referred to as the Developed Oldowan. The earliest true handaxes are known from Konso-Gardula in Ethiopia where they date to 1.4 million years ago. They also abruptly appear in the archaeological record at c. 1.4 million years ago at the sites of Olorgesailie and Kesem-Kebana. Handaxes are found at sites throughout Europe, West and South Asia during Act 3; often they are found in very large numbers. For instance at Olorgesailie in Tanzania, many thousands of handaxes have been found in 16 artifact assemblages around the edge of an ancient lake basin. A notable site in Europe is Boxgrove in southern England, dated to 500,000 years ago, where perfectly preserved scatters of knapping debris from the manufacture of handaxes have been excavated. The only part of the Old World where early humans do not appear to have made handaxes is Southeast Asia. They are also very rare in China. In the regions that they are found, they are not ubiquitous and are absent from many sites at which tools remain similar to Oldowan or Developed Oldowan technology. Such sites include Vertesszöllös in Hungary, Bilzingsleben in Germany and the lowest levels at the stratified sites of Ùbeidiya, Israel, and Swanscombe, England.

The Levallois method is a technique for removing flakes and stone points of predetermined size by careful preparation of the core. It first appears in the archaeological record 250,000 years ago and is widely found in Africa, the Near East and in Europe. Many of the assemblages from North Africa, such as in the cave of Haua Fteah, and the Near East, such as in the caves of Tabūn and Kebara, are dominated by this method. In some assemblages, such as at Pontnewydd in North Wales, the Levallois technique is found together with handaxes.

Wooden artifacts

Artifacts made from wood are extremely rare in the archaeological record, but the few which survive indicate that they were being made by Early Humans. Pointed sticks, which were probably spears, have been recovered from the sites of Clacton-on-Sea and Lehringen and a polished wooden plank has been found at Gesher Benot Ya'aqov in Israel. It is most likely that the working of wood to make artifacts stretches back to the common ancestor, 6 million years ago.

Blade technology

Long thin slivers of flint are referred to as blades rather than flakes, and are usually removed from cores which have been carefully prepared, often into a prismatic shape. The earliest blades are found in the industries termed the Pre-Aurignacian from the cave of Haua Fteah, North Africa, and the Amudian from the Near East, both dating to before 100,000 years ago. But it is not until 40,000 years ago that blade production begins on a systematic scale, after which it becomes the dominant stone working technique throughout the Old World. Blade cores come in various sizes, with the smaller ones referred to as bladelet or micro-blade cores. Blades themselves are often chipped into specific shapes, such as projectile points, endscrapers and burins (chisel-like engraving tools).

Bone artifacts

Although there is evidence of bones being used as tools as much as 500,000 years ago, the first worked artifacts – harpoons made by grinding bones – are only found 90,000 years ago at Katanda in Zaire. These harpoons remain as unique finds for it is not until after 40,000 years ago that another artifact of worked bone is known. After this date bone artifacts are found in all regions of the Old World. For instance, 39,000 years ago arrowheads were made from grinding bone at Border Cave, while in the Near East and Europe bone was carved to make tools such as points and awls. From around 20,000 years ago bone was used to make harpoons, particularly in the societies living in Europe towards the end of the last ice age. Bone needles are first found at 18,000 years ago. The first architecture used the bones of mammoths for dwellings in Russia and Siberia over 20,000 years ago.

Objects of art and personal adornment

Although fragments of red ochre have been found at sites which date to 250,000 years ago, the first objects of art appear 40,000 years ago. The most impressive and abundant of these are in Europe, where beads, necklaces and pendants were made from ivory, animal and human figures were carved and a wide array of abstract and naturalistic images were painted and engraved on cave walls. In Africa slabs of stone painted with animal figures are found dating to 27,500 years ago, while ostrich egg beads date back to 39,000 years ago. In East Asia the first beads are dated to 18,000–13,000 years ago from the cave of Zhoukoudian, while a decorated piece of red deer antler dated to 13,000 years ago has come from Longgupo Cave in China. Engravings made into soft mud on cave walls in Australia have been dated to 23,000–15,000 years ago, while it is likely that some of the rock art stretches back to a date of 40,000 years ago. At Mandu Mandu rockshelter a collection of 20 shell beads has been found dated to 34,000–30,000 years ago.

Computers and other modern props

The first computer, Charles Babbage's analytical engine, was designed in 1834. Less than 160 years later the global computer network called the Internet had been established. These developments took place no more than 90,000 years after the first piece of bone was carved. This contrasts with the more than 2 million years that it took to get from the production of the first stone tool to the carving of that piece of bone. This difference reflects the remarkably rapid rate of technological innovation and change that was hinted at 90,000 years ago, began in earnest 40,000 years ago and continues apace today. Notable landmarks during that 40,000 years were the first use of ceramic technology 26,000 years ago for making clay figurines, which had become widespread for making pots by 8,000 years ago. The first plants and animals were domesticated 10,000 years ago. The first writing began 5,000 years ago, and metal smelting 4,000 years ago. It took only 20,000 years to get from the bow and arrow to the atomic bomb, and 6,000 years from the first wheeled vehicles to spacecraft.

1
2
3
4

ACT 3

ACT 4

ACT 4

ACT 4

ACT 4

Acts 1 and 2: African origins

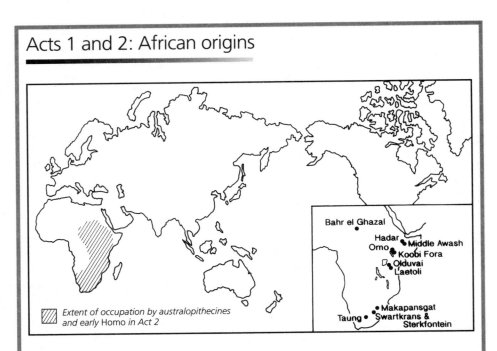

Extent of occupation by australopithecines and early Homo in Act 2

Fossil apes from the period 10–5 million years ago are known from Africa, Europe and Asia and it remains unclear where the common ancestor of 6 million years ago actually lived. But it is most likely to have been East Africa, in light of the diversity of australopithecine fossils from that region and the ape-like features of the earliest of these. Fossils of australopithecines and earliest *Homo* are found from cave deposits in South Africa and from open sites in East Africa. The most important sites in South Africa are Makapansgat, Sterkfontein and Swartkrans, all of which provide a diverse array of animal fossils. It is unlikely that these human ancestors actually occupied the caves and their remains were either washed in, or taken in by carnivores. Of these caves Sterkfontein has *H. habilis* fossils and a stratified sequence of early stone tools. The fossils and early stone tools from East Africa are found eroding from exposed sediments, notably at Hadar, Middle Awash, Olduvai Gorge, Koobi Fora and Omo. Their discovery and dating have been possible due to the faulting and erosion that has occurred in the African Rift Valley which has exposed ancient sediments, and the lenses of volcanic tuffs between these, which can be dated by a variety of radiometric methods.

Act 3: The colonization of Europe and Asia

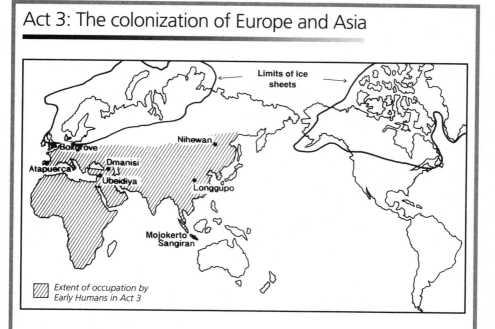

Extent of occupation by
Early Humans in Act 3

H. erectus fossils from Mojokerto and Sangiran on Java have been controversially dated to 1.6–1.8 million years ago, making them almost 1 million years older than previously thought. A tooth possibly dating to 1.9 million years ago and claimed to be early *Homo* has been found at Longgupo Cave in central China. If these new dates are correct, they imply that *H. erectus* dispersed from Africa very rapidly, or that an earlier species of *Homo* had left Africa, and the origins of *H. erectus* may in fact be in Asia itself. There have been claims for Oldowan-like stone tools from the Riwat area of Pakistan dating to 2 million years old, but it remains unclear whether or not these are true artifacts. A human jawbone attributed to *H. erectus* has been recovered from Dmanisi in Georgia. This was found above sediments which have been dated to 1.8 million years ago. It was associated with Oldowan-like stone tools, and most likely dates to between 1.5 and 1 million years ago. As such it may be similar in date to the earliest occupations at Ùbeidiya in western Asia. The earliest archaeological sites from East Asia come from the Nihewan basin in China, which are likely to date to between 0.75 and 1 million years ago. With these early fossils and sites in Asia, the absence of well-dated sites in Europe earlier than 500,000 years ago remains a puzzle. Sites such as Vallonet in France are claimed to date earlier than 1 million year ago, but, as at Riwat, it is unclear that the stone 'tools' are not simply naturally fractured pieces of rock. The earliest dates for human fossils come from Gran Dolina, Atapuerca in Spain where they are dated to 780,000 years ago, although some confirmation for these dates is required. At and soon after 500,000 years ago there are several archaeological sites in Europe. Most notable is Boxgrove in southern England, where handaxes and a part of an early human leg bone have been found.

Act 4: The colonization of Australasia and the Americas

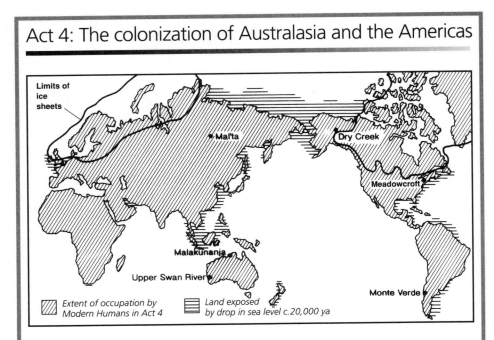

Limits of ice sheets

Mal'ta

Dry Creek

Meadowcroft

Malakunanja

Upper Swan River

Monte Verde

Extent of occupation by Modern Humans in Act 4

Land exposed by drop in sea level c.20,000 ya

Australia is most likely to have been colonized 50,000–60,000 years ago in view of luminescence dates for occupation in Malakunanja II and Nauwalabila rockshelters in the Northern Territory. Other than these sites, the earliest dates are less than 40,000 years old, but this may reflect the 'time barrier' for radiocarbon dating. The site of Upper Swan on the outskirts of Perth is dated to 39,500±2300 years ago, and there are a significant number of sites dated to 35,000–30,000 years ago. Australia was colonized by *H. sapiens sapiens*, but there is some controversy as to whether these represent a dispersing population from Africa, or had evolved locally from *H. erectus* ancestry in Southeast Asia. Human fossils in Australia dating to 30,000–20,000 years ago show considerable variability, ranging from very gracile to very robust anatomy. The Americas were colonized by a route that led through northern Siberia, where the earliest well-dated sites are 35,000 years old. The richest of these is the 25,000-year-old site of Mal'ta which has large quantities of art objects. Entry into the Americas was across the now submerged landmass of Beringia, but the date of this colonization remains unclear. Claims have been made for sites in South America dating to 40,000 years ago, but these are unlikely to be accurate. The earliest well-verified dates come from sites such as Dry Creek in Alaska and Meadowcroft Rockshelter in Pennsylvania at around 12,000 years ago. There are numerous sites dating to between 11,500 and 11,000 years ago, when people appear to have been hunting megafauna such as mammoths. By 11,000 years ago there are many sites in South America, notably Monte Verde. As with Australia, it is likely that colonization was not a single event, but involved numerous influxes of people over a wide time range.

Evolutionary relationships between human ancestors

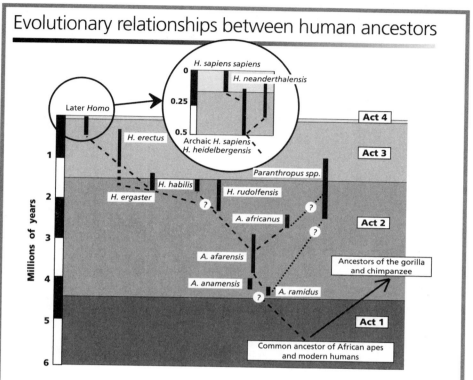

Reconstructing the evolutionary relationships between human ancestors is a task fraught with difficulties due to the paucity of the fossil evidence. This diagram is based on that provided by Bernard Wood (1993), in which the black bars denote the timing of the first and last appearance of a species. Relationships between the australopithecines are particularly hard to establish due to the scarcity of their fossils and their morphological variability: it is often unclear whether one is dealing with the male and female of the same species, or two separate species. Perhaps the most contentious part of the evolutionary tree is the most recent part concerning the origins of *H. sapiens sapiens*. Views about this fall into two broad camps. Some believe that there was a single origin in Africa, and that all existing populations such as Neanderthals in Europe and archaic *H. sapiens* in Asia, were replaced by this new species and made no contribution to the modern gene pool. Others dispute this, arguing for multiple origins of *H. sapiens sapiens* in different parts of the world, evolving from the resident early human populations. Between these two extremes are various other positions, such as those arguing for a dispersing population of modern humans from Africa around 100,000 years ago, but with a degree of interbreeding with the archaic *H. sapiens* populations. The study of human genetics can also provide a means for reconstructing evolutionary history. The limited amount of genetic variability between modern humans suggests that we have had a very recent origin, while measuring the difference between humans and chimpanzees has established the date of the common ancestor at 6 million years ago. Attempts are being made to use the variation in the DNA of human populations in different parts of the world to distinguish between a single or multiple origin for modern humans, and if the former, identify when and where this happened. This book adopts the position of a single African origin followed by a replacement of all archaic *Homo sapiens,* but is sympathetic to the idea of limited hybridization between populations dispersing from Africa and resident early humans.

Changes of scenery during Acts 3 and 4

The Pleistocene climate as recorded in deep sea core V28-238 taken in the Pacific Ocean

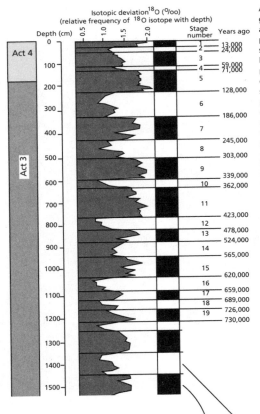

Acts 3 and 4 of prehistory cover the geological periods known as the Middle and Upper Pleistocene. During these the planet experienced a long and complex sequence of climatic changes, dominated by swings from glacial to interglacial phases. We see this alternation most clearly in cores taken from marine sediments. These can be analyzed to provide a record of changes in the ratio of two isotopes of oxygen, which in turn are directly related to climatic fluctuations from glacial to interglacial stages. These cores, which first became available in the 1970s, show that there have been eight cycles from glacial to interglacial during the Middle and Upper Pleistocene. Moreover, there have been numerous smaller oscillations, with marked periods of cold, called stadials, during interglacial periods and conversely periods of warmth, called interstadials, during cold glacial periods.

These climatic oscillations provide us with a chronological structure for the Pleistocene as each climatic stage has a number with glacial periods denoted by even, and warm periods by odd, numbers. Moreover, the fluctuations within a climatic phase are denoted by subscripts of letters. For instance, stage 5 is the whole period of the last interglacial (128,000–71,000 years ago), which is divided up into 5 substages referred to as 5a–5e, with the latter marking the highest sea level. Other particularly important oxygen isotope stages are stage 12 (which is thought to be the Anglian glaciation which covered northern Europe 478,000–423,000 years ago), and stage 2 (which denotes the last glaciation, 24,000–13,000 years ago).

Warm phases
During the warm phases of the Pleistocene the ice sheets melted, resulting in a rise in sea level, cutting areas such as Britain off from continental Europe. As the climate warmed the landscapes were colonized by plants and trees and animal communities were transformed. The marine sediment and ice cores show that the transition to warm phases often involved very rapid periods of global warming.

Cold phases
As global temperatures fell more water became locked up in ice sheets which expanded across high latitudes. In the low latitudes climates became drier. The falling sea levels exposed large areas of landmass which are now flooded. In Europe tundras developed which were exploited by large migratory herds of reindeer. Areas such as the Near East suffered drought conditions.

3 The architecture of the modern mind

WHAT CAN BE LEARNT from the modern mind today that will help us in our quest for the minds of our earliest ancestors?

It helps to start our enquiry briefly not with minds, but with bodies.[1] If we want to find out how people looked or behaved in the past we may go to a museum and look at exhibits of human fossils or stone tools. If it is a good museum there may be a reconstruction, perhaps a hairy Neanderthal crouching at the entrance to a cave cooking food or sharpening a spear. But there is a much easier way to start learning about the past, even about the most ancient of human ancestors. And that is to sit in the bath. As the water cools, you get goose bumps. Your skin reacts in this fashion because our Stone Age ancestors were much hairier than we are today. When they got cold they also got goose bumps, which made their hair stand on end and trap a layer of warm air against their skin. We have (largely) lost the hairy bodies today, but the goose bumps remain. They provide a clue to the way we used to look many millennia ago.

In fact our bodies are a Stone Age detective's paradise. Watching how a gymnast can swing like a gibbon provides a clue that this is what our arms and shoulders were once designed to do. The extent of heart disease in modern Western populations provides a clue that our high fat diet is not what our bodies were designed to consume.[2] Is it the same with our minds? Can the nature of the modern mind betray the nature of the Stone Age mind? Can we find clues in the way we think today to the way that our ancestors thought thousands, even millions, of years ago? We can indeed – although the clues are perhaps not as readily apparent as those concerning our anatomy. In fact we can find more than just clues, for the modern mind has an architecture built up by millions of years of evolution. We can start to reconstruct the prehistory of the mind by exposing that architecture, and then taking it apart.

The mind as a sponge, the mind as a computer

Exposing the architecture of the modern mind is the task of psychologists. But we have all engaged in this activity from time to time: we are all expert mind users. We constantly and compulsively peer into our own minds and wonder what is going on in the minds of others. Sometimes we think we know. Now this is a risky business because we may begin to delude ourselves. Look at the world and it seems to be flat. Look at the mind and it seems to be … well let us start by looking at what the mind does seem to be. And let us start by looking at some of the most fertile and extraordinary minds in existence: those of young children.

Watching my own children develop has in many ways been as helpful to my search for the prehistory of the mind as the academic papers and books that I have read during the last decade. When Nicholas, my son, was almost three years old we were playing with his toy zoo and I asked if he wanted to put the seal into the lake. His eyes glanced at the animal and then he looked at me in silence for a moment. 'Yes', he said, 'but actually it's a walrus'. He was right. I may have got them confused, but my son had meticulous knowledge of his animals. He needed telling just once and the differences between armadillos, aardvarks and anteaters would become embedded in his mind. As with the minds of all children, his seemed to be like a sponge soaking up knowledge. New facts and ideas were sucked into an endless array of empty pores. Moreover, young minds in different parts of the world will soak up different things; they will acquire different cultures. And cultures, so anthropologists tell us, are not just lists of facts about the world, but specific ways of thinking and understanding: the sponge-mind is one that soaks up the processes of thought itself.[3]

The idea that the mind is an empty sponge waiting to be filled is one that pervades both our everyday thinking, and much of academia. The process of acquiring knowledge is about filling up the pores and remembering is about squeezing the sponge. The idea of an IQ test is based on the notion that some sponges are better than others with regard to mopping up and wringing out. The evolution of the human mind appears to be no more than the gradual enlargement of the sponge within our heads.

But this analogy doesn't help us think about how minds solve problems, how they learn. This is more than simply amassing and then regurgitating facts; it is about comparing and combining bits of information. Sponges cannot do this, but computers can. The mind as a *computer* is perhaps an even more persuasive idea than the mind as a *sponge*. We can think of the mind as taking in data, processing it, solving the problem, and making our bodies perform the output. The brain is the hardware, the mind is the software.[4] But what programs are running?

Usually we think of the mind as running a single, powerful general-purpose program. We normally give this program the simple name of 'learning', and say no more. So as the child begins to soak up knowledge it will also start running the general-purpose learning program. One day the child will start entering data about the sounds it hears coming from people's mouths and their actions which follow – the program runs and the child will learn the meaning of words. Another day the input data will be the shape of marks it sees on paper and the adjacent pictures of objects – the child learns to read. Another day the input data may be about numbers on a page, or about balancing on a two-wheeled object and this remarkably flexible computer program we call 'learning' enables the child to understand mathematics or ride a bicycle. The same program just keeps on running, even into adulthood.

If the mind is a computer, how should we think of the minds of our prehistoric ancestors? Easy. Different types of minds are like computers with different memory capacities and processing chips. During the last decade we have seen a dramatic increase in the power and speed of computers and this almost begs to be used as an analogy for the prehistory of the mind. Not long ago I took my children to the Science Museum in London and we looked at the reconstruction of Charles Babbage's analytical engine, the first computer. It is many, many times larger and slower than the tiny laptop computer on which I am writing this book. I wondered whether Babbage's analytical engine and my laptop are analogous to the Neanderthal and the modern mind. Or is a better analogy simply that of having a different amount of memory in your PC?

The mind as a sponge and the mind as a computer. Both ideas are very appealing. Both seem to describe a little of how the mind works. How can the mind seem to be such different types of things at once? It seems so easy to say what the mind is like, and so hard to say what the mind actually is.

But are sponges and computers really good analogies for the mind? The mind doesn't just accumulate information and then regurgitate it. And nor is it indiscriminate in the knowledge it soaks up. My children – like all children – have soaked up thousands of words effortlessly, but their suction seems to lose its power when it comes to multiplication tables. Nor does the mind simply solve problems in the way a computer does. The mind does something else: it creates. It thinks of things which are not 'out there', in the world. Things which *could not* be out there in the world. The mind thinks, it creates, it imagines. This cannot happen within a computer. Computers just do what programs tell them to do; they cannot be truly creative in the way that appears compulsive for a four-year-old child.[5] Maybe when we think of the mind as either a sponge or a computer program we are joining the psychological equivalent of the flat earth society.

In reality what I found provocative when my son declared that 'actually it was a walrus' was not that he was right, but that in a fundamental way he was wrong. How could he possibly have thought that it was a walrus? It was no more than a little piece of moulded orange plastic. A walrus is blubbery and wet, fat and smelly. That little piece of plastic was all these things – but only in his mind.

The ideas of Thomas Wynn and Jean Piaget

My own interest in the origins of the human mind was first sparked not by my children, but by a remarkable paper I read as an undergraduate. In 1979 an American archaeologist by the name of Thomas Wynn had published an article which claimed that by 300,000 years ago the modern mind was already in place.[6] Recall that this is within Act 3 of the play that is our past, before Neanderthals, let alone anatomically modern humans, had appeared on the stage. The evidence that Thomas Wynn used for his claim were the fine symmetrical handaxes made by *Homo erectus* and archaic *Homo sapiens* during the first scene of Act 3.

How did he reach this conclusion? He began by using an idea that has been hotly debated by academics for many years: that the phases of mental development in the child reflect the phases of cognitive evolution of our human ancestors. In jargon, this is referred to as the idea that 'ontogeny recapitulates phylogeny'.[7] This is a 'big idea', and one to which I will return later in this chapter and the next. Think of it as implying that the mind of, say, *Homo erectus* or perhaps a chimpanzee today may have structural similarities to that of a young child, although obviously they will possess a vastly different content. To use this idea, Tom Wynn needed to know what the minds of young children were like; he needed to know the phases of mental development. Not surprisingly he looked to the work of the child psychologist Jean Piaget, by far the most influential figure at that time.

Piaget was a psychologist who firmly believed that the mind is like a computer. According to his theories, the mind runs a small set of general-purpose programs which control the entry of new information into the mind, and which serve to restructure the mind so that it passes through a series of developmental phases.[8] He called the last of these phases, reached when the child is about 12 years old, formal operational intelligence. In this phase the mind can think about hypothetical objects and events. This type of thinking is absolutely essential for the manufacture of a stone tool like a handaxe. One must form a mental image of what the finished tool is to look like before starting to remove flakes from the stone nodule. Each strike follows from a hypothesis as to its effect on the shape of the tool. As a consequence, Tom Wynn felt confident in attributing formal operational intelligence, and hence a fundamentally modern mind, to the makers of handaxes.

To a student of archaeology, this was an absolutely stunning conclusion. Here was someone who could actually read the mind of an extinct human ancestor from the stone tools discarded and lost in prehistory. But could the prehistory of the mind really have been over so soon in the course of human evolution? Did the appearance of art, bone tools and global colonization, the events of Act 4, require no new cognitive underpinnings? This seemed implausible to say the least.

A scrutiny of Tom Wynn's work showed that he had been faultless in using Piaget's ideas. To make a handaxe which was simultaneously symmetrical in three dimensions certainly seemed to involve the types of mental processes that Piaget argued were characteristic of formal operational intelligence. So maybe it was Piaget's ideas that were wrong. This has indeed been the message from many psychologists during the last decade: the mind does *not* run general-purpose programs, and nor is it like a sponge, indiscriminately soaking up whatever information is around. Psychologists have introduced a new type of analogy for the mind: it is like a Swiss army knife. A Swiss army knife? One of those chunky knives with lots of specialized devices, like little scissors and saws and tweezers. Each of these is designed for coping with a very specific type of problem. When the knife is closed up, one wouldn't dream that such a multitude of specialized devices exist. Perhaps our minds are closed to us. But if the mind is a Swiss army knife, how many devices are there? What problems are these designed to solve? How did they get there? And is this analogy any better at helping us understand imagination and creative thought?

Many psychologists since 1980 have addressed such questions. They have adopted terms such as 'modules', 'cognitive domains' and 'intelligences' to describe each of the specialized devices. There are lots of disagreements about the number and nature of the specialized devices, but by scrutinizing their work we will be more successful at exposing the architecture of the mind than when we idly ponder the mind as we play with children. And that architecture looks fundamentally different from the one suggested by Piaget. So now we must follow how this Swiss-army-knife view of the mind has arisen and how it has developed during the last few years.[9]

Fodor's two-tier architecture for the mind

Our starting point is with two big books published in 1983. In fact the first of these books is a small slim volume, but it has some big ideas about the architecture of the mind, and gives some major clues to its past: *The Modularity of Mind*, by Jerry Fodor.[10]

Jerry Fodor is a psycho–linguist with very clear ideas about the architecture of the mind. He proposes that it should be split into two parts which he calls perception, or input systems, and cognition, or the central systems. Their respective architectures are very different; input systems are like the blades on a Swiss army knife and he describes these as a series of discrete and independent 'modules', such as sight, hearing and touch. He includes language as one of these input systems. In contrast the central systems have no architecture at all, or at least their architecture will always remain hidden from us. This is where those mysterious processes happen, known as 'thought', 'problem solving' and 'imagination'. It is where 'intelligence' resides.

Fodor argues that each input system is based on independent brain processes. For instance, those we use for hearing are utterly different from those we use for sight, or for language: they are like different blades within the Swiss army knife that just happen to be contained within the same case. This modularity of input systems is attested by numerous lines of evidence which include their apparent association with specific parts of the brain, the characteristic patterns of development in the child, and their propensity to exhibit specific patterns of breakdown. Fodor also stresses how the input systems operate very quickly and are mandatory: one cannot help to hear, or to see, when given the appropriate stimuli.

While few would contest these features of the input systems, further features proposed by Fodor are more open to controversy. First is the notion that input systems do not have direct access to the information being acquired by other input systems. Hence what I am seeing at this moment is not influenced by what I am hearing. Fodor uses the term 'encapsulated' to describe this feature of the input systems. A second feature is that the input systems have only limited information from the central systems. This, for Fodor, is a crucial architectural feature, for it means that the knowledge possessed by any individual has a limited, perhaps even marginal, influence on the way they perceive the world. A neat example he uses to illustrate this is optical illusions: these persist even when we know that what we are seeing is untrue.

The idea that cognition only marginally influences perception runs counter to the relativist ideas of the social sciences. Recall that when we were thinking about the mind as a sponge, young children were supposed to soak up the knowledge of their culture. Well to the majority of social scientists that knowledge also includes how to perceive the world. Fodor is saying that this is wrong: the nature of perception is already *hard-wired into the mind* at birth. Fodor hates relativism almost as much as he hates fibreglass powerboats, which I assume means he hates it quite a lot.[11]

According to Fodor, input systems are encapsulated, mandatory, fast operating and hard wired. He calls them stupid. As such they contrast with cognition, the 'smart' central system. Fodor argues that we know almost nothing about how the central systems work, other than that they have a series of features which are the opposite of the input systems: they operate slowly, are unencapsulated and domain neutral; in other words, the processes of thought and problem solving turn on the integration of information from all input systems, in addition to that which is being internally generated. Unlike the input systems, the processes of the central systems cannot be related to specific parts of the brain.

The fundamental character of cognition is that it is holistic, the exact opposite of the input systems which are all dedicated to dealing with one specific type of information alone. And this is what Fodor sees as the most puzzling feature of cognition: 'its non encapsulation, its creativity, its holism and its passion for the analogical'.[12] Fodor feels defeated by the central systems, declaring they are impossible to study. For him, 'thought', 'problem solving', 'imagination' and 'intelligence' are unresolvable.

In summary, Fodor believes the mind has a two-tier architecture, the lower one is like a Swiss army knife, the upper one is like ... well we can't say for we have nothing else like it in the world.

At first sight the combination of input and central systems appears to provide a rather odd architecture for the mind, a dramatic and unsightly clash of styles. But Fodor argues that the architect of the modern mind – the processes of human evolution – has in fact come up with a most ingenious design. It is well-nigh perfect for allowing us to adapt to the world around us. Perception has been built to detect what is right in the world: in situations of danger or opportunity a person needs to react quickly and without thinking. According to Fodor 'it is, no doubt, important to attend to the eternally beautiful and true. But it is more important not to be eaten.'[13] At other times, however, one survives by contemplating the nature of the world in a slow, reflective manner, integrating many different types and sources of information. Only by this can one come to recognize the regularities and structure of the world. 'Nature has contrived to have it both ways', Fodor argues, 'to get the best out of fast dumb systems and slow contemplative ones, by simply refusing to choose between them.'[14]

Gardner's theory of multiple intelligences

In the same year that Fodor's book was published, another one appeared: *Frames of Mind: The Theory of Multiple Intelligences*, by Howard Gardner.[15] In some ways this contrasts dramatically with Fodor's work. Gardner is as much concerned with practical matters in terms of devising education policies for schools, as with purely philosophical issues concerning the mind. He also draws on information from more than just psychology and linguistics to bear on the mind, bringing in data from disciplines such as social anthropology and educational studies.

Gardner proposes a very different type of architecture for the mind; he does away with the distinction between input and central systems and instead focuses on the notion of intelligence – which to Fodor is unresolvable. He questions whether there is a single, generalized intellectual capacity – the size of one's sponge, or speed of one's computer – and replaces it with no less than seven different types of intelligence. He claims that these are based in different parts of the brain, having their own dedicated and independent neurological processes. So here too we have a Swiss-army-knife architecture for the mind, with each blade now described as an intelligence.

To identify the multiple intelligences of the mind Gardner uses a stringent set of criteria. For instance, he feels that there should be evidence that the core capacity may become isolated by brain damage, either in terms of losing the capacity (while all others remain unimpaired), or losing all other capacities yet remaining competent in the proposed intelligence. He also feels that one should be able to see a distinct developmental history in the child for the intelligence, and that it ought to be developed to different degrees in different individuals. By using such criteria, Gardner arrives at his set of seven intelligences: his blades for the Swiss army knife of the modern mind.

Gardner's seven intelligences are: linguistic, musical, logical–mathematical, spatial, bodily–kinesthetic and two forms of personal intelligence, one for looking in at one's own mind, and one for looking outward towards others. The function of each intelligence is largely defined by its name. Logical-mathematical is perhaps the closest to what we generally mean when we invoke the word intelligence, as it is ultimately about logical and scientific thought. The awkwardly named bodily-kinesthetic intelligence is about the co-ordination of one's body movements, as exemplified by sportsmen and dancers. Now each of these intelligences meets the criteria that Gardner puts forward. For instance, language certainly seems to rely on its own unique brain processes; and we all probably know children that seem to have particularly advanced levels of musical or logical-mathematical intelligence.

So Gardner suggests that the architecture of the mind is constituted by a series of relatively autonomous intelligences. Not only does he suggest this, but the case is very powerfully made. In doing so, he seems to depart quite radically from the type of architecture proposed by Fodor. Gardner's intelligences are very different from Fodor's modules. The former have a developmental history – their character is heavily influenced by the cultural context of the individual. The blades of Gardner's Swiss army knife are concerned with thinking and problem solving, not just with the acquisition of information as undertaken by a Fodorian module. There is one more fundamental difference. But, ironically, this brings the ideas of Fodor and Gardner much closer together than they initially appear.

While Fodor's modules are absolutely independent from each other, Gardner continuously stresses how interaction between the multiple intelligences is fundamental to the workings of the mind. Gardner emphasizes that 'in the normal course of events, the intelligences actually interact with, and build upon, one another.'[16] It is a characteristic feature of human development, he argues, that young infants have a capacity to build connections between domains. And his book is full of examples of the intelligences working together to create the patterns of behaviour and the cultural achievements of humankind. Indeed it is difficult to conceive of musical intelligence, for instance, not being intimately linked with intricate body movements deriving from bodily-kinesthetic intelligence, or linguistic intelligence being used independently from personal intelligence. So Gardner's position is that, in spite of the independent core processes of each intelligence, 'in normal human intercourse one typically encounters complexes of intelligences functioning together smoothly, even seamlessly, in order to execute intricate human activities.'[17] And the wisest individuals, he suggests, are those who are most able at building connections across domains, as exemplified in the use of metaphors and analogies.

The word 'analogy' immediately takes us back to think of how Fodor described the central systems: they have 'a passion for analogical thought'. Could it be that Fodor could see no modularity in the central systems simply because the intelligences or modules within it function so smoothly together that one is unaware that any modularity exists?[18]

Interlude: Fodor versus Gardner

Let us pause for a moment in this spin through recent thought in psychology to assess how far we have come in exposing the architecture of the mind. Fodor has given us a two-tier architecture, and the role of each tier appears to be of evolutionary interest: one can imagine a mind working with just the input systems, but not with just a central system. Insects and amoebas need input systems, but they don't require the processes of the central systems. So perhaps the latter have been added on sometime during evolution. Gardner has given us a Swiss-army-knife model for the processes of thought which, if the multiple intelligences can truly function together sufficiently smoothly and seamlessly, appears not substantially different from the manner in which Fodor characterized the central systems. So, perhaps the mind is not just a single Swiss army knife, but in fact two knives: one for input systems in which the blades remain truly independent, and one for thought in which the blades are somehow working together for most of the time. But if that is true, why are there separate blades for thought in the first place? Why not have a general-purpose learning/thinking/problem-solving program? Or in other words, a general intelligence? And what confidence can we have that Gardner has identified the correct number and types of blades on the knife? Gardner himself admits that someone else looking at the mind might find a different range of intelligences. To answer these questions we had better think about who put this Swiss army knife/knives of the mind together – that is, about the architect of the mind: the processes of evolution. To do this we must return to our study of recent thought in psychology and meet a gang of psychologists who have been shouting the loudest during the 1990s: the evolutionary psychologists.

Enter the evolutionary psychologists

The leaders of the gang of evolutionary psychologists are Leda Cosmides and John Tooby, two charming people with razor-sharp minds.[19] During the late 1980s and early 1990s they published a succession of papers culminating in a long essay, entitled 'The psychological foundations of culture', published in *The Adapted Mind*, a 1992 book they edited with Jerome Barkow.[20] By adopting an explicitly evolutionary approach their work has challenged many of the conventional notions about the mind – the mind as a sponge, the mind as a general-purpose computer program. In fact it was Leda Cosmides who I saw a few months ago starting a lecture by holding up a Swiss army knife and declaring it to be the mind.[21] I'll refer to Cosmides and Tooby as C&T.

The reason that they parade under the banner of evolutionary psychology is that the gang argue that we can only understand the nature of the modern mind by viewing it as a product of biological evolution. The starting point for this argument is that the mind is a complex, functional structure that could not have arisen by chance. If we are willing to ignore the possibility of divine intervention, the only known process by which such complexity can have arisen is evolution by natural selection.[22] In this regard C&T treat the mind as one treats any other organ of the body – it is an evolved mechanism which has been constructed and adjusted in response to the selective pressures faced by our species during its evolutionary history. More specifically, they argue that the human mind evolved under the selective pressures faced by our human ancestors as they lived by hunting and gathering in Pleistocene environments – the central Acts and Scenes of our prehistory. As that lifestyle ended no more than a fraction of time ago in evolutionary terms, our minds remain adapted to that way of life.

As a consequence of this, C&T argue that the mind consists of a Swiss army knife with a great many, highly specialized blades; in other terms, it is composed of multiple mental modules. Each of these blades/modules has been designed by natural selection to cope with one specific adaptive problem faced by hunter-gatherers during our past. Just as Gardner argued, the mind has more than a capacity for 'general intelligence' – there are multiple specialized types of intelligence, or ways of thinking. As with Gardner's intelligences, it is likely that each module has its own specific form of memory and reasoning process.[23] But the modules of C&T's mind are very different from the intelligences of Gardner. In fact they are far more like Fodor's input processes: they are hard-wired into the mind at birth and universal among all people. Whereas the character of Gardner's multiple intelligences were open to influence by the cultural context in which young minds developed, this is not the case with C&T's modules.

These modules have a critically important feature that we have not come across yet: they are 'content rich'. In other words, the modules not only provide sets of rules for solving problems, but they provide much of the information that one needs to do so. This knowledge reflects the structure of the real world – or at least that of the Pleistocene in which the mind evolved. This information about real-world structure, together with a multitude of rules for solving problems, each contained in its own mental module, is already in a child's mind at birth. Some modules are sparked into action immediately – modules for eye contact with the mother – others need a little time before they get busy, such as the modules for language acquisition.

Now before we look at the types of modules that C&T believe to be within their mind, it is important to understand why they believe the mind is like a Swiss army knife, rather than like a sponge, or a general-purpose computer, or something else. They have three major arguments.

First they suggest that because each type of problem faced by our hunter-gatherer ancestors had a unique form, trying to solve all of them using a single reasoning device would have led to many errors. Consequently, any human who had specialized mental modules dedicated to specific types of problems would have avoided errors and solved them more successfully. That person would have had a selective advantage and his/her genes would have spread in the population, encoding the construction of Swiss army knives in the minds of his/her offspring.

The criteria for choosing sexual partners can illustrate the value of mental modules. If a man is choosing who to have sex with he should avoid someone who is biologically related. But if he is choosing someone to share food with, then he should not avoid kin. Someone using a simple reasoning rule that stated, 'always be friendly to kin', or 'always ignore kin' would not have as much reproductive success as someone with a set of mental rules, each dedicated to a particular problem.

The second argument used by C&T to support the notion of content-rich mental modules is that young children rapidly learn so much about so many complex subjects that it is simply unbelievable that this could happen unless their minds were pre-programmed to do so. This argument was originally known as the 'poverty of the stimulus' and was used by Noam Chomsky with regard to language. How is it possible, he asked, for children to acquire the many and complex rules of grammar from the limited series of utterances they hear from their parents' lips? How could a generalized learning program in the mind possibly deduce these rules, memorize them and then allow a four-year-old child to use them to near perfection? Well, quite simply it couldn't. Chomsky argued that the mind contains a genetically fixed 'language acquisition device' dedicated to learning language, that comes already geared up with a blueprint for grammatical rules. Fodor and Gardner concurred with this viewpoint, which is why both had language as a specialized feature of the mind.

C&T generalize the 'poverty of the stimulus' argument to all domains of life. How can a child learn the meaning of facial expressions, or the behaviour of physical objects, or how to attribute beliefs and intentions to other people, unless that child was helped by content-rich mental modules dedicated to these tasks.

Their third argument is known as the frame problem and is about the difficulty of making decisions. It is the same argument that Fodor used when explaining why stupid input systems exist. Imagine that a prehistoric hunter turned a corner and was suddenly faced with a lion. What should he do? If he had no more than a general-purpose learning program, the time taken to evaluate the intentions of the lion and weigh up the pros and cons of running or staying put might well be too great. He would, as Fodor noted, very probably have been eaten.

The problem with general-purpose learning rules, according to C&T, is that there are no bounds as to what information should be excluded from making a decision, and as to which alternative courses of action should be ignored. Every single possibility should be examined. Our prehistoric ancestors would have quietly starved as they tried to decide where and what to hunt. But if one of the hunters had a specialized mental module for making hunting decisions, which prescribed the types of information to consider and how to process them, he would have prospered. This would, no doubt, have increased his reproductive success, and soon the community would be populated with his offspring, each with this specialized mental module for making hunting decisions.[24]

Now these are powerful arguments. If it is legitimate to think of the mind as a product of natural selection, the case for a Swiss-army-knife design seems overwhelming. So what sort of blades should we find on the knife? This takes us to perhaps the most significant aspect of C&T's arguments: they suggest that we can actually predict what devices should exist within the knife. We do not need to be like Gardner and rely on hunches and guesses. At least, we can predict the blades if we know the types of problems that our prehistoric hunter-gatherers had regularly to face and solve. C&T think that they do and suggest that the mind is teeming with a multitude of modules. These include:

A face recognition module, a spatial relations module, a rigid objects mechanics module, a tool-use module, a fear module, a social-exchange module, an emotion-perception module, a kin oriented motivation module, an effort allocation and recalibration module, a child care module, a social inference module, a friendship module, a semantic-inference module, a friendship module, a grammar acquisition module, a communication-pragmatics module, a theory of mind module, and so on![25]

This extensive and incomplete list of possible modules is perhaps not that different from what Gardner was suggesting. For from such lists one can readily group modules together, such as those about social interaction, or those about physical objects. C&T have called these groupings 'faculties'. As such, these faculties seem similar to Gardner's notion of an intelligence. But the fundamental difference from Gardner's ideas is that his intelligences are arbitrary – no more than his hunches as to what goes on in the mind. C&T, on the other hand, predict what modules should be present by drawing on the fact that the mind is a product of evolution during the Pleistocene in which natural selection can be assumed to have played a dominant role. Moreover, Gardner's intelligences are moulded by the cultural context of development. C&T's are immune to the outside world. But so many modules? Can we really have so many independent psychological processes in our minds? I wonder if such ideas are what Fodor feared when he warned of 'modularity theory gone mad'.[26]

Interlude: Hunter-gatherers and Cambridge dons versus the evolutionary psychologists

Let us break from the psychologists and see how the idea of the modern human mind as the Swiss army knife of a prehistoric hunter-gatherer fares with our experience of the world. Pretty poorly is the answer.

To begin with, consider the idea that the modern mind evolved as a means of solving the problems faced by Stone Age hunter-gatherers in Pleistocene environments. The logical arguments for this are overwhelming: how could it be otherwise? But how then can we account for those things that the modern mind is very good at doing, but which we can be confident that Stone Age hunter-gatherers never attempted: such as reading books and developing cures for cancer. For some of these we may use modules which originally evolved for different, but related, tasks. So modules intended for the acquisition of spoken language might well be co-opted when we learn to read and write. And perhaps we can learn to do geometry because we can use C&T's 'spatial relations module', not now for finding our way around a landscape, but for finding our way around the sides of a triangle.

Other types of non-hunter-gatherer-like thoughts and behaviour may well use some general-purpose learning rules such as associative learning and trial-and-error learning. I group all these together under the title of general intelligence. Even C&T admit that some general-purpose learning rules must exist within the mind. But, if their arguments are correct, these could only solve simple problems. Anything more difficult requires some dedicated, or co-opted, specialized mental processes.

Consider mathematics. Children certainly have a far more difficult time learning the rules of algebra than they do the rules of language. This certainly suggests that the mind is preadapted for learning language but not for mathematics. So perhaps we learn mathematics by using the rules within general intelligence. But could this account for those adults, and indeed children, who are outstanding at mathematics?

Consider the case of a mathematician by the name of Andrew Wiles. In June 1993 he announced that he had a proof for what is known as Fermat's last theorem.[27] Fermat was a 17th-century mathematician who jotted in the margin of a notebook that he had proved that the equation $x^n+y^n=z^n$ has no integer solution when n is greater than 2 and x, y and z are not zero. But he forgot to leave us the proof itself, which ever since has been one of the Holy Grails of mathematics. Wiles claimed he had it: more than a thousand pages of equations utterly unintelligible to the vast majority of people in the world. But someone understood them, and told poor Andrew Wiles that he had got it wrong! One year later a revised proof was submitted, which has been acclaimed as one of the greatest achievements in 20th-century mathematics. Now, if minds are just adapted for solving the problems of hunting and gathering how could this proof have been devised? How indeed could Fermat have thought of a last theorem, or even a first theorem? Could Fermat and Wiles have been using no more than a second-hand cognitive process which had been evolved for another task? Or maybe a general-purpose learning ability? Both of these seem implausible.

Of course it is not just the ability of modern humans to do pure mathematics that poses this problem to Cosmides and Tooby's ideas about the mind. When I first read their work I was a very junior Research Fellow at a Cambridge college, Trinity Hall. Once a week all the Fellows would gather for dinner at High Table. And there I would sit, fresh out of my Ph.D., surrounded by some of the great intellects in the country. People like Sir Roy Calne, the transplant surgeon (and talented artist); Professor John Polkinghorne, who had not only been a professor of mathematical physics but had also been ordained as an Anglican priest; and the distinguished linguist, Sir John Lyons, the Master of the college. On special occasions the honorary Fellows of the college would dine, including the famous physicist Professor Stephen Hawking. Could these surgeons, linguists and theoretical physicists be expanding the boundaries of human knowledge in such diverse and complex fields by using minds which were adapted for no more than a hunter-gatherer existence?

Perhaps we should look at modern hunter-gatherers for a moment and consider how their minds seem to work. The Inuit, Kalahari Bushmen and Australian Aborigines are not relics of the Stone Age. They are just as modern as you and me. They simply have a lifestyle that happens to be the closest analogy for that of the Pleistocene. Indeed by having to hunt and gather for their food, these modern people share many of the adaptive problems faced by Pleistocene hunter-gatherers. Yet there is a vast gulf between the manner in which they appear to think about their activities, and how they should do so according to C& T.

One of C&T's fundamental arguments is that specific types of problems need specific ways to solve them. A girl choosing fruit using the same reasoning devices she uses for choosing a mate is likely to end up with severe stomach ache because she will choose unripe fruit – fruit which seems to have good muscle tone. Yet as soon as we look at modern hunter-gatherers this seems to be precisely what they do; not get stomach ache from eating unripe fruit, but reason about the natural world as if it were a social being.

Nurit Bird-David has lived with people following a traditional hunting and gathering lifestyle in tropical forests, such as the Mbuti of Zaire. She found that all these groups share a common view of their environment: they conceive of the 'forest as parent', it is a 'giving environment, in the same way as one's close kin are giving'.[28] Similarly the Inuit of the Canadian Arctic 'typically view their world as imbued with human qualities of will and purpose'.[29] Modern hunter-gatherers do not live in landscapes composed merely of animals, plants, rocks and caves. Their landscapes are socially constructed. Among the Aborigines of Australia the wells in the landscape are where their ancestors had dug in the ground, the trees are where digging sticks had been placed, and deposits of red ochre where they had shed blood.[30]

2 During the mythological creation period of the Inuit, animals and humans lived together and easily metamorphosed into each other. This picture is from a drawing by Davidialuk Alasuaq and shows a polar bear dressed Inuit-style cordially greeting a male hunter.

This propensity to think of the natural world in social terms is perhaps most evident in the ubiquitous use of anthropomorphic thinking – attributing animals with humanlike minds. Consider the Inuit and the polar bear. This animal is highly sought after and is 'killed with passion, butchered with care and eaten with delight'.[31] But it is also treated in some respects as if it is another male hunter. When a bear is killed the same restrictions apply to activities that can be undertaken as when someone dies in the camp. The polar bear is thought of as a human ancestor, a kinsman, a feared and respected adversary (see Figure 2). In the mythology of the Inuit there was a time when humans and polar bears could easily change from one kind to another. This idea – that in the past humans and non-human animals could be transformed into each other – is indeed a pervasive feature of the minds of hunter-gatherers. It is the basis of totemic thought, the study of which is a foundation stone of social anthropology.[32]

In general all modern hunter-gatherers appear to do precisely what C&T say they should not do: they think of their natural world as if it were a social being. They do not use a different 'blade' for thinking about such different entities. This has been nicely summed up by the anthropologist Tim Ingold. He writes: 'For them [modern hunter-gatherers] there are not two worlds of persons (society) and things (nature), but just one world – one environment – saturated with personal powers and embracing both human beings, the animals and plants on which they depend, and the landscape in which they live and move.'[33] The social anthropologist/philosopher Ernest Gellner goes even further. Writing about non-Western, 'traditional' societies he concludes that 'the conflation and confusion of functions, aims and criteria, is the normal, original condition of mankind.'[34]

The overwhelming impression from the descriptions of modern hunter-gatherers is that all domains of their lives are so intimately connected that the notion that they think about these with separate reasoning devices seems implausible. Killing and eating animals appears to be as much about constructing and mediating social relationships as it is about getting food.[35] Hunter-gatherers have to build huts within their settlements for shelter, but the act of placing a hut at one location rather than another makes an important social statement.[36] Similarly everything that is worn on the body acts both to keep the person warm but also to send social messages about identity and how that person wants to be treated.[37] When designing the shape of an arrowhead hunters take into account the physical properties of the raw material, the functional requirements of the arrowhead, such as whether it should pierce vital organs or slash arteries, and also how the shape can send social messages about either personal identity or group affiliation.[38] In a nutshell, any one action of a modern hunter-gatherer does not address one single adaptive problem. It simultaneously and intentionally impinges on a whole host of problems. If – and it is a very big if – these modern hunter-gatherers are indeed a good analogy for those of the Pleistocene, how could selective pressures have existed to produce a Swiss army knife for the mind?

I have not been lucky enough to sit with Inuit or Kalahari Bushmen at their meal times. But I have sat with Cambridge dons at a High Table and there seems to be little difference in their behaviour. For while the food provided nutrition, it was also used for sending social messages. It was expensive, excessive and exotic, especially when guests were invited to the college: conspicuous consumption acting to bond the group of Fellows together and to establish their prestige. The seating arrangements in the dining hall were as much socially inspired as those of hunter-gatherers when they seat themselves around a fire: the Fellows' High Table literally on a podium, looking down to where the undergraduates would sit. The Master seated in the centre. I remember the many frowns I received from Senior Fellows when I accidentally sat in a place that did not befit my rank. And also the scowls when I forgot to pass the port – similar (but less serious) to those received by a young hunter if he forgets to divide his kill. The gowns that Fellows wear are of course their tribal dress, the different colours and designs used to establish social rank. Cambridge dons and

Kalahari Bushmen, they are all the same. They all have the architecture of the modern mind – which seems to be something fundamentally different from a collection of specialized devices each for solving a unique adaptive problem.

Now one doesn't need to look at exotic human cultures to recognize that what C&T are telling us about the mind runs counter to how people actually seem to think. Let us return to children. Give a child a kitten and she will believe it has a mind like her own: anthropomorphizing appears to be compulsive. Give a child a doll and she will start talking to it, feeding it and changing its nappy. That inert lump of moulded plastic never smiles at her, but she seems to use the same mental process for interacting with it as she uses for interacting with real people.

Now sit with children and watch cartoons on the television. Immediately one enters a world in which every single rule which could have been imposed on their minds by evolution appears to be violated. You will see talking animals, objects that can change shape and come to life, people that can fly. This surreal world is understood effortlessly by young minds. How could this be if the evolutionary psychologists are correct and the child's mind is composed of content-rich mental modules reflecting the structure of the real world? Surely, if that is the case, they should be confused, bewildered, terrified by their cartoons?

So we are left with a paradox. The evolutionary psychologists make a very powerful argument that the mind should be like a Swiss army knife. It should be constituted by multiple, content-rich mental modules, each adapted to solve a specific problem faced by Pleistocene hunter-gatherers. One cannot fault the logic of their argument. I find it compelling. But as soon as we think about Cambridge dons, Australian Aborigines, or young children this idea seems almost absurd. For me it is the human passion for analogy and metaphor which provides the greatest challenge to Cosmides and Tooby's view of the mind. Simply by being able to invoke the analogy that the mind is like a Swiss army knife, Leda Cosmides appears to be falsifying the claim that is being made.

How can we resolve this paradox? I think we should start by looking once again at children's minds, but this time with a little help from another group of experts: the developmental (rather than evolutionary) psychologists.

Child development and the four domains of intuitive knowledge

Are children really born with content-rich mental modules that reflect the structure of the real (Pleistocene) world, as C&T would have us believe? The answer from developmental psychology is overwhelmingly in their favour. Young children seem to have intuitive knowledge about the world in at least four domains of behaviour: about language, psychology, physics and biology. And their intuitive knowledge within each of these appears to be directly related to a hunting and gathering lifestyle long, long ago in prehistory. We have already considered language, so now let us turn to the evidence for these other types of intuitive knowledge, starting with that of psychology.

INTUITIVE PSYCHOLOGY

By the time children reach the age of three years old they attribute mental states to other people when attempting to explain their actions. In particular, they understand that other people have beliefs and desires and that these play a causal role in behaviour. As Andrew Whiten mentions in the introduction to his edited book, *Natural Theories of Mind* (1991), this has been variously described as an 'intuitive psychology', a 'belief–desire psychology', a 'folk psychology' and a 'theory of mind'.[39] The basic concepts of belief and desire that children use, whatever their cultural background, could not be constructed from the evidence available to them during the earliest stages of their development. Consequently these concepts appear to derive from an innate psychological structure – a content-rich mental module which creates mandatory interpretations of human behaviour in mentalistic terms.

The study of this intuitive psychology has been one of the most dynamic fields of enquiry in child development during the last decade. Most interest has focused on what is known as the 'theory of mind' module: an ability to 'read' other people's minds, described for example in the work of Alan Leslie. One of the most interesting proposals is that the condition of autism, in which children have severe difficulties engaging in social interaction, appears to arise from an impairment of this one module. Autistic children seem to be unaware of what other people are thinking, indeed they seem to be unaware that other people may have thoughts in their minds at all. Simon Baron-Cohen has described their condition as 'mindblindness'. Yet autistic children appear to be quite normal in other aspects of thought. It is as if one blade of their mental Swiss army knife has broken off, or got stuck and won't open. All the other blades carry on as normal – or maybe are enhanced as in the cases of people with severe impairments in some areas of mental activity who display prodigious talents in others, the *idiots savants*.[40]

An evolutionary rationale for a theory of mind module was proposed 20 years ago by Nicholas Humphrey.[41] In fact it was Humphrey who delivered evolutionary psychology into the academic world; the current gang have simply picked up as nurse maids during its kindergarten years. In a seminal academic paper entitled 'The social function of intellect',

Nicholas Humphrey argued that when individuals are living within a group, and entering into a diverse set of co-operative, competitive and mutualistic relationships, individuals with an ability to predict the behaviour of others will achieve the greatest reproductive success. Moreover powers of social forethought and understanding – what he termed a social intelligence – are essential for maintaining social cohesion so that practical knowledge, such as about toolmaking and foraging, can be passed around. In other words, there will be selective pressures for abilities to read the contents of other people's minds. We use a clever trick for this: it is called consciousness. We are going to look at Humphrey's ideas in more detail in Chapter 5, when we will also start to come to grips with the idea of consciousness. Here we should simply note that we can both identify selective pressures for a theory of mind module and find evidence in developmental psychology for its existence. C&T seem to be bang on the mark.

INTUITIVE BIOLOGY

Similar evidence exists for an intuitive understanding of biology. Research in child development has shown that children appear to be born with an understanding that living things and inanimate objects are fundamentally different. Children as young as three seem to have a compulsion to attribute an 'essence' to different types of living things and to recognize that a change in manifest appearance does not reflect a change in kind.[42] For instance, Frank Keil has shown that children can understand that if a horse is put into striped pyjamas, this does not turn it into a zebra. Similarly if a dog is born mute and with only three legs, it is nevertheless a dog, which is a barking quadruped.[43] Just as the experience of young children appears inadequate to account for how they acquire language, so too does their experience of the world seem inadequate to account for their understanding of living things.

We are all familiar with this notion of species essence. It is because of this notion that we demand that a severely brain-damaged person should have the same rights as a university professor, or a physically disabled person the same rights as an Olympic sportsman. They are all 'human', whatever their intellectual and physical abilities. Similarly many people feel uncomfortable about the idea of genetic engineering because it often seems to be about combining the essences of two different species.

Another reason for believing in an intuitive biological knowledge is that all cultures share the same set of notions concerning the classification of the natural world, just as all languages share the same grammatical structure. This has been documented by Scott Atran in his book on the *Cognitive Foundations of Natural History* (1990).[44] He describes how all known cultures appear to entertain notions of (1) biological species of vertebrates and flowering plants; (2) sequential patterns of naming , e.g. 'oak', 'shingle oak', 'spotted shingle oak'; (3) taxa constructed by an appreciation of overall patterns of morphological regularity; (4) overarching animal 'life-form' groupings that closely match those of modern zoological classes such as fish and bird; and (5) overarching plant 'life-form' groupings that have ecological significance, such as 'tree', and 'grass', although these have no place in modern botanical taxonomy.

The universality and complexity of the hierarchical classifications of the natural world that people adopt are most parsimoniously (and perhaps only) explained by a shared, content-rich mental module for 'intuitive biology'. It is simply impossible that people could generalize from the limited evidence available to them during development to the complex taxonomies universally adopted, unless they possessed a 'blueprint' for the structures of the living world hard-wired into their minds.

There are further similarities between biological knowledge and that of psychology and language. For instance, just as people seem to be unable to restrain themselves from thinking about other people's actions in terms of a 'belief-desire' psychology, so too do people seem unable to prevent themselves imposing a complex taxonomic classification on the world, even when it is of little utilitarian value. The anthropologist Brent Berlin has shown, for example, that among the Tzeltal Maya of Mexico and the Aguarana Jivar of Peru more than a third of named plants have no social or economic uses, nor are they poisonous or pests.[45] But they are nevertheless named and grouped according to perceived similarities.

Another similarity with notions of beliefs and desires is the ease with which biological information is transmitted. Scott Atran has described how the structure, scope and depth of taxonomic knowledge are comparable in different societies, regardless of the effort put into transmitting that knowledge. The Hanunóo of the Philippines, for example, have detailed botanical knowledge, which they frequently discuss and pontificate about. The Zafimaniry of Madagascar, living in a similar environment and with a similar subsistence organization, have an equally detailed botanical knowledge. But they pass this information on quite informally, with neither instruction nor commentary.

A critical component of this information refers not to the taxonomy of animals and plants, but to their behaviour. There are several cases of cognitive pathologies in which people either lose an intuitive understanding of animal behaviour, or appear to have one enhanced as they lose other types of knowledge. One of the best examples is provided by the clinical neurologist Oliver Sacks, who has described the case of Temple Grandin. She is autistic and cannot decipher even the simplest social exchange between humans. Yet her intuitive understanding of animal behaviour is daunting. Sacks describes his impression of her after spending some time with Temple on her farm:

I was struck by the enormous difference, the gulf, between Temple's immediate, intuitive recognition of animal moods and signs and her extraordinary difficulties understanding human beings, their codes and signals, the way they conduct themselves. One cannot say that she is devoid of feeling or has a fundamental lack of sympathy. On the contrary, her sense of animals' moods and feelings is so strong that these almost take possession of her, overwhelm her at times.[46]

So we have good evidence that the mind has a specialized device for learning about the natural world. I become particularly convinced about this when I see children showing such effortless ease and enjoyment when learning about animals in their games – this reflects their intuitive biology at work. Could such intuitive biology be accounted for by selective pressures on prehistoric hunter-gatherers, as C&T would have us believe? Quite clearly it could. Of all lifestyles, that of hunting and gathering requires the most detailed knowledge of the natural world. This is quite clear when looking at modern hunter-gatherers: they are compulsive and expert naturalists, able to interpret the tiniest clues in their environments as to their implications for the location and behaviour of animals.[47] Their success as hunter-gatherers, often in marginal environments, depends far more on their understanding of natural history than on their technology, or the amount of labour they put into their lives. We can well imagine that in the evolutionary environment of modern humans, those individuals born with content-rich mental modules to facilitate the acquisition of this knowledge would have had a substantial selective advantage.

INTUITIVE PHYSICS

The evidence from developmental psychology appears conclusive: the ease with which children learn about language, other minds and biology appears to derive from a cognitive foundation of innate content-rich mental modules. Such modules appear to be universally shared by all humans. This finding also applies to a fourth cognitive domain: intuitive physics. From a very early age children understand that physical objects are subject to a different set of rules from those which govern mental concepts and living things. It appears impossible for them to have acquired such knowledge from their limited experience of the world.

This has been demonstrated by the psychologist Elizabeth Spelke.[48] She has undertaken sets of experiments with young children to demonstrate that they have an intuitive knowledge about the properties of physical objects. Concepts of solidity, gravity and inertia appear to be hard-wired into the child's mind. While the life experiences of a young child are dominated by that of people, they nevertheless understand that objects have fundamentally different properties. They cannot, for instance, cause 'action at a distance', as a stranger can do when he or she enters a room.

Children understand that the appropriate way to classify physical objects is very different from that needed for living things. The notion of essence is entirely absent from their thought about artifacts. Whereas a dog is a dog is a dog, even if it has three legs, they appreciate that a crate can be something to store things in, or to sit on, or to use as a table or a bed. Unlike living things, the identity of an object depends upon context. It has no essence. It is subject neither to hierarchical classifications nor to ideas about growth and movement.[49]

From an evolutionary point of view the benefit of possessing content-rich mental modules for understanding physical objects is readily apparent. If one risked using ideas appropriate to living things to think about inert objects, life would be full of mistakes. By having an intuitive knowledge of physics one can rapidly draw on culturally transmitted knowledge about those particular objects required for one's lifestyle – perhaps the stone tools needed by prehistoric hunter-gatherers – without having first to learn about how physical objects differ from living things and mental concepts.

Developing minds: the rise and fall of a Swiss-army-knife mentality

In this tussle between our everyday experience of the world and the academic ideas of evolutionary psychologists, the latter seem to have won this second round hands down. There is a mass of ever-accumulating data from developmental psychology that children are indeed born with a great deal of information about the world hard-wired into their minds. This knowledge appears to fall into four cognitive domains: language, psychology, biology and physics. For each of these one can imagine strong selective pressures for the evolution of content-rich mental modules – for the specialized blades on the Swiss army knife which appears to be the mind.

Nevertheless this cannot be a complete account of the mind. Recall for a moment the way in which a child will play with an inert doll, investing it with the attributes of a living being. A critical feature of that child's mind is not simply that she is able to apply the evolutionarily inappropriate rules of psychology, biology and language to play with her inert physical object, but that she is utterly compelled to do so. This compulsion, and the effortless ease with which it is achieved, appears to be just as strong as that to acquire language or a belief-desire psychology.[50] It too must reflect a fundamental feature of the evolved architecture of her mind.

So now let us now climb back into the ring for round three with C&T. And my boxing gloves are going to be a pair of developmental psychologists who have looked at how children's minds change during their first few years of life. As we look at their ideas we must remember that compelling idea introduced earlier in this chapter, that the stages in the development of a child's mind reflect the stages of cognitive evolution in our ancestors: the idea that 'ontogeny recapitulates phylogeny'.

The very young infant: from a generalized to a domain-specific mentality

The conclusive evidence we have seen for content-rich mental modules has predominantly come from children aged two and three. What about their minds before and after this period?

The developmental psychologist Patricia Greenfield has suggested that up until the age of two, the child's mind is not like a Swiss army knife at all; in fact it is like that general-purpose learning program that we met earlier in this chapter.[51] She argues that the capacities for language and object manipulation displayed by the young infant rely on the same cognitive processes: it is only afterwards that modularization occurs.

To make this argument, Greenfield stresses the similarity between the hierarchical organization of object combination and of speech by very young children. With regard to objects, elements are combined to make constructions, while in language, phonemes are constructed to make words. It is only after the age of two that the language explosion occurs; prior to that the child seems to acquire rudiments of language by using learning rules which are not restricted to language alone. The mind is running a simple, general-purpose computer program – it has a general intelligence. Greenfield argues that in this respect the mind of a two-year-old child is similar to that of a chimpanzee, which she also sees as using general-purpose learning processes for manipulating physical objects and symbols – an idea we will explore in Chapter 5. Among humans, it is only after the age of two that the content-rich mental modules containing knowledge about language, physics, psychology and biology overwhelm the general-purpose learning rules.

So we seem to have a strange metamorphosis of the mind from a computer program to a Swiss army knife. Is this metamorphosis like that of a tadpole to a frog, the end of the affair, or is it like that of a caterpillar to a chrysalis – implying that the final, and most startling, change is yet to happen? Annette Karmiloff-Smith believes it is the latter and that the final stage of mental development is like the emergence of a butterfly.[52]

The child: from a domain-specific to a cognitively fluid mentality

In her book *Beyond Modularity* (1992) Karmiloff-Smith concurs with Greenfield that modularization is a product of development. Now for Karmiloff-Smith, the modules which develop are to some extent variable in different cultural contexts – an idea that is anathema to the evolutionary psychologists, but which aligns her work with the ideas of Howard Gardner. She fully accepts the role of intuitive knowledge about language, psychology, biology and physics, which has indeed been conclusively demonstrated by the work of people such as Noam Chomsky, Alan Leslie, Scott Atran and Elizabeth Spelke as we saw above. But for Karmiloff-Smith, these simply provide the kick-start for the development of cognitive domains. Some of the domains/faculties/intelligences that she believes develop in the mind are the same as those which the evolutionary psychologists would accept, such as language and physics. And they are constituted in the same manner: whereas C&T group mental modules into faculties, Karmiloff-Smith divides domains into micro-domains. So within the faculty/domain of language, pronoun acquisition would be described as either a module or a micro-domain, depending on whose book one is reading.

But fundamental to the ideas of Karmiloff-Smith is that the cultural context in which a child develops also plays a role in determining the type of domains that arise. This is due to the plasticity of early brain development. She suggests that 'with time brain circuits are progressively selected for different domain-specific computations'.[53] And consequently, although Pleistocene hunter-gatherers may not have been great mathematicians – their lives did not require it – children today may nevertheless develop a specialized cognitive domain of mathematics. The kick-start to this may lie in one of the modules of intuitive physics or some other aspect of intuitive knowledge that children are born with. In the appropriate cultural conditions this may become elaborated into a fully developed domain of mathematical knowledge, as indeed has been explored by the psychologist David Geary.[54] The mind is still a Swiss army knife; but the types of blades present may vary from person to person. A man who uses a Swiss army knife to go fishing needs a different assortment of blades from one who goes camping.

So Karmiloff-Smith agrees with C&T that the mind of a young child is a Swiss army knife. But for Karmiloff-Smith, this is just a stage prior to the emergence of the butterfly. For she argues that soon after modularization has occurred, the modules begin working together. She uses a very awkward term for this: 'representational redescription' (RR). But what she means is quite simple. The consequence of RR is that in the mind there arise 'multiple representations of similar knowledge' and consequently 'knowledge becomes applicable beyond the special purpose goals for which it is normally used and perceptual links across domains can be forged'.[55] In other words, thoughts can arise which combine knowledge which had previously been 'trapped' within a specific domain.

A very similar idea has been independently proposed by the developmental psychologists Susan Carey and Elizabeth Spelke. They have argued that the emergence of 'mapping across domains' is a fundamental feature of cognitive development, and one which accounts for cultural diversity: 'Although infants the world over share a set of initial systems of knowledge, these systems are spontaneously overturned over the course of development and learning, as children and adults construct, explore and adopt mappings across knowledge systems.'[56]

Accounting for creativity

With these ideas of Karmiloff-Smith, Carey and Spelke we are immediately drawn back to those attributes of the mind that Jerry Fodor and Howard Gardner had found most impressive, and believed to be a fundamental part of its architecture. Recall how Fodor characterized the most puzzling features of the mind as 'its non-encapsulation, its holism, and its passion for the analogical'. Recall how Gardner had described how 'one typically encounters complexes of intelligences functioning together smoothly, even seamlessly, in order to execute intricate human activities.' Gardner had suggested that the wisest of human beings are those who are most able at building connections across domains – or mappings – as exemplified in the use of analogy and metaphor.

Indeed this seems to be the essence of human creativity. In her book *The Creative Mind* (1990), Margaret Boden explores how we can account for creative thought and concludes that this arises from what she describes as the transformation of conceptual spaces.[57] Now for Boden, a conceptual space is much like a cognitive domain, intelligence or faculty that we have been discussing. Transformation of one of these involves the introduction of new knowledge, or new ways of processing the knowledge that is already contained within the domains. In her book she describes how Arthur Koestler had accounted for human creativity, way back in 1964. He had argued that this arises from 'the sudden, interlocking of two previously unrelated skills or matrices of thought'.[58] A matrix of thought sounds suspiciously like one of Gardner's intelligences or C&T's faculties.

The evidence for thought which requires knowledge from multiple cognitive domains is so overwhelming, and this is clearly such a critical feature of mental architecture, that even some evolutionary psychologists have explored how it can be accounted for. There have been two proposals. The first was in fact made 20 years ago by Paul Rozin, who joins Nicholas Humphrey as one of the midwives of evolutionary psychology. Rozin developed ideas very similar to those of C&T.[59] He argued that the processes of evolution should result in a host of modules within the mind, which he described as 'adaptive specializations' (C&T's technical term, coined 20 years later, was 'Darwinian Algorithms'). But the critical question that he asked is how can behavioural flexibility evolve? C&T suggest that this comes from simply adding more and more specialized devices to the Swiss army knife. Rozin, on the other hand, argued that some form of accessibility between mental modules/domains is the critical feature in both child development and evolution: the 'hall mark for the evolution of intelligence ... is that a capacity first appears in a narrow context and later becomes extended into other domains'.[60] That statement could easily switch places with that by Karmiloff-Smith written almost two decades later: 'knowledge becomes applicable beyond the special purpose goals for which it is normally used'.

All of these arguments by Fodor, Gardner, Karmiloff-Smith, Carey, Spelke and Rozin appear to do away with a strictly modular architecture for the fully developed modern mind. This lack of modularity appears essential to creative thought. But the cognitive scientist Dan Sperber has argued that we can have it both ways – a strictly modular but also a highly creative modern mind.[61] He has argued that during the course of evolution the mind has simply evolved another, and rather special, module. This he calls the 'module of metarepresentation' (MMR). This name is almost as awkward as Karmiloff-Smith's term representational redescription and indeed there is a fundamental similarity in their ideas: the multiple representations of knowledge within the human mind. Whereas the other modules of the mind contain concepts and representations of things, such as those about dogs and what dogs do, Sperber suggests that this new module only holds 'concepts of concepts' and 'representations of representations'.

Sperber explains himself by using an example not about dogs but about cats. Now somewhere deep within our minds, we have a concept of 'cat' which is linked to our intuitive knowledge about living things. This conceptual cat cannot bark, because that is not in the cat essence. As we are told something new about cats it initially enters our minds into the MMR. From there, anything about cats that is compatible with our existing concept of cats is combined with, and may slightly change, that concept. So the MMR is like a clearing house, through which new ideas must pass before they can find a home. But even when they have found their home, they are free to come back and visit the clearing house whenever they like. Some new ideas, such as that cats might bark, do not have a proper home to go to. And consequently they just stay in the clearing house. Now in this clearing house all sorts of mischief can occur. Ideas from different modules, and those which have no home to go to, can get together in some peculiar ways. For instance, knowledge about dogs can get mixed up with knowledge about physical objects and with knowledge about beliefs and desires, so that when a child is given a toy dog – an inert lump of stuffed material – he or she makes it behave like a dog, while also giving it human-like beliefs, desires and intentions.

How could this clearing house have evolved? Or if this clearing house is not really present, how could evolution have drilled holes between the walls of our cognitive domains to let knowledge flow between them or to get replicated in different parts of the mind, as Gardner, Karmiloff-Smith and Rozin suggest? To find some kind of an answer we need to know the Prehistory of the Mind. For this crossing over between domains is after all exactly what C&T argued should not happen in evolution, since it can lead to all sorts of behavioural mistakes. I might go for lunch and see a bowl of plastic bananas. Rather than checking whether or not these yellow objects conform to what I know about edible things (i.e. that they are not made of plastic) I might just bite into them. And all because of some mischief in my mental clearing house that led knowledge of inert physical objects and of (once) living things to get mixed up.

I'm back from lunch and there was not a plastic banana in sight. Actually there was never a risk of eating one as the mind doesn't seem to make mistakes like that. We can create wild and wacky concepts, but often (not always) we seem very able at separating these from the real world. Yet the ability to think of such concepts has certainly evolved, and psychologists can offer no answers as to why this is the case. The only psychologists to have thought seriously about evolutionary issues, C&T, have no explanation as to how or why the multitude of mental modules they believe exist in the mind can lead to such ideas. For they are committed to the idea of the mind as a Swiss army knife.

In this chapter we have seen that the mind is more than simply a Swiss army knife. It may not be an indiscriminate sponge or a computer with a single all-purpose program, as earlier theorists would have it, but nor is it solely a Swiss army knife. It is too creative and unpredictable for that. So perhaps the ideas of Karmiloff-Smith, Carey, Spelke and Sperber about a kind of clearing house can be reconciled with those of Cosmides and Tooby, if seen in an evolutionary context. It is the task of the next chapter to propose just such a framework.

4 A new proposal for the mind's evolution

THE 'GUIDES' who took us around the modern mind in the previous chapter were interested in how the mind works today, and how it develops during childhood. But my interest is with evolutionary history. Since I am trained as an archaeologist I can hardly help trying to identify evolutionary phases whenever faced with a complex structure – whether that structure is a building of stone or the modern mind. Let me give you a taste of how we need to approach the mind by briefly recounting my own experience of an archaeological excavation.

During my summer vacations when a student I worked on the excavation of the medieval Benedictine Abbey of San Vincenzo in Molise, Italy.[1] I supervised the investigation of a particularly complex building, known as the 'South Church'. This involved exposing, recording and interpreting a large series of walls, floors and tombs: the remnants from a remarkable palimpsest of buildings. How could the walls and other remains be made to yield up the secrets of the building's history – its architectural phases and their dates? Much of archaeology entails the painstaking scraping away of the past, layer by layer. It also requires the study of complex intercuttings of certain walls by others, to deduce which are earlier, which later. Those walls must then be dated by reference perhaps to the different types of pottery found in the floor deposits that abut them. All these techniques of archaeological detection are then brought together to recreate as best one can the architectural phases of the building. In the case of the South Church, we deduced that there had been five phases in all, spanning the first 1,000 years AD and culminating in an elaborate multi-storey building housing many of the precious relics of the Abbey. The transitions between each phase had involved the demolishing and constructing of walls, the laying of new floors, the addition of new storeys, and the blocking of doors.

When I look at the evidence about the modern mind provided by the psychologists in the previous chapter, I am reminded of our work at the South Church at San Vincenzo – or indeed any modern church or cathedral. The task of this chapter is the task that we faced after having amassed the information from the South Church excavations: identifying a series of architectural phases.

In this short chapter I will propose an evolutionary history for the mind in terms of three architectural phases. This will provide the framework for the rest of my study – the archaeological data we are going to explore in later chapters will be used to evaluate, refine, develop and date this framework. Without a provisional framework we would be simply swamped with data, knowing neither what we should be looking for nor what it might mean. In order to propose these phases I will draw on the theories outlined in the previous chapter. I will also draw on one of the biggest ideas in biology, one that has been significant in studies of evolution since the time of Aristotle, although the last two decades has seen it lose its once preeminent position: recapitulation, or 'ontogeny follows phylogeny'.

I briefly introduced this idea in the previous chapter. In essence recapitulation proposes that the sequence of developmental stages that a juvenile of a species goes through, its ontogeny, reflects the sequence of adult forms of its ancestors, its phylogeny. Ernest Haeckel stated this idea in his biogenetic law of 1866: 'ontogeny is the short and rapid recapitulation of phylogeny'.[2] Haeckel had thought that during the course of evolution the rate of development had accelerated, and consequently ancestral adult forms had been pushed back, or 'telescoped into', the juvenile stages of descendants.

The origin and history of this idea have been traced in the seminal book by Stephen Jay Gould entitled *Ontogeny and Phylogeny* (1977). He explains that parallels between development and evolution pervade the biological world and that for many scientists of the 19th and early 20th centuries recapitulation appeared to be the key for understanding the past. Gould quotes the biologist E. Conklin writing in 1928: 'recapitulation promised to reveal not only the animal ancestry of man and the line of his descent but also the method of origin of his mental, social and ethical faculties.'[3] Jean Piaget, the most influential developmental psychologist of the 1960s and 1970s, was sympathetic to the idea of parallels between ontogeny and phylogeny, although he did not adopt an explicit position regarding recapitulation. But as I noted in the previous chapter, the archaeologist Thomas Wynn was drawn to the notion of recapitulation as a means to infer the intelligence of our ancestors by relying on the developmental phases for the mind as proposed by Piaget. Indeed the psychologist Kathleen Gibson has recently written that 'ontogenetic perspectives have become the rule, rather than the exception, among serious scholars of cognitive and linguistic evolution.'[4]

Today biologists take a rather more liberal view of the relationship between ontogeny and phylogeny than that adopted by Haeckel. As

Stephen Jay Gould explains, while there is evidence for the accelerated development of some traits, just as Haeckel proposed, and hence the pushing of ancestral adult forms into the juvenile stages of descendants, there is also evidence for the converse: the slowing up of the development of other traits so that certain juvenile features of ancestors appear in the adult descendants. This is referred to as neoteny, and is thought to be as common as recapitulation. It is most dramatically illustrated by the manner in which juvenile chimpanzees have a striking resemblance to adult humans – a similarity that is lost as chimpanzees mature. Consequently if there is any value in the notion of recapitulation, it will be found in the study of individual organs, rather than organisms as a whole.

Gould devotes much of his book to neoteny, demonstrating that this is of critical importance for understanding human evolution. But as both Kathleen Gibson and the psycho-linguist Andrew Lock have argued, while neoteny may help explain the morphological development of modern humans, this cannot account for the development of intelligence and knowledge.[5] These do not remain infantile during development, as does the shape of the skull, for instance. And so, if there are parallels between the development and the evolution of the mind, recapitulation rather than neoteny is a more likely scenario.[6]

I am going hesitantly to adopt the notion of recapitulation and propose a series of architectural phases for the evolution of the mind. My hesitation is for two reasons. First, as Gould describes in *The Mismeasure of Man* (1981), the idea of recapitulation 'provided an irresistible criterion'[7] for late-19th-century and 20th-century scientists to rank human groups as higher or lower. It provided pseudo-scientific support for racist and sexist ideas. So, although these ideas reflect a misunderstanding and misuse of recapitulation, one must always use it with great caution. The second reason for my hesitation is that I have no theoretical conviction that recapitulation of the evolution of the mind during development necessarily occurs. If it does, I am sure that it is likely to be manifest in some broad parallels rather than any strict correspondence of phylogenetic and ontogenetic stages.

Whether or not recapitulation of the mind is correct, it provides a means to establish the framework of hypothetical architectural phases which is needed to continue with my study.[8] Indeed it would seem a missed opportunity verging on academic negligence if I were to ignore the idea of recapitulation. After all, I am already in possession of information about the development of the mind in the child, as described in the previous chapter, and by the end of my study I also intend to have information about the evolution of the mind acquired from the materials of the archaeological and fossil records. So by adopting the notion of recapitulation an intriguing prospect looms: will we see the developmental stages of the minds of children today paralleled in the evolution of human ancestral minds?

In the previous chapter we looked at the work of several developmental psychologists, notably Patricia Greenfield, Annette Karmiloff-Smith, Susan Carey and Elizabeth Spelke. It will be largely by drawing on their work that I will suggest the architectural phases for the evolution of the mind. I say largely because I believe that there were also clues provided by all the psychologists whose work we considered in that chapter, clues which in fact support the proposed phases as drawn from studies of child development.

Three phases for the evolution of the mind

Let me now simply state the three broad architectural phases for the evolution of the mind that will serve as the framework for interpreting the archaeological and fossil data in later chapters, prior to elaborating on these in the rest of this chapter.

Phase 1. Minds dominated by a domain of general intelligence – a suite of general-purpose learning and decision-making rules.

Phase 2. Minds in which general intelligence has been supplemented by multiple specialized intelligences, each devoted to a specific domain of behaviour, and each working in isolation from the others.

Phase 3. Minds in which the multiple specialized intelligences appear to be working together, with a flow of knowledge and ideas between behavioural domains.

The correspondence between these and the development processes described in the previous chapter should be clear. The first is paralleled by the domain-general learning processes identified as critical to the very young infant; the second parallels the modularization of the mind with the development of domain-specific thought and knowledge; and the third parallels what Karmiloff-Smith describes as 'representational redescription' and Carey and Spelke describe as 'mapping across domains' – when knowledge becomes available for use in multiple domains of activity.[9]

These three broad phases are suggested as no more than a hypothetical framework for guiding the rest of my study. I want to spend the remainder of this chapter elaborating on this framework. There are further clues yet to be extracted from the observations about the modern mind made by the psychologists we considered in the previous chapter.

It is also important to clarify the relationship between development and evolution. As Stephen Jay Gould stressed in *Ontogeny and Phylogeny*, when we talk about evolution, we are normally just talking about the evolution of the adult forms of past species. But just as with any individual today, an australopithecine or member of an early *Homo* species went through a period of development, possibly with his/her mind going through a series of substantial changes. There is, therefore, considerable potential for confusion between the development and evolution of the mind. Let me try to clarify the relationship by pursuing an analogy of the mind as a cathedral.

The mind as a cathedral

We can think of the mind of each individual as a new cathedral being built as he or she develops from an infant to a mature adult. It is built according to an architectural plan encoded in the genetic constitution of that individual, as inherited from his/her parents, and under the influence of the particular environment in which he/she develops. As we all vary in our genetic constitution and/or developmental environment, we all have a unique mind. But as members of the same species, we share substantial similarities in the architectural plans that we inherit and the minds we develop.

This situation has been the same for all our ancestors. But the architectural plans have been constantly tinkered with by evolution. Random changes were brought about by genetic mutations. Most of these changes had no effect on the mind. A few had negative effects: these 'damaged' plans did not survive for long in the gene pool because the individuals with such minds were out-competed by other individuals for resources and for mates. Some other mutations resulted in beneficial effects, enabling individuals to compete more successfully and pass on to the next generation these 'improved' architectural plans. Of course, while these mutations were happening, the environment was also changing. Our ancestors constantly faced new types of problems, requiring new types of thought processes for their solution – different types of buildings are appropriate in different types of environment.

With the joint effects of variation caused by random genetic mutations, inheritance, differential reproductive success, and constant environmental change, the suite of architectural plans evolved. In other words, it was shaped by natural selection.[10] The architectural plans may have been continually tinkered with, but no plan was ever started again from scratch. Evolution does not have the option of returning to the drawing board and beginning anew; it can only ever modify what has gone before. This is, of course, why we can only understand the modern mind by understanding the prehistory of the mind. It is why ontogeny may contain clues to phylogeny. It is why we can look at the cathedral of the modern mind and find clues to the architecture of past minds.

We also know that even though two cathedrals may have shared the same architectural plan, they will not have looked exactly the same due to the unique environments in which they were built. Different types of stone, topographic settings and workforces would have been available. It is impossible to separate the influence of the building environment and the architectural plan on the finished cathedral, claiming for instance that a particular feature is due to one or the other. Similarly when trying to understand the character of a modern mind, it is impossible to separate the effects of genes and the developmental environment.

In the last chapter we looked at several different modern cathedrals – the minds of young children and mature adults, the minds of Cambridge dons and Kalahari Bushmen, the minds of brilliant mathematicians and those who suffer from cognitive pathologies such as autism. We were guided by various psychologists, each trying to identify the common and significant features of modern minds, but each stressing different features. To my mind they all rather neglected the importance of architectural joints and how buildings change in design and function throughout their long histories. This, of course, was not their concern: their interest was in how the modern mind works today. But my concern is with architectural history, so let me now return to those three phases I stated above and elaborate these by pursuing my analogy of the mind as a cathedral (see Box p. 67).

Phase 1
Minds dominated by a central nave of generalized intelligence.
The minds of the first proposed phase have no more than a single nave in which all the services take place; these are the processes of thought. Information is delivered to this nave via a series of input modules – earlier versions of those that Jerry Fodor described when looking at the modern mind. The nave does not contain the complex central systems that Fodor saw within the mind. It is a nave of general intelligence, which has few traces surviving in the modern mind. Two of our guides – Patricia Greenfield and Annette Karmiloff-Smith – found traces of this type of intelligence in the minds of young children. Two other guides, John Tooby and Leda Cosmides, acknowledged that traces of this nave might be somewhere in the modern mind, but were not inter-ested in searching for them, believing that general intelligence plays a limited role in the modern mind. Of course, if I had chosen another guide – Jean Piaget – he would have seen little else but this nave in all

The mind as a cathedral

N.B. These are schematic, metaphorical illustrations. They carry no implications for the spatial location of cognitive processes within the brain.

Phase 3: Two possible architectural plans for Phase 3 minds.
These represent minds of people living by hunting and gathering. For those with other lifestyles, it is likely that other types of specialized intelligences will develop, although social and linguistic intelligence are likely to be universal.

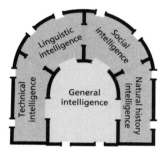

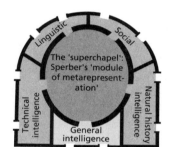

Phase 2
Minds with a 'nave' of general intelligence and multiple 'chapels' of specialized intelligences. It remains unclear how that of language is related to the other cognitive domains. As we can assume that all minds of this phase were of people living by hunting and gathering, the three 'chapels' are social, technical and natural history intelligence.

Phase 1
Minds with a 'nave' of general intelligence. The 'doors' represent the passage of information from modules concerned with perception.

Evolutionary time

the minds we visited. This general intelligence would have been constituted by a suite of general-purpose learning and decision-making rules. Their essential features are that they can be used to modify behaviour in the light of experience in any behavioural domain. But they can only produce relatively simple behaviour – the rate of learning would be slow, errors would be frequent and complex behaviour patterns could not be acquired.

Phase 2
Minds in which isolated chapels of specialized intelligences are built.
Minds of this second proposed phase are distinguished by the construction of a series of 'chapels' of specialized intelligences, as Howard Gardner called them, alternatively known as cognitive domains or faculties, as described by Leda Cosmides and John Tooby. Just as the greater number of side chapels in Romanesque cathedrals of the 12th century reflect the increasing complexity of church ritual at that time, so too do these chapels reflect the increasing complexity of mental activity.

The nave of general intelligence remains as an essential feature of the architectural design. But the services of thought within the nave are now overshadowed by those of greater complexity being undertaken in each of the chapels. Bundles of closely related mental modules relating to one specific domain of behaviour are found within each specialized intelligence. Some of the modules may in fact have been present in Phase 1, where they would have been scattered around the nave rather than being grouped together in the appropriate isolated specialized intelligence.

Each specialized intelligence looks after a specific domain of behaviour and is essential to the functioning of the mind as a whole. All knowledge about the domain is contained within that chapel and cannot be found anywhere else within the mind. Learning within these behavioural domains is now rapid and with a minimum of errors. Complex behavioural patterns can be acquired, and these can be easily modified due to new experience relating to that specific behavioural domain. So in Phase 2 we have minds with multiple specialized intelligences, or chapels of the mind. How many chapels were there, and what domains of behaviour were they dedicated to?

We know that the architectural plans for these minds evolved, and the minds themselves developed, while people were living as hunter-gatherers. And we saw in the last chapter that the modern mind still has modules that provide us with an intuitive knowledge of biology, physics and psychology. These modules are likely to be the surviving foundations of the chapels/intelligences which were once built in the minds of this second phase. Consequently there are likely to have been at least three dominant chapels/intelligences in the second phase:

1. The traces of an intuitive psychology imply a chapel of **social intelligence,** used for interacting with other human individuals, and including modules for 'mind reading'.
2. Similarly the traces of an intuitive biology within the modern mind suggest that there was once a chapel of **natural history intelligence** – a bundle of modules concerned with understanding the natural world, an understanding essential to life as a hunter-gatherer.
3. Intuitive physics may be the surviving foundations of a chapel of **technical intelligence** that once existed in the minds of some of our early ancestors, housing the mental modules for the manufacture and manipulation of stone and wooden artifacts, including those for throwing such artifacts.[11]

A critical design feature of these chapels is that their walls are thick and almost impenetrable to sound from elsewhere in the cathedral. There is no access between the chapels. In other words, knowledge about different behavioural domains cannot be combined together. Moreover the modules used for thinking within each intelligence are largely restricted to that intelligence alone. There may be some exceptions: on some occasions modules may indeed be used in an inappropriate domain of behaviour – a module evolved for social interaction being used for interacting with animals – but when this happens the module cannot work effectively. We may think of this as the sounds emanating from one chapel being heard in a heavily muffled and indistinct form elsewhere in the cathedral.

Minds in this second proposed phase of cognitive evolution use the chapels for thinking complex thoughts about toolmaking, natural history and social interaction. But when a single thought is required which could benefit from knowledge or modules from more than one chapel – such as thoughts about designing a tool for hunting a specific animal – the mind must rely on general intelligence. Consequently, thought and behaviour at 'domain-interfaces' would appear far simpler than that within a single domain. Nevertheless, the nave remains an essential part of the building, for without it the structure would simply collapse.

There may be a fourth chapel within the cathedrals of this phase: that of **linguistic intelligence**. As we saw in the previous chapter, this is also constituted by a bundle of mental modules. But could linguistic intelligence ever have been isolated from the other intelligences of the mind? Unlike them it serves no function in itself – people do not talk about grammar for its own sake. And we saw in the previous chapter how Jerry Fodor characterized language as one of the 'input' processes rather than as a feature of the central systems. So at present, while we recognize that a chapel of linguistic intelligence may have existed, we cannot specify its architectural relationship to general intelligence and the other specialized intelligences. This will have to wait until we have acquired further evidence later in this book.

The previous chapter gave us a large number clues to the existence of this evolutionary phase of the modern mind, which partly reflects my choice of guides. One of the biggest clues came from the study of child development. Annette Karmiloff-Smith describes how, after having passed through a phase in which thought is dominated by general intelligence, children develop 'domain-specific' thought processes. Because of the highly variable environments in which children develop today, the numbers and types of domains are quite variable – they are not those which are necessarily appropriate to a hunter-gatherer way of life. They are, however, built upon, or in Karmiloff-Smith's term 'kick started' by, the surviving foundations of the Phase 2 specialized intelligences.

Phase 3
Minds in which the chapels have been connected, resulting in a 'cognitive fluidity'.

The minds of the third phase share a new architectural feature: direct access between the chapels. With this feature, knowledge once trapped within different chapels can now be integrated together. It is not quite clear how this direct access was achieved. Some of our guides described how they could see knowledge crossing between domains/intelligences, as if passing through doors and windows which had been inserted in the chapel walls. But one of our guides, Dan Sperber, thought he could see a 'superchapel' – his module of metarepresentation. In this superchapel, knowledge from specialized intelligences is replicated in much the same way that Karmiloff-Smith argued that knowledge becomes replicated in different parts of the mind during development. Clearly we need more evidence before the specific architectural design of Phase 3 minds can be described; all we know at present is that the combining of thoughts and knowledge of the different specialized intelligences is possible and that this has significant consequences for the nature of the mind.

As occurred in Phase 1, a 'single service' of thought can be conducted. But these single services of Phase 3 draw upon and harmonize the previously isolated services practised perhaps for millennia within each of the chapels of Phase 2. For instance, Howard Gardner stresses how in the modern mind complexes of intelligences function smoothly and seamlessly together; Paul Rozin, Annette Karmiloff-Smith, Susan Carey and Elizabeth Spelke have written about the importance of knowledge being used in multiple domains of thought. Moreover, the single service now has a complexity that was previously absent: for this single service is what Jerry Fodor described as the central system of the mind.

Experience gained in one behavioural domain can now influence that in another. Indeed distinct behavioural domains no longer exist. And brand new ways of thinking, subjects to think about and ways to behave arise. The mind acquires not only the ability but a positive passion for metaphor or analogy.

The differences between the Phase 2 and Phase 3 minds are analogous to those between Romanesque and the succeeding Gothic cathedrals of stone. In Gothic architecture sound and light emanating from different parts of the cathedral can flow freely around the building unimpeded by the thick heavy walls and low vaults one finds in Romanesque architecture. In a Gothic design, sound, space and light interact to produce a sense of almost limitless space. Similarly, in the Phase 3 mental architecture, thoughts and knowledge generated by specialized intelligences can now flow freely around the mind – or perhaps just around the superchapel. As both Arthur Koestler and Margaret Boden recognized, when thoughts originating in different domains can engage together, the result is an almost limitless capacity for imagination. So we should refer to these Phase 3 minds as having a 'cognitive fluidity'.

Why the tinkering of evolution led to the ability to combine thoughts and knowledge from specialized intelligences, and indeed why the specialized intelligences were constructed in the first place, remains unclear. But this is not important at this stage in our enquiry. All we need at present is a basic architectural history.

How should we date the different phases of our architectural history? When in the course of human evolution did the architectural plans encode information for the construction of no more than a central nave? When were chapels first built? Were they built simultaneously, or introduced piecemeal so that there was a gradual change from Phase 1 to Phase 2 buildings? How did the chapel of linguistic intelligence fit in? When was the direct access between chapels first created? How was this direct access achieved, by the construction of a superchapel, or simply a series of doors and windows?

These questions are similar to those a medieval archaeologist might ask when devising a programme of excavations to refine an architectural history. They are the questions we need to answer when we turn to examine the archaeological and fossil evidence for the evolution of the mind in later chapters. But a good archaeologist never rushes to dig holes. First he or she searches for further clues in the modern world. He or she looks around the landscape to find a building dating to an early period and not subjected to later construction work which might have destroyed the original design. Indeed a few years after digging at San Vincenzo I was able to accompany the director of those excavations to southern Albania where we saw intact 9th-century monastic buildings. These had been constructed with architectural plans similar to those used for the buildings at San Vincenzo, but which we had struggled to reconstruct from no more than wall fragments and foundations.

So for one more chapter we must remain in the modern world. But the landscape we must now explore is not occupied by churches and abbeys; it is one populated by chimpanzees. We must try to expose the architecture of the chimpanzee mind, because this is likely to share features with that of the common ancestor of 6 million years ago. In this sense we can now raise the curtain on Act 1 of our prehistory.

5 Apes, monkeys and the mind of the missing link

ACT I OF OUR PREHISTORY begins 6 million years ago. But, as we saw in Chapter 2, the stage is bare and our actor, the missing link, is absent. There are no bones or artifacts to inspect which might give clues to past behaviour and past mental activity. How then can we reconstruct the mind of this distant ancestor? To what architectural phase should we assign her mind? Phase 1, with no more than a general intelligence? Or perhaps Phase 2, with one or more specialized cognitive domains working alongside, but blocked off from each other and a general intelligence? How can we use the mind of the missing link to help in understanding the prehistory of the mind? These are all challenging questions to answer.

Our only hope is to take a look at that great ape from whom our fore-bears diverged on the ancestral family tree 6 million years ago: the chimpanzee.

There is a long history in science of using the chimpanzee as an analogy for our earliest human ancestor.[1] This assumes that there has been minimal cognitive evolution during the last 6 million years along the ape line. We can indeed be confident that there has not been significant evolution in terms of brain processing power, for the brain size of the chimpanzee at about 450 cc is not significantly less than that of the aus-tralopithecines and a figure that seems reasonable for the missing link. Similarly, as we go back in time from *H. erectus*, to *H. habilis*, to *A. afaren-sis* and *A. ramidus*, anatomy becomes increasingly ape-like in character – more and more like that of living chimpanzees. And if we look at the archaeological record that chimpanzees leave behind them, it is practi-cally indistinguishable from that of our earliest ancestors because it hardly exists at all. There are no more than a few stone flakes (uninten-tionally created when hammering nuts) which can barely be dis-tinguished from flakes created by natural processes. Such flakes are likely to have been lost within the litter of nature.

So we will follow convention and assume that the mind of the chim-panzee is a good approximation for the mind of the missing link. What does the behaviour of chimpanzees tell us about the architecture of their minds? Let us start with a type of behaviour which was once thought to be uniquely human – the manufacture and use of tools – and ask whether chimpanzees have a chapel of technical intelligence.

Technical intelligence: Chimp the toolmaker?

Fifty years ago it was generally believed that humans were the only species to make and use tools, summed up in the epithet 'Man the toolmaker'. Then in the late 1950s Jane Goodall began to study wild chimpanzees at Gombe in Tanzania and soon described how the chimpanzees stripped leaves off sticks to use as probes for ants and to make fishing sticks for termites.[2] Since that time many other observations of chimpanzee tool manufacture and use have been made by researchers such as by Bill McGrew and Christophe and Hedwige Boesch. We now know that a wide range of tools are made, and used for a variety of tasks, by chimpanzees.[3] In addition to catching insects, small sticks are used for acquiring honey, removing nuts from their shells, picking bits of brain from skulls and cleaning eye orbits. Leaves are crushed together to form a sponge to gather up ants or water. Leaves are also used by chimpanzees to clean the cranial cavities of prey, and to clean themselves. They even use leaves as a plate – a plate to catch their own faeces which are then inspected for undigested food items. In the forests of West Africa chimpanzees use hammers and anvils to crack open nuts (see Figure 3). In sum, chimpanzees appear adept at manufacturing and manipulating physical objects. Does this imply that they have specialized cognitive processes dedicated to such tasks – does their mental architecture have a chapel of technical intelligence? Or do chimpanzees simply rely on the processes of general intelligence, such as trial-and-error learning, for making and using tools?

As a first stab at answering this question we might consider how complex chimpanzee tool behaviour appears to be: the more complex it

3 A chimpanzee using a stone hammer and anvil to crack open nuts.

is, the more likely it is to arise from specialized cognitive processes. Bill McGrew, author of the most comprehensive study of chimpanzee material culture,[4] firmly believes that chimpanzee tool use is of considerable complexity. Indeed, in an (in)famous article written in 1987, he directly compared the toolkits of chimpanzees to those of Tasmanian Aborigines and concluded that they were at an equivalent level of complexity. For this comparison McGrew chose to measure complexity by counting 'technounits', which is simply an individual component of a tool, whatever material that component is made from and however it is used. So a hoe used by, say, a peasant farmer, comprising a shaft, a blade and a binding, has three technounits, while the suite of computerized robots operated by a modern car worker has perhaps three million technounits.

When McGrew measured the technounits in the tools of the Tasmanian Aborigines and those of the Tanzanian chimpanzees he found that the mean number of technounits per tool was not substantially different. All chimpanzee tools and most of the Aboriginal tools were made from a single component. The most complex Aboriginal tool, a baited hide, had only four technounits. All other tools, such as spears, stone missiles, ropes, hides and baskets, appeared to be directly comparable in their technounit complexity to the termite sticks and leaf sponges of the chimpanzees. Consequently if the modern mind, as possessed by Tasmanian Aborigines, has an intuitive physics then we should also attribute this to the chimpanzee mind.

McGrew's conclusion, however, is unhelpful. The tools of the peasant farmer may have several million fewer components than those of the factory worker, but they may require far greater skill and knowledge to use effectively. Once the computers and robots are in place, pressing a button can build a car, but to till the ground a hoe needs to be manipulated with care.

Counting technounits as a measure of tool complexity can also be seen to be of limited value when we consider how the tools are made. One requires a tool to make a sharpened stick. This may simply be a flake of stone, but nevertheless that flake must be found or, more likely, struck from a nodule. A termite probe can be made by simply tearing off the leaves and biting the stick to an appropriate length. When Aborigines make tools their physical actions are unique to toolmaking: there is nothing comparable in other domains of human behaviour to the chipping of stone or the whittling of a stick. When chimpanzees make tools they simply use the same set of actions which are employed in feeding: removing twigs from bushes, stripping leaves, biting them into shorter pieces.[5]

McGrew did in fact address manufacturing complexity in his comparison of Aboriginal and chimpanzee tools, and again argued that the similarities outweigh the differences. But I find some of his examples unconvincing. For instance, Aborigines regularly use a production principle of 'replication' when making their tools. This is the combining of several identical elements, as in a bunch of tied-up grass. McGrew argued that chimpanzees also use this principle – but the only example he could find was that of a leaf sponge, a crushed mass of essentially identical leaves.

Aborigines also regularly use 'conjunction', which is the joining of two or more technounits together. But only one single example of conjunction by a chimpanzee has ever been witnessed. This was on 16 January 1991, when Testuro Matsuzawa observed Kai, an old female chimpanzee, take two stones for nutcracking, one for the hammer and one for the anvil.[6] To steady the anvil she placed another stone below it to act as a wedge. Until there are other examples, I'm not convinced that this is sufficient evidence that chimpanzees employ conjunction in their tool-making – something that is present in practically every single tool made by humans.

The gist of my argument should now have become clear: we cannot attribute chimpanzees with specialized cognitive processes dedicated to the manipulation and transformation of physical objects i.e. a technical intelligence. Further confirmation of this can be found when we look at the distribution of tool use among different chimpanzee groups – although this evidence is normally used to argue the exact converse. Chimpanzees appear to have cultural traditions regarding tool use.[7] Only the chimpanzees of the Tai forest in West Africa extract bone marrow with sticks; the chimpanzees of Mahale in Tanzania do not use tools to probe for ants, although they feed upon these insects. Similarly those of the Tai forest do not go ant fishing, although they do go ant eating. Unlike chimpanzees of Gombe, the Mahale and Tai chimpanzees do not use tools for personal hygiene.

These differences cannot be explained on genetic or ecological grounds alone: chimpanzee tool use appears to be largely based on tradition. This finding has been like a blast of trumpets for those who have wanted to minimize the differences between chimpanzee and human behaviour. For it seems to say that chimpanzees are like humans: animals with culture. But I interpret this finding rather differently. Human cultural traditions rarely impinge on the use of simple tools for simple tasks, especially when they dramatically increase the efficiency with which that task is completed (as is the case with using sticks for termite fishing). All human groups use knives, for instance. Human cultural traditions are usually about different ways of doing the same task, rather than whether that task is undertaken or not. To take a trivial example, Frenchmen used to wear berets and Englishmen bowlers, but they both wore hats. Chimpanzee tool-use traditions appear fundamentally different from human cultural traditions. The failure of Tai chimpanzees to use termite sticks is most likely to arise simply from the fact that no individual within that group has ever thought of doing such a thing, or discovered it accidentally, or managed to learn it from another chimp before that chimp forgot how to do it, or passed away with his great tool-use secret. This is not cultural behaviour; it is simply not being very good at thinking about making and using physical objects. It is the absence of a technical intelligence.

This conclusion can be strengthened when we actually look at the pattern of learning about tool use. Recall that the intuitive physics and technical intelligence within the human mind facilitate rapid and efficient learning about the world of objects. Now if we see chimpanzees struggling to learn about the simplest object manipulation tasks, this may indicate that their minds lack such intuitive knowledge. And this is precisely what we do see.

We commonly think of chimpanzees as very rapid learners – a species that has mastered the art of imitation. Indeed we commonly use the verb 'to ape' as another way of saying 'to imitate'. But this is far from the truth: chimpanzees do not seem to be very good at imitating behaviour at all. In fact, some primatologists argue that chimpanzees cannot imitate – all that happens is that their attention is drawn to certain objects and then learning takes place on a trial-and-error basis.[8] So if one chimpanzee sees another poking sticks in a hole and licking the termites off, and then starts to do something similar, this is unlikely to be imitation in terms of understanding both the goal of the action and the means to achieve it. It is more likely that his attention was simply drawn to sticks and holes. This is perhaps why in more than 30 years of observation of chimpanzee tool use there have been no technological advances: each generation of chimpanzees appears to struggle to attain the technical level attained by the previous generation.

Unfortunately we lack systematic studies of how techniques such as termite fishing and ant dipping are acquired by chimpanzees, although there are various reports of juveniles watching their mothers at work and 'playing' with sticks.[9] Christophe and Hedwige Boesch, however, have made a detailed study of the acquisition of the nutcracking technique as used by the chimpanzees in the Tai forest of West Africa.[10] For you, me or most young children this technique is easy. A nut is placed on an anvil and struck with a hammer. Yet juvenile chimpanzees appear to have great difficulty in learning to do this. They do not fully acquire the skill before adulthood and require four years of practice before any net benefits are achieved. Juveniles seem to spend a lot of time hitting hammers directly against anvils without putting a nut between them, or bringing nuts to anvils without hammers.

Here is a summary of the evidence about toolmaking and using by chimpanzees. Their tools are very simple. They are made by using physical actions common to other domains of behaviour. They are used for a limited range of tasks, and chimpanzees appear to be rather poor at thinking about new ways to use tools. They are slow at adopting the tool-use methods currently practised within their group. Now these attributes do not constitute the type of behavioural repertoire that we would expect if the chimpanzee mind had a technical intelligence devoted to manipulating and transforming physical objects. They are much more like those we would expect from the use of a general intelligence – processes such as trial and error and associative learning – which are not specifically designed for making and using tools.

Natural history intelligence: mental maps and hunting behaviour

Chimpanzee tool use is predominantly about getting food. So we must now turn to foraging and ask whether the chimpanzee mind has a natural history intelligence in terms of a suite of cognitive processes dedicated to acquiring and processing information about resources, such as plants, animals and raw materials.

Chimpanzees certainly appear to be very adept at making foraging decisions, for they display goal-directed movements towards particular food patches. Such behaviour is likely to derive from a detailed knowledge about the spatial distribution of resources – a continually updated mental map – and knowledge of the ripening cycles of many plants. Some of the most detailed observations of chimpanzee foraging behaviour have been made by Richard Wrangham.[11] He studied the Gombe chimpanzees of Tanzania and concluded that they have an intimate knowledge of their environment, being excellent botanists and able to discriminate between subtle visual clues of species type or plant condition. By using such botanical knowledge and a mental map chimpanzees were able to move directly to patches with ripe plant material.

Wrangham could find no evidence, however, that chimpanzees could find food patches about which they had no prior knowledge. To do so would have necessitated the development of hypotheses for food distribution – an insightful and complex use of knowledge to create a new idea about the world, which is one of the hallmarks of a specialized intelligence. Chimpanzees appear to rely on noticing and remembering sufficient information about the environment on their daily travels.

The possession of mental maps in chimpanzees has been demonstrated by formally testing their ability to find and remember the location of objects hidden in enclosures.[12] But the most interesting study has been undertaken by Christophe and Hedwige Boesch regarding the transport of hammers and nuts to anvils in the West African Tai forest.[13] By monitoring the movement of hammerstones, weighing them and measuring the distance between trees, the Boeschs inferred that the chimpanzees have a spontaneous means of measuring the distance between two locations in the forest – a means as accurate as the Boeschs' own measuring ropes, even when there are intervening obstacles such as fallen trees and rivers. They claim that chimpanzees are able to abstract and compare distances between sets of paired locations, identify the shortest of these, and include the influence of the weight of the hammer to be transported when deciding where to aim for. This mental feat is all the more impressive when one recognizes that mental maps need continual updating to account not only for the movement of hammers, but also the activity of other nutcracking chimps. Indeed one of the reasons for the few sub–optimal decisions appears to be that a hammerstone had been expected in one location, but had already been moved by other individuals.

It is most likely that this well–developed mental mapping exhibited by Tai chimpanzees derives from the need to exploit patchy resources under conditions of poor visibility. This has indeed been proposed as a general explanation for the evolution of intelligence among primates[14] – before intelligence was thought of as a Swiss army knife of specialized devices.

These observations by Wrangham and the Boeschs leave us in a rather equivocal position regarding the possibility of a specialized domain of natural history intelligence. Certain elements of this appear to be present: the interest and ability to build up a large database of natural history knowledge and the processing of this to make efficient foraging decisions. Yet this is effectively no more than rote memory – there does not seem to be a creative or insightful use of that knowledge. And we must remember that many animals, particularly birds, construct very elaborate mental maps for the distribution of resources.[15] We need to look for further evidence regarding chimpanzee interaction with the natural world, which we can find by considering a rather more challenging type of foraging behaviour – hunting.

In 1989 the Boeschs published a detailed study of the hunting behaviour of the Tai chimpanzees in which they undertook a comparison with hunting by the chimpanzees of Gombe and Mahale.[16] The Tai chimpanzees appear to be very proficient hunters; on over 50 per cent of their hunting events clear hunting intentions were apparent within the group before any prey had been seen or heard. In contrast, all the hunts by the Gombe and Mahale chimpanzees appear to be opportunistic.

The Tai chimpanzees concentrate on one type of prey, colobus monkeys, while those of Gombe and Mahale regularly hunt bushpigs, bushbuck and blue duiker. This difference can be explained on ecological grounds alone, as young duiker are rare in the Tai forest and bushpigs live in relatively large groups and are difficult to hunt.

With regard to hunting success, this is considerably higher among the Tai chimpanzees. It appears to reflect the fact that they hunt in larger groups within which there is a relatively high degree of cooperation. When the Gombe chimpanzees hunt in groups they tend to chase the prey in different directions, which serves to confuse it. In contrast the Tai chimpanzees disperse under the prey, often out of sight of each other, but all remain focussed on the same victim. As the hunt progresses they reunite when cornering their victim.

Why do the Tai chimpanzees show this greater degree of intentionality and cooperation in their hunting activity? The Boeschs argue that it reflects the challenge of hunting in a thickly forested environment in which visibility is limited to about 20 metres (65 feet). There is, however, an alternative to this argument. In the Tai forest the chimpanzee hunters rely on acoustic clues to locate their prey. The Boeschs give several examples of this, such as how a hunting group will alter their direction when they hear the grunting of forest hogs. In more open environments, such as in Gombe and Mahale, a chimpanzee will need to have as much, if not greater, reliance on visual clues, such as the sight of the animal and its tracks left on the ground. Now visual clues may be inherently more difficult for a chimpanzee to use. This is certainly the case with vervet monkeys, who seem unable to understand the danger implied when they see the signs that their predators are nearby, such as the trail left by a python or the carcass from a recent leopard kill.[17] If chimpanzees are also relatively poor at drawing inferences from visual clues – as appears to be the case[18] – then hunting in relatively open environments may be more difficult than in those environments in which acoustic clues are dominant.

My suspicion that hunting by Tai chimpanzees may appear more complex than it really is finds a little support in a curious anecdote provided by the Boeschs. They describe an incident in which a group of infants and juveniles had caught a very young blue duiker and were playing with it. An adult female joined the play session, during which the animal was killed by their rough behaviour. Yet throughout, the adult males showed no interest and the carcass of the animal was abandoned without being eaten. This appears rather bizarre in view of the excitement shown by the males whenever a small colobus monkey was killed. It would be very difficult to imagine a human hunter ignoring such an opportunistic kill; it is not the sort of behaviour one expects if a specialized domain of natural history intelligence is present.

To summarize, the cognitive basis for the chimpanzee's interaction with the natural world is difficult to assess. On the one hand there is the acquisition of large amounts of information, and the processing of it to make efficient foraging decisions. On the other hand there appears to be a marked absence of a creative use of such knowledge; foraging behaviour appears to be characterized by a significant degree of inflexibility. And there is severe doubt that chimpanzees are proficient at reading the mass of visual clues available in the environment. The most reasonable conclusion is to attribute the chimpanzee mind with some microdomains enabling the construction of mental maps, but not a fully developed natural history intelligence.

Social intelligence: Machiavellian behaviour and the role of consciousness

Now let us turn to the cognitive basis of social interaction. In 1988 a remarkable collection of papers was published in a book entitled *Machiavellian Intelligence: Social Expertise and the Evolution of Intellect in Monkeys, Apes and Humans.*[19] Edited by Dick Byrne and Andrew Whiten, some of the papers had been originally published more than 30 years ago. They all contributed to making one major argument: that there is something very special about the cognitive processes used for social interaction. These processes lead to social behaviour which is fundamentally more complex than that found in any other domain of activity. In effect they argued that monkeys and apes have a discrete domain of social intelligence, constituted by a whole bundle of mental modules. The term Machiavellian seemed particularly apposite since cunning, deception and the construction of alliances and friendships are pervasive in the social life of many primates.

One of the key papers re-published in that volume was 'The social function of intellect' by Nicholas Humphrey that I briefly referred to in Chapter 3. That had set out the problems that group living poses to primates and the need for specialized cognitive processes to compete successfully within the social milieu. Picking up on this argument, Byrne and Whiten described the tangled social web in which chimpanzees, and many other primates, live. Such animals need to:

balance a diverse range of competitive and co-operative options. Individuals may compete not only over mates, but (for example) over feeding resources, sleeping sites, location in the group (which may affect not only feeding, but predator avoidance), allies, grooming partners, playmates and access to infants, and they may cooperate with each other not only in mating, but in (for example) grooming and support in agnostic encounters.[20]

It sounds a lot harder than pulling a few leaves off a twig to make a termite stick or building up a mental map of plant distribution.

One of the best accounts of this tangled social web within which chimpanzees live is Franz de Waal's marvellous description of the chimpanzee politics he witnessed during his observations of a colony at the Burgers' zoo, Arnhem.[21] He provides a story of ambition, social manipulation, sexual privileges and power takeovers that would put any aspiring politician to shame – and it was all done by (Machiavellian-minded) chimpanzees. For instance, de Waal describes a two-month-long power struggle between the two eldest males, Yeroen and Luit. This began with Yeroen as the dominant male and proceeded through a series of aggressive encounters, bluff displays and reconciliation gestures to the social isolation and eventual dethronement of Yeroen. To achieve this, Luit carefully nurtured the support of the females within the group, who began as Yeroen's supporters. When Yeroen was present, Luit ignored the females; but when Yeroen was out of sight he paid them attention and played with their children. And before an intimidation display against Yeroen, Luit systematically groomed each female in turn as if to arouse their support. Luit's eventual success depended upon a coalition he developed with another male, Nikkie. During conflicts with Yeroen, Luit relied upon Nikkie to fight off Yeroen's supporters, the females. Nikkie had much to gain by this. He began with very low status in the group, being ignored by the females, yet he became second-in-command in the hierarchy above the females and Yeroen once Luit became leader. As soon as this happened, Luit's social attitudes changed. Rather than being the source of conflict he became the champion of peace and stability. When females were fighting he broke up the contests without taking sides and hit anyone who continued fighting. In other situations Luit prevented the escalation of conflict within the group by supporting the weaker participant in a conflict. He would chase away Nikkie, for instance, when Nikkie attacked Amber, one of the females. After a few months as the dominant male, Luit was himself toppled from power by Nikkie. And this was only achieved by Nikkie developing a powerful coalition with none other than Yeroen.

The two centrepieces of social intelligence are the possession of extensive social knowledge about other individuals, in terms of knowing who allies and friends are, and the ability to infer the mental states of those individuals. When we watch chimpanzees engage in deception of others, we can be confident that both are working together smoothly. Dick Byrne and Andrew Whiten have given many examples of deception used by apes.[22] Here are three of them. Female gorillas have been seen to engineer situations carefully in which they and a young male become separate from the bulk of the group, especially the dominant male. They then copulate, suppressing the cries that normally go with this act. Male chimpanzees are just as cunning. When courting females in the presence of a higher-ranking competitor, they have been seen to place a hand over their erect penis so that it remains visible to the female but hidden from the viewpoint of the other male. Deception is as useful for stealing food as it is for stealing sex. Another incident Byrne and Whiten relate is one in which a high-ranking individual left an area in which another individual had been concealing food items. He left as if suspecting nothing, but then peeped from behind a tree until the food was exposed. And then he stole it.

David Premack has explored the character of the 'theory of mind' that chimpanzees possess by laboratory experiments.[23] In one experiment a chimpanzee called Sarah was instrumental in allowing one of her carers to acquire food items because she had control of the button which opened the door to the cabinet in which the food was placed. Behind this door the cabinet was divided into two halves, one stocked with good food items such as cakes, and the other with bad food items such as rubber snakes and even a cup of faeces about which the carer had gestured to Sarah her utter disgust. In the experiment the carer entered the room and Sarah pressed the button which opened the cabinet door so that the carer reached in and took something from the side with the good food items. This was repeated many times. Then Sarah was allowed to watch an 'intruder', a human unknown to Sarah, prise open the cabinet and switch the locations of the good and bad food items. The next time the carer entered Sarah knew about the switch and she should also have known that the carer did not know. If the door was opened the carer would place her hand in a very inappropriate place. Yet Sarah pressed the button as usual.

Premack uses this experiment to argue that the chimpanzee's theory of mind is rather less sophisticated than that of humans. For Sarah appeared unable to hold within her mind a representation of her own knowledge, as well as that of the carer's which was different from her own. Premack argues that attributing knowledge which is different from one's own to another individual is beyond the mind capabilities of a chimpanzee. Yet isn't this precisely what chimpanzees are doing in the cases of deception? The naughty chimp with the erect penis is surely holding representations of his own, the dominant male's and the female's knowledge of his sexually excited state in his mind all at the same moment. I suspect that the reason that Sarah seemed unable to do this was because her carer was not another chimpanzee. Reading the minds of other chimpanzees may be difficult but attainable; crossing the species boundary and reading the mental state of a human may simply be impossible for chimpanzees.

This returns us to the notion – discussed in Chapter 3 – that the theory of mind module within the domain of social intelligence is likely to have evolved to facilitate interaction with other members of one's social group. The essence of a theory of mind is that it allows an individual to predict the behaviour of another. Social life is about building and testing hypotheses – unlike decision making in chimpanzee foraging activity, which is simply rote memory. Nicholas Humphrey argues that this is the biological function of consciousness.[24] In effect we explore our own mind and use it as the best model we have for the mind of another individual. We reflect on how we would feel and behave in a particular context and assume that another individual will do likewise. This is a very powerful argument for the evolution of reflexive consciousness: it is elegant, makes common sense and conforms to all we understand about evolution. It persuades me that chimpanzees have a conscious awareness of their own minds. But if Humphrey is correct, this conscious awareness should extend only to their thoughts about social interaction. If consciousness is a trick to predict the behaviour of others, there is no evolutionary reason why chimpanzees should have a conscious awareness about their (limited) thoughts about toolmaking or foraging. Yet our own conscious awareness seems to cover our thoughts about all domains of activity. We will see as this prehistory of the mind unfolds that the broadening of conscious awareness has a very critical role to play in creating the modern mind.

Our next task is to look at the would-be Dr Doolittles, those who have tried to talk with the animals.

A linguistic capacity? Chatting with chimps

Chimpanzees cannot talk to us because they do not have the vocal apparatus to do so. But do they have the cognitive basis for language? If we could plug a chimpanzee into a pair of vocal cords, would the chimpanzee have much to say? Well we cannot do this, but the next best thing has been to teach chimpanzees the use of sign language.

In the 1960s Beatrice Gardner and her husband and research colleague Allen Gardner trained a chimpanzee called Washoe to use sign language.[25] Washoe lived in a caravan next to their house and whenever in his presence they signed to him and to each other. Washoe learnt to sign back. Within three years he had acquired at least 85 signs and could hold a 'conversation' with humans and make requests. 'Gimme tickle, gimme, gimme tickle' is not the most profound and articulate request ever made, although it may have been one of the most sincere. Washoe's most acclaimed statement during his time as the star performer of the chimpanzee world occurred when he saw a swan and signed water and then bird in quick succession. A swan is indeed a water-bird.

During the same decade David Premack embarked on a series of language experiments with Sarah, whom we met just a moment ago.[26] Premack used plastic chips of different colours and shapes, each of which was represented by a different object. Using these he argued that Sarah could be seen to understand abstract concepts such as 'same', 'different', 'colour of' and 'name of'.

In the early 1970s a long-term research programme was begun at the Yerkes Language Research Centre in the U.S. by Duane Rumbaugh and Sue Savage-Rumbaugh.[27] They used symbols on a computer keyboard to represent words. They claimed to demonstrate that chimpanzees were able to classify objects by semantic class, such as 'fruit' or 'tool'. More importantly, they argued that their experiments demonstrated a correspondence between what chimpanzees intend to say and what they actually do say. The use of symbols by chimpanzees, they argued, is not simply a series of tricks or conditioned routines, but involves an understanding of the significance of utterances in much the same way as humans.

The validity of these experiments and results did not go unchallenged. At Columbia University a study was made of the 'linguistic' capacity of a chimpanzee called Nim Chimpsky by Herbert Terrace.[28] He concluded that the claims made by the Gardners, by Premack and by Rumbaugh's group were false. They had, he argued, all inadvertently exaggerated the linguistic abilities of their chimpanzee students by adopting a poor methodology that did not preclude simple associative learning or even random signing. In the academics' desire to see evidence for a linguistic ability they over-interpreted their data; any movement that could conceivably be a sign was recorded as one. So was Washoe's 'waterbird' just a chance association of two words that happened to make a meaningful combination in the context of when they were uttered?

In 1979 Terrace and his colleagues published an academic paper which posed a question: can an ape create a sentence? They gave a simple answer. No. In a series of academic papers during the early 1990s Sue Savage-Rumbaugh and her colleagues have been giving the opposite answer. Yes, they have argued, chimpanzees can create a sentence. Or at least the new star performer of the chimpanzee world can. This is a pygmy chimpanzee or bonobo who goes by the name of Kanzi.[29]

Kanzi was not formally taught to use symbols in the manner of previous apes. He was simply encouraged to use them by being placed in a learning environment that had as many similarities with a natural situation as was possible. Consequently Kanzi and his siblings were reared in a 55-acre forest and much of their communication was related to normal chimpanzee-type activities, such as looking for food.

Kanzi's learning process involved understanding a spoken word and its referent, and then learning the symbol for it on a computer keyboard. By the age of six Kanzi could identify 150 different symbols upon hearing the spoken word. He could also understand the meanings of sentences when different words were strung together to make novel requests not previously encountered. When he was eight, Kanzi's linguistic abilities were formally compared with those of a two-year-old girl called Alia. She was the daughter of one of Kanzi's carers and had developed in a similar environment. Their linguistic abilities appeared to be markedly similar.

Sue Savage-Rumbaugh and her colleagues have laid great stress on what appears to be Kanzi's ability to use rules of grammar. He appeared to adopt some of the grammatical rules used by his carers. For instance, there seemed to be a progressive ordering of words in two-word phrases away from a random combination towards the order used in English, in which an action word precedes an object word. So Kanzi became more prone to say 'bite ball' and 'hide peanut' and rather less prone to say 'ball bite' and 'peanut hide'.

They also claim that Kanzi has 'invented' his own rules of grammar. For example, Kanzi frequently makes two-word combinations of action words. A statistical analysis of these utterances demonstrated that certain words, such as 'chase', 'tickle' and 'hide', were more likely to be in the first position, while other words were more likely to come second, such as 'slap' and 'bite'. Savage-Rumbaugh and her colleagues argued that this ordering reflects the sequence in which events occur: the first word tends to be an invitation to play, while the second describes the content of the play that follows. In such cases, Kanzi combines words with grammatical rules. He creates sentences.

But they are not very good sentences. In fact they are awful, whether compared with those of William Shakespeare or any three-year-old child. Savage-Rumbaugh and her colleagues acknowledge that Kanzi's range of vocabulary and use of grammatical rules is not as advanced as that of a three-year-old. But they do not recognize the yawning gulf that in fact exists. The gulf has been stressed by the linguist Steven Pinker.[30]

By the age of three a child frequently strings ten words together by the use of complex grammatical rules. By the age of six a child will have a vocabulary of about 13,000 words. Young children are constant commentators on the world around them and on what others say. Almost the entire sample of Kanzi's utterances are demands for things; his comments on the world are extremely rare.

Indeed the whole pattern of acquiring language is so radically different between apes and humans that it is difficult to imagine how ape language could ever have been thought of as anything other than a very weak analogy for that of humans. A much stronger analogy appears to be bird song. As the biologist Peter Marler once described, there are several important points of similarity between the way that children acquire language and young birds acquire their song.[31] Both learn the correct pattern of vocalization from adults. Both have a critical period during which the learning of language/song is at a premium. The 'subsong' of young birds appears to be analogous to the babbling of young children. There is also a similarity in terms of the brain structures which enable language/song to be learnt. In both birds and humans these are found in the cerebral cortex, while in primates vocalizations are controlled by other parts of the brain, such as the brain stem.[32]

The similarities between acquisition of language by children and that of song by young birds are as striking as the differences from 'language' acquisition by chimpanzees. Song plays a much more important role in the life of birds than does vocalization in the life of non-human primates; it is possibly as important as the role of language among humans. We should therefore perhaps expect that both birds and humans will have specialized cognitive processes designed for the rapid acquisition of complex song/language, traits that may be less developed, perhaps even absent among non-human primates. Convergent evolution has meant that these bird-song and human-language modules are strongly analogous. It is perhaps not surprising that the most impressive non-human linguist is not an ape, but an African Grey parrot called Alex.[33]

Steven Pinker's description of chimpanzee linguists as 'highly trained animal acts' may be a bit harsh. But we do not appear to be witnessing in these language acquisition experiments the release of some latent linguistic ability, trapped in the animals' minds by the absence of vocal cords. We simply see clever chimps at work, using aspects of general intelligence such as associative learning to understand the links between a set of signs and their referents, and how to combine those signs to gain rewards. Using a general-purpose learning rule for language acquisition can take a chimpanzee only so far when learning vocabulary and grammar: that distance appears to be similar to the 'language' of a two-year-old human child. And recall, as we saw in the previous chapter, that up to the age of two human children may also be using generalized learning rules for language – the language explosion only occurs after that age, with specialized language modules coming into operation. But no such thing happens in the chimpanzee mind. There is no linguistic intelligence.

Brick walls or open windows? Thought at domain interfaces in the chimpanzee mind

We have tried to established the cognitive processes that lie behind tool use, foraging, social behaviour and 'language' acquisition by chimpanzees. How is the architectural plan of the chimpanzee mind shaping up?

There appear to be three main features (see Figure 4). The first is a general intelligence, which includes modules for trial and error learning, and associative learning. These are used for a wide range of tasks: making foraging decisions, learning about tool use, acquiring an understanding of symbolic meanings. We should not minimize the importance of this general intelligence: chimpanzees are without doubt clever chimps. Secondly, there is a specialized domain of social intelligence. This enables a chimpanzee's interaction with the social world to be an order of magnitude greater in complexity than its interaction with the non-social world, involving aspects such as hypothesis formation which are evidently lacking from foraging behaviour and tool use. Thirdly, there is a small set of mental modules concerned with building up large mental databases about resource distribution, an incipient natural history intelligence.

This proposed suite of features for the mental architecture of the chimpanzee has been identified by looking at toolmaking, foraging, linguistic and social behaviour in isolation from each other. It can be strengthened when we look at the interfaces between them.

Consider that between toolmaking and foraging. This seems to be so fluid that differentiating between them is impossible. The Tai chimpanzees seem very proficient at choosing hammerstones of the appropriate weight for cracking the specific type of nuts they have acquired.[34] Similarly they manufacture sticks of appropriate size for the job in hand: small sticks for extracting bone marrow and nuts, longer and thinner sticks for ant dipping and getting honey.[35] The Gombe chimpanzees select stems and grass blades of an appropriate size for termite fishing and bite them to optimize their length or rejuvenate the stiffness of the ends. Bill McGrew has described how Kate, a rehabilitated chimpanzee

4 *The chimpanzee mind.*

in the Gambia, used four tools in succession to acquire honey from a bees nest in a hollow tree.[36] Each tool appeared to be very well chosen for the particular stage that she had reached in this delicate task.

In general, chimpanzees appear very good at making and choosing tools which are just right for the job in hand. This is indeed what we should expect if both toolmaking and foraging are using the same mental processes, general intelligence.

Now consider the interface between social behaviour and toolmaking. This seems quite the opposite, characterized by an awkwardness and what appears to be many missed opportunities. Consider the social interactions between mothers and their infants in the context of using hammers and anvils to open nuts in the Tai forest.[37] It is not surprising, in view of the nutritional value of nuts but the difficulty of nutcracking, that mothers help their infants acquire the skill. They may leave a hammer on an anvil, or nuts close by an anvil. Moreover, active teaching appears to have been observed. The Boeschs report two instances in which mothers saw their infants having difficulty in cracking nuts and provided demonstrations of how to solve the problem. In one case the correct positioning of a nut on an anvil prior to striking was demonstrated, while in the other the proper way to grip a hammerstone was shown to an infant who immediately seemed to adopt the grip with some success.

What is remarkable, however, is that such active teaching, or even passive encouragement, should be so rare. The two instances that the Boeschs describe constitute less that 0.2 per cent of almost 1,000 maternal interventions in nutcracking seen during 4,137 minutes of observation. Why don't they do more of it? The time and effort juveniles invest in cracking nuts is substantial, as is the nutritional benefit once the skill is attained. We have seen evidence that chimpanzees are able to imagine what is going on inside the mind of another chimpanzee, so should not a mother be able to appreciate the problems her offspring is facing when trying to use tools? It would seem to make very great evolutionary sense for mothers to provide their offspring with more instruction. But they don't. It seems a missed opportunity. It appears that this capacity for imagining the thoughts of another individual does not extend to thoughts about toolmaking but is restricted to those of the social domain alone.

Nor do chimpanzees use material culture in their social strategies. We have seen these to be Machiavellian in character: deception, cunning, ambition are rife. Chimpanzees *seem* to use any means possible to gain social advantage – but in fact they don't. For they do not employ material culture to this end. No chimpanzee has ever been seen wearing or using material items to send social messages about status and aspiration. Imagine if our politicians acted with the same self-restraint in their competitive posturing: no pin-striped suits and no old school ties. Material culture is critical to the Machiavellian social antics of modern humans, but is strangely absent from those of chimpanzees. If social status is so important to them, why not use tools to maintain it? Why not display the head of a little monkey that one had killed, or use leaves to exaggerate the size of one's chest? The failure of chimpanzees to act in this way seems another missed opportunity at this awkward cognitive interface between social behaviour and tool use.

There seems to be a brick wall between social and tool behaviour – the relationship between these lacks the fluidity that exists between foraging and tool use. We can explain this brick wall by the very different types of cognitive processes used by chimpanzees to interact with physical objects (general intelligence) and those used for social interaction (social intelligence). In short they seem unable to integrate their thoughts about toolmaking with their thoughts about social interaction. They may be able to read each other's minds, but not when a mind is 'thinking' about tool use. I suspect that this is because they have no mental awareness of their own knowledge and cognition concerning making and using tools. These are not part of their conscious awareness.

The existence of this brick wall between general and social intelligence is not to say that there is no relationship between social and tool-making behaviour at all. Clearly there is, because the patterns of social behaviour provide the means by which knowledge about tool use is maintained within a group. As the Boeschs have noted, it is probably no coincidence that the Tai chimpanzees have both the most complex patterns of tool use and the greatest degree of social complexity among chimpanzee groups.[38] The food sharing that occurs from mothers to juveniles is probably essential in order to allow the juveniles time and energy to invest in learning the nutcracking technique. The intensity of social life in chimpanzee groups is also essential for maintaining the tool-use traditions, which require constant watching of other individuals and hence unsolicited opportunities for being stimulated to use tools. The critical point is that the relatively higher frequency of tool use among chimpanzees living in socially complex groups is simply a *passive* reflection of that social complexity; the tools are not playing an active role within social strategies.

I suspect that the same relationship holds between social and foraging behaviour, especially hunting patterns. There are indeed 'traditions' regarding animal exploitation that do not appear to have an ecological explanation. There are some striking culinary preferences: 'Tai chimpanzees keep the rump or the ribcage for last, consistently share the brain, and always swallow their leaf wadges. By contrast, Gombe chimpanzees keep the brain, which they rarely share, for last, spit out their leaf wadges, suck the blood of their prey, and eat with delight the fecal content of the large intestine.'[39] Butchery differences are interesting: Tai chimpanzees tend to kill their prey by disembowelling them, while Gombe chimpanzees smash the heads of their prey against tree trunks or rocks, or tear them apart by their limbs. Like tool traditions, these appear to play a passive role in social interaction; they are nothing like the culinary and butchery traditions between human groups, which have an active role in defining social identity.

More generally, the exploitation of resources appears to have no direct social implications. Food sharing among chimpanzees is tolerated theft rather than the provisioning of individuals to build up social obligations, as among humans. Even among the Tai chimpanzees, food sharing is essentially a passive reflection of social structure, rather than an active means to manipulate social relationships. The apparent effectiveness of Tai chimpanzees at hunting is a consequence of large group size, a high degree of mother-juvenile sharing, and an abundance of acoustic clues, rather than evidence for a natural history intelligence.

Further evidence to support the proposed mental architecture for the chimpanzee is what happens to chimpanzees when they are taken into captivity and come under the influence of socially complex, tool proficient, linguistically talented humans. We do not see any fundamental change in the complexity of chimpanzee social behaviour. The social strategies they adopt in captivity are essentially the ones they adopt in the wild. But just look at what happens to their toolmaking and using capacities. These become highly elaborated, with chimpanzees even learning to flake stone nodules. Indeed many primates suddenly become proficient tool users in captivity when provided with appropriate stimulus. And the same happens with chimpanzees' 'linguistic abilities' – a capacity for using symbols suddenly emerges. Now recall from the previous two chapters that one of the fundamental attributes of a specialized intelligence built upon intuitive knowledge is that the behavioural skills need only minimal stimulus from the social and natural environment to develop. If chimpanzees had a 'technical intelligence' we would expect to see them performing very little better with tools in the laboratory than in the wild; on the other hand, if they are simply clever chimps in terms of having general intelligence, the more stimulus and encouragement they receive, the better tool and language users they are likely to become. This seems to be precisely what we observe. Social behaviour, on the other hand, is already built upon a base of specialized cognitive processes and is not significantly influenced by an increased intensity of social interaction when in captivity.

The origins of social intelligence

Let me summarize the arguments of this chapter. We wanted to interpret the action of Act 1 of our prehistory in this chapter, but the theatre was in darkness and our actor was missing. To compensate for this we have considered the behaviour of the chimpanzee, assuming that the chimpanzee mind has a similar architecture to that of the common ancestor of 6 million years ago.

We watched the chimpanzee make and use tools, learn to use symbols in the laboratory, go foraging and hunting and engage in complex social strategies. Our interpretation of this behaviour is that the chimpanzee mind has a powerful general intelligence, a specialized domain of social intelligence, and a number of mental modules which are used for building up a large database about resource distributions. If we return to the analogy of the mind as a cathedral and our proposed architectural history for the mind, it can be suggested that the mind of the 6-million-year-old ancestor is at the interface between Phase 1 and Phase 2. We now know that the chapels were not built simultaneously; the first erected was the chapel of social intelligence.

When did a specialized domain of social intelligence first appear in the primate mind? To answer this we must first look to another common ancestor, ancestral to ourselves, chimpanzees and monkeys. This common ancestor appears to have lived about 35 million years ago and is likely to have possessed a mind similar to that of the monkeys which live today.[40]

Robert Seyfarth and Dorothy Cheney drew on years of field observations and experiments to 'look inside' the monkey mind in their 1990 book *How Monkeys See the World*. They found a rather less powerful general intelligence than the one we found inside the chimpanzee mind; one that did not lead monkeys to use tools in the wild, although it enabled them to learn tool use when given sufficient stimulus in laboratory contexts. Cheney and Seyfarth also found evidence for a specialized domain of social intelligence in the monkey mind which, as in that of chimpanzees, was closed off from general intelligence. Monkeys seem able to solve problems in the social world far more effectively than problems in the non-social world, even when those problems appear essentially the same. They can, for instance, rank the social status of their conspecifics, but cannot rank the amount of water in a series of containers. And they have a thirst for social knowledge, but an indifference to that about the non-social world.[41] But the social intelligence of monkeys appears less complex and powerful than that of chimpanzees. Monkeys appear unable to work out what other monkeys are thinking, or indeed that they may be thinking at all: they have no theory of mind module. And place a monkey in front of a mirror and he gets upset at the other monkey who has suddenly entered the room: unlike chimpanzees and gorillas, they cannot recognize themselves and have no concept of self.[42]

Now let us look at yet another common ancestor. We will venture even further back in time to look at the common ancestor to humans, apes, monkeys and lemurs. This common ancestor lived as much as 55 million years ago, and probably had a mind much like that of modern lemurs. Dick Byrne and Andrew Whiten have suggested that this mind has a general intelligence, but lacks any cognitive processes specialized for social behaviour.[43] The interaction that lemurs have with their social worlds appears to be no more complex than that with the non-social world.

To summarize, a specialized domain of social intelligence first appeared in the course of human evolution after 55 million years ago. This gradually increased in complexity with the addition of further mental modules, such as that for a theory of mind between 35 and 6 million years ago. As this domain of social intelligence increased in complexity, so too did the capacity for general intelligence. And mental modules first appeared relating to foraging activity, enabling the mind to construct large databases of resource distribution.

Act 2 of our prehistory is now almost upon us. The programme notes have told us that actors will now appear, and a candle will be lit to watch them by. Time has flown. It is now 4.5 million years ago. Has there been any new building work in the cathedral of the mind?

6 The mind of the first stone toolmaker

THE FIRST SCENE of the second act begins 4.5 million years ago and has three actors, *A. ramidus*, *A. anamensis* and *A. afarensis*. As I noted in Chapter 2, we can learn a certain amount about their behaviour from the few fossil fragments of these species that survive, but we have no direct evidence of their toolmaking – if indeed they made tools at all – and foraging activities. With the start of scene two at 2.5 million years ago there is a rush of actors on to the stage: first the later australopithecines and then by 2 million years ago the earliest members of the *Homo* lineage. The fossil fragments of these show significant anatomical and thus behavioural developments, such as the appearance of more effective bipedalism – habitual walking on two legs – a behavioural event to which I will return later in this book. Moreover we can see our ancestors setting off in two different evolutionary directions. The australopithecines went down a route of ever-increasing robusticity as specialized plant-grinding machines, while early *Homo* took a more cerebral route of increasing brain size. It is the mind of the earliest *Homo* which is the subject of this chapter.

There are likely to have been several species of early *Homo* at this time, but I will use the shorthand in this chapter of referring to one single species, *H. habilis*. Although the fossil remains of *H. habilis* are sparse, they are more substantial than those of the gracile australopithecines living prior to 2 million years ago, and we thus have more opportunities to make inferences about behaviour and mental activity. Moreover we now have direct evidence for foraging and toolmaking in the form of scatters of stone tools and the debris from their manufacture, as well as scatters of bone fragments of the animals that were exploited. It is only in a very few cases, however, that we can confidently attribute these archaeological remains to *H. habilis*. Many of the stone tools may have been made by the australopithecines, who may also have been responsible for some of the scatters of animal bone fragments. But I will follow convention in this chapter by assuming that the majority of the archaeological remains do indeed derive from the activity of *H. habilis*. My aim is to reconstruct the architecture of the mind of *H. habilis*. I must start with the hardest evidence available, Oldowan stone tools, and ask whether there was a specialized domain of technical intelligence.

Technical intelligence: do the first stone tools mark a cognitive breakthrough?

Oldowan artifacts are named after the site of Olduvai Gorge in East Africa, where they have been found eroding from sediments. Numerous other locations in East and South Africa have yielded similar artifacts. They are principally made from basalt and quartzite[1] and come in a range of shapes and sizes. Some are flakes removed from nodules, others are the remnant nodules themselves, referred to as cores. A few of the flakes have had smaller flakes removed from them. Are these artifacts indicative of specialized cognitive processes of a kind that seem absent from the mind of the common ancestor 6 million years ago? In the 4 million years that have elapsed since that ancestor, has evolution created a technical intelligence?

We need to start by asking how different these stone artifacts are from the tools made from plant material used by chimpanzees. By definition they are different: they are made from stone. Some archaeologists have felt that that is the end of the matter and that in all other respects the Oldowan and chimpanzee technologies are essentially the same.[2] But this misses two important differences, which have considerable implications for the mental processes underlying tool manufacture. First, although the function of Oldowan artifacts remains unclear, there is little doubt that some were made to make other tools – such as the production of a stone flake to sharpen a stick.[3] The making of a tool to make another tool is unknown among chimpanzees. It involves holding in one's mind the qualities of two contrasting types of raw material, such as stone and wood, and an understanding of how one can impinge on the other.

A second point is that when a chimpanzee makes a termite stick, the bits that must be removed from the twig are strongly dictated by the nature of the material and the future task themselves – you cannot poke a stick down a hole when it has got leaves on, and it is clear where these should be detached. But *H. habilis* had a more difficult task when removing bits from stone nodules. Just hitting a nodule in a random fashion is either unlikely to make any impact at all, or it will shatter the rock into many tiny pieces. To detach the type of flakes one finds in the sites of Olduvai Gorge, one needs to recognize acute angles on the nodules, to select so-called striking platforms and to employ good hand–eye co-ordination to strike the nodule in the correct place, in the right direction and with the appropriate amount of force[4] (see Figure 5). Members of *H. habilis* were working stone nodules in a fundamentally different manner from the way chimpanzees work their raw materials. They could indeed locate appropriate angles and adjust the force and direction of their striking actions.

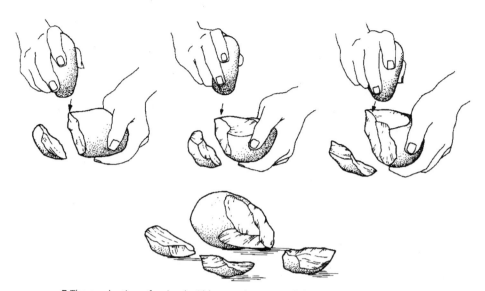

5 *The production of a simple Oldowan chopper and the resultant flakes.*

In 1989 Tom Wynn and Bill McGrew, both of whom we have already met in this prehistory, suggested that a chimpanzee could make Oldowan-like stone tools. This has now been tested. And they can't. Or at least that linguistic star of the chimpanzee world, Kanzi, is unable to do so. And if he can't it seems unlikely that other chimpanzees can. Nicholas Toth, the foremost expert on Oldowan technology, and his colleagues motivated Kanzi to want sharp-edged cutting tools, tempting him with treats locked in a box tied with string. Kanzi was shown the principles of producing stone flakes and provided with rocks. He did indeed learn to produce stone flakes, cut the string and win his reward. But he didn't win Nicholas Toth's vote as a modern Oldowan toolmaker. For Kanzi has never developed the concept of searching for acute angles, using flake scars as striking platforms or controlling the amount of force in percussion. His failure to do this does not reflect a lack of adequate manual dexterity, for Kanzi has learnt to do things like tie shoelaces and undo buttons. And it seems implausible, although a possibility, that he may learn the Oldowan-type flaking strategies with more practice.[5]

Now if Kanzi cannot produce Oldowan-like artifacts, what implications does this have for the minds of those who did 2 million years ago? There are two possibilities. The first is that a more powerful general intelligence had evolved so that the techniques of Oldowan technology could gradually be learnt, with presumably many trials and a lot of error. Alternatively, specialized cognitive processes dedicated to the manipulation and transformation of stone nodules had appeared – an intuitive physics in the mind of *H. habilis*. Perhaps even a technical intelligence.

If this is the case then our best bet for when it appeared is in the short interval between Scenes 1 and 2 of this second act of prehistory. Recall that just at the end of the first scene, between 3 and 2 million years ago, there were props scattered on the stage although we could see no actors to use them. Well these props are the tools of the Omo industrial tradition, which precedes the Oldowan. They are only found in a few places in East Africa, notably at Omo itself and at the site of Lokalalei in West Turkana.[6] These 'tools' are little more than smashed nodules, requiring less technical skill to make than those of the Oldowan. Indeed, they look like the sort of stone flakes that Kanzi can produce. So perhaps we are witnessing a greater need for stone flakes within the behavioural repertoire of the forebears of *H. habilis* prior to 2 million years ago, which then provided the selective pressures for the specialized cognitive mechanisms we see expressed in the Oldowan technology.

We should tread very carefully here, however, for while Oldowan stone tools appear beyond the cognitive capacities of chimpanzees, they are nevertheless extremely simple artifacts by human standards. As Nicholas Toth has shown, the aim of Oldowan artifact makers appears to have been simply to produce flakes with sharp edges, and nodules which could be held in the hand while having sufficient mass for tasks such as breaking open bones for marrow. In the 1970s archaeologists spent much time dividing Oldowan artifacts into different 'types', like polyhedrons, spheroids and choppers. These are easily thought of as equivalent to our 'types' of tools today, such as hammers, saws and screwdrivers. But we now know that this was too complex a classification. Oldowan artifacts in fact show a continuous pattern of variability. The form of the artifact can be explained simply by the character of the original nodule, the number of flakes removed and the sequence in which they were detached. We can see no evidence for an intentional imposition of form.[7] We should also note that although working stone is technically more demanding than stripping leaves off twigs, the Oldowan toolmakers, mainly using stone such as basalt and quartzite, appear to have been unable to work more intractable rocks such as cherts.[8] For this we must wait until the next act of our prehistory.

We must conclude, therefore, on a rather equivocal note. On the one hand the making of Oldowan stone tools requires an understanding of fracture dynamics that appears beyond the capacity of the chimpanzee mind. On the other hand the stasis in Oldowan technology, the absence of imposed form and the preference for the easier raw materials prevent us attributing *H. habilis* with a technical intelligence beyond that of a few micro-domains.

Natural history intelligence: the rise of the meat eaters?

While Oldowan stone tools are likely to have been used for a variety of purposes, their main function was probably the processing of animal carcasses. The sharp flakes were most likely used to cut hide and tendons, and to remove pieces of meat. The heavy nodules were probably employed to smash apart joints, or to break open bones to remove marrow.[9] This takes us, therefore, to a second aspect of *H. habilis* lifestyles for which we might expect specialized cognitive processes to have evolved: interaction with the natural world. In the previous chapters we saw that chimpanzees are capable of building up substantial mental databases of resource distribution. I attributed this to the presence of dedicated mental modules for this task. But the lack of hypothesis building and the creative use of knowledge about resource distribution suggested that attributing chimpanzees with a domain of natural history intelligence was unwarranted. Is there any evidence that it had evolved by the time of *H. habilis*?

To answer this we must focus on the one major difference from the behaviour of the chimpanzee/common ancestor that we can be confident about – members of *H. habilis* were consuming larger quantities of meat. We know this because many archaeological sites dating between 2 and 1.5 million years ago have large numbers of fragments of animal bones intermingled with stone artifacts. These dense accumulations are normally assumed to have derived from meal times – Mary Leakey described these sites as 'living floors'.

During the 1980s a vast amount of attention was paid to these bone fragments, engendering a vociferous and acrimonious debate as to how they should be interpreted. The fragments are those found at sites such as HAS at Koobi Fora, a 1.6-million-year-old scatter of stone artifacts and animal bones, dominated by those of a hippopotamus.[10] Or those at FLK 22, Olduvai Gorge where 40,172 bone fragments and 2,647 stone artifacts were found and have been studied in immense detail – this is one of the most intensively studied sites from any period or region in the whole world.[11] The problem with these bone fragments is that they are usually extremely small, and it is often not clear from what type of bone they derived, let alone the types of animal to which they belonged. When these animals can be identified, it is clear that *H. habilis* exploited a wide range of species, including zebras, antelopes and wildebeest.

The debates about *H. habilis* lifestyles were initiated by the publications of the late Glynn Isaac.[12] He proposed that these dense artifact and bone scatters represented 'home bases' – places where *H. habilis* shared food and the care of infants. Food sharing was the critical feature. Isaac suggested that the wide range of species typically represented on these

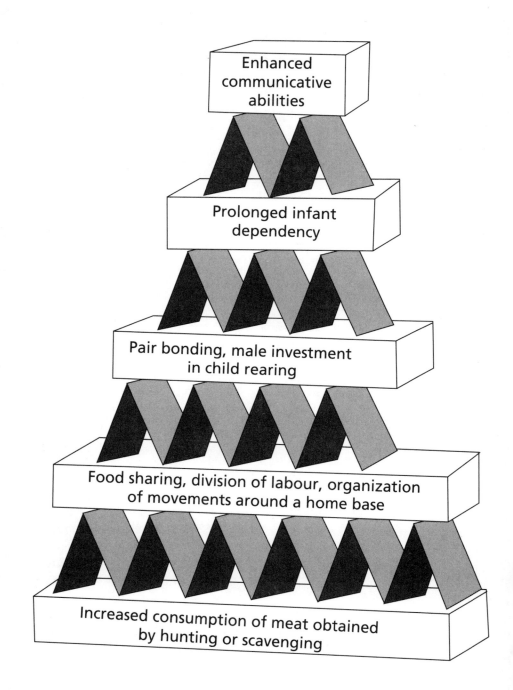

6 *Glynn Isaac's home base and food sharing hypothesis as a stack of cards. If Isaac's conclusion that early* Homo *was consuming a large quantity of meat is wrong, then all his other ideas concerning social behaviour and cognition come tumbling down.*

sites implied that members of *H. habilis* were transporting foodstuffs from different types of ecological zones in the landscape to a central place. Food sharing was the basis for a pyramid of inferences – some would say a house of cards – culminating in the presence of prolonged infant dependency and linguistic communication (see Figure 6). The home base model was published in the late 1970s and transformed the field of Palaeolithic archaeology, shifting it away from mere descriptions of stone artifacts and subjective guesses as to what they might mean.[13] For a few years it became widely accepted. And then in 1981 Lewis Binford published one of the truly significant archaeological books of the last 30 years, *Bones: Ancient Men and Modern Myths*,[14] which further transformed the study of the earliest archaeological sites.

During the 1980s Lewis Binford was the big-punching heavyweight of Palaeolithic archaeology. He took on all comers about how the stone tools and bone fragments of the archaeological record should be interpreted. His strength in debate came from a knowledge about how the archaeological record is formed – the processes of decay and change that affect the items that hunter-gatherers leave behind them in the millennia until they are found by archaeologists. He had acquired this knowledge in the Arctic and the Australian desert where he lived with modern hunter-gatherers, making meticulous records of their activities, what is thrown away and how this would look to an archaeologist.

Binford argued that there was no evidence for the transport and consumption of large quantities of meat. Instead, he suggested that members of *H. habilis* acquired just tiny morsels of meat, if indeed any at all. They were not merely scavengers, but 'marginal scavengers'. They did no more than take the tit-bit leftovers at the bottom of the hierarchy of meat eaters on the African savannah, trailing in after the lions, the hyenas and the vultures had had their fill (see Figures 7 and 8). Take away the large meat packages, and Isaac's home bases and his pyramid of inferences come tumbling down.

Following Binford's first onslaught against Isaac's model in 1981 a lengthy debate ensued, often with Isaac's students rather than himself arguing the case for hunting or scavenging from freshly killed carcasses by *H. habilis* and hence the maintenance of large meat parcels in the diet.[15] New models were proposed, supplementing the home base and marginal scavenging hypotheses. Binford himself developed the theme of marginal scavenging into a 'routed' foraging model in which the movements of foragers were constrained around a series of fixed points in the landscape, such as trees used for shade.[16] Richard Potts suggested that members of *H. habilis* were creating caches of unworked stone nodules or artifacts at strategic points in the landscape to minimize search

7, 8 *Glynn Isaac's and Lewis Binford's contrasting models for early* Homo *lifestyles. In the upper figure we see early* Homo *living in large social groups and using specific nodes in the landscape as home bases for the sharing of food. At these home bases co-operative behaviour involving the division of labour is planned. In the lower figure we see Lewis Binford's interpretation of the same evidence in which individuals, or at most small groups, scavenge morsels of meat and marrow from carcasses, trailing in after other predators and scavengers.*

time for stone when a carcass had been located.[17] Robert Blumenschine suggested that members of *H. habilis* concentrated their activities in woodland near water sources, since this provided a scavenging niche not being exploited by other species.[18]

Yet in spite of the intensity of research, our understanding of *H. habilis* subsistence patterns remains limited, with no consensus about the extent of hunting and scavenging, the use of central places or of routed foraging. Two factors explain this lack of consensus. First, the archaeological record is probably just too poorly preserved to make inferences about *H. habilis* lifestyles with regard to day-to-day activities.[19] Second – and rather more optimistically – the true answer to the *H. habilis* lifestyle is probably that it was marked by diversity; a flexibility between hunting and scavenging, and between food sharing and feed-as-you-go, to suit the particular ecological circumstances of the moment. *H. habilis* is likely to have been behaviourally flexible, a non-specialized forager. The only type of animal exploitation that appears absent from the Olduvai assemblages is the marginal, scrounging type of scavenging.[20]

It is indeed most likely that meat eating was a regular part of the diet of *H. habilis*.[21] In addition to the animal bones, sometimes showing butchery cutmarks from the stone tools found at archaeological sites, the relatively large brain of *H. habilis* implies the consumption of a high-quality diet, measured in terms of calorific intake per unit of food. The brain is a highly expensive organ in terms of the quantity of energy it consumes. As the anthropologists Leslie Aiello and Peter Wheeler have argued, to compensate for the amount of energy used by an enlarged brain, the requirements of another part of the body must be reduced to maintain a stable basal metabolic rate.[22] They argue that this has to be the gut; as the brain gets bigger, the gut has to get smaller. And the only way for the gut to get smaller is by increasing the quality of the diet, such as by the consumption of greater quantities of meat as opposed to plant foods. So the fact that *H. habilis* has a brain size significantly larger than the australopithecines suggests that meat had become a larger part of the diet – whether or not the intellectual challenge of finding animal carcasses provided a selective pressure for brain enlargement. Indeed, as will be argued below, the need to live within larger groups was probably a far more important selective pressure in this regard.

Behavioural flexibility involving meat eating implies cognitive complexity. Does this in its turn imply the existence of a specialized natural history intelligence? What new cognitive capacities would regular meat eating have required from the mind of *H. habilis*?

In view of the prevalence of tooth and gnaw marks on the bones from early archaeological sites, animal carcasses appear to have been competed for by several carnivores and scavengers, and many of these competitors would have been a threat to the members of *H. habilis*. Knowledge of carnivore behaviour and distribution would therefore appear to have been critical to early *Homo*: competing carnivores may have provided both a threat and an indication of a possible scavenging opportunity. In this light it would seem improbable that *H. habilis* could have exploited the carcass niche if it had not mastered the art of using inanimate visual clues, such as animal footprints and tracks. In contrast to monkeys, chimpanzees and the 6-million-year-old common ancestor, members of *H. habilis* are likely to have been able to read the visual clues indicating that a carnivore was in the vicinity.

On a more general level, the switch to a higher meat diet may have required a more sophisticated ability to predict resource locations than that needed by the predominantly vegetarian australopithecine forebears. Random searching for animals or carcasses, or even for the visual clues which indicate carcass location, is unlikely to have been feasible within such predator-rich environments. Unlike plant foods, animals are mobile and carcasses can disappear within a relatively short space of time, eaten by carnivores ranging from hyenas to vultures.[23] Simply building up an information store and mental map of their distribution – as we saw chimpanzees can do for plant and hammerstone distributions – would be inadequate. Members of *H. habilis* are likely to have needed one further cognitive trick – the ability to use their natural history knowledge to develop hypotheses about carcass/animal location.

The evidence that members of *H. habilis* were engaging in prediction about resource distribution comes from the recovery of stone nodules away from their raw material source and incomplete sets of knapping debris at archaeological sites. These reflect the transport of unworked nodules and stone artifacts across the landscape. Such artifacts were not carried for great distances – 10 km appears to be the very maximum and transport distances are usually much shorter.[24] Indeed the predominant pattern remains one of extremely local use of raw materials. Yet the fact that some items were transported, possibly to create caches, indicates that *H. habilis* had mental maps of raw material distribution, and could anticipate the future use of artifacts for subsistence activities.[25] There appear to be three important differences between *H. habilis* artifact transport, and that of hammerstones by Tai forest chimpanzees. First, *H. habilis* artifact transport occurs over a larger spatial scale than the transport of hammerstones by chimpanzees. Second, chimpanzees transport stone to fixed locations (nut trees), whereas the carcass destinations for *H. habilis* artifacts were continually changing. Third, it is as likely that members of

H. habilis transported the foodstuffs that needed processing to the tools (rather than just the other way around), and very often both tools and foodstuffs were transported from separate sources to a third location.

So far in this section the evidence from the archaeological record has been in favour of a considerable development of mental modules for interaction with the natural world. But there is some conflicting evidence, guarding against the inference of an evolved natural history intelligence. For one thing, much of *H. habilis* activity appears to be constrained to a narrow range of environments in comparison to the humans who appear in the fossil record after 1.8 million years ago. At a coarse spatial scale, it appears unlikely that any *Homo* prior to *H. erectus* moved out of their African evolutionary environment.[26] Even within the region of East Africa the activity of *H. habilis* was focused in a narrow range of microenvironments, as compared with the wide range of environments exploited by *H. erectus*, let alone modern humans. Much of the activity of *H. habilis* appears to have been 'tied' to the edges of permanent water sources.[27]

This tethering to natural features for the foci of activities appears to be reflected in the 'stacking' of archaeological sites in Olduvai Gorge. Sites such as FLK North I and MNK Main-II consist of vertical distributions of artifacts through several stratigraphic layers.[28] Hominids appear to have repeatedly returned to such locations in spite of fairly substantial changes in fauna, climate and landscape. The diversity of the faunal remains on the sites, with regard to body size and habitat preference, suggests that members of *H. habilis* did range quite widely into a variety of microenvironments when procuring animal parts. The fact that these were repeatedly transported to the same type of environmental context implies the absence of the behavioural flexibility indicative of a full natural history intelligence.[29]

Let me summarize the evidence we have for the mind of *H. habilis* regarding interaction with the natural world. We can start from the basis of an ability to construct large mental databases and maps for resource characteristics and distributions, as this was found in the mind of the common ancestor in the previous chapter. This now appears to be supplemented with abilities to develop hypotheses concerning resource location and to use inanimate visual clues. On the other hand members of *H. habilis* remained within a rather narrow environmental setting, and within that appear to be tethered to natural features for much of their activity. We seem to have reached a similar conclusion to that concerning technical intelligence: evolution has been at work laying further foundations for a chapel of natural history intelligence, but the walls are yet to be completed and general intelligence continued to play a dominant role in thought about the natural world.

A burgeoning social intelligence: safety in numbers

In the last chapter we saw that the common ancestor to modern humans and the chimpanzee at 6 million years ago already had a discrete domain of social intelligence. How, if at all, had the nature of social intelligence changed by the time of *H. habilis*?

To address this question we must begin with a short digression and think about the problems of group living, soap operas and brain size. As a general rule the more people that one chooses to live with, the more complex life becomes: there is a wider choice of possible partners with whom to share food or sex, and each of those partners will have a greater number and more diverse relationships with other members of the group. It is a considerable challenge to keep track of who is friends with whom, who are enemies, and who bear grudges or desires, and then to try to decide with whom to make friends without upsetting your other friends. We have all had some experience of this. In fact we seem to quite enjoy the social manoeuvrings that become paramount as groups enlarge, especially if we are bystanders. Why else are soap operas so popular? As a new character enters the script we watch the havoc caused to existing social relationships. Somebody often gets heartache, while someone else gets a headache.

It is therefore not surprising to find that among living primate species there is a strong positive relationship between group size and brain size – species which tend to have a terrestrial lifestyle in large groups also tend to have bigger brains. They need the brain processing power to keep track of the increased number of social relationships that arise as groups increase in size. This was discovered by the anthropologist Robin Dunbar who consequently argued that among living primates brain size is a direct measure of social intelligence.[30] Dick Byrne concurs with this result by finding a strong positive relationship between brain size and the frequency of deception in social strategies – the more complex the social scene, the more devious you are going to need to be to win more friends without winning more enemies.[31]

Now a critical question for reconstructing the prehistory of the mind is whether these relationships hold for extinct primates, like the australopithecines and *H. habilis*. The reason that they may not is that, as we have seen, the mind of *H. habilis* had a greater number of mental modules for making tools and interacting with the natural world than in any living primate and these must take up some brain processing power. Nevertheless, those domains seem only to have just got off the ground by 2 million years ago and so the relationship that exists for living primates between brain size and group size may also be applicable for *H. habilis*.

Robin Dunbar used the cranial volume of the fossil skulls of *H.*

habilis to estimate brain size. He then plugged these figures into an equation he had derived from living primates relating brain size to group size, to predict that australopithecines would have been living in groups with a mean size of 67 individuals, and a member of *H. habilis* with its larger brain size would usually have had about 82 other members of *H. habilis* for company. These compare with a predicted group size for chimpanzees of 60 individuals. The group sizes are for something that Dunbar refers to as the 'cognitive group', that is the number of individuals of whom one has social knowledge, as opposed to with whom one might live on a daily basis.

There is good circumstantial evidence that *H. habilis* would have been living in larger groups than his ancestors. If we again look at modern primates, there appear to be two ecological situations in which primates choose to live in larger groups, and suffer the accompanying social challenges.[32] One of these is when they face a high risk from predators. In that case it is better to be with some friends because then you can work together to fend off an attack, or failing that you might hope that the attacker will eat one of your friends rather than yourself. Now we know that our earliest ancestors did become the prey of carnivores – we have skulls pierced with the teeth marks of leopards to prove it.[33] And we know that their predilection for morsels of meat from carcasses may have been pitting them against hyenas. At just 1.5 m (under 5 ft) tall and 50 kg (110 lbs) in weight at most,[34] and with no more than a few lumps of stone to throw, they were not particularly well equipped for hand-to-hyena combat. So group living seems a necessity for *H. habilis*.

The other ecological condition which favours group living is when food comes in large parcels that are irregularly distributed around the landscape. Finding these may not be easy, but once found there is plenty of food to be had. So it is often beneficial to live within a relatively large group, search for food packages individually or in pairs, but then share food with other group members. On the next day it may be someone else who is the lucky one and finds the food. This scenario is likely to apply to *H. habilis* searching for carcasses on the savannahs of East Africa 2 million years ago. Indeed the archaeologist Mark Lake has demonstrated the plausibility of such an idea by building a computer simulation model of *H. habilis* searching for carcasses and seeing how well different individuals get on when they are lonely introverts or social extroverts.[35] The gregarious loudmouths consistently win the prize of the smelly rotting carcass.

We have therefore good ecological criteria for believing that *H. habilis* would be choosing to live in relatively large groups, and their large brain size implies that they had the social intelligence to do so. In other words the enlarged brain of the *H. habilis* suggests that the domain of social intelligence has become yet more powerful and complex. What might the new elements have been? We can only speculate, but one possibility is that they could cope with more 'orders of intentionality' than could their chimpanzee-like ancestors.

'Orders of intentionality' is a term that the philosopher Daniel Dennett introduced to help us think about how social intelligence works.[36] If I believe you to know something, then I can cope with one 'order of intentionality'. If I believe that you believe that I know something, then I can cope with two orders of intentionality. If I believe that you believe that my wife believes that I know something, then I can cope with three orders of intentionality. We modern humans regularly encounter three orders of intentionality – or at least we do if we believe soap operas, which often revolve around beliefs of what others believe a third party believes, and which often turn out to be false beliefs. Five orders of intentionality seem to be our limit. Daniel Dennett demonstrated this quite effectively when he asked if 'you wonder whether I realize how hard it is for you to be sure that you understand whether I mean to be saying that you recognize that I can believe you to want me to explain that most of us can keep track of only about five or six orders of intentionality under the best of conditions'.[37] Under the best of conditions chimpanzees are likely to manage just two orders of intentionality. Perhaps the new architectural features in the chapel of social intelligence had increased this to three or four in early *Homo*.

Incipient language? Investigating brain casts and social grooming

In the preceding passage I suggested that members of *H. habilis* had probably been 'gregarious loudmouths'. All sorts of animals can become loudmouths in a metaphorical sense when they want to threaten another animal or show off to the opposite sex. Peacocks are loudmouths with their tails, so too are gorillas when they beat their chest and sticklebacks when their stomachs go red. Members of *H. habilis* were surely loudmouths in this sense – displaying to impress the opposite sex, or to assert their authority with the group. But were they literally loudmouths, with plenty of words to speak? Did they have a capacity for language?

In the last chapter we could try and chat to chimps, whether by gestures or with computer keyboards. But now we have no more than *H. habilis* fossil bones and stone tools to interrogate. Looking more closely at stone tools is not going to be of any help. Language is a modularized cognitive capacity, reliant on its own unique neural processes. In contrast, as we saw in Chapter 3, the object manipulation and vocalizations of very

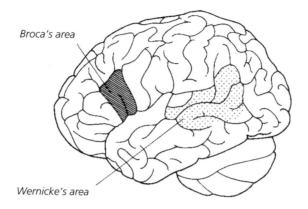

9 *A side view of the brain showing the locations of Broca's area and Wernicke's area. These are thought to be associated with the production and the comprehension of language.*

young children prior to their development of language, as well as those of chimpanzees, derive from 'general intelligence' rather than language modules. When we see a child making a hierarchically structured object we can infer that this child also makes hierarchically structured vocalizations, even if we can only see those objects. But fully developed language relies on mental modules specialized for language alone; we cannot infer the existence of these in the mind of *H. habilis* from the character of the physical objects being made.[38]

Can we infer a linguistic capacity from the shape of the brain itself? The neural processes which provide the capacity for language appear to be concentrated in specific areas of the brain, principally in the left hemisphere. Within this area, two regions appear to be particularly important: Broca's area and Wernicke's area[39] (see Figure 9). People who have suffered damage to either of these lose some of their linguistic capacity. Damage to Broca's area appears mainly to affect the use of grammar, while that to Wernicke's area affects comprehension. Damage to the connecting tissue between these areas, or to the tissue that connects these areas to the rest of the brain, can also result in severe language defects. But the relationships between specific parts of the brain and specific features of language are complex and little understood; all that we can be truly confident about is that certain areas of the brain are important for language.

So what do the brains of *H. habilis* look like? Can we see a development of Broca's and Wernicke's areas? The closest we can get to looking at their brains is to look at casts of the insides of their fossilized skulls.[40] We must hope that the humps and bumps on these casts reflect the humps and bumps of the brain of *H. habilis*. A risky business to say the least. Remember that these fossils have remained within the ground for as much as 2 million years, often becoming fossilized under the massive weight of overlying sediments. Humps and bumps on these casts are perhaps as likely to reflect the squashes and strains of the fossilization processes as much as the structure of the brain.

The fossil skull of a 2-million-year-old *H. habilis* specimen from Koobi Fora, referred to as KNM-ER 1470, is particularly well preserved. This has been examined by Phillip Tobias, one of the foremost authorities on the evolution of the brain. He is confident that a significant development of Broca's area can be seen, which has been confirmed by the work of another leading specialist, Dean Falk. In contrast, no such development of Broca's area can be seen in the brains of the australopithecines.[41]

Another clue to the presence of a linguistic intelligence may come not from the shape of the brain, but simply from its size. The two people who have thought about this in most detail have reached rather opposing conclusions.

The neuroscientist Terrence Deacon has argued that the enlargement of the brain that occurs with the first members of the *Homo* lineage involved a disproportionate increase of the part of the brain known as the pre-frontal cortex.[42] By drawing on extensive studies of the neural circuits involved in primate vocalizations and human language, Deacon argued that this relative enlargement of the pre-frontal cortex would have led to a re-organization of connections within the brain which would have favoured the development of a linguistic capacity – although whether that was sufficiently developed 2 million years ago to be termed language remains unclear.

The anthropologist Robin Dunbar looked at the size of the brain of *H. habilis* from a very different perspective.[43] Recall that we have already referred to his work regarding the relationship between brain size and group size – living within a larger group requires more brain-processing power to keep up with the ever-changing sets of social relationships. When living in groups, primates have to transfer information between each other and the principal way they do this is by grooming each others' bodies – picking out all the fleas and the lice. Who one chooses to groom, how long one grooms, and who you let watch while you do it, function as much to send social messages as to get rid of parasites. In the Burgers' zoo chimpanzee group that we looked at in the previous chapter grooming between males reached a peak when their relationships were unstable. Grooming sessions among the males lasted nine times as long in periods when there was an oestrus female in the group; de Waal suggests that the grooming may amount to 'sexual bargaining'.

Dunbar found that as group size increases, so too does the amount of time that primates spend grooming. This is not because there are more lice about but because one has to invest more and more time in social communication. But grooming is time consuming, and there are other things to do such as finding food to eat. Dunbar reckons that the longest any primate can afford to groom others is about 30 per cent of its time budget. Once above that limit, the individual may be a mastermind at social relationships, but be very hungry and lack the energy to exploit this knowledge to his or her social advantage.

So what can be done when group size is so large that even spending 30 per cent of one's time grooming leaves one ignorant of many important social relationships within the group? Well, maybe another means for transferring social information could be used – or in evolutionary terms would be selected for. Dunbar suggests that that other means is language. He argues that language evolved to provide a means for exchanging social information within large and socially complex groups, initially as a supplement to grooming, and then as a replacement for it. Language can do this because it is a much more efficient way of transferring information. An ambidextrous chimp may be able to groom two of his mates at once, but an articulate human can chat away to whoever is listening.

We will explore this social origin theory of language more thoroughly in the next chapter, but here we must ask whether *H. habilis* could have achieved the transfer of sufficient social information by grooming alone. Dunbar fed his estimates for the group size of *H. habilis* into his equation relating group size to grooming time, derived from his study of living primates. He found that early *H. habilis* just manages to dip under the 30 per cent threshold, with a social grooming time requirement of 23 per cent. With such a high percentage of time required for grooming it is likely that those individuals who could reduce their grooming time by inferring social information from the vocalizations of others, or who could begin to embed social information into their own vocalizations, may have gained some selective advantage.

The anthropologist Leslie Aiello suggests that these vocalizations may have been analogous to the chattering observed in Gelada baboons today and functioned to spread feelings of mutual content and well-being.[44] Perhaps they may also have been analogous to the purring of a cat when it is stroked. Or perhaps it is the sighs of pleasure when we stroke each other. These oohs, aahs, and ouches are social communication: do some more of this please, a little less of that. Dunbar has in fact argued that in our more intimate moments we return to our ancient means of social communication – physical grooming – although we now lack the body hair and (hopefully) the lice and the fleas.

Opening a crack in the cathedral door

Some cathedrals and churches are easier to get into than others. One of the churches I recently visited was in the small town of Angles in France. The main doors were locked and we had to search for a small side entrance. When inside it was initially so dark that we could hardly see our way around. Visiting that church was like trying to visit the mind of *Homo habilis*. With such a poorly preserved archaeological record, and no living species to provide an adequate analogy, finding a way into this prehistoric mind has been very difficult. The Oldowan stone tools have perhaps been able to prise apart a crack in the cathedral door. But peeping through this has been like the first few moments in the church at Angles, it all looks very dark and gloomy: it is hard to see what the basic architectural design actually is, let alone appreciate any of the details.

When my eyes grew accustomed to the lack of light in the church at Angles I was startled by the simplicity of the building; there was just a simple nave with bare stone walls and plain wooden pews. A few candles were burning in a small chapel. For some reason I had expected it to be more elaborate – architecturally more complex with ornate decorations. I feel the same about what I have managed to see of the mind of *H. habilis*. The first appearance of stone tools sounds such a grand event in human prehistory – indeed it is the starting point for the discipline of archaeology – that we expect it to be marked by some major cognitive event. But the mind of *H. habilis* at 2 million years ago seems to have been little more than an elaborate version of the mind of the common ancestor of 6 million years ago, with no fundamental changes in design (see Figure 10). Let me quickly summarize what we have seen in the mind of *H. habilis*.

OUR SOCIALLY PRECOCIOUS ANCESTOR

The toolmaking and foraging behaviour of *H. habilis* is certainly more complex than that of chimpanzees and what we expect of the common ancestor. Both the production of stone tools and the regular exploitation of animal carcasses are likely to have required specialized cognitive processes of a type absent from the chimpanzee mind. *H. habilis* appears to have been able to understand the fracture dynamics of stone and to have constructed hypotheses about resource distributions, both of which are likely to be beyond the capacity of general intelligence that dominates the toolmaking and foraging behaviour of the chimpanzee. Yet these specialized cognitive processes in the mind of *H. habilis* do not appear to be embedded within a matrix of other specialized processes relating to the same domain of activity. General intelligence appears to have continued to play an important role in conditioning toolmaking and foraging behaviour of *H. habilis*. And as a consequence, the making of stone arti-

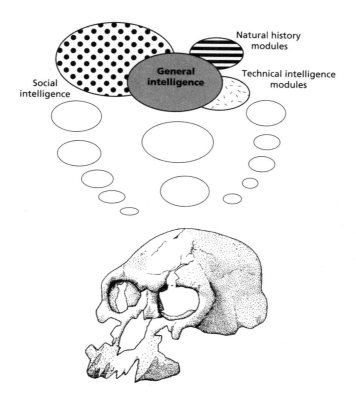

10 *The mind of early* Homo. *The drawing depicts the* H. habilis *skull known as KNM-ER 1470. This was discovered in 1972 at Koobi Fora, Kenya, and dates to 1.9 million years ago.*

facts and the exploitation of animal carcasses appear to be thoroughly integrated. They seem to be part of a single stream of activity, just as we recognized for the tool–using and foraging behaviour of the chimpanzee.

Social intelligence has become more complex and powerful than that within the mind of the chimpanzee. But it remains just as isolated from the thoughts about toolmaking and foraging as in the chimpanzee mind. There is no evidence that *H. habilis* used tools in social strategies. As noted above, the form of Oldowan artifacts appears to reflect no more than the character of the original nodule and the number of flakes removed. There is no imposition of social information on to the tools, as is pervasive among modern humans. Similarly, there are no examples in the archaeological record of spatial structure on archaeological sites which might reflect a social use of space. Material culture was not used in social strategies, even though we must conclude that those social strategies were even more complex and Machiavellian than we see among chimpanzees today.

Yet this increased social complexity is likely to have had a passive influence over the foraging and technical behaviour of *H. habilis*. As we saw in the previous chapter, the complexity of the tool-using and hunting behaviour of the Tai chimpanzees, as compared with those of Gombe, can partly be attributed to their larger group size and more intense social relationships. These provide greater opportunities for social learning and the cultural transmission of behavioural patterns. From this perspective, much of the increase in behavioural complexity of *H. habilis* over that of the common ancestor, in terms of the manufacture of stone tools and the exploitation of animal carcasses, might simply be accounted for as a spin-off from increased social complexity. The frequent use of the term 'food sharing' when discussing the behaviour of early *Homo* is probably misleading. It is more appropriate to view this as 'tolerated theft'. In terms of the play that is our past, the extra power and complexity of social intelligence appears to be the most important feature to explain the action of the second scene of Act 2.

In summary, the architectural plans inherited by members of *H. habilis* encoded the construction of a mental cathedral that appears to have had the same basic design as that encoded in the mind of the common ancestor 6 million years ago. The nave was larger, the chapel of social intelligence more elaborate, the walls of the chapels of technical and natural history intelligence a little higher and incorporating more modules. But those chapels remained incomplete.

7 The multiple intelligences of the Early Human mind

ACT 3 OF PREHISTORY, from 1.8 million to 100,000 years ago, is the most puzzling period of our past. The quality of the archaeological record is substantially improved over that of Act 2, often enabling detailed and accurate reconstructions of past behaviour to be made. But when we study that behaviour, it frequently seems almost bizarre in its nature. It appears fundamentally different from what went before and from what comes afterwards in that rush towards the present day in Act 4.

While we still have much to learn about our ancestors of Act 2, discussed in the previous chapter, we can nevertheless accept that their ways of life were fine-tuned adaptations to the African woodland and savannahs between 4.5 and 1.8 million years ago. Because their lifestyles are so alien to us, it seems clear how they should be studied: once we have reconstructed the behaviour of the earliest *Homo*, for instance, we try to understand it as if we were an ecologist trying to understand the behaviour of any other primate species. We can also feel confident about how we should approach the performance of Act 4, especially in the second and third scenes after 60,000 years ago. During that period the pace of cultural change is so fast that it feels familiar, because this is precisely what we are accustomed to in our own short lives. And for the majority of these scenes we have a single type of human improvising the script – ourselves, *H. sapiens sapiens*. So we try to be more like an anthropologist than an ecologist when explaining human behaviour in Act 4.

Between these two periods we find the no-man's land of Act 3, where neither ecologist nor anthropologist can tread with confidence. Indeed this also applies to much of the first scene of Act 4, particularly when we are looking at the behaviour of the final Neanderthals. During these periods some features of the actors' behaviour seem so familiar to us that we could readily believe that they have the modern mind; but in other ways their behaviour appears as alien as that of the earliest *Homo* on the African savannah. Act 3 is indeed a period full of puzzles – we will come across eight of them within this chapter. Each actor seems to be like the man that Charles Colton was thinking about when he wrote early in the last century that 'Man is an embodied paradox, a bundle of contradictions'.[1] The task of the next two chapters is to unravel this bundle to see what type of mind is hidden inside.

Let us begin by reminding ourselves of the salient points of the third act.

Act 3 has an exciting start: the appearance of *H. erectus* 1.8 million years ago, followed by new types of stone tools, handaxes, 1.4 million years ago. Through the course of this act we watch how *H. erectus* diversifies and evolves into a range of new human ancestors. While the size of the brain appears to have remained stable between 1.8 and 0.5 million years ago – as *H. erectus* and her immediate descendants colonized much of the Old World – this period is brought to a close by a return to a period of rapidly expanding brain size, similar to that which had happened 2 million years ago, and which ends at around 200,000 years ago with the brain at an equivalent size to that of Modern Humans today. The new larger-brained actors after 500,000 years ago are classified as types of archaic *H. sapiens* in Africa and China, while in Europe the scant fossil remains are referred to as *H. heidelbergensis*. This last species then seems to give rise to *H. neanderthalensis* – the Neanderthals – found in Europe and the Near East after about 150,000 years ago and which survives in Europe until as late as 30,000 years ago. For this chapter I am going to group all of these actors together and refer to them as 'Early Humans' to distinguish them from *H. sapiens sapiens* appearing at the start of Act 4, whom I will refer to as 'Modern Humans'.

While these evolutionary events were occurring, the scenery was going through a hectic series of changes. This period of our past is dominated by a succession of global environmental changes as the planet went through at least eight major glacial–interglacial cycles. If we look at Europe, we can see the landscapes repeatedly changing from ice-covered tundras, to thick forests and back again, with accompanying changes in animal fauna. And even within one climatic phase, there were a host of shorter-term climatic fluctuations – successions of years, or even individual years, when the climate was abnormally cold or warm, wet or dry.

So with regard to the evolution of human anatomy and climatic change, Act 3 is teeming with action. But the props that the actors are using do not seem to match this tempo of change. After the initial appearance of the handaxe at 1.4 million years ago, we have a single major technical innovation at around 250,000 years ago with the appearance of a new production technique called the Levallois method. But other than this there seem to be hardly any changes in material culture. Indeed many of the props seem little different from those used by *H. habilis* on the African savannah in Act 2. As a whole, the archaeological record between 1.4 million and 100,000 years ago seems to revolve around an almost limitless number of minor variations on a small set of technical and economic themes.

By the start of Act 3, over 4 million years have passed since the time of the common ancestor. This has taken us to a mind with two dominant features: a bundle of mental modules dedicated to social interaction alone, which can be characterized as a discrete social intelligence, and a suite of generalized learning and problem-solving rules which are used irrespective of the behavioural domain and are referred to as general intelligence. Supplementing these are a number of specialized mental modules which relate to understanding physical objects and the natural world, although these appear to be relatively few in number. We must now see what happens to this mind during the next act of prehistory.

As I have just indicated, there are several different types of human ancestors during this act, each of whom is likely to have had a slightly different type of mental architecture. I say 'slightly' because I am going to start with the premise that the similarities between their mental architectures are more significant than the differences. My aim in this chapter is to try to reconstruct the architecture for a generic Early Human mind, drawing freely on data from the different types of Early Humans of this act. Indeed I will also step into the start of Act 4, when looking at the behaviour of the last of the Neanderthals – behaviour that appears to be no different from that of Act 3, but which can be reconstructed in rather more detail. Only at the end of this chapter will I try to draw some distinctions between the mental architectures of *H. erectus* and *H. neanderthalensis*, thereby exploring the evolution of the mind during the course of Act 3.

This act is full of behavioural paradoxes, if not plain contradictions. A theme running through this chapter will be how Early Humans appear to be so much like Modern Humans in some respects, yet so remarkably different in others. I believe that these puzzles and paradoxes are in fact the key to reconstructing the architecture of the Early Human mind. In order to proceed, we must consider the evidence for each of the four cognitive domains I defined in Chapter 4 – technical, natural history, social and linguistic intelligence – as well considering how these interacted, if at all. So let us start once again with technical intelligence and the evidence from stone tools.

Technical intelligence: imposing symmetry and form

We must begin by recognizing a quite dramatic increase in technical skill over that possessed by *H. habilis* in Act 2. The most characteristic artifact produced by Early Humans was the handaxe. Even a brief look at handaxes indicates a number of significant differences from those artifacts produced within the Oldowan tradition. They often display high degrees of symmetry, sometimes simultaneously in three dimensions, and indi-

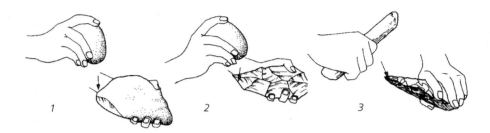

1   2   3

11 *The production of a symmetrical handaxe involves three major stages. Beginning with either a large flake or a nodule (1), a hard hammer of stone is used to achieve the basic shape by detaching flakes from alternate sides of the artifact (2). The handaxe is finished by using a 'soft' hammer, of either bone, antler or wood, to remove 'thinning' flakes (3) and to achieve the final form of the artifact.*

cate that the knapper was imposing form on to the artifact, rather than just creating sharp edges as with an Oldowan chopper.

To achieve such symmetry and form, longer knapping sequences were required. These can be appreciated from the refitting of knapping debris from sites such as Boxgrove in southern England, where handaxes were made 500,000 years ago.[2] To make a handaxe, great care must be paid to the initial selection of the stone nodule with regard to its shape, quality and likely fracture dynamics. Manufacture involves roughing out the handaxe using a stone hammer followed by final shaping, often with a 'soft' hammer made of bone or wood (see Figure 11). Flakes are removed from alternate sides of the artifact in turn, which is why the technique is often described as bifacial knapping, and the artifacts as bifaces. A soft hammer can detach flakes with shallow scars to create an artifact that is relatively thin. Prior to the removal of each thinning flake, the edge of the artifact may be ground for a few moments or have small flakes removed, in preparation for a strike.

The difficulty in achieving a symmetrical handaxe of a specified form has been stressed by Jacques Pelegrin, who has many years' experience at replicating handaxes. He has explained how the goal of the knapper is not simply to obtain a sharp cutting edge but to extricate an artifact of a specific form independent from the starting shape of that nodule. Planning ahead is essential if symmetry is to be achieved, and maintained as the piece is developed. The knapper needs to assess both what is desirable and what is possible, and achieve such ends by blows of a specific force and direction at specific points on the artifact. Each nodule worked by a knapper will have its own unique characteristics and challenges. Consequently to produce standardized forms, the knapper needs to exploit and adapt his or her toolmaking knowledge, rather than just follow a fixed set of rules in a rote fashion.[3] This final point is particularly important since many collections of handaxes from single sites are of very similar shape and size. If we assume that the original nodules are unlikely to have been exactly the same shape, then we have a fine example of the imposition of a specified form.[4]

Many of the above comments regarding the technical difficulty in producing handaxes also apply to the use of the Levallois method – the archetypal knapping technique used by the Neanderthals. Indeed, the Levallois method may involve even greater technical skill that that required to make handaxes.[5] The essence of the method is the removal of a flake, the size and shape of which is predetermined by the preparation of the core. The core is created with two distinct surfaces. One of these is domed, with flake scars to guide the removal of a flake. The other surface is the striking platform. If flake removal is to be successful, the angle between these two surfaces, the angle at which the core is struck and the force used must all be precisely right. Otherwise the detached flake may plunge over the side of the core, or deviate to one side or the other.

A modern-day flintknapper and archaeologist has recently remarked that 'even today, there are few students of lithic technology that ever achieve a Neanderthal's level of expertise in producing good Levallois cores or flakes, while the number of contemporary flint knappers that have successfully mastered the technique for producing good Levallois points probably number less than a score'.[6] He goes on to argue that the production of a blade from a prismatic core – as is characteristic of the Upper Palaeolithic period beginning 40,000 years ago in Act 4 – is 'incomparably easier' than the manufacture of a Levallois point (see Figure 12).

The Neanderthal stone technology from the Near East illustrates the technical sophistication of the Levallois technique. Consider, for instance, the demanding process by which Levallois points were produced at Kebara Cave between 64,000 and 48,000 years ago.[7] After the cortex of the core had been removed, flakes were struck from the core to create a convex profile in both the longitudinal and transverse directions. Following this, a special type of striking platform was created, referred to as a *chapeau de gendarme*. This has a central protrusion which aligns with the axis of the 'Y' form on the main ridge on the dorsal side of the core created by the initial preparation. This combination then acts to guide the removal of a flake so that the desired symmetrical point is obtained. The Kebara Neanderthals removed several Levallois flakes from each core before restoring its convexity to enable a further sequence of Levallois points to be removed. These points were most frequently used just as they came off the core; no further shaping was required.

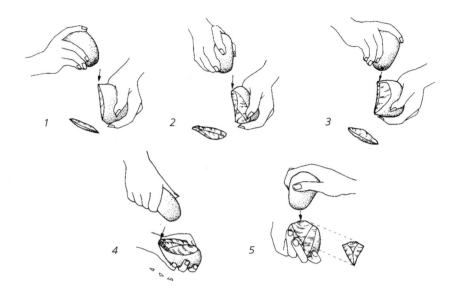

12 *To make a Levallois point one must remove flakes from the surface of a core to leave a series of ridges on a domed surface (1–3) which will then guide the removal of the final pointed flake. A striking platform is prepared perpendicular to the domed surface of the core (4) and the Levallois point removed by a single blow (5).*

As with the making of handaxes, it is critical to appreciate that Levallois flakes cannot be successfully removed by a mechanical adherence to a set of rules. Each nodule of stone has unique properties and a unique 'pathway' through the nodule must be found. Nathan Schlanger has described this when exploring the knapping actions undertaken 250,000 years ago by the Early Human who made 'Marjories core', a Levallois core from the site of Maastricht-Belvédère in the Netherlands that has had many of the waste flakes refitted.[8] Schlanger stresses how the knapper needed to have used both visual and tactile clues from the core, to have constantly monitored its changing shape, and to have continually adjusted his or her plans for how the core should develop.[9]

The technical intelligence of Early Humans is also apparent from the range of raw materials that they worked. Some of the earliest handaxes indicate an ability to work raw materials with less predictable patterns of fracture than those of the Oldowan. Consider, for instance, the collection of artifacts containing handaxes stratified immediately above the Oldowan at Sterkfontein in South Africa.[10] In this we see the introduction of a new raw material, diabase, and much better use of the difficult rock types, such as quartzite and chert. Indeed, throughout the Old World we find bifacial and Levallois flaking methods being applied successfully to relatively intractable materials.[11]

Moreover we can see a clear preference in some sites for making particular types of artifacts from particular types of raw materials. For instance, at Gesher Benot in Israel, a site more than 500,000 years old, basalt was preferentially used for handaxes, while limestone was used for choppers. Similarly at the site of Terra Amata in southern France, one of the earliest occupations in Europe, limestone was used for choppers and bifaces, while flint and quartz were used for the small tools.[12]

Puzzling over technical conservatism

We have seen evidence for an advanced technical intelligence among Early Humans. There can be little doubt that in terms of understanding the fracture dynamics of stone, and putting that understanding into practice to make stone artifacts conforming to a series of preconceived mental templates, Early Humans possessed equivalent abilities to the Modern Humans of Act 4. But, when we consider other features of Early Human technology, we see types of behaviour that are in dramatic contrast to those of Modern Humans. There are indeed four puzzles about Early Human technology:

Puzzle 1. Why did Early Humans ignore bone, antler and ivory as raw materials? Although there is evidence that Early Humans used pieces of unworked bone, such as for hammers when making handaxes, there are no carved artifacts made from bone, antler or ivory. A few pieces have scratches on the surfaces, or even chips removed from their edges – although it is often difficult to distinguish these from carnivore gnawing. But there is nothing remotely requiring the type of technical skill that is so readily apparent from stone tools. If Early Humans had been working materials such as ivory and bone, we would surely have some of the results in the enormous collections of bones which are found intermingled with the stone artifacts made by Neanderthals from sites such as Combe Grenal in France and Tabūn in the Near East. Both of these have long sequences of occupation horizons with many thousands of stone tools and animal bones. Consequently we cannot invoke poor preservation to explain the absence of carved bone artifacts. Nor can we explain it by invoking anatomical constraints in terms of Early Humans' lack of manual dexterity. Even though the anatomy of the Neanderthal hand differed slightly from that of *H. sapiens sapiens*,[13] Neanderthals seem to display equivalent sophistication to Modern Humans in their manipulation of stone artifacts during manufacture. Moreover, Early Humans made simple wooden artifacts, such as the sharpened sticks from Clacton in Britain and Lehringen in Germany, and a 'polished plank' from Gesher Benot in Israel, which required similar motor movements to working bone. And finally we cannot explain the absence of bone, antler and ivory artifacts by suggesting that they would have been of little value to Early Humans. These raw materials have physical properties, such as an ability to sustain impacts without fracturing, which give them advantages over stone when making projectiles for hunting large ungulates,[14] an activity which we will see was a central element of Early Human lifestyles. So why did they ignore such raw materials?

Puzzle 2. Why did Early Humans not make tools designed for specific purposes? Microscopic analysis of the edges of stone tools has shown that the stone artifacts of Early Humans were typically used for a wide range of tasks. Moreover there appears to be no relationship between the form of a tool and its likely function.[15] Handaxes, or simple flakes, appear to have been used as general-purpose tools, such as for woodworking, chopping plant material, cutting animal hides and removing meat. The generalized nature of Early Human tools is particularly noticeable for spear points. These show hardly any variability in size and shape across the Old World, although many different types of animals were hunted. As we will see in Chapter 9, Modern Humans of the Upper Palaeolithic – 40,000–10,000 years ago – made an immense diversity of spear and projectile points indicating that specific types of weapons were made to hunt specific types of game.[16] Early Humans do not appear to have done this. In fact nor did the earliest Modern Humans in the first scene of Act 4.

Puzzle 3. Why did Early Humans not make multi-component tools? There is nothing to suggest that *H. erectus* hafted any stone artifacts. Neanderthals appear to have been the first to do this with the stone points they made using the Levallois method. Those points found in the caves of the Near East have breakage and wear patterns consistent with hafting and their use as spear points.[17] Hafting involves making a shaft, ensuring the end is the appropriate size and shape, acquiring the binding and resin and then using these to achieve a secure attachment. It is a time-consuming business, but transforms the effectiveness of hunting weapons. From the evidence of the fracture patterns of the Levallois points from the Near East, it is clear that Early Humans had mastered the technique. The odd thing, however, is that these hafted tools remained so few in number and with so few components. If one stone flake can be attached, why not create artifacts with multiple components which, in view of their dominance among later hunter-gatherers, appear to have been considerably more efficient? So if Early Humans had mastered the art of combining different types of raw materials to make composite artifacts, why did they stop at making such simple tools? The most complex tool that Neanderthals made is unlikely to have had more than two or three parts.

Puzzle 4. Why did Early Human stone tools show such limited degrees of variation across time and space? Perhaps the most startling feature of the stone technology of Early Humans is its limited degree of variability. In Chapter 2 I quoted the archaeologist Glynn Isaac who remarked on the 'shuffling of the same essential ingredients' of Early Human technology for more than a million years of 'minor, directionless change'. Other prominent archaeologists have also stressed this puzzling aspect of Early Human technology. For instance, Lewis Binford has written how we have collections of handaxes 'from many different environments in Africa, western Europe, the Near East and India, and, except for possible minor variations that can be understood in terms of the types of raw materials available for those artifacts' production and distribution ... no patterned differentiations convincingly covary with grossly different environments.'[18] Large-scale statistical analyses of handaxe shape have supported such views.[19] Similarly with regard to the period after 200,000 years ago, Richard Klein, one of the authorities on the behaviour of archaic *H. sapiens* in South Africa, has described how their toolkits have little to distinguish them from those of the Neanderthals living in the Near East and Europe.[20] Why was there no degree of variability in technology to match that of environment? Why was there such limited innovation?

One possible solution to these puzzles is simply that Early Humans had no need for tools made from organic materials other than wood, or with specialized functions, or of many component parts. But this solution can easily be seen to be inadequate: when we consider the interaction between Early Humans and their natural environment, we see that many Early Humans appear to have been under considerable adaptive stress that could have been alleviated by such tools. So before finding the solution to these puzzles we must consider the nature of this interaction with the environment, and in so doing examine a second cognitive domain of the Early Human mind: natural history intelligence.

Natural history intelligence: expanding minds, expanding territories

Natural history intelligence is an amalgam of at least three sub-domains of thought: that about animals, that about plants and that about the geography of the landscape, such as the distribution of water sources and caves. As a whole it is about understanding the geography of the landscape, the rhythms of the seasons, and the habits of potential game. It is about using current observations of the natural world to predict the future: the meaning of cloud formations, of animal footprints, of the arrival and departure of birds in the spring and autumn.

Were Early Humans natural historians *par excellence* like modern hunter-gatherers? In the previous chapter we arrived at a rather equivocal situation for the earliest members of the *Homo* lineage. We concluded that their success as hunters, gatherers and scavengers on the savannah of East Africa implied an ability to use natural history clues, such as footprints, and the ability to develop hypotheses about resource distribution. These abilities are likely to have gone far beyond those of the 6-million-year-old common ancestor we considered in Chapter 5. But we nevertheless characterized these abilities as a small cluster of micro-domains, too limited in number and scope to deserve the title of a natural history intelligence.

The most obvious indication that we should now be prepared to use this title for a component of the Early Human mind is the colonization of landscapes outside Africa. Recall from Chapter 2 that *H. erectus* or his descendants had begun living in Southeast Asia and perhaps China by 1.8 million years ago, western Asia by 1.0 m.y.a., and Europe perhaps by 0.78 m.y.a. and certainly by 0.5 m.y.a.

While these new environments varied greatly from one another, they were all substantially more seasonal than the low latitudes of Africa. If the earliest *Homo* had mastered low-latitude savannah environments, Early Humans had the capacity to learn about a much wider range of new environments, most notably those of the high latitudes with their very different landscapes, resources and climates. The increased technical intelligence discussed above, and the developments in social organization and language that we will consider below, may well have facilitated the exploitation of new environments. But ultimately the Early Humans would have needed to understand the habits of new types of game, the distribution of new plants and a new set of environmental clues. Consequently the presence of Early Humans from Pontnewydd Cave, North Wales, in the far northwest corner of the Old World to the Cape of South Africa implies a sophisticated natural history intelligence.

Yet Early Humans remained absent from several regions of the Old World, and made no entry into Australasia or the Americas. Clive Gamble, one of the foremost authorities on Early Human behaviour, has recently reviewed the evidence for global colonization and concluded that Early Humans were unable to cope with very dry and very cold environments.[21] These appear to have been too challenging, even if Early

Humans had a well-developed natural history intelligence and were able to make artifacts such as handaxes.

The manner in which Early Humans exploited these diverse environments, particularly in the first scene of Act 3, remains unclear. We only rarely find the animal bones which derived from Early Human hunting and scavenging activity, and those we have are often very poorly preserved.[22] But the evidence we do have suggests that Early Humans had been eclectic and flexible foragers, using a mixture of plant gathering, scavenging and hunting. In the second scene of Act 3 and the first scene of Act 4, the period between 200,000 and *c.* 60,000 years ago, the interaction between Early Humans and the natural world becomes a little clearer. So let us now explore the natural history intelligence of Early Humans by considering one specific actor in one specific part of the Old World: the Neanderthals of western Europe.

THE NEANDERTHALS: SURVIVING AGAINST THE ODDS

If the stone tools of the Neanderthals are impressive, then so too is the fact that these Early Humans lived successfully in the particularly challenging glaciated landscapes of Europe. The demands of living in such high latitudes, predominantly open tundra, cannot be underestimated.

The faunal remains from caves and open sites indicate very diverse animal communities. Among the herbivores were mammoth and woolly rhino, bison, deer and horse, reindeer, ibex and chamois. The carnivore element included species that today are only found in very different environments, such as cave bear, hyena, lion and wolf.[23] In general the animal communities appear to have been substantially more diverse than any in the modern world.

With this diversity of game, it might initially appear that Neanderthals were living in a Garden of Eden; but far from it. Acquiring the necessities of life – food, shelter, warmth – would have been immensely challenging. The animal and plant resources may have been diverse, but they are not likely to have been abundant. Each animal would have been linked into a complex foodweb resulting in frequent and unpredictable fluctuations in their numbers. And with the frequent environmental changes, whether these were from an advance or a retreat of the ice sheets, or even a few years of relative warmth or cold, the composition and links of these foodwebs would have been constantly changing. Even within a single year, the availability of plants and game would have shown dramatic variations over the seasons, with a marked deterioration during the winter months.[24]

The problems that Neanderthals faced in such environments were further exacerbated by their technology, or rather their lack of it. As I have discussed, Neanderthals appear to have mastered very complex sequences of stone tool production. Yet in spite of this technical proficiency, the range of tools appears remarkably narrow, and to have made a limited contribution to coping with the glaciated landscapes.

It is important here to appreciate the type of technology that modern hunter–gatherers such as the Inuit (Eskimo) use to survive in glaciated landscapes. These modern hunter–gatherers are as reliant upon a highly complex technology as they are upon their detailed knowledge of the natural world and an extensive series of social alliances between groups.[25] They have tools with multiple components and various complex facilities, including those for storing foodstuffs to cope with seasonal shortages.[26] To make their tools they use a wide array of raw materials, notably bone and ivory. Many of their tools are 'dedicated' to very specific tasks (see Box p. 127). As I noted above, there is no evidence that Neanderthals, or indeed any Early Humans, had such technologies. This reliance of Modern Humans on a complex and diverse technology to exploit glaciated landscapes makes the technologically-simple Neanderthal achievement particularly impressive – an achievement that lasted over 200,000 years.

That life was never easy for the Neanderthals is demonstrated by the fact that they died so young: 70–80 per cent of individuals were dead by the age of 40. Not only were Neanderthals living on the edge of the Old World, they were quite literally living on the edge of life itself. A very high proportion of Neanderthals suffered from stress fractures, and degenerative diseases. In fact they show a very similar pattern of physical injuries to rodeo riders today.[27] It would indeed be difficult to think of any group of people more in need of a wide variety of tools, or ones dedicated to specific tasks.

So how did they survive? As the environmental conditions would not have favoured substantial plant gathering, Neanderthals must have been reliant upon exploiting game, particularly during the harsh winter months. The collections of animal bones from Neanderthal occupations in the caves of western Europe typically represent many different species, but are dominated by large herbivores such as red deer, reindeer, horse and bison. These bones have been subject to intense debate concerning whether they reflect opportunistic scavenging by Neanderthals or well-planned game hunting.[28]

The most important bone collections are those from the cave site of Combe Grenal in southwest France. These have been studied by Phillip Chase who looked at the types of bones present, examining whether they would once have provided large quantities of meat or just tit-bit morsels from scavenged carcasses. He also examined the location of cutmarks

Tool complexity of Inuit hunter-gatherers

The most complex tool Early Humans appear to have made was a short thrusting spear created from a stone point hafted on to a wooden shaft. In contrast modern Inuit hunter-gatherers routinely make and use tools with many components, and which are 'dedicated' to killing specific types of animals in specific circumstances. The anthropologist Wendell Oswalt has made a study of Inuit technology and shown that tools for killing terrestrial mammals, such as caribou, similar to the reindeer hunted by the Neanderthals, typically have several components and are made from several raw materials such as stone points, antler foreshafts and wooden shafts. It is likely that the bone artifacts from the earliest Upper Palaeolithic sites after 40,000 years ago came from tools of equivalent complexity. The most complex tools used by the Inuit were for marine hunting, such as this harpoon for sealing employed by the Angmagsalik hunters of Greenland. This was carried on the side of a kayak and launched when a seal came into sight. Wendell Oswalt (1973, 137–8) describes its component parts:

Reconstruction of a hafted Levallois point as made by Neanderthals.

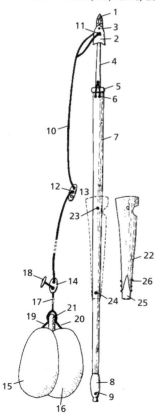

The stone point (1) was attached to the toggle head of bone (2) with a peg (3), and the distal end of the ivory foreshaft (4) fitted into a hole at the base of the harpoon head. The proximal end of the foreshaft fitted into a hole in the top of the bone socketpiece (5) and was held in place by thongs (6) which passed through a hole in the foreshaft and through two holes in the wooden shaft (7). At the base of the shaft was a bone counterweight (8) held with pegs (9). The harpoon line (10) was attached to the harpoon head through two holes (11), and it extended through two holes in a bone clasp (12). A third hole in the clasp was fitted over a bone peg (13) wedged into the shaft. The line continued on to another bone clasp (14) to which the end was tied. The floats (15, 16) were held by a single line (17) which ended in a toggle bar (18) where it was attached to a line leading from the harpoon head. The double floats consisted of two blown-up sealskins which were bound together at the middle, presumably with a thong, and had thongs which closed the opening at the head end of each (19, 20). A section of wood (21) which served to join the floats at the front was forked at the ventral surface in order to fit over a strap across the rear decking of the kayak.... The harpoon was launched with a throwing-board (22) and was readied for throwing by fitting the two bone pegs (23, 24) in the shaft through matching holes in the throwing-board. The throwing-board consisted of a strip of wood with a bone inset at the distal end (25) held in place with a series of bone pegs (26).

from stone tools on the bones, which can indicate how the animals were butchered and thus how they were acquired. Chase concluded that the Neanderthals at Combe Grenal were proficient hunters of reindeer and red deer. The method by which bovids and horse were exploited is more equivocal and is likely to have been a mix of hunting and scavenging.[29] Other cave sites, such as Grotta di Sant'Agostino in western Italy, have also yielded conclusive evidence that Neanderthals were hunters, in that case of red and fallow deer.[30] This hunting activity is likely to have been undertaken with short thrusting spears, requiring that the hunters got close to their prey, perhaps by stranding the animals in marshes or rivers.[31]

Neanderthals also scavenged animals which had either been killed by other predators, or died natural deaths, as demonstrated at the site of Guattari in western Italy.[32] Clive Gamble has stressed the likely importance of scavenging during the winter months when game would have been scarce and Neanderthals may have been dependent upon locating and then thawing frozen carcasses, a food niche not open to other predators.[33] Indeed, it is most likely that hunting and scavenging were alternative tactics open to Neanderthals which they chose to employ in the appropriate circumstances.

We have seen, therefore, that Neanderthals survived in Europe by employing a mixture of scavenging and hunting. The Early Humans in the Levant (Neanderthals) and those in South Africa (archaic *H. Sapiens*) employed a similar mix of subsistence tactics, adapted to their particular resource characteristics.[34] How could Early Humans have achieved such effective patterns of subsistence, particularly in the harsh glaciated landscapes of Europe, in view of their limited technological repertoire?

There appear to be three answers. The first is that they lived in large groups which mitigated the dangers of a failure in the food supply for any single individual or subgroup of foragers. We will consider the evidence for this below. A second reason is that they worked very hard. The Neanderthal short lifespan partly reflects physically demanding lives.[35] Their lower limbs were particularly robust in character, which, together with other postcranial anatomical features and a high frequency of stress fractures, indicates that Neanderthals were habitually engaged in prolonged periods of locomotion involving strength and endurance.[36] Their large nasal apertures and projecting noses are likely to have been partly to get rid of excess body heat during prolonged bouts of activity.

But simply having lots of friends and working hard would not have been enough. The third, and most important, answer to their technologically-challenged survival must be within their minds. The circumstantial evidence is conclusive: Neanderthals (and other Early Humans) must have possessed a sophisticated understanding of their environment and the animals within it; they had an advanced natural history intelligence.

Natural history intelligence would have been essential for building mental maps of their environment – maps at a vastly greater geographical scale than those used by chimpanzees that we considered in Chapter 5. One of the critical features of these mental maps would have been the location of rockshelters and caves. These were needed for shelter and warmth. Neanderthal clothing is likely to have been rather unsophisticated, as they lacked the technology to make sewn garments – bone needles are first found at 18,000 years ago, well into Act 4.[37] The evidence for Neanderthal occupation in caves is often marked by extensive layers of ash and evidence of burning. These have traditionally been interpreted as 'home bases', but a novel idea is that they may have principally served as 'defrosting chambers' for carcasses.[38] Whatever the role of caves, Neanderthals' mental maps of the location of caves and rockshelters, and an ability to infer the presence of resident carnivores, would have been essential for survival.

A natural history intelligence would also have been essential for hunting. Neanderthals would have needed to get close to game for an effective use of their short thrusting spears. For this they had to understand animal behaviour and how to entice prey into disadvantaged situations: planning is essential to effective hunting, and knowledge of animal behaviour is essential to effective planning. Neanderthals could only have been successful at hunting large game if they had mastered the use of visual clues such as hoofprints and faeces, and possessed an intimate knowledge of the habits of their game. Successful scavenging behaviour would also have relied on a natural history intelligence, perhaps even more so than for the earliest *Homo* on the African savannah. The prediction of carcass location, rather than random searching, would have been a necessity. This would require not only a knowledge of animal behaviour, including the hunting patterns of predators whose prey might be scavenged, but also of the physical processes that lead to the movement, burial and exposure of carcasses.

In summary, a well-developed natural history intelligence appears to have been essential for Early Human lifestyles as inferred from the archaeological record. And surely it must have been a natural history intelligence as sophisticated as that of modern hunter-gatherers, who have the advantage of highly complex, multi-component tools. Indeed, without the use of complex tools, Early Humans are likely to have relied even more heavily on a natural history intelligence than do Modern Humans. They literally must have thought their way through the hazards of living by hunting and gathering in glaciated landscapes.

Yet even this well-developed natural history intelligence may have been inadequate when the environments in northern Europe became very harsh during the height of one of the later ice ages of the Pleistocene period. At those times Neanderthals employed a further strategy for survival: they left. Similarly Neanderthals seem to have been unable to cope with the thickly forested woodland of northwest Europe at 125,000 years ago, a period of climatic warmth squeezed in between two periods of cold tundra environments and expanded ice sheets.[39] We should also note that while Early Humans were effective big-game hunters, they do not appear to have systematically exploited small game, birds and fish. Even their big-game hunting appears to have been restricted to the killing of individuals or at least small groups of animals. It is only with behaviourally modern hunter-gatherers beginning in Act 4 that we find systematic mass slaughters. So as with their manufacture of tools, in some ways Early Humans appear to be very modern, and in others they seem to be very distant human ancestors.

Solving the puzzle of Early Human technology

Having established that Neanderthals – as our representatives of Early Humans – possessed both a technical intelligence, as manifest in their stone tools, and a natural history intelligence, as manifest in their hunting activities and indeed their mere survival in ice age Europe, we must return to our four puzzles about Early Human technology. As will become apparent, there is I think a simple solution to these enigmas: a barrier between the technical and natural history intelligences within the Early Human mind – a barrier like that of a thick wall dividing two chapels in a medieval cathedral. Let us consider each of the puzzles in turn.

The first was the absence of artifacts made from bone, antler or ivory. This can only be explained by recognizing that Early Humans could not think of using such materials for tools: these materials were once parts of animals and animals were thought about in the domain of natural history intelligence. The conceptual leap required to think about parts of animals using cognitive processes which had evolved in the domain of inert, physical objects appears to have been too great for Early Humans.

Do the few examples of minimally scratched and chipped bone by Early Humans indicate that this cognitive barrier was occasionally overcome? Perhaps they do, for the fact that they were chipped suggests that they may have been thought of as stone. For instance, Paola Villa has described a piece of elephant bone from the site of Castel di Guido in Italy, at least 130,000 years old, which has a series of scars from where it had been struck as if it were a nodule of stone. She interprets the piece as an attempt to make a handaxe out of bone.[40] Alternatively the scratching and chipping of bone may simply reflect the use of general intelligence – which could never achieve artifacts of any complexity, or develop working methods appropriate to these raw materials. Indeed, general intelligence is likely to have supplied the cognitive processes for the working of wood as a raw material.

A cognitive barrier preventing the integration of knowledge about animal behaviour and toolmaking also appears to explain the second puzzle, the absence of artifacts dedicated to specific activities. As we saw above, Early Humans relied on general-purpose tools – they did not design specific tools for specific tasks. To do so would have required an integration of technical and natural history intelligence. For instance, if one wishes to design a projectile to kill one type of animal, say a red deer, in a particular situation then one must think about the animal's anatomy, pattern of movement and hide thickness, while also thinking about the raw material and how to work it. We have seen that Early Humans could think in complex ways about these things, but they do not seem to have been able to think about them in this manner at the same time. When activity at the domain interface of toolmaking and hunting was required, this was undertaken by general intelligence and resulted in behavioural simplicity.

This also explains the third puzzle: the absence of tools with multiple components. Among modern hunter-gatherers these are principally produced with specific types of prey in mind. The most complex tools, for example, are found among groups such as the Inuit and are used for hunting marine mammals (see above).[41] Each of the components is designed for solving a specific problem concerned with locating, killing and retrieving an animal. If animals and tools cannot be thought about in such an integrated fashion, it seems unlikely that tools with more than a few components would ever be produced.

This same cognitive constraint might be invoked to explain the fourth puzzling feature about Early Human technology: its remarkable conservatism across time and space. There can be little doubt that the behaviour of Early Humans varied across the inhabited part of the Old World as they encountered different types of resources, competed with different type of carnivores and coped with different climatic regimes. They had an advanced natural history intelligence which enabled them to adapt to new resources. If the chimpanzees of Gombe and the Tai forest can have such different feeding patterns as we saw in Chapter 5, we should expect no less of Early Humans. Yet, when viewed at this scale, technology shows minimal variation. The making of stone tools simply does not appear to be fully integrated with subsistence behaviour and the reason must be that thought about stone tools was inaccessible to thought about natural history. As archaeologists we are left with a million years of technical monotony that *mask* a million years of socially and economically flexible behaviour.

This is not to argue that there was no relationship between the types of environments exploited by Early Humans and the types of tools they made. Different environments provided different types of raw materials. If only small nodules were available, or the stone was of poor quality, Early Humans were restricted in the types of stone artifacts they could make. Moreover, access to raw material sources was influenced by the manner in which people moved around the landscape, and the extent of vegetation and snow cover. When access appears to have been restricted, such as in France when snow cover was particularly thick or in west-central Italy when wide-ranging scavenging behaviour resulted in infrequent visits to raw material sources, we see Early Humans using their raw materials more conservatively. For instance, we see repeated re-sharpening of artifacts, or the adoption of knapping methods which could remove a relatively large number of flakes from a single nodule of stone.[42] But this variability in technology is no more than a *passive reflection* of past environments and the manner in which they were exploited, requiring only general intelligence to make simple cost/benefit decisions about raw material use.[43]

Now let us consider social intelligence.

Social intelligence: expanding minds, expanding social networks

The social intelligence of Early Humans is both the easiest and the most difficult of our cognitive domains to assess. The easy part is that we can simply assert that *H. erectus*, Neanderthals and other Early Humans are likely to have possessed a complex social intelligence given its existence in non-human primates and the earliest *Homo*, as we have seen in Chapters 5 and 6. If chimpanzees have a theory of mind and engage in cunning Machiavellian social tactics, there can be little doubt that Early Humans were at least as socially intelligent. We can indeed find substantial evidence for the existence of a domain of social intelligence – perhaps one as complex as that of Modern Humans – within the Early Human mind. This evidence comes not from the tools and animal bones they left behind, but from their anatomy and from the environments within which they lived.

The most significant piece of evidence is the size of the Early Human brain, and the implications this has for the average size of social groups – which, as I discussed in the previous chapter, is a proxy measure for the degree of social intelligence. Recall how the biological anthropologist

Robin Dunbar demonstrated a strong correlation between brain size and the average group size for living non-human primates.[44] Using estimates for the brain size of Early Humans, and extrapolating from this relationship, Leslie Aiello and Robin Dunbar predict that *H. erectus* would have lived in groups with a mean size of 111, archaic *H. sapiens* in groups of 131, and Neanderthals in groups of 144, not significantly different from the group size for Modern Humans of about 150.[45] These are not predictions for the day-to-day groups within which Early Humans lived, but for the number of individuals about whom any one person had social knowledge. There are many problems with this study which make me cautious about the specific figures. Aiello and Dunbar, for example, ignore the complex technical and foraging behaviour of Early Humans, which must have used some brain-processing power and contributed to brain expansion. Yet Dunbar provides some supporting evidence for these predictions in terms of the group sizes of Modern Humans in recently documented hunter-gatherer societies.[46] In view of such inferences we have good reason to expect that Early Humans, especially those after 200,000 years ago, were as socially intelligent as Modern Humans.

Living in large groups – though probably not as large as Dunbar suggests – would appear to make ecological sense for Early Humans. In many regions of the world they are likely to have been at risk from carnivores, a danger alleviated, as we saw in the last chapter, by group living. Even so, we know of several cases in which Early Humans seem to have fallen victim to carnivores.[47] The character of the food supply would also have encouraged the formation of large groups. Food is likely to have come predominantly in 'large packages' in the shape of animal carcasses, either hunted or scavenged. This would have been especially true in the glaciated tundra-like environments of Europe. One 'large package' could have fed many mouths, thus encouraging Early Humans to live within large groups.[48] Moreover the chances of finding and killing an animal on one's own or in a small group would have been minimal.[49]

While in most circumstances the appropriate social strategy would have been to live in large social groups, in some environments Early Humans would have found it more advantageous to live in relatively small groups. There are many disincentives to group living, such as competition for resources and aggressive encounters between group members, the frequency of which are likely to have increased with the size of the group.[50] It is most likely that when Early Humans in Europe were living in relatively wooded environments, such as during warmer interludes between the advances of the ice sheets, they would have formed much smaller groups. Thick vegetation provides a means to evade and escape potential predators, and plant resources are more evenly distributed and provide food in smaller packages than animal carcasses. Consequently we should expect Early Humans to have constantly altered their group size in accordance with environmental conditions. This would require an adjustment of social relationships between individuals. The capacity for such social flexibility is at the heart of social intelligence.

Early Human skeletal remains may provide one further glimpse of complex social relations. Neanderthals clearly took care of their sick and elderly – those who could only make a limited contribution, if any, to the welfare of the group. A classic example of this is the Neanderthal from Shanidar Cave in Iraq who appears to have lived for several years in spite of having suffered head injuries and a crushing of the right side of his body, possibly from a cave rock fall, and blindness in his left eye. It is unlikely that he could have moved very far at all and yet he lived for several years with these severe injuries, no doubt being cared for by other members of his social group.[51]

Social intelligence: the contradictory evidence from archaeology

The anatomical and environmental evidence I have so far considered supports the idea that Early Humans frequently lived in large groups and had an advanced level of social intelligence. Yet as soon as we turn to the archaeological evidence we find some more puzzles. If we accept – as we must – that the brain size of Early Humans implies a high degree of social intelligence, resulting in Machiavellian social tactics adopted by individuals often living in large groups, then four more aspects of the archaeological record are very odd indeed:

Puzzle 5. Why do the settlements of Early Humans imply universally small groups? Archaeologists attempt to make inferences concerning past group size and social organization from the spatial extent of archaeological sites and the distribution of artifacts and features within the sites.[52] This is not an easy task when dealing with the sites of Act 3: poor preservation and the limited extent of many excavations make it very difficult to assess the original area of an occupation. Nevertheless, the leading authorities on the archaeological record of Early Humans have all agreed that such data indicate that they were living in very small groups as compared with Modern Humans. For example, Lewis Binford describes groups of Neanderthals as 'uniformly small',[53] while Paul Mellars suggests that 'communities ... were generally small ... and largely lacking in any clear social structure or definition of individual social or economic roles'.[54] Randall White has described Neanderthal social organization as 'internally un- or weakly differentiated'.[55] Similarly Olga Soffer, the leading authority on the archaeology of the Central Russian Plain, argues that Neanderthals lived in 'small sized groups' and that there was an 'absence of social differentiation'.[56] As is evident, there is a dramatic contrast between these views about group size among Early Humans gained from the archaeological record, and those of the biological anthropologists such as Robin Dunbar gained by looking at Early Human brain size.

Puzzle 6. Why do distributions of artifacts on sites suggest limited social interaction? It is not only the size of Early Human occupation sites that is very different from those of Modern Humans. They also show very different distributions of artifacts and bone fragments. Rather than being found in patterned arrangements, such as around hearths or huts, artifacts and bones are found in seemingly randomly distributed piles of knapping and butchery debris.[57] It is as if each individual or small group were operating with no desire to observe and interact with other group members – quite the opposite of what is expected from high social intelligence. Indeed, Clive Gamble interprets the lack of spatial structure as reflecting an episodic behavioural pattern – a 15-minute culture.[58] But an essential feature of the advanced social intelligence implied by Early Human brain size is a long time depth to social relationships.

Puzzle 7. Why is there an absence of items of personal decoration? A characteristic feature of all Modern Humans, whether they are prehistoric hunter-gatherers or 20th-century business people, is that they use material culture to transmit social information. As I have noted already, this is an essential part of our complex social behaviour – it is unimaginable how sufficient social information could be passed between people living in large social groups without the help of material culture. Yet we have no evidence that Early Humans were doing this: no beads, pendants or necklaces, or paintings on cave walls. There are a few pieces of bone that are claimed to have been pierced by Neanderthals, but it is likely that the piercing was done by the canines of carnivores. And a few pieces of red ochre found in Early Human sites in South Africa may imply body painting.[59] Yet if they do, then the absence of any actual artifact for body decoration in more than 1.5 million years of prehistory becomes even more bizarre.

Puzzle 8. Why is there no evidence for ritualized burial among Early Humans? This is a puzzle because while there is clear evidence that Neanderthals were burying some individuals in pits, there is no evidence of graveside ritual accompanying such acts, nor of the placing of artifacts within the pits/graves along with the dead, as is characteristic of Modern Humans. Isolated burials of Neanderthals have been found in several caves, such as Teshik Tash, La Ferrassie and Kebara. It was once believed that a 'flower burial' had occurred in Shanidar Cave, high pollen frequencies in the soil seeming to indicate that the body of a deceased Neanderthal had been covered with a wreath of flowers. But this pollen is now believed to have been blown into the cave, or even brought in on workmen's boots.[60]

The significance of these Neanderthal burials remains unclear. They may simply represent an hygienic disposal of corpses so as not to attract scavenging carnivores. Alternatively the act of burial, and the resulting existence of a grave within an occupied cave, may reflect the importance of ancestors in on–going social relations. And it is this which makes the absence of any ritual and grave-goods so puzzling.

Solving the enigma of social intelligence

In summary, the evidence for the social intelligence of Early Humans leaves us with a paradox. The brain size of Early Humans and the environmental evidence appear conclusively to show an advanced level of social intelligence; the archaeology shows the exact converse – it implies that Early Humans lived in small groups apparently with little or no social structure. A resolution to this paradox is quite simple: archaeologists are making a major mistake in their interpretation of the data. They are assuming that the Early Human mind was just like the modern mind – that there was a cognitive fluidity between social, technical and natural history intelligences. We can only make sense of the archaeological record, and solve the puzzles we have found, by recognizing that these were isolated from each other. Just as there was a cognitive barrier between technical and natural history intelligence, so too were there barriers between these and social intelligence.

This provides a ready solution to why the character of Early Human sites appears to suggest a simple social behaviour, while brain size implies a sophisticated social intelligence. If technical intelligence was not integrated with social intelligence, there is no reason to expect that social activity and technical activity took place at the same place in the landscape. We know that it did for Modern Humans, epitomized by the manufacture or repair of tools while people were seated around a hearth and engaged in conversation. Because of this intimacy between technical and social activities, the artifact distributions of Modern Humans may well reflect the size of social groups and their social structure. But the artifact scatters left by Early Humans have no such implications. They show no more than where tools were made and used: the complex social behaviour and large social aggregations of Early Humans took place elsewhere in the landscape, perhaps no more than a few metres away – and are archaeologically invisible to us today (see Figures 13 and 14). Similarly, the butchering and sharing of food is as much a social as an economic activity among modern hunter-gatherers today, and consequently the distribution of butchery remains provides information about social behaviour. But if social and natural history intelligence were not linked, the animal bones from the sites of Early Humans will provide no information about past social behaviour.

Food sharing is nonetheless likely to have been prevalent in Early Human society because food sources would often have come in large packages – animal carcasses. Moreover, the relatively large brain size of Early Humans, particularly Neanderthals and archaic *H. sapiens*, suggests that nursing mothers would have required a high-quality diet to meet the feeding demands of the infant. The provisioning of females with meat appears a very likely scenario – it is difficult to imagine how a nine-months pregnant Neanderthal, or one with a young infant, could have survived without some provisioning of food by either other females or perhaps her sexual partner. Yet the articulation of food within a social relationship could have been handled by general intelligence.

As we will see in the next chapter, the provisioning of pregnant or nursing mothers with food may be the behavioural context for a selective pressure for an integration of social and natural history intelligence. But this comes later in human evolution. The provisioning and sharing of food among Early Humans appear to have been handled by general intelligence in view of the absence of spatial patterning in artifact and bone distributions on sites. I therefore suspect that the formalized rules for food sharing found in many modern hunter-gatherer groups were lacking among Early Humans. These often involve very strict rules which define which part of a carcass should go to which relative.[61] The carcass is itself interpreted as a map of social relations within the group – the distribution of meat provides a means to reinforce those social relationships. Food sharing among Early Humans was probably a rather simpler affair. Similarly I doubt if feasting took place of the kind seen in the Potlatches of the Northwest Coast Indians of America or the pig feasts among New Guinea Highlanders. In these ritualized feasts, food is used as a medium for social interaction rather than to appease hunger.

General intelligence is also likely to have been adequate to build the links between interaction with the social and natural environments required for coordinating group hunting. It seems improbable that either hunting or scavenging could have been successful without some degree

13, 14 *Modern and Early Human spatial behaviour compared. In the upper figure we see how Early Humans undertook activities such as social interaction, making stone tools and butchering carcasses in spatially discrete locations. Among Modern Humans of the Upper Palaeolithic, for whom the boundaries between different types of activities were much more blurred, each activity was undertaken within the same spatial area. The result for archaeologists are two very different types of archaeological record.*

of social cooperation, either in these activities themselves, or in terms of sharing information. But we must be careful not to exaggerate the extent of social cooperation required here: we can see cooperative hunting and information-sharing in many different types of animals, including lions and chimpanzees, as I described in Chapter 5.

The most persuasive piece of evidence for a cognitive barrier between social and technical intelligence is the absence of any artifacts used for body decoration, such as beads and pendants. The manufacture of these objects involves a type of thinking equivalent to that for making specialized hunting weapons, as I described above. One needs to keep in mind the social purposes of these artifacts – such as to communicate social status or group affiliation – while performing the technical acts themselves. If social and technical intelligence are closed to each other, the opportunities for making such artifacts is lost. Due to this cognitive barrier, any body decoration by Early Humans would need to have been undertaken by using general intelligence alone. This in its turn would have meant that such body decoration sent only very simple social messages, or perhaps merely drew attention to parts of the body. Indeed it is this sort of behaviour that probably explains the pieces of red ochre found at an extremely small number of Early Human archaeological sites.

In summary, the relationship between the technical and social intelligence of Early Humans appears to mirror that between technical and natural history intelligence. Just as tools were not made for specific forms of interaction with the natural world, nor were they made for specific patterns of social interaction. Just as the limited variation in technology provides a very poor reflection of the diversity of hunting and gathering behaviour, so too does the limited variability in settlement size provide a poor reflection of social variability and complexity.

A further similarity, however, is that past patterns of social behaviour may be *passively reflected* in Early Human technology. For instance, it is apparent that those European Early Humans before 100,000 years ago who were living in small social groups in wooded environments did not make complex artifacts such as handaxes and lacked strong toolmaking traditions. A good example of these are the Early Humans who made the tools classified as the Clactonian industry in southern England, dating to before 250,000 years ago and lacking any handaxes. In contrast those who probably lived on tundra-like environments in large groups had very strong traditions, such as in the shapes of handaxes which seem to have been copied from generation to generation. Those who lived in southern England both before and after those who made Clactonian tools used the same raw materials to produce very fine handaxes. The Clactonian toolmakers simply had fewer other toolmakers to observe, and did so less frequently. Consequently there was little stimulus to enable the intuitive physics within their minds to mature into a technical intelligence, as happened when Early Humans lived in large social groups on open tundras.[62]

We must now turn to language.

A social language

There are three features of the fossil crania of Early Humans which can be used to draw inferences concerning linguistic capacities: brain size, neural structure as inferred from the shape of the brain, and the character of the vocal tract.

With regard to brain size, the most important point is also the simplest: the brain sizes of the majority of *H. erectus*, and all archaic *H. sapiens* and Neanderthals, fall within the range of that of Modern Humans. Indeed the mean brain size of Neanderthals is rather larger than that of anatomically Modern Humans.[63] Now recall that in the previous chapter I introduced the ideas of Robin Dunbar that related brain size to group size, and group size to the amount of social grooming required to maintain social cohesion. He suggested that the maximum percentage of time a primate can devote to grooming without interfering with other activities (such as foraging) is about 30 per cent. By the time of archaic *H. sapiens*, *c.* 250,000 years ago, the predicted grooming time had risen to almost 40 per cent. Leslie Aiello and Robin Dunbar have argued that to alleviate this, the use of language with a significant social content would have been essential.[64]

On such evidence Aiello and Dunbar concluded that the basis of the language capacity appeared early in the evolution of the genus *Homo*, at least by 250,000 years ago. A critical feature of their argument is that the subject matter of the earliest language was social interaction; it was in effect a 'social language'. There was thus a co-evolution of increasing group size/social intelligence and a capacity for language. Evidence for this may indeed be found in the structure of the brain. The prefrontal cortex is not only the area of the brain responsible for many aspects of language, but also that where the ability to reflect on one's own and other people's mental states, which I have argued is a central fact of social intelligence, are found.[65] The general-purpose character of language as we know it today, and its symbolic features evolved, Aiello and Dunbar argued, at a later date – although how much later is left unclear in their work. On a far more intuitive basis, it is indeed difficult to imagine how an Early Human could have had a brain size equivalent to that of ourselves today, but lacked a linguistic capacity.

Further support for a linguistic capacity can be found by looking at the shape of the Early Human brain, as reconstructed from the bumps on the insides of their crania. We saw in Chapter 6 that *H. habilis* appears to have had a well-developed Broca's area, which is conventionally associated with speech. Broca's area also appears well formed on the *H. erectus* cranium of KNM-WT 15000,[66] a particularly well-preserved 12-year-old boy dating to 1.6 million years ago and found at East Turkana in Kenya. With regard to more recent Early Humans, palaeoneurologists have argued that the brain shape is practically identical to that of Modern Humans. Ralph Holloway, in particular, has argued that both Broca's and Wernicke's areas can be identified on Neanderthal brain casts and that they show no difference from their appearance on the brains of Modern Humans.[67]

A third source of evidence for a linguistic capacity is the nature of the vocal tract of Early Humans. There has been a long history of efforts at reconstructing the vocal tract, particularly for the Neanderthals.[68] Since it is principally composed of soft tissue – the larynx and pharynx – one must rely on consistent relationships between the organization of soft tissue and those parts of the cranium that can survive in an archaeological context. The most recent reconstructions imply that the Neanderthal vocal tract would not have differed significantly from that of Modern Humans: Neanderthals would have had essentially modern powers of vocalization and speech.

This has received support from the discovery of a hyoid bone, surviving in a Neanderthal skeleton buried in Kebara Cave in Israel and dated to 63,000 years ago.[69] The hyoid is a bone that can provide detailed information about the structure of the vocal tract. Its movement affects the position and movement of the larynx to which it is attached. That found at Kebara, lying in an undisturbed position with the mandible and cervical vertebra, is virtually identical to that of a Modern Human with regard to its shape, muscular attachments and apparent positioning. This implies that the morphology of the vocal tract of this Neanderthal was not significantly different from that of Modern Humans. If the cognitive capacity for language was present, there appears no reason why the full range of human sounds could not have been produced.

Of course the 'if' in the last statement is a rather big 'if'. On purely logical grounds, however, it would be a little odd if Neanderthals had the vocal structures but not the cognitive capacity for speech. The structure of the human vocal tract differs markedly from other animals in having a single rather than a two-tube system. As a result adult humans carry with them the possibility of fatal choking by food becoming lodged in the pharynx. The selective disadvantage of this is over-ridden by the selective benefits of the wide range of vocalizations – and thus articulate speech – that can be made with this particular structure.[70] It would be evolutionarily bizarre indeed if Neanderthals were exposed to the possibility of choking, without being able to complain about their food.

All the fossil evidence I have briefly reviewed is ambiguous and open to different interpretations. Yet during the last few years the argument that both archaic *H. sapiens* and Neanderthals had the brain capacity, neural structure and vocal apparatus for an advanced form of vocalization, that should be called language, is compelling.

If humans began using language to talk about their social relationships, did they also start to use it to talk about toolmaking, plant gathering and hunting before the end of Act 3? In other words, had language become transformed to have the general-purpose functions which are familiar to us today – a means to communicate information irrespective of the behavioural domain? It might indeed be argued that it would have been too difficult to have acquired, say, the Levallois method for flake production without verbal instruction. Or that the cooperation implied by hunting and scavenging could not have been achieved without talking about game movements. Countering such arguments, one might point out that *H. erectus*, the earliest of Early Humans, appears to have been a very proficient toolmaker and forager even though his/her linguistic capacity is likely to have been rather limited. Moreover, if language was used within the technical and natural history domains of behaviour as frequently and effectively as in the social domain, we would expect a greater integration between behaviour in these domains. Communication by spoken language is, after all, the means by which Dan Sperber proposed that the metarepresentational module would evolve, as was described in Chapter 3.

Consequently, I am in sympathy with the suggestion from Robin Dunbar that language first evolved to handle social information, and I believe that it remained exclusively a 'social language' for the whole of Act 3.

The Early Human mind

We have now looked at all four specialized cognitive domains of the Early Human mind, and the nature of the connections between these domains. The Early Human mind we have found is illustrated in Figure 15. This is what may be described as a generic Early Human mind, because I have constructed it by freely drawing on evidence from different types of Early Humans, although the quality of the evidence has led me to focus on the Neanderthal mind which this diagram fits most closely. The archaeological data have been too sparse or ambiguous to deal with each

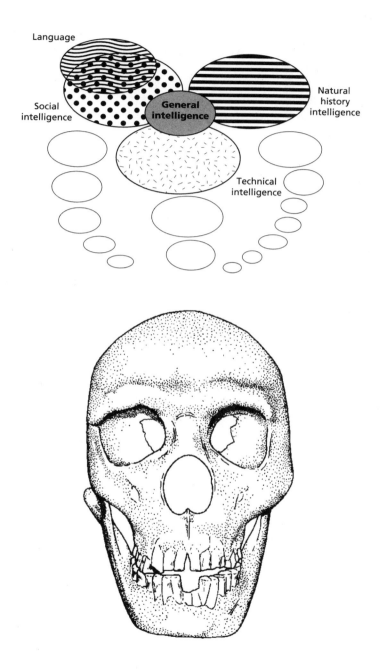

15 *The Neanderthal mind. The drawing depicts the Neanderthal skull known as Shanidar I, a man who had suffered substantial injuries and was probably blind in his left eye. This model for the mind is also applicable to archaic H. sapiens after c. 200,000 years ago.*

type of Early Human in turn and to identify the cognitive variability that no doubt existed between them. There are nevertheless some pointers as to what those differences may have been.

There was a very significant enlargement of brain size during the course of Act 3, from the value of 750–1250 cc for earliest *H. erectus* to 1200–1750 cc for Neanderthals. This was not a gradual increase: brain size appears to have been at a plateau between 1.8 million and 500,000 years ago, and then to have rapidly increased in association with the appearance of archaic *H. sapiens* and then the Neanderthals. In view of the arguments I have made and reviewed in this chapter, we should expect such an expansion to reflect a growth in both social intelligence and linguistic capacity. Indeed my hunch is that this expansion in brain size reflects the change to a form of language with an extensive lexicon and a complex series of grammatical rules, although remaining a 'social language'.

Thus while *H. erectus*'s vocalizing capacity may have been considerably enhanced over that of any living primate, it remained too simple to be called language. As Leslie Aiello has noted, the anatomy of the most complete *H. erectus* skeleton, KNM-WT 15000, suggests that the muscle control essential for the fine regulation of respiration in human speech was absent.[71] We should perhaps think of *H. erectus* as having been able to produce a wide range of sounds in the context of social interaction which related to feelings of contentment, anger or desire and which mediated social relationships. But compared with Modern Humans, the range of sounds and their meanings would have been limited, with none of the grammatical rules that allow an infinite number of utterances to be made from the finite number of sounds available. Perhaps very elaborate versions of cat purring is an appropriate analogy.

A case can also be made that the Levallois method, appearing roughly at the end of the period of brain expansion (250,000 years ago), is more technically and cognitively demanding than bifacial knapping used to make handaxes. And consequently the appearance of the new method may reflect an increase in technical intelligence. I rather doubt this, however, and suspect that it is a reflection of more intense social interactions which enabled greater amounts of technical knowledge to be passively and unintentionally transmitted. Similarly, it is clear that the high latitudes of Europe were occupied rather later than those of Asia, perhaps as much as a million years after *H. erectus* had first moved out of Africa. This late entry into Europe is surprising and one may wonder whether there was some feature of Pleistocene environments in Europe which were beyond the cognitive capacities of the earliest Early Humans to cope with – perhaps the degree of seasonal variation. A case can be

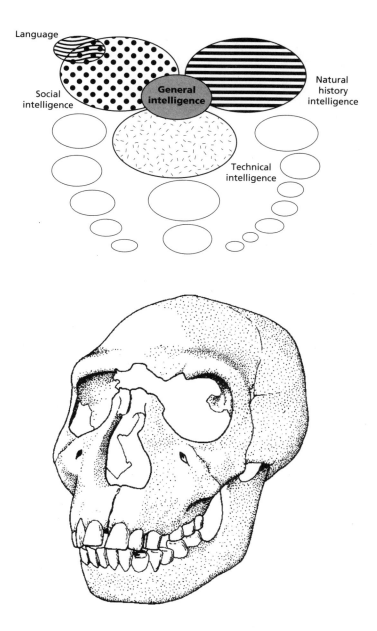

16 *The mind of H. erectus. The drawing depicts the skull denoted by KNM-WT 15000, otherwise known as the Nariokotome boy. This was discovered in Kenya in 1984 and dates to around 1.6 million years ago.*

made therefore, although a weak one, for some increase in natural history intelligence during the course of Act 3. But the fundamental difference between the mind of *H. erectus* and *H. neanderthalensis* lies in the extent of linguistic intelligence (see Figure 16).

In conclusion, we can safely state that in spite of linguistic differences, all Early Humans shared the same basic type of mind: a Swiss-army-knife mentality. They had multiple intelligences, each dedicated to a specific domain of behaviour, with very little interaction between them. We can indeed think of the Early Human mind as a cathedral with several isolated chapels within which unique services of thought were undertaken, each barely audible elsewhere in the cathedral. We have reached Phase 2 in the architectural history proposed in Chapter 4. Early Humans seem to have been so much like us in some respects, because they had these specialized cognitive domains; but they seem so different because they lacked a vital ingredient of the modern mind: cognitive fluidity.

8 Trying to think like a Neanderthal

BEFORE WE LOOK at what happened to the mind at the start of Act 4 with the appearance of the first Modern Humans, we must ask an important question: what would it have been like to have had the mind of an Early Human such as a Neanderthal?

To address this question we must return to the issue of consciousness. In this book I am following Nicholas Humphrey's argument that consciousness evolved as a cognitive trick to allow an individual to predict the social behaviour of other members of his or her group. Humphrey suggested that it evolved to enable us to use our minds as models for those of other people. At some stage in our evolutionary past we became able to interrogate our own thoughts and feelings, asking ourselves how we would behave in some imagined situation. In other words, consciousness evolved as part of social intelligence.

This has significant consequences for how the stream of subjective states of awareness and sentience which would have been experienced by Neanderthals contrasts with that inside our minds today. In the Neanderthal mind social intelligence was isolated from that concerning toolmaking and interaction with the natural world. With regard to our cathedral of the mind analogy, consciousness was firmly trapped within the thick and heavy chapel walls of social intelligence – it could not be 'heard' in the rest of the cathedral except in a heavily muffled form. As a consequence, we must conclude that Neanderthals had no conscious awareness of the cognitive processes they used in the domains of technical and natural history intelligence.

Now before pursuing this proposal I must enter the caveat that consciousness is a multifaceted phenomenon that no one really understands. Whether Daniel Dennett did indeed explain consciousness in his 1991 book *Consciousness Explained* is a moot point. Some suggest that he merely explained it away. There appear to be at least two different types of consciousness.[1] There is the type that we refer to as 'sensation', such as our awareness of itches on our body, colour and sounds. Nicholas Humphrey calls this a 'lower order' of consciousness than that which relates to reasoning and reflection about one's own mental states. It is this higher order of 'reflexive consciousness' which I suspect was lacking from the Neanderthal mind in connection with toolmaking and interaction with the natural world, although it was present with regard to their thoughts about the social world.

I believe that Early Humans experienced the type of consciousness when making their stone tools that we experience when driving a car while engaged in conversation with a passenger. We finish the journey with no memory of the roundabouts, traffic lights and other hazards we negotiated and appear to have passed safely through these without thinking about driving at all. As Daniel Dennett has remarked, while this type of driving is often described as a classic case of 'unconscious perception and intelligent action', it is in fact a case of 'rolling consciousness with swift memory loss'.[2]

When Early Humans engaged in their toolmaking and foraging they may well have experienced this type of 'rolling consciousness'. It resulted from the heavy 'muffling' of consciousness when it is 'heard' from outside the chapel of social intelligence. In other words, when the mental modules that create consciousness were applied in domains different from those they had evolved to serve, they could not work effectively. This left Neanderthals with a rolling, fleeting, ephemeral consciousness about their own knowledge and thoughts concerning toolmaking and foraging. There was no introspection.

This argument is perhaps easier to accept when dealing with the 6-million-year-old common ancestor and the 2-million-year-old *H. habilis* than it is with the Neanderthals. Neither of the former had particularly advanced thought processes for toolmaking and natural history and consequently consciousness about these does not appear as a major issue. But with the Neanderthals, or indeed any type of Early Human, it is a struggle to imagine what it could possibly have been like to be such a skilled toolmaker or natural historian, but not be aware of the depth of one's knowledge or the cognitive processes that one uses. We find it extremely difficult to imagine making a tool without at the same time thinking in detail what the tool will be used for and then utilizing those thoughts in designing the artifact. Similarly when choosing what clothes (i.e. material artifacts) to wear in the morning, we automatically think about the social contexts within which we will find ourselves that day.

We have to struggle so hard to imagine what it may have been like to have had a Swiss-army-knife-type mentality that the plausibility of such a mentality is called into question. How could a Swiss-army-knife-like mind possibly have existed? But in moments of such doubt we can remind ourselves that we have many complex cognitive processes going on inside our minds about which we have no awareness. Indeed, we are probably aware of only a tiny fraction of what goes on inside our minds. For example, we have no conscious awareness of those processes we use to comprehend and generate linguistic utterances. We are not aware of the great number of linguistic rules we use in our everyday speech, or of the many thousands of words that we know the meaning of. Generating grammatically correct, meaningful utterances is perhaps the most complex thing we do – the number of cognitive processes we use is likely to be far in excess of those needed by Neanderthals to make their stone tools – and we do it with no conscious awareness of what is going on inside our minds.

Daniel Dennett has stressed the importance of other types of unconscious thought. To prove their existence he gives the example of knocking your coffee cup over your desk: 'In a flash, you jump up from the chair, narrowly avoiding the coffee that drips over the edge. You were not conscious of thinking that the desk top would not absorb the coffee, or that coffee, a liquid obeying the law of gravity, would spill over the edge, but such unconscious thoughts must have occurred – for had the cup contained table salt, or the desk been covered with a towel, you would not have leaped up'.[3]

A different example of unconscious thought is perhaps the most persuasive argument that Early Humans could have made their stone tools and gone foraging with limited, if any, conscious awareness of the thought processes and knowledge that they were using. Some unfortunate people suffer sudden loss of functions in their higher brain stem which results in 'petit mal' seizures. These involve a loss of conscious experience. Yet the sufferers are still able to continue with their activities, whether they be simply walking, or even driving cars or playing pianos. They continue with these goal-directed activities, which involve selective responses to environmental stimuli, with no conscious awareness of their thought processes. When acting in this way their behaviour takes on a rather mechanical nature – something to which we will return in a later chapter – but they nevertheless continue to perform their complex activities.[4]

I am not suggesting that the Early Human mind was equivalent to someone today suffering a petit mal seizure. I simply use this example as a further demonstration that the absence of conscious awareness about one's thought processes would not mean that those thought processes were not occurring and could not lead to complex forms of behaviour. If people can drive cars and play pianos without conscious awareness, then the possibility of Neanderthals making stone tools and foraging without conscious awareness becomes more plausible.

Plausible, perhaps, but still practically impossible to imagine. Yet this difficulty in imagining what it may have been like to have thought as a Neanderthal may simply reflect a constraint on our own type of thinking put in place by evolution. At the heart of Nicholas Humphrey's ideas about the evolution of consciousness is the notion that it enables us to use our own minds as a model for the minds of other people. Thinking that other people think in the same way as us appears to have been of immense evolutionary value. But the corollary of this is that we find it inherently difficult to think that another human (of whatever species) thinks in a manner that is fundamentally different from our own.

We are perhaps not in quite as bad a position as was the philosopher Thomas Nagel when he famously asked, writing in 1974, 'what is it like to be a bat?'. We are, after all, much closer in evolutionary terms to Neanderthals than to bats. Nagel didn't want to know what it would be like for him to be a bat, but what it is like for a *bat* to be a bat. 'If I try to imagine this', he wrote, 'I am restricted to the resources of my own mind, and those resources are inadequate to the task. I cannot perform it either by imagining additions to my present experience, or by imagining segments gradually subtracted from it, or by imagining some combination of additions, subtractions, and modifications'.[5]

All we can ever achieve then is perhaps a fleeting experience of how a Neanderthal may once have thought as we for example concentrate on some task and block out the rest of the world from our minds. But this experience lasts no more than an instant. As with Nagel and his bats, we are unable to know what it was like for a *Neanderthal* to have been a Neanderthal. Evolution has guarded against this possibility and we are left struggling with the idea of a Swiss-army-knife mentality for Early Humans.

But to help us with this struggle we have the archaeological record, the empirical evidence, perhaps worth more than all the theorizing by philosophers and psychologists. It is indeed the often bizarre nature of this record that is the most compelling argument for a fundamentally different type of human mind. So much of Early Human behaviour looks modern, epitomized by the technical skill apparent from stone tools. But so much else looks positively weird: the monotony of industrial traditions, the absence of tools made from bone and ivory, the absence of art. All of this is epitomized by the 'type' artifact of Early Humans, the handaxe. As the archaeologist Thomas Wynn has recently stated, 'it would be difficult to over-emphasize just how strange the handaxe is when compared to the products of modern culture'.[6] It seems to me that the only way to explain the archaeological record of Early Humans is by invoking a fundamentally different type of mind from that which Modern Humans possess.

9 The big bang of human culture: the origins of art and religion

THERE WAS a cultural explosion in the fourth and final act of our past. This happened in the time period 60,000–30,000 years ago, which marks the blurred start of the second scene of Act 4. The start of the act itself is marked by the entry of the final, and sole surviving, actor, *H. sapiens sapiens* at 100,000 years ago. This new actor appears immediately to have adopted certain forms of behaviour never previously seen in the play. Most notable are the making of bone artifacts in southern Africa, and the placing of parts of animals into human burials in the Near East – the only two areas of the world where 100,000-year-old *H. sapiens sapiens* fossils are known. But other than these glimpses of something new, the props of *H. sapiens sapiens* in the first scene of Act 4 are almost identical to those of the Early Humans. I will therefore refer to these first *H. sapiens sapiens* as Early Modern Humans. The cultural explosion only occurs after they have been on the stage for at least 40,000 years. And consequently it is the start of Scene 2, and not the first appearance of *H. sapiens sapiens*, which archaeologists denote as one of the major turning points in prehistory, referring to it in an ungainly phrase as the 'Middle/Upper Palaeolithic transition'.

In this chapter I want to look at the behaviour of *H. sapiens sapiens* in the first two scenes of Act 4 – immediately before and after this transition – and ask how their minds were different from those of Early Humans. But I want to take the two scenes in reverse order, beginning with the dramatic cultural changes which happened after 60,000 years ago, notably the origin of art.

Now recall that by the start of Act 4 the cathedral of the modern mind is almost complete. The four chapels of technical, natural history, social and linguistic intelligence, the traces of which we saw when we looked at the modern mind in Chapter 3, are in place. But the walls of these chapels are solid; the chapels are closed to each other, trapping within them the thoughts and knowledge of each specialized intelligence – except for the flows between the chapels of linguistic and social intelligence. To constitute the modern mind, the thoughts and knowledge located in all these chapels must be allowed to flow freely around the cathedral – or perhaps within one 'superchapel' – harmonizing with each other to create ways of thought that could never have existed within one chapel alone.

Archaeologists have often described the Middle/Upper Palaeolithic transition as a cultural explosion. Recall from Chapter 2 that it is at, or soon after, this transition that Australia was colonized, that bone tools became widespread (after having made their very first appearance in Act 4 Scene 1), and wall paintings were created. Scene 2 of Act 4 is a frenzy of activity, with more innovation than in the previous 6 million years of human evolution. As the start of this scene is so often described as a cultural explosion, it seems obvious to ask whether this noise is an explosion at all; perhaps it is the sound of doors and windows being inserted into the chapel walls, or even the noise of a 'superchapel' being constructed. In other words, the start of the final phase of our architectural history of the mind.

It is quite easy to think of the Middle/Upper Palaeolithic transition as a cultural explosion, or a big bang – the origins of the universe of human culture. Indeed a 'big bang' is the shorthand description I will use in this chapter. Yet if we look a little more closely at the boundary between Scenes 1 and 2 we see that there is not so much a single big bang as a whole series of cultural sparks that occur at slightly different times in different parts of the world between 60,000 and 30,000 years ago. The colonization of Australia, for instance, seems to reflect a cultural spark which happened between 60,000 and 50,000 years ago, yet at this time all remained relatively quiet elsewhere in the world. In the Near East a cultural spark happened between 50,000 and 45,000 years ago when the Levallois technology was replaced by that of blade cores. The cultural spark in Europe seems not to have been until 40,000 years ago with the appearance of the first objects of art. Indeed, it is perhaps only after 30,000 years ago that we can be confident that the hectic pace of cultural change had begun in earnest throughout the globe. Some archaeologists go so far as to deny that there is such a thing as a major transition at all, and view the cultural changes as no more than the result of a long process of gradual change. They suggest that the new types of artifacts that appear in the archaeological record during Act 4 reflect better preservation and recovery rather than new forms of behaviour.[1] But I disagree.

As with the majority of archaeologists I believe something fundamental occurs at the Middle/Upper Palaeolithic transition, even if at slightly different times in different parts of the world. There have been several ideas previously put forward as to what this fundamental thing might be. These include notions about the 're-structuring of social relations',[2] the appearance of economic specialization,[3] a technological 'invention' similar to that which caused the transition to agriculture 30,000 years later,[4] and the origin of language.[5] I think that these are all

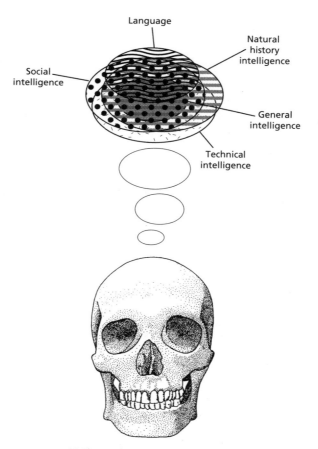

17 *The modern hunter-gatherer mind.*

wrong: either they are merely consequences rather than causes of the transition, or they fail to recognize the complexity of social and economic life of the Early Humans.

My explanation of the big bang of human culture is that this is when the final major re-design of the mind took place. It is when the doors and windows were inserted in the chapel walls, or perhaps when a new 'super-chapel' was constructed. The modern mind might thus be represented as in Figure 17. With these new design features the specialized intelligences of the Early Human mind no longer had to work in isolation. Indeed I believe that during the last two decades of research the explanation for the Middle/Upper Palaeolithic transition has been found – not by archaeologists but by the cognitive scientists whose work we examined in Chapter 3.

Recall how Jerry Fodor finds the 'passion for the analogical' to be a central feature of the distinctly non-modular central processes of the mind and how Howard Gardner believes that in the modern mind multiple intelligences function 'together smoothly, even seamlessly in order to execute complex human activities'. We saw how Paul Rozin concluded that the 'hall mark for the evolution of intelligence ... is that a capacity first appears in a narrow context and later becomes extended into other domains' and Dan Sperber had reached a similar idea with his notion of a metarepresentational module, the evolution of which would create no less than a 'cultural explosion'. Also recall the ideas of Annette Karmiloff-Smith regarding how the human mind 're-represents knowledge', so that 'knowledge thereby becomes applicable beyond the special-purpose goals for which it is normally used and representational links across different domains can be forged', which is so similar to the notion of 'mapping across knowledge systems' as proposed by Susan Carey and Elizabeth Spelke, and the ideas of Margaret Boden regarding how creativity arises from the 'transformation of conceptual spaces'.[6]

None of these cognitive scientists was writing about the Middle/Upper Palaeolithic transition. Nor were they necessarily writing about the same aspects of the modern mind: some were addressing child development while others were discussing cognitive evolution, or simply how we think as we go about our daily lives. But their ideas share a common theme: that in both development and evolution the human mind undergoes (or has undergone) a transformation from being constituted by a series of relatively independent cognitive domains to one in which ideas, ways of thinking and knowledge flow freely between such domains. Although they did not know it, Gardner, Rozin, Boden and the others were providing the answer to the Middle/Upper Palaeolithic transition.

At least I think they were. It is the purpose of this chapter and the next to evaluate this proposition. I will begin by asking whether such developments can explain the new types of behaviour we see early on in Act 4, when people continued to live by hunting and gathering during the period we call the Upper Palaeolithic. In the Epilogue I will take us a little bit closer to the present day and lifestyles that are familiar to us by considering the origin of agriculture.

We must start with the event of Act 4 that at last brings some colour to the play: the appearance of art.

What is art?

We cannot discuss the origin of art unless we agree what we are talking about. Art is another of those words pervading this book which defy easy definition, words like mind, language and intelligence. As with those words, the definition of art is culturally specific. Indeed many societies who create splendid rock paintings do not have a word for art in their language.[7] The communities of the Upper Palaeolithic are likely to have had a very different concept of art (if one at all) from that which is the most popular today: non-utilitarian objects to be placed on pedestals in galleries. Yet these prehistoric hunter-gatherers were producing artifacts which we regard as priceless today, and which are very readily placed on pedestals in our own galleries and museums. Let us for a moment consider the earliest pieces of art known to us, before generalizing about their essential qualities.

In the debris left from Act 3 a few pieces of scratched stone and bone have been found which some have claimed to be of symbolic significance, such as a bone from Bilzingsleben in Germany with incised parallel lines.[8] I doubt if there is any justification for such claims, and these objects should be excluded from our admittedly ill-defined category of art. The majority can be explained as by-products of other activities, such as cutting plant material on a bone support – but there may be some exceptions to which I will return below.

Membership of the elite group of artifacts that we call 'art' must go to those which are either representational or provide evidence for being part of a symbolic code, such as by the repetition of the same motifs. The earliest phase of the Upper Palaeolithic provides us with examples of both.

In terms of representational art we can do no better than start with the ivory statuette from Hohlenstein-Stadel in southern Germany, some 30,000–33,000 years old (see Figure 18). This is a figure of a man with a lion's head carved from the tusk of a mammoth, a remarkable combination of technical expertise and powerful imagery. It was found shattered in tiny pieces and meticulously restored to provide us with the earliest work of art known.[9] Also from southern Germany at this time we have a series of animal figures carved in ivory including felines and herbivores such as mammoth, horse and bison. Some of these have incised markings on their bodies.[10]

Contemporary with this representational art, we find images which appear to be part of a symbolic code being created in southwest France (see Figure 19). These are predominantly 'V'-shaped signs engraved on to limestone blocks in the caves of the Dordogne. Although they have been traditionally described as images of vulvas, archaeologists now discount the idea that they have any simple representational status. The critical feature is that the motifs which have the same form are repeatedly engraved.[11]

18 *The lion/man ivory statuette from Hohlenstein-Stadel, southern Germany, c. 30,000–33,000 years old. Height 28 cm.*

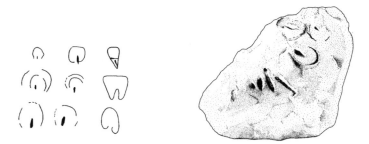

19 *(Right) Engraved symbols on a small boulder, 60 cm wide, from Abri Cellier, Dordogne, France, c. 30,000–25,000 years old. Images such as these are repeated in other sites in southwest France during this period, including Abri Blanchard, Abri de Castanet and La Ferrassie, as illustrated on the left.*

Along with these pieces of art, the period between 40,000 and 30,000 years ago saw the first production of items for personal decoration such as beads, pendants and perforated animal teeth. At the site of La Souquette in southwest France ivory beads were carved to mimic sea shells.[12] At the same time as, or soon after, these items were being produced the first caves in southwest Europe were being painted with images of animals, signs and anthropomorphic figures, a tradition which would culminate in the paintings of Lascaux at around 17,000 years ago.[13] Indeed some of the paintings in Chauvet Cave in the Ardèche region of France, a cave discovered as recently as 18 December 1994, have been dated as being 30,000 years old. The 300 or more paintings of animals in this cave – including rhinoceroses, lions, reindeer, horses and an owl – are quite remarkable. Many of them are highly naturalistic and demonstrate an impressive knowledge of animal anatomy and outstanding artistic skill. The cave is perhaps on a par with Lascaux, and certainly with Altamira in Spain, with regard to the spectacular nature of its art.[14] Although this is the very first art known to humankind, there is nothing primitive about it.

While the production of art was most prolific in Europe, it was a worldwide phenomenon by, or soon after, 30,000 years ago. In southern Africa the painted slabs from Apollo Cave are well dated to 27,500 years ago while wall engravings in Australia date back beyond 15,000 and perhaps to 40,000 years ago.[15] Art remains rare, or even absent in several regions of the world until 20,000 years ago. But that is just 20,000 years after its first appearance in Europe – an almost insignificant amount of time when set against the more than 1.5 million years that Early Humans lived without art.

The variability in the intensity with which art was produced can be attributed to variation in economic and social organization, which in turn can be largely attributed to environmental conditions. The archaeological record shows us that Stone Age art is not a product of comfortable circumstances – when people have time on their hands; it was most often created when people were living in conditions of severe stress. The florescence of Palaeolithic art in Europe occurred at a time when environmental conditions were extremely harsh around the height of the last ice age.[16] Yet there is unlikely to have been a human population living under more adaptive stress than the Neanderthals of western Europe. But they produced no art. They lacked the capacity to do so.

There can be little doubt that by 30,000 years ago this capacity was a universal attribute of the modern human mind. What does it entail? While the definition of a visual symbol is notoriously difficult, at least five properties are critical:

1. The form of the symbol may be arbitrary to its referent. This is one of the fundamental features of language, but also applies to visual symbols. For instance, the symbol '2' does not look like two of anything.[17]

2. A symbol is created with the intention of communication.[18]

3. There may be considerable space/time displacement between the symbol and its referent. So, for example, I might draw a picture about something that happened long in the past, or what I imagine may happen some time in the future.

4. The specific meaning of a symbol may vary between individuals and indeed cultures. This often depends upon their knowledge and experience. A Nazi swastika has a different meaning to a young child, than to a Jew whose family was lost in the Holocaust. The swastika is in fact an ancient symbol, found in cultures as far apart as Mexico and Tibet.

5. The same symbol may tolerate some degree of variability, either deliberately or unintentionally imposed. For instance, we are able to read different people's handwriting although the specific forms of the letters are variable.

These properties of visual symbols become particularly apparent when we consider the art created by recent hunter-gatherers, such as the Aboriginal communities of Australia. The last decade has seen a tremendous development in our understanding of this art.[19] We now know that even the simplest of images, such as a circle, can have many different referents. Among the Walpiri of the Central Australian Desert, for example, a circle can represent an almost unlimited number of referents: campsites, fires, mountains, waterholes, women's breasts, eggs, fruit and other items. The intended meaning of the circle in any one composition can only be identified by the associated motifs. Such simple geometric motifs may have a wider range of possible meanings than complex naturalistic images[20] (see Box p. 158).

Naturalistic images, perhaps of animals or ancestral beings, can also

Complex meanings in simple designs of hunter-gatherer art

The complex and multiple meanings that may be found in the simplest geometric designs found in Palaeolithic art can be illustrated with an example from the art of the Australian Aborigines. The social anthropologist Howard Morphy has described how many of their paintings have a basic geometric template underlying the design. Each part of the template may encode a series of meanings. For instance, consider the image below which has two 'loci', (a) and (b).

At locus (a), the following meanings are encoded: 'well', 'lake', 'vagina'. At locus (b) the meanings 'digging stick', 'river' and 'penis' are encoded. Consequently three different interpretations of this image would be a river flowing into a lake, a digging stick being used to dig a well, and a penis going into a vagina. All three of these are 'correct' interpretations, but each is appropriate in a different social context. Moreover, the interpretations may be connected within a single mythic sequence:

> A kangaroo ancestor was digging a well with a digging stick. When he finished, a female wallaby bent down to drink the fresh water, and the kangaroo seized his opportunity to have sexual intercourse with her. The semen flowed out of her body and into the waterhole. Today a river flows into the lake at that place and the kangaroo's penis was transformed into a digging stick which can be seen as a great log beside the lake.

If such simple geometric designs can 'encode' such complex meanings, and by doing so express the transformational aspects of Ancestral Beings, one can only wonder at the types of meanings encoded in the geometric designs from the Palaeolithic period.

have complex and multiple meanings. An Aboriginal child, lacking in knowledge about the Dreamtime (the mythical past/present), may initially interpret images in a literal fashion. To a child, images of fish, for instance, are about fishing which is an economically important activity for many Aboriginal groups. Such literal interpretations can be described as the 'outside' meanings of the art – they are learned in the context of daily life and are in the public domain. As the child matures and acquires knowledge about the ancestral world, the same image will be interpreted in a more metaphorical sense, often relating to the actions of the Ancestral Beings. There may be various levels of these, each requiring additional knowledge about the ancestral past, which may be restricted to certain classes of individuals. Consequently these are described as 'inside' meanings. For example, the child may gradually learn how fish are a potent symbol of spiritual transformation of both birth and death. They are good to paint not just because they are good to eat, but also because they are good to think. The metaphorical meanings of fish images, concerning birth and death, do not replace the literal interpretation concerning the practice of fishing, they are complementary. As a result, many images have different meanings to different people depending on their access to knowledge about the ancestral past.[21]

Whatever meaning is attributed to an image, that image is most likely to be displaced in time and space from the inspiration for the image. The waterhole referred to by a circle may be far away, while the Ancestral Being has no clear location in either time or space.

We can find many of these features in the rock art tradition of other modern hunter-gatherers, such as the San of southern Africa.[22] Indeed, we cannot doubt that the images created in the Upper Palaeolithic also had complex symbolic and multiple meanings involving those five properties listed above. Archaeologists are more likely to have success at reconstructing the 'outside' meanings of this art, rather than the 'inside' meanings which require access to the lost mythological world of the prehistoric mind – a world to which I will return at the end of this chapter when I consider the origins of religious ideas.

Cognitive fluidity and the origins of art

Having considered some of the properties of visual symbols, let us consider what mental attributes are involved in creating and reading them. There are at least three:

1. The making of a visual image involves the planning and execution of a preconceived mental template.

2. Intentional communication with reference to some displaced event or object.

3. The attribution of meaning to a visual image not associated with its referent.

From what we established in the previous chapter – and as I will explain below – it is likely that Early Humans were competent in each of these cognitive processes. They are likely to have existed in as complex and as advanced a state as in the Modern Human mind. So why no art? The answer would appear to be that although they possessed these processes, they were found in different cognitive domains. They were inaccessible to each other and the origin of art only occurred following a marked increase in the connections between cognitive domains. So where in the Early Human mind were these processes located?

The making of marks on objects is something that happens unintentionally in the course of activities by many animals – marks such as hoofprints, scratches on trees and gnawmarks on bones. Some non-human animals also create marks intentionally: chimpanzees have created striking paintings in laboratories, although these do not appear to have symbolic meanings and are not created in the wild.[23] I would interpret such 'artistic achievements' in the same manner as the 'linguistic' achievements of chimpanzees – as the product of a generalized learning capacity. The earliest members of the *Homo* lineage we encountered in Chapter 6 were making marks with stone tools on bones in the process of butchery. We also have the series of artifacts made by Early Humans which have incised lines on them, such as a fossil nummulite from Tata in Hungary, which appears to have a line intentionally engraved perpendicular to a natural crack to make a cross and is thought to be 100,000 years old, and the marked bone from Bilzingsleben[24] in Germany (see Figure 20). Although it has yet to be demonstrated, I am sympathetic to the idea that some of these lines may have been intentionally created, and I will return to how they should be interpreted shortly. Similarly, the few pieces of red ochre from Early Human sites in southern Africa – no more than a dozen from the period prior to 100,000 years ago[25] – may suggest that archaic *H. sapiens* were marking their bodies. But there is no reason to believe that this is equivalent to the symbolic behaviour involved in producing objects of art. What we need to find in the mind of Early Humans is a capacity to intentionally create marks or objects of a preconceived form.

This can indeed be found – in the domain of technical intelligence. We have seen that Early Humans were regularly imposing form on to their stone artifacts. Handaxes and Levallois flakes required the extraction of objects of a preconceived form from nodules of stone. In view of such technical intelligence, the failure to make three-dimensional objects of art cannot reflect difficulties in conceiving of objects 'within' a block of

20 Fragment of a rib of a large mammal from Bilzingsleben, Germany. On its surface there is a series of parallel lines, each engraved by the repeated application of a stone tool probably by a Neanderthal. Length 28.6 cm, width 3.6 cm.

stone or ivory, or the mental planning and manual dexterity to 'extract' them. The cognitive processes located in the domain of technical intelligence used for making stone artifacts appear to have been sufficient to produce a figurine from an ivory tusk. But they were not used for such ends.

With regard to the second of the three critical cognitive capacities for art, intentional communication, this was established in the previous chapter as a critical feature of Early Human social intelligence. Indeed Early Humans were probably as dependent on intentional communication as are modern humans today. Among the last of the Early Humans this capacity became manifest in spoken language; in the earlier ones it was probably restricted to vocalizations too simple to be described as language, as well as gesture. In Chapter 5 we saw that both monkeys and apes also engage in intentional communication, suggesting that this capacity has had a long evolutionary history: there can be little doubt that not only Early Humans, but also the common ancestor and the earliest *Homo* were engaging in frequent, intentional communication.

The third element of a capacity for art is an ability to attribute meaning to inanimate objects or marks displaced from their referents.[26] Can this ability be found within one of the cognitive domains of Early Humans? It certainly can: the capacity to attribute meaning to the unintentionally made tracks and trails of potential prey is a critical component of natural history intelligence. As I have argued in previous chapters, the ability to draw inferences from marks such as footprints most likely reaches back to when earliest *Homo*, or indeed australopithecines, began hunting and scavenging on the African savannah. These inferences often include the type, age, sex, state of health and current behaviour of the animal which made them.

The unintentionally made marks left by animals share a number of properties with the intentionally made 'marks' or symbols of Modern Humans, such as paintings on rock faces or drawings in the sand.[27] They are inanimate. They are both spatially and temporally displaced from the event which created them and that which they signify. Footprints, just like symbols, must be placed into an appropriate category if correct meaning is to be attributed. For instance, the hoofprint of a deer will vary depending upon whether it is made in mud, snow or grass, just as the drawing of a symbol will vary according to rock surface and the individual style of the artist. The marks left by animals will often be non-representational. While the hoofprint of a deer may look like the base of the hoof, it does not look like the event that is inferred from it, such as the passing of a male stag. Many marks have no visual resemblance to the animal which created them, such as the parallel lines left by the wriggling of a snake. And finally, the meaning of marks will vary according to the knowledge of the person viewing the mark, in a similar way that the meaning of symbols vary. For example a child may identify a hoofprint as coming from a deer, whereas a mature and skilled hunter may be able to infer that the deer is a pregnant female which passed two hours ago.

These points of similarity suggest that the same cognitive processes which are used to attribute meaning to marks unintentionally made by animals would be equally effective at attributing meaning to marks intentionally created by humans. But we have no evidence that they were used for such purposes before the arrival of Modern Humans.

The three cognitive processes critical to making art – mental conception of an image, intentional communication and the attribution of meaning – were all present in the Early Human mind. They were found in the domains of technical, social and natural history intelligence respectively. But the creation and use of visual symbols requires that they function 'seamlessly and smoothly together' (to quote Gardner). This would require 'links across domains' (to quote Karmiloff-Smith). And the result would be a 'cultural explosion' (to quote Sperber).

We do see a cultural explosion beginning 40,000 years ago in Europe as the first works of art were produced and I would suggest that this can be explained by new connections between the domains of technical, social and natural history intelligence. The three previously isolated cognitive processes were now functioning together, creating the new cognitive process which we call visual symbolism, or simply art (see Box p. 163).

If I had to choose just one feature of the earliest art to support this argument it would be that the very first images are of such technical skill and emotive power. No analogy can be drawn between the origins of art in evolutionary time and the development of artistic skills by a child. The latter consists of a gradual change from scribbles to representational images, and then a gradual improvement in the quality of those images. For some young artists one can then see a gradual understanding of how to use line and colour to convey not just a record of what is seen but one's feelings for it. There is nothing gradual about the evolution of the capacity for art: the very first pieces that we find can be compared in quality

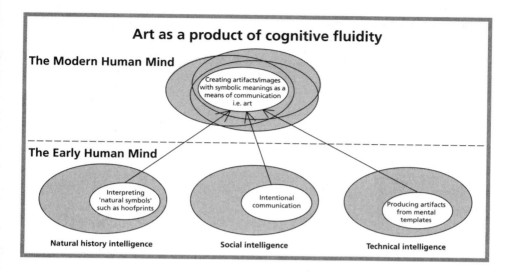

with those produced by the great artists of the Renaissance. This is not to argue that the ice age artists themselves did not go through a process of learning; we can indeed find many images which appear to be those drawn by children or apprentice artists.[28] But the abilities to impose form, to communicate and to infer meaning from images, must have already been present in the Early Human mind – although there was no art. All that was needed was a connection between these cognitive processes which had evolved for other tasks to create the wonderful paintings in Chauvet Cave.

But before we leave the origins of art we must return to those scratched pieces of bone and ivory made by Early Humans, such as from Bilzingsleben and Tata. If – and it is a big if – these lines were intentionally made, how can they be accounted for? I suggest that they reflect the maximum amount of symbolic communication that can be achieved by relying on general intelligence alone. Early Humans may have been able to associate marks with meanings by using their capacities for associative learning alone. But relying on this would have severely constrained the complexity of the marks and meanings. There is a similarity between the simplicity of the toolmaking capacities of chimpanzees as compared with those of Early Humans, and the simplicity of Early Human intentional markings as compared with those of Modern Humans. Chimpanzees rely on general intelligence for toolmaking, just as Early Humans relied on general intelligence for 'symbolic' communication. As a result, chimpanzees and Early Humans appear to 'underachieve' in these activities in light of their accomplishments in behavioural domains for which they have specialized intelligences.

Humans as animals, animals as humans: anthropomorphism and totemism

The new flow of knowledge and thought processes between cognitive domains of the modern mind can be readily seen not only in the existence of art, but also in its contents. Consider once again the image in Figure 18. This figure has a lion's head and human body. We cannot prove, but equally cannot doubt, that it represents a being in the mythology of the Upper Palaeolithic groups of southern Germany. Whether it is an image of an animal that has taken on certain human attributes – reflecting anthropomorphic thinking – or a human who is descended from a lion – reflecting totemic thought – we do not know. But, whichever of these is correct (and the answer is probably both), the ability to conceive of such a being requires a fluidity between social and natural history intelligences.

Images like this pervade not only the art of Upper Palaeolithic groups, but that of almost all hunter–gatherer societies, and indeed those living by agriculture, trade and industry.[29] We have many spectacular examples from prehistory. In the art of the Upper Palaeolithic they include the 'sorcerer' from Trois-Frères – a painted figure that has an upright posture, legs and hands that look human, but the back and ears of a herbivore, the antlers of a reindeer, the tail of a horse, and a phallus positioned like that of a feline (see Figure 21) – as well as a bird-headed man from Lascaux and a female figurine from Grimaldi Cave paired back to back with a carnivore.[30] Indeed one of the paintings in the newly discovered Chauvet Cave, some of which are dated to 30,000 years old, is a

21 *The sorcerer from Trois-Frères, Ariège, France, as drawn by Henri Breuil. Height 75 cm.*

figure with the head and torso of a bison and the legs of a human. Similarly the prehistoric hunter-gatherers who lived 7000 years ago in the forests of Europe after the ice had retreated made monumental carvings of fish/humans at the site of Lepenski Vir on the Danube.[31] As I noted in Chapter 3, among the modern hunter-gatherers described by anthropologists, animals are frequently attributed with human-type minds.

Anthropomorphic thinking is something that pervades our own everyday lives. We indulge in anthropomorphic thinking in our relations with pets by attributing to them feelings, purposes and intentions. This may indeed be reasonable with regard to dogs and cats, but with a moment's reflection it seems far-fetched with regard to pets such as goldfish. We seem unable to help anthropomorphizing animals – some claim that it is built into us by both nature and nurture – and while this gives us considerable pleasure, it is a problem that plagues the study of animal behaviour, for it is unlikely that animals really do have human-like minds.[32] Anthropomorphism is a seamless integration between social and natural history intelligence (see Box p. 166). The very first pieces of Palaeolithic art indicate that it stretches back to the cultural explosion of 40,000 years ago. But I doubt if it goes back any further.

Totemism is the other side of the human/animal coin. Rather than attributing animals with human characteristics, it involves embedding human individuals and groups within the natural world, epitomized by tracing descent from a non-human species. The study of totemism – and attempts to define it – formed the core of social anthropology as it developed during the 19th century. Between 1910 and 1950 major works on totemism were produced by the pioneers of social anthropology including Frazer, Durkheim, Pitt-Rivers, Radcliffe-Brown and Malinowski. Such works provided the foundations for Levi-Strauss' *The Savage Mind*. This in turn has been followed as from the 1970s by a renewed surge of interest in totemism.[33]

In the light of this long history of study, it is not surprising that totemism has been defined and interpreted in a variety of ways. Lévi-Strauss' position is perhaps the most widely known: animals are not just good to eat but also 'good to think'. He viewed totemism as the practice of humanity brooding on itself and its place in nature. To his mind, the 'study of natural species, provided nonliterate and prescientific groups with a ready-to-hand means of conceptualizing relations between human groups'.[34]

Whether or not this is a correct interpretation, we may simply note three features of totemism that are particularly relevant for an understanding of the evolution of the modern mind. First, when broadly defined, totemism is universal among human groups who live by a

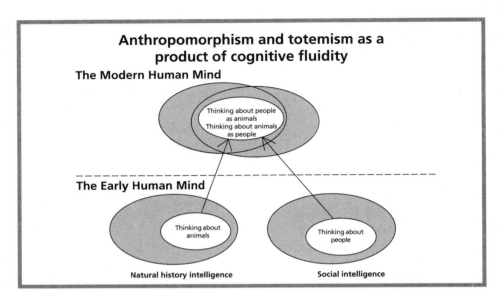

Anthropomorphism and totemism as a product of cognitive fluidity

hunting-gathering lifestyle; second, it requires a cognitive fluidity between thinking about animals and people; and third, on the basis of archaeological evidence it is likely to have been pervasive in human society since the start of the Upper Palaeolithic. The evidence we can invoke here includes that of imagery in Palaeolithic art and that from burials, such as at the 7800-year-old cemetery at Oleneostrovski Mogilnik in Karelia where we find two clusters of graves, one associated with effigies of a snake, and the other with effigies of an elk.[35] In contrast, we have no reason to believe that Early Human society was structured on a totemic basis.

We must also note here that it is not just other living things which are thought of as possessing human qualities. Hunter-gatherers do not just live in a landscape of animals and plants, rocks, hills and caves. Their landscapes are socially constructed and full of meaning. Once again the Aboriginal communities of Australia provide a good example. The wells in their landscape are where ancestral beings dug in the ground, the trees where they had placed their digging sticks and the deposits of red ochre where they had bled.[36] John Pfeiffer has argued that the encompassing of the features of the landscape in a web of myths and stories is of great utility to the Aborigines, for it helps them to remember enormous quantities of geographic information.

Whether or not this is the case, when we look at a region such as that of southwest France in which we find both a range of topographic features universally attributed with social and symbolic meanings by modern hunter-gatherers,[37] and caves and rockshelters covered with paintings, we can be in no doubt that the Upper Palaeolithic hunters were also living in a landscape full of symbolic meanings.

It is useful to recall here the words of Tim Ingold that I quoted in Chapter 3: 'For them [modern hunter-gatherers] there are not two worlds of persons (society) and things (nature), but just one world – one environment – saturated with personal powers and embracing both human beings, the animals and plants on which they depend, and the landscape in which they live and move.'[38] The anthropomorphic images and painting of caves and rockshelters that begin after 40,000 years ago suggests that the earliest Upper Palaeolithic hunter-gatherers had a similar attitude to the social and natural worlds: they were one and the same. One consequence, of benefit to us today, is that they expressed this view within their art, creating some of the most powerful and beautiful images ever made. But this collapse of the cognitive barrier between the social and natural worlds also had significant consequences for their own behaviour, for it fundamentally changed their interaction with the natural world. It is to this that we must now turn.

A new proficiency at hunting: special strategies, special tools

The hunter-gatherers of the Upper Palaeolithic were hunting the same types of animals as the Early Humans. In Europe, for instance, reindeer, red deer, bison and horse continued as the mainstay of their economies, while in southern Africa animals such as eland, cape buffalo and seals remained the most important prey. What differed, however, is the manner in which these animals were hunted. Modern Humans appear to have been considerably more proficient at predicting game movements and planning complex hunting strategies.

This is readily apparent from Europe. Almost all the sites of Early Humans have a mix of animal species, suggesting that these were hunted as individuals on an opportunistic basis. The site of Combe Grenal in southwest France is typical in this regard. Each occupation level usually contains a few individuals of each of the types of large game being hunted. As the climate grew colder, animals such as reindeer become more prevalent in the occupation deposits, while red deer increase during periods of relative warmth. The Neanderthals were simply hunting whatever animals were available – although as I indicated in the last chapter, we should certainly not minimize their achievement at exploiting such game.

The first Modern Humans in Europe hunted in a very different fashion. Although they continued to kill individual animals, or at most small groups, they began to specialize on specific animals at specific sites.[39] Consequently many sites are dominated by one species alone, very often reindeer. Indeed certain sites seem to have been selected for ambush hunting, indicating that Modern Humans were much better at predicting the movements of animals than Early Humans. This becomes very apparent when we look at hunting methods in the period *c.* 18,000 years ago, when the last ice age was at its peak. At about this time, Modern Humans shifted from hunting individual and small groups of animals to slaughtering mass herds of reindeer and red deer. These are likely to have been attacked at critical points on their annual migration routes when the animals were constrained in narrow valleys, or when crossing rivers.[40]

The same contrast between Early and Modern Humans can be seen in other parts of the Old World. In northern Spain, for example, animals such as ibex began to be hunted for the first time. This is significant because, as the archaeologist Lawrence Straus has written, ibex hunting required 'elaborate strategies, tactics, weapons and ... logistical camps'. By 'logistical camps' he refers to sites specifically located for ibex hunting.[41] Similarly on the Russian Plain, Olga Soffer has described how the first Upper Palaeolithic hunters were locating sites for exploiting specific animals at specific times of the year. She suggests that they were taking greater account of the seasonal and long-term fluctuations in animal numbers and behaviour patterns.[42] The same can be seen in southern Africa. For instance, Richard Klein has suggested that a new awareness of the seasonal variation in seal numbers had arisen, and was being used to plan hunting trips to the coast. This replaced a more opportunistic pattern of hunting and scavenging.[43]

In general, the Modern Humans of the Upper Palaeolithic appear to have had a significantly greater ability both to predict the movements of animals and to use that knowledge in their hunting strategies. How were they managing to do this? The answer lies in what has already been a major theme of this chapter: anthropomorphic thinking. This is universal among all modern hunters and its significance is that it can substantially improve prediction of an animal's behaviour. Even though a deer or a horse may not think about its foraging and mobility patterns in the same way as Modern Humans, imagining that it does can act as an excellent predictor for where the animal will feed and the direction in which it may move.

This has been recognized in several studies of living hunter-gatherers, such as among the G/Wi and the !Kung of the Kalahari, the Valley Bisa of Zambia and the Nunamiut of the Canadian Arctic. Anthropomorphizing animals by attributing to them human personalities and characters provides as effective a predictor for their behaviour as viewing them with all the understanding of ecological knowledge possessed by Western scientists.[44] The anthropologist Mary Douglas sees the similarity in the categories used for understanding the natural and social worlds as primarily being of practical value in terms of understanding and predicting the ways of animals. She suggests that this is of far more importance than using the natural world for addressing profound metaphysical problems about the human condition, as proposed by Lévi-Strauss.[45]

Anthropomorphic thinking, therefore, has clear utilitarian benefits. Yet the new powers of prediction would have been of limited value had Modern Humans not also been able to develop new types of hunting weapons. And we do indeed see a striking elaboration of technology at the start of the Upper Palaeolithic. In Europe, Modern Humans could make all those types of tools which Neanderthals, with their Swiss-army-knife mentality, could not even think about: tools which required an integration of technical and natural history intelligences.

For example, we see many new types of weapons made from bone and antler, notably harpoons and spearthrowers. Experimental studies using replica artifacts have shown that these were very effective at piercing animal hides and organs.[46] We see many new types of stone projectile points, and find associations between specific types of points and specific types of animals.[47] We can see evidence for complex, multi-component tools being made, such as in the presence of microliths – small blades of flint used as points and barbs. Lying at the heart of these new technological innovations was the switch to 'blade technology', which provided standardized 'blanks', each of which could be turned into part of a highly specialized tool (see Figure 22).

It is not simply the introduction of new tools at the start of the Upper Palaeolithic which is important. It is how these were then constantly modified and changed. Throughout the Upper Palaeolithic we can see the processes of innovation and experimentation at work, resulting in a constant stream of new hunting weapons appropriate to the prevailing environmental conditions and building on the knowledge of previous generations. As the environments became very harsh at the height of the last ice age 18,000 years ago, large points were manufactured, specialized for ensuring that large game would be despatched on the tundra. As the climate began to ameliorate, and a wider range of game became available, hunting technology became more diverse, with an emphasis on multi-component tools.[48] Lawrence Straus has appositely described this as a Palaeolithic arms race.[49] Such behaviour, geared to maintaining if not maximizing hunting efficiency, is markedly different from the monotony of the hunting tools of Early Humans during the equally variable environments that they exploited. It could only have arisen owing to a new connection between natural history and technical intelligence.

The design of hunting weapons is perhaps the best example of this new type of thinking, but it also resulted in a wide range of other technological developments. For instance, by 18,000 years ago people in North Africa were using grinding stones for preparing plant material. Such artifacts required integrated thought about the characteristics of both stone and plant material.[50] The elaboration in the range of scraping and engraving tools used for such tasks as cleaning hides and carving bone required thought about the nature of animal products during the process of tool manufacture. And perhaps most impressive of all is the development of facilities for trapping animals, such as small game or fish, and the technology for storing food, whether it be reindeer meat during the Upper Palaeolithic or hazelnuts once forests had spread across Europe after the end of the last ice age 10,000 years ago.[51] The design and use of all these involve an integration of natural history and technical knowledge, resulting in a constant innovation of new technology.

Art as stored information

Many of the new bone and antler tools of the Upper Palaeolithic carried elaborate designs engraved on to their surfaces, or were even carved into animal figures themselves, such as the spearthrower from Mas d'Azil (see Figure 23). Indeed it is very difficult to draw any division between what is a piece of 'art' and what is a 'tool', and such artifacts epitomize the absence of any boundaries between different domains of activity. Many of the art objects can indeed be thought of as a brand new type of tool: a tool for storing information and for helping to retrieve information stored in the mind.

The simplest tools of this new type are pieces of bone with incised parallel lines. The most complex have many hundreds of marks made by a number of different tools, creating a complex pattern on the face of the artifact, such as on the Taï plaque from eastern France (see Figure 24).[52] The interpretation of these has always been controversial. When first discovered they were described as *'tailles de chasse'* – hunting tallies recording the number of animals killed. A range of other interpretations have since been made, for example that they record the number of people attending social gatherings and lunar calendars.[53]

Detailed microscopic study of such artifacts by Alexander Marshack and Francesco D'Errico has confirmed that on several of them the marks come in such regular patterns that they appear to be a system of notation.[54] These artifacts are likely to have acted as a form of visual recording device, most probably about environmental events. They look very similar to notched and engraved artifacts made by modern hunter-gatherers which are known to have been mnemonic aids and recording

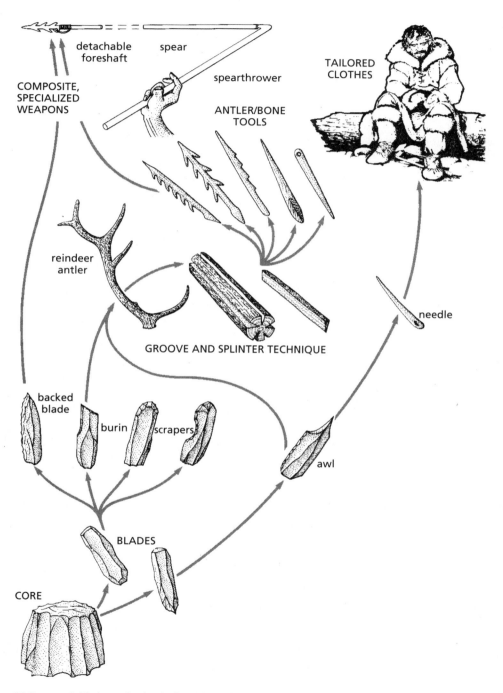

22 Systematic blade production in the Upper Palaeolithic was a means to produce standardized 'blanks' that could be easily modified for use in a wide range of multi-component tools.

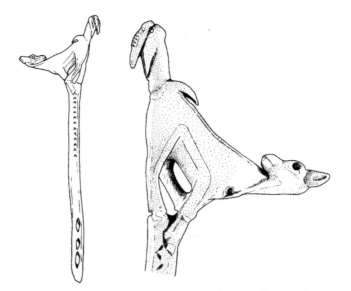

23 *Antler spearthrower from Mas d'Azil, Ariège, France. This depicts an ibex that is either giving birth, or excreting a large turd on which two birds are perched. Total length 29.6 cm.*

devices, such as the calendar sticks made from ivory by the Yakut people of Siberia.[55]

Like the engraved pieces of bone, cave paintings also appear to have been used to store information about the natural world, or at least facilitate its recall by acting as a mnemonic device. Indeed, these paintings have been described as the 'tribal encyclopedia' by John Pfeiffer.[56] I myself have suggested that much of the animal imagery within this art served to help recall information about the natural world stored within the mind.[57] For instance, I have argued that the manner in which many of the animals were painted makes direct reference to the ways in which information was acquired about their movements and behaviour. In some images, while the animals were painted in profile, their hooves were painted in plan, as if hoofprints were being depicted to facilitate the memorizing and recall of tracks seen while in the environment, or even the teaching of children. Similarly the choice of imagery itself was selective towards those animals which provide knowledge about forthcoming environmental events. The bird imagery is particularly telling, dominated as it is by ducks and geese, which are likely to have been migratory. Modern hunters in glaciated environments keep a very close lookout for the annual arrival and departure of such birds, since such information gives a clue as to when the big freeze of the winter, or the spring thaw, will happen. Some of the most evocative images of this type are ivory carvings of geese in flight found at the Siberian site of Mal'ta, where the hunters had relied on mammoths for food but no doubt eagerly watched for the passing of migrating birds indicating the arrival of spring.[58]

The way in which Upper Palaeolithic cave paintings may have functioned to help store information about the natural world is perhaps analogous to the way in which Wopkaimin hunter-horticulturalists of New Guinea use the bones from the animals they hunt. These bones are placed on the rear walls of their houses where they are described as 'trophy arrays'. But they are carefully arranged to act as a mental map for the surrounding environment to facilitate the recall of information about that environment and animal behaviour. They thus play an important role in decision-making about use of resources and improving the predictions about animal location and behaviour.[59] There is clear patterning in the arrangement of animal figures in the cave paintings of the Upper Palaeolithic.[60] Michael and Anne Eastham have suggested that the paintings and engravings in the caves of the Ardèche region of France served as a model or a map for the specific terrain around the caves.[61]

In summary, although the specific roles that prehistoric artifacts may have played in the management of information about the natural world remain unclear, there can be little doubt that many of them served to store, transmit and retrieve information. Major benefits of this will have been enhanced abilities to track long-term change, to monitor seasonal fluctuations and to devise hunting plans. Many of the paintings, carvings and engravings of Modern Humans were tools with which to think about the natural world.

Sending social messages: objects of personal adornment

Beads, pendants and other items of personal decoration first appear at the start of the Upper Palaeolithic. They too arise from the new cognitive fluidity of the mind – an integration between technical and social intelli-

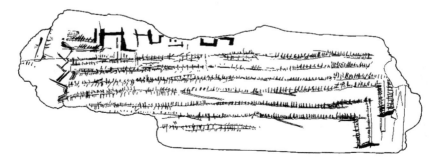

24 *Engraved bone plaque from Grotte du Taï, Drôme, France. Length, 8.8 cm.*

gence. Such artifacts are initially found in abundance in occupation deposits of caves in southwest France, and are particularly important during the very harsh climatic conditions at around 18,000 years ago.[62] They are often found in burials, most dramatically on the 28,000-year-old burials at Sungir in Russia (see Box p. 175). Describing beads and pendants as 'decoration' risks belittling their importance. They would have functioned to send social messages, such as about one's status, group affiliation and relationships with other individuals, just as they do in our own society today. And of course these messages need not have been 'true'; beads and pendants provide new opportunities for deception in the kind of social tactics that we saw are prevalent even among chimpanzees. To have produced such artifacts required not only specialized social and technical intelligences – as possessed by Early Humans – but also an ability to integrate these.

It is likely that all types of artifacts, including those that might appear to be mundane tools for hunting or even processing animal hides, became imbued with social information at the start of the Upper Palaeolithic.[63] In effect the 'goal posts' of social behaviour were moved; whereas for Early Humans the domains of hunting, toolmaking and socializing were quite separate, these were now so integrated that it is impossible to characterize any single aspect of Modern Human behaviour as being located in just one of these domains. Indeed as Ernest Gellner stated: 'the conflation and confusion of aims and criteria, is the normal and original condition of mankind'.[64]

The rise of religion

Many of the new behaviours I have been describing, such as the anthropomorphic images in the cave paintings and the burial of people with grave goods, suggest that these Upper Palaeolithic people were the first to have beliefs in supernatural beings and possibly an afterlife. We are indeed seeing here the first appearance of religious ideologies. This can be explained by the collapse of the barriers that had existed between the multiple intelligences of the Early Human mind.

Just as we did with art, we must first reach some agreement on quite what we mean by the notion of religion. While it is difficult to identify features universal to all religions, there are nevertheless a series of recurrent ideas. The importance of these has been stressed by the social anthropologist Pascal Boyer in his 1994 book *The Naturalness of Religious Ideas*. Boyer explains that a belief in non-physical beings is the most common feature of religions; it may indeed be universal. In fact, ever since the classic work of E.B. Tylor in 1871 on *Primitive Cultures*, the idea of non-physical beings has been taken for the very definition of

Sending social information by material culture: the Sungir burials

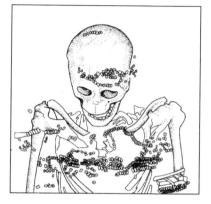

The burials at Sungir, Russia, have been dated to 28,000 years old. They consist of the graves of a 60-year-old man, and a joint burial of a male and a female adolescent. Each of these individuals were decorated with thousands of ivory beads, which had probably been attached to clothing. The archaeologist Randall White has studied these graves and provides the following descriptions:

The man was adorned with 2936 beads and fragments arranged in strands found on all parts of his body including his head, which was apparently covered with a beaded cap that also bore several fox teeth. His forearms and biceps were each decorated with a series of polished mammoth-ivory bracelets (25 in all), some showing traces of black paint.... Around the man's neck he wore a small flat schist pendant, painted red, but with a small black dot on one side....

The supposed small boy was covered with strands of beads – 4903 of them – that were roughly 2/3 the size of the man's beads, although of exactly the same form. Unlike the man, however, he had around his waist – apparently the remains of a decorated belt – more than 250 canine teeth of the polar fox. On his chest was a carved ivory pendant in the form of an animal. At his throat was an ivory pin, apparently the closure of a cloak of some sort. Under his left shoulder was a large ivory sculpture of a mammoth. At his left side lay a medial segment of a highly polished, very robust human femur, the medullary cavity of which was packed with red ochre. At his right side ... was a massive ivory lance, made from a straightened woolly mammoth tusk.... Near it is a carved ivory disc which sits upright in the soil.

The supposed girl had 5274 beads and fragments (also roughly 2/3 the size of the man's beads) covering her body. She also wore a beaded cap and had an ivory pin at her throat, but her burial contains no fox teeth whatsoever. Nor does she have a pendant on her chest. However, placed at each of her sides there was a number of small ivory 'lances', more appropriate to her body size than that accompanying the boy. Also at her side are two pierced antler batons, one of them decorated with rows of drilled dots. Finally, she was accompanied by a series of three ivory disks with a central hole and lattice work, like that adjacent to the supposed boy's burial.

(White 1993, 289–292)

religion itself. Boyer notes three other recurrent features of religious ideologies. The first is that in many societies it is assumed that a non-physical component of a person can survive after death and remain as a being
with beliefs and desires. Second, it is very frequently assumed that certain people within a society are especially likely to receive direct inspiration or messages from supernatural agencies, such as gods or spirits. And
third, it is also very widely assumed that performing certain rituals in an
exact way can bring about change in the natural world.

If we look at the archaeological evidence from the start of the Upper
Palaeolithic, we get hints that each of these features was present. Few can
doubt that the painted caves, some of which were located deep underground, were the locus for ritual activities. Indeed the anthropomorphic
images within this art, such as the sorcerer from the cave of Les Trois-
Frères, are most easily interpreted as being either supernatural beings or
shamans who communicated with them. As was most forcefully argued
by the French prehistorian André Leroi-Gourhan, these painted caves
are likely to reflect a mythological world with concepts as complex as
those of the Dreamtime held by the Australian Aborigines.

In addition to the art we have the evidence from the burials. It is difficult to believe that such investment would have been made in burial ritual,
as at Sungir, had there been no concept of death as a transition to a non-
physical form. Indeed, since only a tiny fraction of the Upper Palaeolithic
population seems to have been buried, it is likely that these people played
a special religious role within their society.

Pascal Boyer has explored how the characteristics of supernatural
beings as found in religious ideologies relate to the intuitive knowledge
about the world genetically encoded in the human mind. In Chapter 3 I
described three types of intuitive knowledge, that regarding psychology,
biology and physics, and argued that these 'kickstarted' the formation of
cognitive domains or multiple intelligences during child development.
Boyer argues that a typical feature of supernatural beings is that they
have characteristics which violate this intuitive knowledge.

For example, Boyer explains that the supernatural beings of religious
ideologies commonly violate intuitive biological knowledge. While they
may have bodies, they do not undergo the normal cycle of birth, matura-
tion, reproduction, death and decay. Similarly, they may violate intuitive
physics by being able to pass through solid objects (as with ghosts) or
simply be invisible. Nevertheless, supernatural beings also have a tendency to conform to some intuitive knowledge; for instance, they are very
frequently intentional beings who have beliefs and desires like normal
human beings. The Ancestral Beings of the Australian Aborigines provide an excellent example of such entities which both violate and con-

form to intuitive knowledge of the world. On the one hand, they have very weird characteristics, such as existing in both the past and the present. On the other hand, in many of the stories they play tricks and engage in deception in a manner which is very human.[65] A more familiar example to many people will be the gods of Greek legends who have supernatural powers but also suffer jealousies and petty rivalries much like those of normal people.

Boyer argues that it is this combination of violation of, and conformity to, intuitive knowledge that characterizes supernatural beings in religious ideologies. The violations make them something different, but by conforming to some aspects of intuitive knowledge people are able to learn about them; if there was nothing about supernatural beings which conformed to intuitive knowledge of the world, the concept of them would simply be too difficult for the human mind to grasp.

An alternative way of viewing this feature of supernatural beings is as a mixing up of knowledge about different types of entities in the real world – knowledge which would have been 'trapped' in separate cognitive domains within the Early Human mind. For example, Early Humans would have known that rocks are not born and do not die like living things. And Early Humans would also have known that people have intentions and desires, while inert nodules of stone do not. Because they had isolated cognitive domains, there was no risk of the Early Human mind getting these entities mixed up, and arriving at a concept of an inert object that is neither born nor dies, but which nevertheless has intentions and desires. Such concepts, which Boyer argues are the essence of a supernatural being, could only arise in a cognitively fluid mind.

Boyer himself suggests that a combination of knowledge about different types of entities explains another recurrent feature of religious ideologies – the fact that some individuals are believed to have special powers of communication with supernatural beings. At the heart of this notion, Boyer argues, is the belief that some people have a different 'essence' from others in the group. I discussed the notion of essence in Chapter 3, where it was explained to be a critical feature of intuitive biology, a means by which even young children are able to classify animals into different species. Boyer explains the differentiation of people into different social roles, exemplified by that of shaman, as an introduction of the notion of essence into thought about the social world. In other words, it is a consequence of cognitive fluidity.

We cannot, of course, reconstruct the religious ideologies of the earliest Upper Palaeolithic societies. But we can be confident that religious ideologies as complex as those of modern hunter-gatherers came into existence at the time of the Middle/Upper Palaeolithic transition and have remained with us ever since. This appears to be another consequence of the cognitive fluidity that arose in the human mind, which resulted in art, new technology, and a transformation in the exploitation of the natural world and the means of social interaction.

Towards cognitive fluidity: the mind of Early Modern Humans

The new cognitive fluidity transformed the human mind and all aspects of human behaviour (see Figure 25). It is not surprising that with new abilities to use materials such as bone and ivory for tools, and to use artifacts to store and transmit information, humans were able to colonize new areas of the world. At around 60,000 years ago a second major pulse of movement across the globe began, following that of the first Early Humans to leave Africa more than 1.5 million years ago. As Clive Gamble has described in his recent study of global colonization,[66] Australasia was colonized by extensive sea voyages, and then the North European Plain, the arid regions of Africa and the coniferous forests and tundra of the far north were colonized soon after 40,000 years ago. Early Humans may have temporarily entered these environments, but they did not remain on a long-term basis. Modern Humans not only colonized them but used them as stepping stones to the Americas and the Pacific islands.

The emergence of a cognitively fluid mentality provides the answer to the Middle/Upper Palaeolithic transition. But remember that this transition does not happen until half-way through Act 4. The start of that act is defined by the appearance of *H. sapiens sapiens* in the fossil record at 100,000 years ago. We must complete this chapter by asking how the minds of these Early Modern Humans – those who lived before the Middle/Upper Palaeolithic transition – were different from those of the Early Humans of Act 3 (who also continued into the first scene of Act 4), and the Modern Humans who lived after the Middle/Upper Palaeolithic transition, among whom we must include ourselves.

There is, I believe, a simple answer to this question. The Early Modern Humans seem to have been achieving some degree of integration between their specialized intelligences, but not gaining the full cognitive fluidity that arose after 60,000 years ago. Their minds were a half-way house between a Swiss-army-knife and a cognitively fluid mentality.

We can see this most clearly in the Near East, where we find the remains of Early Modern Humans in the caves of Skhūl and Qafzeh dating to between 100,000 and 80,000 years ago. While their stone tools are practically indistinguishable from those of the Neanderthals who used the cave of Tabūn before the Early Modern Humans arrived (c. 180,000–90,000 years ago), and Kebara after they left (63,000–48,000

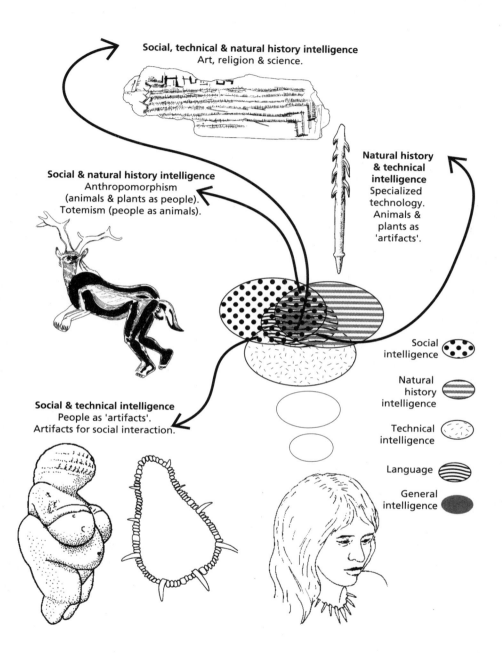

Social, technical & natural history intelligence
Art, religion & science.

Social & natural history intelligence
Anthropomorphism
(animals & plants as people).
Totemism (people as animals).

Natural history & technical intelligence
Specialized technology.
Animals & plants as 'artifacts'.

Social & technical intelligence
People as 'artifacts'.
Artifacts for social interaction.

Social intelligence

Natural history intelligence

Technical intelligence

Language

General intelligence

25 The cultural explosion as a consequence of cognitive fluidity.

years ago), the Early Modern Humans seem to have had two unique features to their behaviour.

The first is that they placed parts of animal carcasses within human graves. For instance, in the cave of Qafzeh a child was found buried with the skull and antlers of a deer. At Skhūl one of the burials contained a body which had been laid on its back, with the jaws of a wild boar placed within its hands.[67] These seem to imply ritualized burial activity, and a belief in religious ideologies. Recall that while Neanderthals did bury some individuals, there is no evidence for the intentional placing of items within the graves, or for any ritual activity associated with the act of burial.

The second contrast concerns the hunting of gazelle. This was the most important animal hunted by both Neanderthals and Modern Humans, and both appear to have used short thrusting spears with stone points. But their hunting patterns were quite different. The Early Modern Humans used their caves on a seasonal basis, and probably expended less physical energy in their hunting behaviour. In addition, they appear to have needed to repair their spears less frequently.[68] In other words, they were hunting with greater degrees of planning and more efficiently than the Neanderthals. This, in turn, is likely to reflect an enhanced ability at predicting the location and behaviour of their prey.

At first glance these two differences between the Early Modern Humans and the Neanderthals of the Near East appear unrelated. But there is in fact a very significant relationship: both derive from an integration of natural history and social intelligence in the minds of Early Modern Humans. As I argued earlier in this chapter, improvements in the ability to predict animal behaviour over what can be achieved with a natural history intelligence alone probably derive from anthropomorphic thinking, as is universal among living hunter-gatherers. I also discussed how concepts of religious belief arise from cognitive fluidity, particularly the integration of natural history and social intelligence. The placing of animal parts within the burials of Early Modern Humans implies that some associations were being made between people and animals, probably reflecting some form of totemic thought. It is significant, I think, that artifacts were not placed within the burials, which is common practice during the Upper Palaeolithic. This suggests that technical intelligence remained isolated within the Early Modern Human mind. This is indeed confirmed by the fact that in spite of their abilities at predicting the behaviour of gazelle, Modern Humans continued to use the same types of hunting weapons as the Neanderthals. They do not appear to have been designing more effective hunting weapons, which would have arisen if technical and natural history intelligence had been integrated,

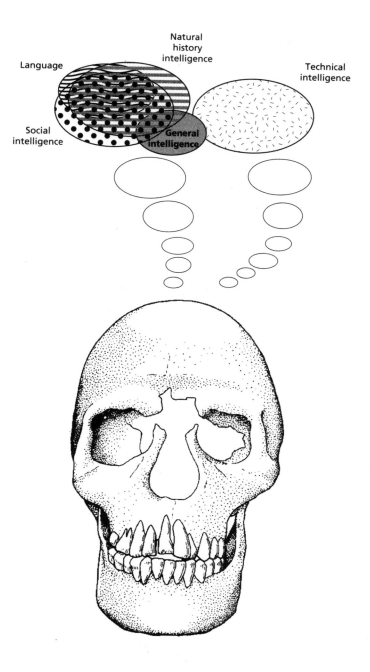

26 *The Early Modern Human mind. The drawing depicts the skull known as Qafzeh 9 dating to c. 100,000 years ago. This is from a young adult who appears to have been buried with a child at its feet.*

nor were they investing their stone tools with social information, as would have arisen if technical and social intelligence were integrated.

In summary, the minds of the Early Modern Humans of the Near East seem to be a half-way house between the Swiss-army-knife mentality of Early Humans and the cognitively fluid mentality of Modern Humans (see Figure 26).

We reach a similar conclusion when we consider the Early Modern Humans of South Africa. Their fossils, found in the caves of Klasies River Mouth and Border Cave, are less well preserved than those of the Near East, but date to the same time period of around 100,000 years ago. The South African specimens contain some archaic features and this region is likely to have been the original source of *H. sapiens sapiens*.[69]

The long stratified sequence of archaeological deposits in Klasies River Mouth is of most interest.[70] It covers the period between around 140,000 years ago and 20,000 years ago. Towards the end of this sequence, at around 40,000 years ago, we see a change in stone technology from a predominantly flake to a blade production method, which denotes the Middle/Upper Palaeolithic transition – although in Africa this is referred to by archaeologists as the change from the Middle to Later Stone Age. Prior to this event, the stone tools in almost the whole of this sequence are very similar to those made by Early Humans elsewhere in the African continent during Act 3, even though those after 100,000 years ago appear to have been made by Early Modern Humans, the first *H. sapiens sapiens*.

However, the levels likely to correlate with the first appearance of Early Modern Humans are notable for a significant increase in the quantity of red ochre.[71] Some of these pieces seem to have been used as crayons. The pieces of red ochre remain quite rare, less than 0.6 per cent of the artifacts from any one layer, but are nevertheless at much higher frequencies than in sites associated with Early Humans. Indeed there are no pieces of red ochre known prior to 250,000 years ago, and only a dozen pieces before 100,000 years ago. Red ochre is also found at other sites in southern Africa after this date, and there have even been claims that it was mined at Lion Cavern in Swaziland. It remains unclear what the Early Modern Humans were doing with the ochre. As the anthropologists Chris Knight and Camilla Powers have argued, body painting is the most likely explanation, since there are no objects of art known in South Africa prior to 30,000 years ago, nor are there any beads or pendants.[72]

A few other traces can be found of new types of behaviour by the Early Modern Humans in southern Africa. In Border Cave there appears to have been a burial of an infant within a grave dating to between 70,000 and 80,000 years ago. This is the only burial known from the Middle Stone Age of the region and it is notable for not only being that of an Early Modern Human, but for also containing a perforated *Conus* shell that had originated more than 80 kilometres away.[73] Another innovation – alongside the more widespread stone flake technology – was the introduction of small blades, made from higher quality stone and chipped into forms which would not be out of place in the Upper Palaeolithic of Europe. These blades look as if they were designed for multi-component tools.[74] A final type of novel behaviour is the working of bone. The most dramatic evidence comes from the sites at Katanda in Zaire, where bone harpoons with multiple barbs have been found. These are as complex as any bone artifact from the Upper Palaeolithic of Europe. They were made by grinding and are at least 90,000 years old – making them 60,000 years earlier than any other known examples. They are associated with typical Middle Stone Age stone artifacts.[75]

If we are indeed dealing with a single type of human in southern Africa after 100,000 years ago, then the mentality of the Early Modern Humans appears to drift in and out of cognitive fluidity. It is as if the benefits of partial cognitive fluidity were not sufficient for this mental transformation to have been 'fixed' within the population. The minds of these Early Modern Humans seem like those of the Early Modern Humans of the Near East in showing some degree of cognitive fluidity, but one that did not match what arose after the start of the Upper Palaeolithic.

Nevertheless, this partial cognitive fluidity was to prove absolutely critical in giving Early Modern Humans the competitive edge as they spread from Africa and the Near East throughout the world between 100,000 and 30,000 years ago. The Early Modern Humans of the Near East are likely to be representatives of – or at least closely related to – the source population of *H. sapiens sapiens* that left Africa, spread into Asia and Europe and replaced all existing Early Humans.[76]

The strongest evidence for this replacement scenario is the limited amount of genetic diversity among living humans today. Although there is considerable controversy as to how modern genetic variability should be interpreted, there is strong evidence that there has been a recent and severe 'bottleneck' in human evolution. In general, living Africans have a higher degree of genetic variability than people elsewhere in the world, suggesting that as the first *H. sapiens sapiens* left Africa there was a considerable loss of genetic variation. This implies that for a short period of time there was a very small breeding population. One recent estimate has suggested no more than six breeding individuals for 70 years, which would reflect an actual population size of around 50 individuals, or 500 individuals if this bottleneck lasted for 200 years.[77]

If the Early Modern Humans of the Near East are indeed part of this source population, or closely related to them, then as they spread throughout the world, they took with them their partially cognitively fluid minds. This feature of their mentality was presumably encoded within their genes. It was their integration of natural history and social intelligence which enabled them to compete successfully with resident Early Human populations, pushing the latter into extinction – although the possibility of some hybridization remains. And consequently we find *H. sapiens sapiens* in China at 67,000 years ago, represented by the fossil skull from Liujang.[78]

At slightly different times in different parts of the world the final step to a cognitively fluid mind was taken. This was the integration of technical intelligence with the already combined social and natural history intelligences. That all *H. sapiens sapiens* populations dispersed throughout the world took this final step – a case of parallel evolution – was perhaps inevitable. There was an evolutionary momentum to cognitive fluidity; once the process had begun it could not be halted. It appears that as soon as a set of adaptive pressures arose in each area, technical intelligence became part of the cognitively fluid mind, the final step on the path to modernity.

In this chapter I have argued that the events of Act 4 can be explained by the emergence of cognitive fluidity in the human mind. This process began with the very first appearance of *H. sapiens sapiens* and its culmination caused the cultural explosion that archaeologists call the Middle/Upper Palaeolithic transition. But, as in so much of science, answering one question merely raises another. How did it happen? How did the thoughts and knowledge escape from their respective chapels of the Early Human mind?

10 So how did it happen?

IN AN EARLIER chapter I suggested that we should view the past as if it were a drama. The interest in such a play is not so much the action, but what is going on in the minds of the actors when various events occur and actions are undertaken. I have concluded that the diverse range of new behaviours that appear in Act 4 of the play derive from a fundamental change in mental architecture. Thoughts and knowledge which had been previously trapped within chapels of specialized intelligence could now flow freely around the cathedral of the mind – or at least a part of it – harmonizing with each other to create new types of thoughts as part of an almost limitless imagination: a cognitively fluid mentality.

Explaining the rise of the flexible mind

My argument remains incomplete, because I have yet to explain how the new cognitive fluidity arose. I believe the explanation relates to changes in the nature of language and consciousness within the mind. Let me start my explanation with a simple proposition: once Early Humans started talking, they just couldn't stop.

To understand how this led to cognitive fluidity we must first recall that in previous chapters I have followed the proposals of Robin Dunbar that the language of Early Humans was a 'social language' – they used language as a means to send and receive social information. This contrasts with our language today which is a general-purpose language, playing a critical role in the transmission of information about the non-social world, although a social bias remains. Now although the language of Early Humans can be characterized as a social language – and for the Early Humans after 250,000 years ago, as a language with an extensive lexicon and grammatical complexity – I believe there would nevertheless have been 'snippets' of language about the non-social world, such as about animal behaviour and toolmaking.

These would have arisen from two sources. The first is general intelligence. As I argued in Chapter 7, general intelligence was extremely important in the Early Human mind as it conditioned behaviour at the domain interfaces, such as the use of tools for hunting and use of food for establishing social relationships. As a result, behaviour at these domain interfaces remained extremely simple, because general intelligence could not access the cognitive processes located within each of the specialized intelligences. General intelligence is also likely to have enabled Early Humans to associate particular vocalizations with non-social entities and consequently produced 'snippets of conversation' about the non-social world – which would have been few in number and lacking in grammatical complexity. Indeed these snippets are likely to have been similar in complexity to the use of symbols by chimpanzees when trained in laboratories which, as I argued in Chapter 5, arises simply from possessing a general intelligence, rather than any linguistic capacity. The non-social 'language' of Early Humans may thus have amounted to a small range of 'words', used predominantly as demands, and with no more than two or three being strung together in a single utterance. They would have contrasted with the grammatically complex and diverse flow of utterances relating to the social world produced by Early Humans arising from their specialized social and linguistic intelligences. Yet the non-social vocalizations may have been embedded within this social language.

A second way for snippets of non-social conversation to arise may have been that the specialized intelligences were never totally isolated from each other, although the degree of isolation was sufficient to prevent them working together. I gave an example of this in Chapter 8 when I suggested that although Neanderthals may have lacked reflexive consciousness about their toolmaking and foraging activities, they may have had a fleeting, ephemeral, rolling consciousness about these – a 'snippet of consciousness', insufficient to have provided any introspection about their thoughts and knowledge in these domains. I explained why this may have been the case by using my analogy of the mind as a cathedral. The 'sounds' of reflexive consciousness at work may have seeped through the chapel walls of social intelligence, and then seeped into the chapels of technical and natural history intelligence, arriving in a heavily muffled or watered down form. I gave another example in Chapter 7 when I noted that in those very rare instances when Early Humans did work bone, they chipped it as if it were stone. This implies that if technical intelligence was indeed being used, it was not working effectively, since chipping is an inappropriate method for working bone. So we may also imagine that seeping in through the walls of social and linguistic intelligence were the muffled thoughts and knowledge coming from the chapels of technical and natural history intelligence. Consequently these were also available for use by linguistic intelligence when generating utterances.

What would have happened to these snippets of language about the non-social world? They must have entered the minds of other individuals as part of the flow of social language and have been decoded by linguistic intelligence and interpreted by social intelligence. In other words, the chapel of social intelligence began to be invaded by non-social information. Those individuals who could exploit these invasions to increase their own knowledge about the non-social world would have been at a selective advantage. They would have been able to make more informed decisions about hunting and toolmaking, enabling them to compete more successfully for mates and provide better care for offspring.

Further selective advantage would have been attained by those individuals who could add more non-social linguistic snippets into conversation, such as by introducing questions about animal behaviour or toolmaking methods. Perhaps these were individuals who, due to random changes made in the architectural plans they inherited, had particularly permeable walls between their specialized intelligences. These talkative individuals were gaining their selective advantage by exploiting the non-social knowledge of other individuals by using language, as opposed to relying on behavioural observations alone. As a consequence, social language would very rapidly (in evolutionary time) have moved to a general-purpose language; my guess would be in the time period between 150,000 and 50,000 years ago. Natural selection, the most important architect of the mind, simply would not have allowed this opportunity to improve the exchange of non-social information, and hence increase reproductive success, to pass by.[1]

There is evidence of this switch from a social to a general-purpose language surviving in our conversation today. As Robin Dunbar described, we still predominantly talk about social issues – we have a love of gossip. Moreover, when we talk about physical objects we often appear to ascribe to them an intrinsic tendency towards motion and imply that they possess 'minds' as if they are living, social beings. This has been explained by the linguist Leonard Talmy.[2] He argues that sentences such as 'the book toppled off the shelf' and 'the ball sailed through the window' imply that these objects move under their own power, since they are equivalent in their structure to sentences such as 'a man entered the room'. More generally, utterances appear to use the same range of concepts and structures whether they are referring to mental states, social beings or inert objects – which linguists refer to as the 'thematic relations hypothesis'.[3] They assume that the original use of language was for the last of these, and those concepts became transferred into utterances about the social/mental world by 'metaphorical extension'. Yet it makes more sense to see it the other way round: the structure of language arose when talking about the social world and was metaphorically extended for talking about physical objects.

The superchapel of the mind

Returning to our evolutionary scenario of a switch from social to general-purpose language, we must ask what happened to the chapel of social intelligence as it began to be invaded by non-social ideas and information? The cognitive scientist Dan Sperber has provided the answer: it became a type of superchapel in the cathedral of the mind. As we saw in Chapter 3, he described this superchapel as the 'module of metarepresentation' (MMR). He suggested that the MMR is an expanded version of the theory of mind module, although my position conceives of it as an expanded – perhaps even exploded – version of a more general domain of social intelligence. Sperber states: 'As a result of the development of communication, and particularly of linguistic communication, the actual domain of the meta-representational module is teeming with representations made manifest by communicative behaviours.... An organism endowed with ... a meta-representational module ... may form representations of concepts and beliefs pertaining to all conceptual domains, of a kind that the modules in those domains might be unable to form on their own.'[4] (see Figure 27)

The critically important point that Sperber is trying to express is that knowledge about the world comes to be represented in two different locations within the mind – within the specialized cognitive domain where it 'belongs', and within what had been the domain of social intelligence but which now contains knowledge about both the social and the non-social world. Indeed, the multiple representations of knowledge within the mind is a critical feature of Annette Karmiloff-Smith's idea for how cognitive fluidity arises during development.

This idea helps us understand what often appear to us to be contradictory views held by living hunter-gatherers, and indeed any Modern Human, about their world. Recall, for instance, the attitude to the polar bear held by the Inuit that I described in Chapter 3. This animal is thought of as a fellow kinsman, but it is also killed and eaten with delight. This combination of a deep respect for the animals they hunt, often expressed in terms of social relationships, and the lack of any qualms about actually killing them appears to be universal among hunter-gatherers. Such a combination of attitudes appears contradictory to us, until we appreciate that knowledge about these animals may be contained in two different cognitive domains – one where it relates to natural history and the problems of securing food, and one where it is mixed up with social intelligence. Another example is the attitude of the Australian Aborigines to their landscapes. To exploit these they rely upon a profound understanding of ecology. They are expert natural historians with detailed knowledge about the cycles of life and death. Yet they also

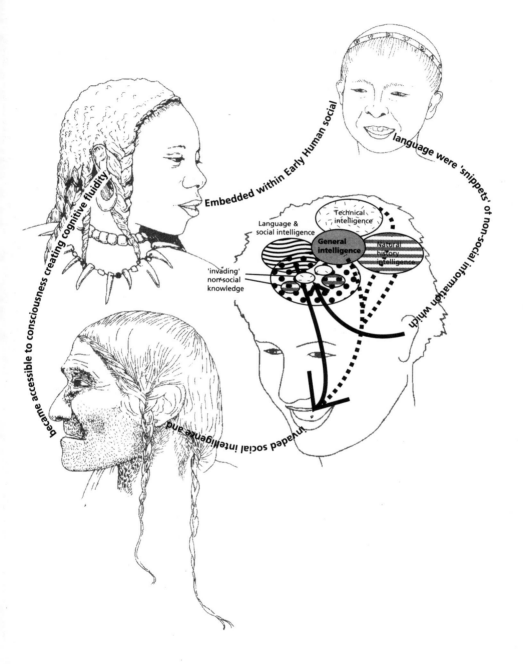

Embedded within Early Human social language were 'snippets' of non-social information which

became accessible to consciousness creating cognitive fluidity

invaded social intelligence and

Technical intelligence

Language & social intelligence

General intelligence

Natural history intelligence

'invading' non-social knowledge

27 The role of language in creating cognitive fluidity.

understand their landscape as continuously created by Ancestral Beings, who have no respect for any laws of ecology. There is no contradiction or confusion in the Aboriginal mind: they simply have two mental representations of their environment, located in different cognitive domains.

Sperber suggested that the invasion of social intelligence by non-social information would trigger a 'cultural explosion'.[5] We do, of course, see precisely that cultural explosion at the start of the Upper Palaeolithic, and indeed see a rumbling anticipation of it after the first Modern Humans enter the play of our past 100,000 years ago. And as part of that cultural explosion we see the appearance of concepts and beliefs which no single domain could create by itself, concepts such as art and religion.

A new role for consciousness

A critical feature of the change to a cognitively fluid mind was a change in the nature of consciousness. Throughout this book I have followed Nicholas Humphrey's arguments that (reflexive) consciousness evolved as a critical feature of social intelligence: it enabled our ancestors to predict the behaviour of other individuals. But just like any other micro-domain of social intelligence, consciousness was not accessible to thought in other cognitive domains – there is no reason to expect Early Humans to have had an awareness about their own knowledge and thought processes concerning the non-social world (other than the ephemeral rolling consciousness I described in Chapter 8). But if, via the mechanism of language, social intelligence starts being invaded by non-social information, the non-social world becomes available for reflexive consciousness to explore. This is, in essence, the argument that Paul Rozin made in 1976 regarding the evolution of advanced intelligence. The critical feature of his notion of accessibility was the 'bringing to consciousness' of the knowledge which was already in the human mind but located within the 'cognitive unconsciousness'.[6]

Quite how much knowledge was brought to a level of conscious awareness is unclear. As I discussed in Chapter 8, a large proportion of our mental activity is likely to remain closed to us in our unconscious mind. Craftspeople, for instance, often appear unaware of the technical knowledge and skills they are using. When asked how they undertake tasks such as throwing a pot they often have difficulty explaining what they do unless they can provide a demonstration. Actions do indeed speak louder than words when technical knowledge is trapped within a specialized cognitive domain. This emphasizes the importance of verbal teaching of technical skills, which only began at the start of the Upper Palaeolithic as is implied by the spatial proximity of knapping debris produced by skilled and unskilled knappers at sites such as Etiolles in France and Trollesgave in Denmark.[7] When knowledge is acquired by verbal instruction it is by definition passed into what had once been the chapels of social and linguistic intelligences, where it becomes available for reflexive consciousness.[8]

The new role for consciousness in the human mind is likely to have been the one identified by the psychologist Daniel Schacter. In an article written in 1989 he argued that, in addition to creating the subjective feelings of 'knowing', 'remembering' and 'perceiving', consciousness should be viewed as 'a global database that integrates the output of modular processes.' He goes on to argue that such an 'integrative mechanism is crucial in any modular system in which processing and representations of different types of information are handled in parallel by separate modules.'[9] In the Early Human mind, general intelligence was the only device available to play this integrating role, and it hardly played it at all. But because language acted as the vehicle for delivering non-social thoughts and knowledge into the chapel of social intelligence, consciousness could start to play this new integrating role within the cathedral of the mind.

We have seen the consequence of integrating knowledge from separate domains in the previous chapter – a vast increase in human creativity. A final argument that consciousness is playing a fundamental role in achieving this integration and resulting creativity comes from the philosopher John Searle. In his 1992 book *The Rediscovery of the Mind*, he considered those sufferers of petit mal seizures that I referred to in Chapter 8. Recall that during their seizures they were able to continue with their goal-directed behaviour but without any consciousness. Referring to the change in the manner in which they undertook their activities, such as piano playing, Searle writes: 'the patients were performing types of actions that were habitual, routine and memorized ... normal human conscious behaviour has a degree of flexibility and creativity that is absent from ... [these] ... cases of unconscious drivers and unconscious pianists.... One of the evolutionary advantages conferred on us by consciousness is the much greater flexibility, sensitivity and creativity we derive from being conscious.'[10]

Early Humans did not lack consciousness altogether; it was simply restricted within their domain of social intelligence. And consequently their social interactions showed considerable flexibility, sensitivity and creativity. But this was markedly absent from their non-social activity – as anyone who has had the task of describing handaxe, after handaxe, after handaxe will know. But as soon as language started acting as the vehicle for delivering non-social information and ideas into the domain of social intelligence, reflexive consciousness could also get to grips with the non-social world. Individuals could now become introspective about their non-social thought processes and knowledge. As a result, the whole of human behaviour was pervaded with the flexibility and creativity that is characteristic of Modern Humans.

Nursing females, cognitive fluidity and extended childhood

The scenario I have offered for the evolution of cognitive fluidity suggests that by 150,000 years ago the Swiss-army-knife mentality was beginning to break down. Those individuals who were able to exploit snippets of non-social conversation were at a selective advantage as they could integrate knowledge which had been 'trapped' within specialized intelligences. We can, I think, identify one particular class of individual within these societies who would have been under particular selective pressure to achieve cognitive fluidity: sexually mature females.

Females at any time during human evolution were only able to give birth to relatively small-brained infants. This is due to the anatomy of the pelvis which needs to be narrow to allow efficient walking on two legs.[11] Consequently the offspring of Modern Humans have a brain size no larger than that of a newborn chimpanzee – about 350 cc. Yet unlike the chimpanzee, in the immediate period after birth the human brain continues to grow at the same rate as that of a foetus. By the age of four a human brain has tripled in size, and when maturity is reached it is around 1400 cc, four times the size at birth. In contrast the chimpanzee brain has only a small postnatal increase in size to around 450 cc.[12] During the period of brain growth after birth, human infants have a very high degree of dependency on adults. There are substantial demands on the mothers to supply the energy to fuel the growth of the infant brain, and indeed anatomy in general. These demands would have become particularly strong during the second period of rapid brain expansion that began after 500,000 years ago.

The social anthropologist Chris Knight and his colleagues have argued that the Early Modern Human females solved the problem of how to 'fuel' the production of increasingly large-brained infants by extracting 'unprecedented levels of male energetic investment'.[13] They suggest that coordinated behaviour by females forced males to provide them with high-quality food from hunting. An important element of the female action was a 'sex strike' and the use of red ochre as 'sham menstruation'. They describe this as the first use of symbolism and find evidence for it in the increase of red ochre after 100,000 years ago associated with the Early Modern Humans of southern Africa.

While I am sceptical about their ideas of coordinated female action, they have identified a social context in which food becomes critical in negotiating social relationships between the sexes. In this context 'snippets' of language about food and hunting may have been especially valuable in the social language between males and females. Females, in particular, may have needed to exploit this information when developing their social relationships with males. This may indeed explain why the first step towards cognitive fluidity, as seen in the behaviour of the Early Modern Humans of the Near East, was an integration of social and natural history intelligence.

The increase in the time between birth and maturity that arose as brain size enlarged during the course of human evolution[14] has another consequence for the switch from a Swiss-army-knife to a cognitively fluid mentality. This is simply that it provides the time for connections between specialized intelligences to be formed within the mind. As I described in Chapter 3, the developmental psychologist Annette Karmiloff-Smith has argued that the mind of a modern child passes through a phase during which cognition is essentially domain-specific, after which knowledge becomes applicable beyond the special-purpose goals for which it is normally used. In Chapter 7 I argued that the cognitive development for young Early Humans effectively ceased after the specialized domains of thought had arisen and before any connections had been built. Consequently, with regard to development, the source of cognitive fluidity must lie in a further extension of the period of cognitive development.

There is indeed evidence in the fossil record that child development of Modern Humans is considerably longer than that of Early Humans. This comes in the form of the skeletal remains of the few Neanderthal children that exist. These show that Neanderthal children grew up rather quickly, developing robust limbs and a large brain at an early age compared with Modern Humans. A particularly important specimen comes from the site of Devil's Tower on Gibraltar and dates to around 50,000 years ago. This consisted of no more than five fragments, but reconstructions have shown it to be of a three- or four-year-old child. The teeth of this child demonstrate that dental eruption occurred earlier than in Modern Humans. Of more interest, however, is that at this young age the brain size of this Neanderthal, at 1400 cc, was approaching that of a mature adult. Such a rapid rate of brain expansion appears to be a general feature of Neanderthal children, being found in several other specimens.[15] The most recently discovered and best-preserved Neanderthal child is a two-year-old from Dederiyeh Cave in Syria. This appears to have possessed a brain size equivalent to that of a six-year-old Modern Human.[16]

In essence, there was no time for cognitive fluidity to arise before the development of the Neanderthal mind – and I assume the Early Human mind in general – had ceased. Unfortunately we lack any child skulls of the 100,000-year-old Early Modern Humans from the Near East, or those of the first Upper Palaeolithic hunter-gatherers. But my guess would be for a gradual extension of the period of development between 100,000 and 50,000 years ago.

The rise of the modern mind: an overview

Let me conclude this chapter by summarizing my explanation for the evolution of cognitive fluidity. The seeds were sown with the increase of brain size that began 500,000 years ago. This was related to the evolution of a grammatically complex social language. The utterances of this language, however, carried snippets of non-social information as well. Those individuals who were able to exploit such non-social information gained a reproductive advantage. In particular, females who were nursing infants for prolonged periods – and therefore unable to feed themselves adequately – would have come under selective pressure to adapt in this way, because their patterns of social interaction with males had become bound up with a need for food. As social language switched to a general-purpose language, individuals acquired an increasing awareness about their own knowledge of the non-social world. Consciousness adopted the role of an integrating mechanism for knowledge that had previously been 'trapped' in separate specialized intelligences.

The first step towards cognitive fluidity appears to have been an integration between social and natural history intelligence that is apparent from the Early Modern Humans of the Near East, 100,000 years ago. This is before Modern Humans dispersed into Asia and Europe where they either replaced or interbred with existing Early Human populations. The final step to a full cognitive fluidity occurred at slightly different times in different populations between 60,000 and 30,000 years ago. This involved an integration of technical intelligence, and led to the changes in behaviour that we refer to as the Middle/Upper Palaeolithic transition. In other words, it created a cultural explosion: the appearance of the modern mind.

11 The evolution of the mind

THE CRITICAL STEP in the evolution of the modern mind was the switch from a mind designed like a Swiss army knife to one with cognitive fluidity, from a specialized to a generalized type of mentality. This enabled people to design complex tools, to create art and believe in religious ideologies. Moreover, as I argue in the Boxes on pp. 196–97 and 198, the potential for other types of thought which are critical to the modern world can be laid at the door of cognitive fluidity. So too can the rise of agriculture as I will explain in the Epilogue to this book – for agriculture and its consequences do indeed constitute the cultural epilogue to the evolution of the mind.

The switch from a specialized to a generalized type of mentality between 100,000 and 30,000 years ago was a remarkable 'about turn' for evolution to have taken. The previous 6 million years of evolution had seen an ever-increasing specialization of the mind. Natural history, technical and then linguistic intelligence had been added to the social intelligence that was already present in the mind of the common ancestor to living apes and humans. But what is even more remarkable is that this recent switch from specialized to generalized ways of thinking was not the only 'about turn' that occurred during the evolution of the modern mind. If we chart the evolution of the mind not just over the mere 6 million years of this prehistory, but over the 65 million years of primate evolution, we can see that there has been an oscillation between specialized and generalized ways of thinking.

In this final chapter I want to put the modern mind in its truly long-term context by charting and explaining this long-term oscillation in the nature of the mind. Only by doing so can we appreciate how we are products of a long, slow gradual process of evolution and how we differ so much from our closest living relative, the chimpanzee. And in doing so I want firmly to embed the evolution of the mind into that of the brain, and indeed the body in general. I must begin by introducing some rather shadowy new actors who now appear in a long prologue to the play that is our past (see Figure 28).[1]

Sixty-five million years of the mind

We must start 65 million years ago with a creature known as *Purgatorius*, represented by sparse cranial and dental fragments coming from eastern

Racist attitudes as a product of cognitive fluidity

In Chapter 9 I argued that cognitive fluidity led to anthropomorphic and totemic thinking, since the accessibility between the domains of natural history and social intelligence meant that people could be thought of as animals, and animals could be thought of as people. The consequences of an integration of technical and social intelligence are more serious. Technical intelligence had been devoted to thought about physical objects, which have no emotions or rights because they have no minds. Physical objects can be manipulated at will for whatever purpose one desires. Cognitive fluidity creates the possibility that people will be thought of in the same manner.

We are all aware of such racist attitudes in the modern world, typified in the treatment of racial minorities. The roots of denying people their humanity would appear to stretch back to the dawn of the Upper Palaeolithic. Perhaps this is indeed what we see with the burial of part of a polished human femur with one of the children at Sungir 28,000 years ago and the defleshing of human corpses at Gough's Cave in Somerset, England, 12,500 years ago, which were discarded in the same manner as animal carcasses. Early

Humans, with their Swiss-army-knife-like mentality, could not think of other humans as either animals or artifacts. Their societies would not have suffered from racist attitudes. For Neanderthals, people were people, were people. Of course those early societies could not have been peaceful Gardens of Eden with no conflict between individuals and groups. The idea that our ancestors may have lived in an idyllic state of cooperation and harmony was shown to be nonsense as soon as Jane Goodall, in her 1990 book *Through a Window* about the chimpanzees of Gombe, described how she saw bloodthirsty brutal murder and cannibalism of one chimpanzee by another. There can be little doubt that Early Humans engaged in similar conflicts as they attempted to secure and maintain power within their groups, and access to resources. But what Early Humans may have lacked were beliefs that other individuals or groups had different types of mind from their own – the idea that other people are 'less than human' which lies at the heart of racism.

The social anthropologists Scott Atran and Pascal Boyer have both independently suggested that the idea that there are

Montana, USA. This animal was a member of a group known as the plesiadapiforms. *Purgatorius* appears to have been a mouse-sized creature which lived on insects. The best preserved of its group was known as *Plesiadapis*: about the size of a squirrel, it fed on leaves and fruit (see Figure 29).

It is unclear whether or not the plesiadapiforms should be classified as primates. They lack characteristic primate features in certain regions of their skulls and in their mode of locomotion, as far as these can be reconstructed from fragmentary fossil remains. It is in fact possible that rather than being primates, the plesiadapiforms shared a common ancestor with the earliest true primates which appeared after 55 million years ago. In view of this uncertain evolutionary status, plesiadapiforms are best described as 'archaic primates'.

different human races comes from a transfer into the social sphere of the concept of 'essences' for living things that, as we saw in Chapter 3, is a critical part of intuitive biology. This transfer appears to happen spontaneously in the minds of young children. As another social anthropologist, Ruth Benedict, made clear in her classic 1942 study entitled *Race and Racism*, believing that differences exist between human groups is very different from believing that some groups are inherently inferior to others. For this view, which we can call racism, we seem to be looking at the transfer into the social sphere of concepts about manipulating objects, which indeed do not mind how they are treated because they have no minds at all. My argument here is that the cognitive fluidity of the Modern Human mind provides a potential not only to believe that different races of humans exist, but that some of these may be inferior to others due to the mixing up of thoughts about humans, animals and objects. There is no compulsion to do this, simply the potential for it to happen. And unfortunately that potential has been repeatedly realized throughout the course of human history.

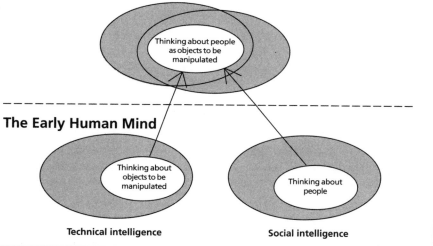

The Modern Human Mind

Thinking about people as objects to be manipulated

The Early Human Mind

Thinking about objects to be manipulated

Thinking about people

Technical intelligence

Social intelligence

Our concern is with the type of mind that should be attributed to these creatures. It would seem appropriate to characterize their pattern of behaviour as more directly under the control of genetic mechanisms than of learning. A strict division between these – between 'nature' and 'nurture' – has long been rejected by scientists. Any behaviour must be partly influenced by the genetic make-up of the animal and partly by the environment of development. Nevertheless, the relative weighting of these varies markedly between species, and indeed between different aspects of behaviour within a single species.

It is useful here briefly to consider some findings from laboratory studies on the learning capacities of different types of animals. These studies require animals to solve problems, such as about getting food by pressing the correct levers, and have shown that primates as a whole have

Humour as a product of cognitive fluidity

Here is a joke:

> A kangaroo walked into a bar and asked for a scotch and soda. The barman looked at him a bit curiously and then fixed the drink. 'That will be two pounds fifty' said the barman. The kangaroo pulled out a purse from his pouch, took out the money and paid. The barman went about his business for a while, glancing from time to time at the kangaroo, who stood sipping his drink. After about five minutes the barman went over to the kangaroo and said, 'You know, we don't get many kangaroos in here.' The kangaroo replied, 'At two pounds fifty a drink, it's no wonder.'

This joke was quoted by Elliot Oring in his 1992 book *Jokes and their Relations* to illustrate what he believes to be a fundamental feature of successful humour: 'appropriate incongruities'. In this joke there are lots of incongruities: kangaroos walking into bars, speaking English and drinking scotch. But the response of the kangaroo to the barman's remark is an 'appropriate incongruity' due to the way the barman framed his remark. This implied that there were scotch-drinking, English-speaking kangaroos around, but that they simply were not visiting his particular bar.

It is readily evident that the potential to entertain ideas that bring together elements from normally incongruous domains arises only with a cognitively fluid mind. Had Neanderthals known about kangaroos, scotch and bars, they could not have thought of the incongruous situation of kangaroos buying a drink because their knowledge about social transactions would have been in one cognitive domain and that about kangaroos in another. And consequently their Swiss-army-knife mentality may have denied them what seems to be an essential element of a sense of humour.

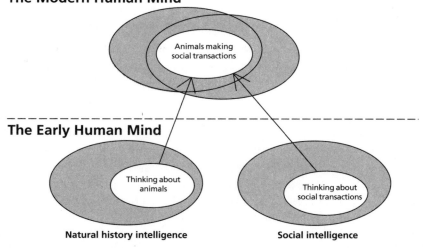

The Modern Human Mind

Animals making social transactions

The Early Human Mind

Thinking about animals

Thinking about social transactions

Natural history intelligence

Social intelligence

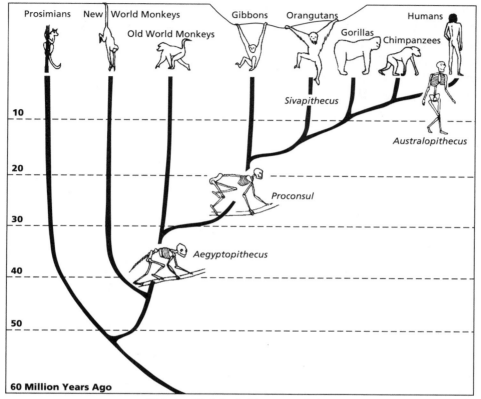

Prosimians   New World Monkeys   Gibbons   Orangutans   Humans

Old World Monkeys   Gorillas   Chimpanzees

Sivapithecus

10

Australopithecus

20

Proconsul

30

Aegyptopithecus

40

50

60 Million Years Ago

28 *A simplified chart of human evolution.*

29 Plesiadapis.

a greater capacity for learning than other animals, such as rats, cats and pigeons. By 'learning', I am referring here to what I have called throughout this book 'general intelligence' – a suite of general-purpose learning rules, such as those for learning associations between events. Only primates appear able to identify general rules that apply in a set of experiments, and to use the general rule when faced with a new problem to solve. While rats and cats can solve simple problems, they do not show any improvement over a series of learning tasks.[2]

Returning to the plesiadapiforms, and remembering that they may not be primates at all, it would seem likely that they would fall in with the rats and the cats on such tasks, rather than with the primates. In other words, we should attribute them with a minimal general intelligence, if one at all. The lives of the plesiadapiforms were probably dominated by relatively innately specified behaviour patterns, that arose as a response to specific stimuli and which were hardly modified at all by experience. We could indeed think of the plesiadapiform mind/brain as being constituted by a series of modules, encoding highly specialized knowledge about patterns of behaviour. To put it in other words, they possessed a type of Swiss-army-knife mentality.

The plesiadapiforms declined in abundance around 50 million years ago. This coincided with a proliferation of rodents, which probably outcompeted the plesiadapiforms for leaves and fruit. However, by around 56 million years ago two new primate groups had appeared, referred to as the omomyids and the adapids. These are the first 'modern primates' and looked similar to the lemurs, lorises and the tarsier of today. These first modern primates were agile tree dwellers, specialized for eating fruit and leaves. The best preserved is *Notharctus*, whose fossil remains come from North America (see Figure 30).

The most notable feature of these early primates is that they were the first to possess a relatively large brain. By this I mean that they had a brain size larger than what one would expect on the basis of their body size alone when compared with other mammals of their time period.[3] In general, larger animals need larger brains, simply because they have more muscles to move and coordinate. Primates as a group, however, have brains larger than would be predicted by their body size alone. The evolution of this particularly large brain size is described as the process of encephalization – and we can see that it began with these early primates of 56 million years ago.

I referred to this group at the end of Chapter 5 when we were considering the evolution of social intelligence. As I noted, if their minds were similar to those of lemurs today, it is unlikely that they possessed a specialized social intelligence. It is probable, however, that they pos-

30 Notharctus.

sessed a 'general intelligence', supplementing the modules for relatively innately specified behaviour patterns. The biological anthropologist Katherine Milton has argued that the selective pressure for this general intelligence was the spatial and temporal 'patchiness' of the arboreal plant resources they were exploiting. Simple learning rules allowed primates to lower the food acquisition costs and improve foraging returns.[4] Yet general intelligence may also have had benefits in other domains of behaviour, such as by facilitating the recognition of kin.

It is at this date, therefore, of about 56 million years ago, that we have the first 'about turn' in the evolution of the mind. We can see a switch from a specialized type of mentality possessed by archaic primates, with behavioural responses to stimuli largely hard-wired into the brain, to a generalized type of mentality in which cognitive mechanisms allow learning from experience. Evolution appears to have exhausted the possibilities for increasing hard-wired behavioural routines: an alternative evolutionary path was begun of generalized intelligence.

General intelligence required a larger brain to allow the information processing required to make simple cost/benefit calculations when choosing between behavioural strategies, and to enable knowledge to be acquired by associative learning. For a larger brain to have evolved, these early modern primates would have needed to exploit high-quality plant foods such as new leaves, ripe fruits and flowers – as is confirmed by their dental features. Such dietary preferences were essential in order to permit a reduction in gut size and consequently the release of sufficient metabolic energy to fuel the enlarged brain while maintaining a constant metabolic rate.[5]

The next important group of primates come from Africa, notably the sedimentary deposits of the Fayum depression in Egypt. The most important of these is *Aegyptopithecus*, which lived around 35 million years ago. This was a fruit-eating primate, living in the tall trees of monsoonal rainforests. Its body appears to have been adapted for both climbing and leaping. Like all the previous primates, it was a quadruped committed to moving on all four limbs. The most important primate fossils from the period 23–15 million years ago are likely to represent several species, but are referred to as *Proconsul*. These fossils are found in Kenya and Uganda, and show both monkey-like and ape-like features (see Figure 31).

The mind of *Aegyptopithecus* probably differed from that of *Notharctus* and the other early modern primates in two major respects. First the domain of general intelligence became more powerful – giving greater information processing power. The second change is of more significance: the evolution of a specialized domain of social intelligence.

If we follow the scenario put forward by Dick Byrne and Andrew Whiten, by 35 million years ago there was a form of social intelligence which resulted in significantly more complex behaviour in the social domain than in the interaction with the non-social world – as I discussed

31 Proconsul.

in Chapter 5. This domain of social intelligence evolved thanks to the reproductive advantage it gave individuals in terms of being able to predict and manipulate the behaviour of other members of the group. As argued by Leda Cosmides and John Tooby, those individuals with a suite of specialized mental modules for social intelligence are likely to have had more success at solving the problems of the social world. In other words, by 35 million years ago evolution seems to have exhausted the possibilities of improving reproductive success by enhancing general intelligence alone: an evolutionary turn around was made which began an ever-increasing specialization of mental faculties that continued until almost the present day.

It is during this period that Andrew Whiten's characterization of brain evolution as deriving from a 'spiralling pressure as clever individuals relentlessly selected for yet more cleverness in their companions' is appropriate.[6] As Nicholas Humphrey has described, when intellectual prowess is correlated with social success, and if social success means high biological fitness, then any heritable trait which increases the ability of an individual to outwit his fellows will soon spread through the gene pool.[7]

This 'spiralling pressure' probably continued in the period between 15 and 4.5 million years ago, during which the fossil record is particularly sparse.[8] It was in this time period, at around 6 million years ago, that the common ancestor of modern apes and humans lived, and it was with this missing actor that I began the play of our past. Byrne and Whiten suggest that by the time of the common ancestor, social intelligence had become sufficiently elaborated to involve abilities at attributing intentions to other individuals and to imagining other possible social worlds.

When the fossil record improves after 4.5 million years ago, the australopithecines are established in East Africa and possibly elsewhere in that continent. As we saw in Chapter 2, the best preserved of these, *A. afarensis*, displays adaptations for a joint arboreal and terrestrial lifestyle. As can be seen in Figure 1, the fossils between 3.5 and 2.5 million years ago suggest that this was a period of stability with regard to brain size. Why should the 'spiralling pressure' for ever greater social intelligence, and consequently brain expansion, have come to an end – or at least a hiatus? The probable answer is that evolution now confronted two severe constraints: bigger brains need more fuel, and bigger brains need to be kept cool. With regard to fuel, brains are very greedy, requiring over 22 times more energy than muscle tissue while at rest. With regard to temperature, an increase of only 2°C (3.6°F) can lead to impaired functioning of the brain.[9]

The australopithecines are likely to have been mainly vegetarian and lived in the equatorial, wooded savannahs. This lifestyle constrained the amount of energy that could be supplied to the brain, and exposed them to constant risk of overheating. Brain expansion could therefore not have occurred, even if the selective pressures for it had been present.

Had it not been for a remarkable conjunction of circumstances, it is likely that australopithecines would still be foraging in Africa and that the *Homo* lineage would not have evolved. But as we saw in Figure 1, at around 2 million years ago there started a very rapid period of brain expansion, marking the appearance of the *Homo* lineage. This could only have arisen if the constraints on brain expansion had been relaxed – and of course if selective pressures were present. When trying to explain how this happened, the interrelationships between the evolution of the mind, the brain and the body become of paramount importance. There are two behavioural developments in this period which are of critical importance: bipedalism – habitual walking on two legs – and increased meat eating.

The evolution of bipedalism had begun by 3.5 million years ago. Evidence for this is found in the anatomy of *A. afarensis* (see Figure 32), and, more dramatically, by the line of australopithecine footprints preserved at Laetoli in Tanzania. The most likely selective pressure causing the evolution of bipedalism was the thermal stress suffered by the australopithecines when foraging in the wooded savannahs of East Africa. With their tree–climbing and tree-swinging ancestry, the australopithecines had a body already conditioned for an upright posture. The anthropologist Peter Wheeler has shown that by adopting bipedalism australopithecines could achieve a 60 per cent reduction in the amount of solar radiation they experienced when the sun was overhead. Moreover, the energetic costs of locomotion would have been reduced. Bipedalism enabled australopithecines to forage for longer periods without the need for food and water, to forage in environments which had less natural shade, and thus to exploit foraging niches not open to other predators who were more heavily tied to sources of shade and water.[10] The shift to increasingly efficient bipedalism may have been partly related to the environmental change to more arid and open environments that occurred in Africa at around 2.8 million years ago,[11] increasing the value of reducing exposure to solar radiation by adopting an upright posture.

Bipedalism required a larger brain for the muscle control needed for balance and locomotion. But bipedalism and a terrestrial lifestyle had several other consequences for brain enlargement. Some of these have been discussed by the anthropologist Dean Falk.[12] She explains how a new network of veins covering the brain must have been jointly selected for with bipedalism to provide a cooling system for the brain – or a 'radiator' as she describes it. Once in place, the constraint of overheating on

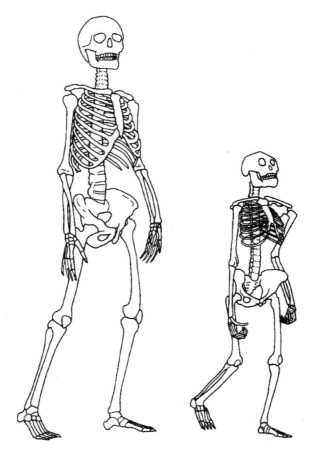

32 *A comparison of the size and posture of 'Lucy' (right) – A. afarensis – and a Modern Human female (left). Lucy was about 105 cm (3 ft 5 in) tall, with notably long arms.*

further expansion of the brain was relaxed as this radiator could easily be modified. Consequently the possibility (not necessity) arose of further brain enlargement.

Dean Falk also suggests that bipedalism would have led to a reorganization of the neurological connections within the brain: 'once feet had become weight bearers (for walking) instead of graspers (a second pair of hands) areas of cortex previously used for foot control were reduced thus freeing up cortex for other functions'.[13] This of course went with the 'freeing' of the hands, providing opportunities for enhanced manual dexterity for carrying and toolmaking. There may also have been significant changes in the perception of the natural environment due to an increase in the distances and directions regularly scanned; and a change in the social environment by an increase in face-to-face contact, enhancing the possibilities for communication by facial expression.

Perhaps the most significant consequence of bipedalism, however, is that it facilitated the exploitation of a scavenging niche. A 'window of opportunity' was opened to exploit carcasses during periods of the day when carnivores needed to find shade. As Leslie Aiello and Peter Wheeler have discussed, with an increasing amount of meat in the diet, the size of the gut could be further reduced, releasing more metabolic energy to the brain while maintaining a constant basal metabolic rate.[14] And in this way a further constraint on the enlargement of the brain was relaxed.

The main selective pressures for brain enlargement no doubt continued to come from the social environment: the spiralling pressures caused by socially clever individuals creating the selective pressure for even more social intelligence in their companions. And this pressure itself was present due to the need for large social groups that a terrestrial lifestyle in open habitats required, partly as a defence against predators.

Confirmation of the importance of the social environment for the expansion of brain size was found in Chapter 6. As we saw in that chapter, it is clear that the Oldowan stone tools of early *Homo* demanded more knowledge to make than those which chimpanzees use today, and therefore those likely to have been used by the australopithecines. But this knowledge probably arose from the enhanced opportunities for social learning in larger groups rather than as a consequence of selection for a domain of technical intelligence. Similarly, the narrow range of environments exploited by early *Homo* suggests that a discrete domain of natural history intelligence had not yet evolved and that the information requirements for scavenging were also being met as a by-product of living in larger social groups.

In my reconstruction of the evolution of the mind I only found the first evidence for distinct domains of natural history and technical intelligence at 1.8–1.4 million years ago with the appearance of *H. erectus*, and the technically demanding handaxes. What were the causes, conditions and consequences for these new domains of intelligence?

The ultimate cause for these new specialized intelligences was the continuing competition between individuals – the cognitive arms race that had been unleashed when the constraints on brain enlargement had been relaxed. But the evolution of these specific intellectual domains may well reflect the appearance of a constraint on any further enhancement of social intelligence itself. As Nicholas Humphrey noted, 'there must surely come a point when the time required to solve a social argument becomes insupportable'.[15] So, just as the possibilities of increasing reproductive success by enhancing general intelligence alone by natural selection had been exhausted by 35 million years ago, we might also conclude that the 'path of least resistance' for a further evolution of the mind in the conditions existing at 2 million years ago lay not in enhanced social intelligence but in the evolution of new cognitive domains: natural history and technical intelligence.

In other words, those individuals gaining most reproductive success were the ones who were most efficient at finding carcasses (and other food resources) and most able to butcher them. These individuals gained a better quality of diet, and spent less time exposed to predators on the savannah. As a result, they enjoyed a better state of health, could compete more successfully for mates, and produced stronger offspring. With regard to toolmaking, behavioural advantage was gained by those individuals who were able to have ready access to suitable raw materials for removing meat and breaking open bones of a carcass. The advantages of artifacts such as handaxes may well have been that they could be carried as raw material for flakes, as well as used as a butchering tool themselves. Experimental studies have repeatedly shown that they are very effective general-purpose tools.

Bipedalism, the scavenging niche, the existence of raw materials, the competition from other carnivores – these were all conditions that enabled the enhanced intellectual abilities at toolmaking and natural history to be selected for. Had one of these conditions been missing, we might still be living on the savannah.

The most significant behavioural consequence of these new cognitive domains was the colonization of large parts of the Old World. The evolution of a natural history and technical intelligence thus opened up a further window of opportunity for human behaviour. Within less than 1.5 million years, our recent relatives were living as far apart as Pontnewydd Cave in north Wales, the Cape of South Africa and the tip of Southeast Asia. There could be no more effective demonstration that the Swiss-army-knife mentality of Early Humans provided a remarkably effective adaptation to the Pleistocene world. Indeed, there appears to have been no further brain enlargement and no significant changes in the nature of the mind between 1.8 and 500,000 years ago.

This is not to argue that all minds were exactly the same; the *H. erectus* and *H. heidelbergensis* populations that dispersed throughout much of the Old World were living in diverse environments, resulting in subtle differences in the nature of their multiple intelligences. An example I gave in Chapter 7 referred to juveniles living in relatively small social groups in wooded environments during interglacial periods who will have had less opportunity to observe toolmaking, and whose minds consequently will not have developed the technical skills found in other Early Human populations.

The fourth cognitive domain to have evolved in the Early Human mind was that of language. It is likely that as far back as 2 million years ago, selective pressures existed for enhanced vocalizations. In this book I have followed Robin Dunbar's and Leslie Aiello's arguments that language initially evolved as a means of communicating social information alone rather than information about subjects such as tools or hunting. As group sizes enlarged, mainly due to the pressures of a terrestrial lifestyle, those individuals who could reduce the time they needed to spend in building social ties by grooming – or who acquired greater amounts of social knowledge with the same time investment – were reproductively more successful.

Just as the tree-living ancestry of the australopithecines enabled bipedalism to evolve, so too did bipedalism itself make possible the evolution of an enhanced vocalization capacity among early *Homo*, and particularly *H. erectus*. This has been made clear by Leslie Aiello.[16] She has explained how the upright posture of bipedalism resulted in the descent of the larynx, which lies much lower in the throat than in the apes. A spin off, not a cause, of the new position of the larynx was a greater capacity to form the sounds of vowels and consonants. In addition, changes in the pattern of breathing associated with bipedalism will have improved the quality of sound. Increased meat eating also had an important linguistic spin off, since the size of teeth could be reduced thanks to the greater ease of chewing meat and fat, rather than large quantities of dry plant material. This reduction changed the geometry of the jaw, enabling muscles to develop which could make the fine movements of the tongue within the oral cavity necessary for the diverse and high-quality range of sounds required by language.

The linguistic capacity was intimately connected with the domain of social intelligence within the Early Human mind. But technical and natural history intelligence remained isolated from these, and from each other. As I discussed in Chapter 7, this created the distinctive characteristics of the Early Human archaeological record, appearing very modern in some respects, but very archaic in others.

As I explained at the end of Chapter 7, while *H. erectus* probably possessed a capacity for vocalizing substantially more complex than what we see in apes today, it is likely to have remained relatively simple compared with human language. The evolution of the two principal defining features of language, a vast lexicon and a set of grammatical rules, seems to be related to the second spurt of brain enlargement that happened between 500,000 and 200,000 years ago. Yet even with these elements present, it remained in essence a social language. Explanations for this second period of brain enlargement are less easy to propose than for the initial spurt, which is clearly related to the origin of bipedalism and a terrestrial lifestyle.

One possibility is that the renewed brain enlargement relates to a further expansion of the size of social groups, resulting in those individuals with enhanced linguistic capacities being at a selective advantage. But the need for large group size is unclear – even remembering that this refers to the wider 'cognitive group', not necessarily the narrower group within which one lives on a day-to-day basis. Aiello and Dunbar suggest that it may simply reflect the increase in global human population and the need for defence not against carnivores, but other human groups.[17]

Yet here again another new window of opportunity arose for evolution. As soon as language acted as a vehicle for delivering information into the mind (whether one's own or that of another person), carrying with it snippets of non-social information, a transformation in the nature of the mind began. As I suggested in Chapter 10, language switched from a social to a general-purpose function, consciousness from a means to predict other individuals' behaviour to managing a mental database of information relating to all domains of behaviour. A cognitive fluidity arose within the mind, reflecting new connections rather than new processing power. And consequently this mental transformation occurred with no increase in brain size. It was, in essence, the origins of the symbolic capacity that is unique to the human mind with the manifold consequences for hunter-gatherer behaviour that I described in Chapter 9. And, as we can now see, this switch from a specialized to a generalized type of mentality was the last in a set of oscillations that stretches back to the very first primates.

As I discussed in Chapter 10, one of the strongest selective pressures for this cognitive fluidity is likely to have been the provisioning of females with food. The expansion of the brain had resulted in an extension of infant dependency which increased the expenditure of energy by females and made it difficult for them to supply themselves with food. Consequently male provisioning is likely to have been essential, resulting in a need for connections between natural history and social intelligence. It is perhaps not surprising, therefore, that these cognitive domains appear to have been the first two to have become integrated – as is apparent from the behaviour of the Early Modern Humans of the Near East – to be followed somewhat later by technical intelligence. Moreover, the prolonged period of infancy provided the time for cognitive fluidity to develop.

This transition to a cognitively fluid mind was neither inevitable nor pre-planned. Evolution simply capitalized on a window of opportunity that it had blindly created by producing a mind with multiple specialized intelligences. It may be the case that by 100,000 years ago the mind had reached a limit in terms of specialization. It might be asked why cognitive fluidity did not evolve in the other types of Early Humans, the Neanderthals, or the archaic *H. sapiens* of Asia. Well, there may indeed be a trace of cognitive fluidity between social and technical intelligence in the very latest Neanderthals in Europe, as they seem to start making artifacts whose form is restricted in time and space, and consequently may be carrying social information.[18] Yet before this could develop fully, they were pushed into extinction by the incoming Modern Humans, who had already achieved full cognitive fluidity.

Cognitive fluidity enabled people to engage in new types of activities, such as art and religion. As soon as these arose the developmental contexts for young minds began to change. Children were born into a world where art and religious ideology already existed; in which tools were designed for specific tasks, and where all items of material culture were imbued with social information. At 10,000 years ago the developmental contexts began to change even more fundamentally with the origins of an agricultural way of life, which, as I will explain in my Epilogue, is a further product of cognitive fluidity. As I described in Chapter 3, with these new cultural contexts, the hard-wired intuitive knowledge within the minds of growing infants may have 'kick-started' new types of specialized cognitive domains. For instance, a young child growing up in an industrial setting may no longer have developed a 'natural history intelligence'. Instead, in some contexts, a specialized domain for mathematics may have developed, kick-started by certain features of 'intuitive physics', even though no prehistoric hunter-gatherer had ever developed such a domain.

The hectic and ongoing pace of cultural evolution unleashed by the appearance of cognitive fluidity continues to change the developmental contexts of young minds, resulting in new types of domain-specific knowledge. But all minds develop a cognitive fluidity. This is the defining property of the modern mind.

Oscillations in the evolution of the mind

If we stand back from this 65 million years, we can see how the selective advantages during the evolution of the mind have oscillated from those individuals with specialized intelligence, in terms of hard-wired modules, up to 56 million years ago, to those with general intelligence up to 35 million years ago, and then back again to those with specialized intelligence in the form of cognitive domains up until 100,000 years ago.

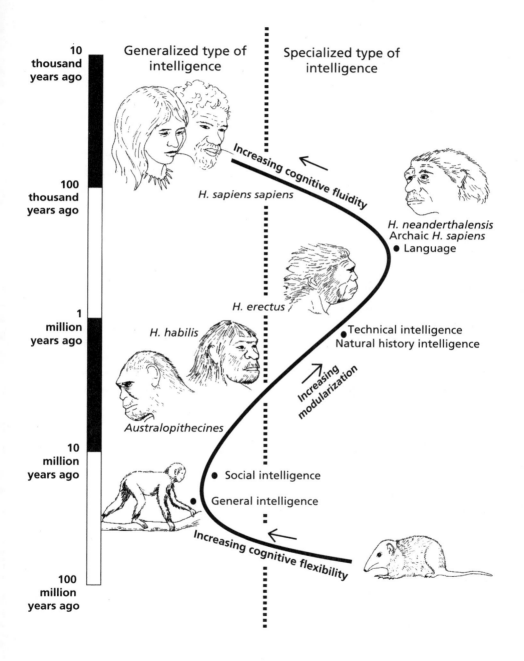

33 The evolution of human intelligence.

The final phase of cognitive evolution involved a further switch back to a generalized type of cognition represented by cognitive fluidity.

In the light of this evolutionary trajectory, as illustrated in Figure 33, it is not surprising that the modern mind is so frequently compared with that of a chimpanzee. Both have a predominantly generalized type of mentality (although chimpanzees have a specialized, isolated social intelligence), and therefore both look superficially similar. When we look at chimpanzees and modern hunter-gatherers we see a very smooth fit in each case between their technology and subsistence tasks. Both are very adept at making 'tools for the job'. Chimpanzees often behave in a similar way to humans, especially when they are taught and encouraged by humans to make tools, or paint pictures or use symbols. We are led to believe that the chimpanzee and the human mind are essentially the same: that of Modern Humans simply being more powerful because the brain is larger, resulting in a more complex use of tools and symbols. The evolution of the mind, as I have documented in the preceding pages, shows this to be a fallacy: the cognitive architecture of the chimpanzee mind and the modern mind is fundamentally different.

Yet this poses an important question. If the end point of cognitive evolution has been to produce a mind with a generalized type of mentality, superficially similar to the generalized type of mentality of the chimpanzee (excepting social intelligence) and the one we attribute to our early primate ancestors, then why did it bother to go through a phase of multiple, specialized intelligences which had limited integration? Why did natural selection not simply build on general intelligence, gradually making it more complex and powerful?

The answer is that a switch between specialized and generalized systems is the only way for a complex phenomenon to arise, whether it is a jet engine, a computer program or the human mind. Indeed my colleague Mark Lake believes that repeated switching from general-purpose to specialized designs is likely to be a feature of evolutionary processes in general.[19] To explain it let me return to one of the first analogies for the mind that I used in this book: the mind as a computer. Actually, let me be more specific and characterize the mind as a piece of software, and natural selection as the computer programmer – the designer. Both are common analogies, but no more. The mind/brain is as much a chemical soup as a series of electronic circuits, and natural selection has no goal; it is in Richard Dawkins memorable phrase the 'Blind Watchmaker'.[20] Let us briefly consider how natural selection blindly wrote the computer programs of the mind.

How is a complex piece of software produced? There are three stages. First one must write an overall plan for the program, often in the form of a series of separate routines that are linked together. The aim of this stage is simply to get the program to 'run', for all the routines to work together. This is analogous to natural selection building the general intelligence of our early primate ancestors: no complexity but a smoothly functioning system. The next stage is to add the complexity to the program *in a piecemeal fashion*. A good programmer does not try to add the required complexity to a program as a whole and all at once: if this is attempted, de-bugging becomes impossible and the program repeatedly crashes. The faults cannot be located and they pervade the system.

The only way to move from a simple to a complex program is to take each routine in turn, and develop it on an independent basis to perform its own specialized and complex function, ensuring that it remains compatible with the initial program design. This is what natural selection undertook with the mind; specialized intelligences were developed and tested separately, using general intelligence to keep the whole system running. Only when each routine has been developed on an independent basis does a programmer glue them back together in order simultaneously to perform their complex functions as an advanced computer program. This integration is the third and final stage of writing a complex program. Natural selection did it for the mind by using general–purpose language and consciousness as the glue. The result was the cultural explosion I described in Chapter 9.

In this regard, natural selection was simply being a very good (though blind) programmer when building the complex modern mind. If it had tried to evolve the complex, generalized type of modern mind directly from the simple, generalized type of mind of our early ancestors, without developing each cognitive domain in an independent fashion, it would simply have failed. Moreover, it is perhaps not surprising that we have found in this book a similar sequence of changes in the cognitive development of the child as in the cognitive evolution of the species.

The cognitive origins of science

Knowing the prehistory of the mind provides us with a more profound understanding of what it means to be human. I have used it to understand the origins of art and religion. And I must draw this book to a close by considering the third of the unique achievements of the modern mind, science, which I referred to in my introductory chapter, since this will lead us to identify the most important feature of our cognitively fluid minds.

Science is perhaps as hard to define as art or religion.[21] But I believe there are three critical properties. The first is the ability to generate and test hypotheses. This is something which, as I argued in previous chapters, is fundamental to any specialized intelligence: chimpanzees are evidently generating and testing hypotheses about the behaviour of other individuals when they engage in deceptive behaviour by using their social intelligence. I argued that early *Homo* and Early Humans were needing to generate and test hypotheses about the distribution of resources, especially carcasses for scavenging, by using their natural history intelligence.

A second property of science is the development and use of tools to solve specific problems, such as a telescope to look at the moon, a microscope to look at a flea, or even a pencil and paper to record ideas and results. Now although the hunter-gatherers of the Upper Palaeolithic did not make telescopes and microscopes, they were nevertheless able to develop certain dedicated tools by being able to integrate their knowledge of natural history and toolmaking. Moreover, they were using material culture to record information in what the archaeologist Francesco D'Errico has described as 'artificial memory systems':[22] the cave paintings and engraved ivory plaques of the Upper Palaeolithic are the precursors of our CD-Roms and computers. The potential to develop a scientific technology emerged with cognitive fluidity.

So too did the third feature of science. This is the use of metaphor and analogy, which are no less than the 'tools of thought'.[23] Some metaphors and analogies can be developed by drawing on knowledge within a single domain, but the most powerful ones are those which cross domain boundaries, such as by associating a living entity with something that is inert, or an idea with something that is tangible. By definition these can only arise within a cognitively fluid mind.

The use of metaphor pervades science.[24] Many examples are widely known, such as the heart as a mechanical pump and atoms as miniature solar systems, while others are tucked away in scientific theories, such as the notion of 'wormholes' in relativity theory and 'clouds' of electrons in particle physics. Charles Darwin conceived of the world in metaphor 'as a log with ten thousand wedges, representing species, tightly hammered in along its length. A new species can enter this crowded world only by insinuating itself into a crack and popping another wedge out.'[25] The biologist Richard Dawkins is a master at choosing appropriate metaphors to explain evolutionary ideas, such as 'selfish' DNA, 'natural selection as a blind watchmaker' and 'evolution as a flowing river'. Mathematicians are prone to talk about their equations and theorems using terms such as 'well behaved' and 'beautiful', as if they were living things rather than inert marks on pieces of paper.

The significance of metaphors for science has been discussed at length by philosophers, who recognize that they play a critical role not only in the transmission of ideas but in the practice of science itself. In his 1979 essay entitled 'Metaphor in Science', Thomas Kuhn explained that the role of metaphor in science goes far beyond that of a device for teaching and lies at the heart of how theories about the world are formulated.[26] Much of science is perhaps similar to Daniel Dennett's description of the study of human consciousness – a war of competing metaphors.[27] Such a battle has indeed been fought in this book. If we could not think of the mind as a sponge, or a computer, or a Swiss army knife, or a cathedral, would we be able to think about and study the mind at all?

In summary, science like art and religion, is a product of cognitive fluidity. It relies on psychological processes which had originally evolved in specialized cognitive domains and only emerged when these processes could work together. Cognitive fluidity enabled technology to be developed which could solve problems and store information. Of perhaps even greater significance, it allowed the possibility for the use of powerful metaphors and analogy, without which science could not exist.

Indeed, if one should want to specify those attributes of the modern mind that distinguish it not only from the minds of our closest living relatives, the apes, but also our much closer, but extinct, ancestors, it would be the use of metaphor and what Jerry Fodor described as our passion for analogy. Chimpanzees cannot use metaphor and analogy, because with one single type of specialized intelligence, they lack the mental resources for metaphor, not to mention the language with which to express it. Early Humans could not use metaphor because they lacked cognitive fluidity. But for Modern Humans, analogy and metaphor pervade every aspect of our thought and lie at the heart of art, religion and science.

The human mind is a product of evolution, not supernatural creation. I have laid bare the evidence. I have specified the 'whats', the 'whens' and the 'whys' for the evolution of the mind. I have explained how the potential arose in the mind to undertake science, create art and believe in religious ideologies, even though there were no specific selection pressures for such abstract abilities at any point during our past. I have demonstrated that we can only understand the nature of language and consciousness by understanding the prehistory of the mind – by getting to grips with the details of the fossil and archaeological records. And I have found the use of metaphor and analogy in various guises to be the most significant feature of the human mind. I have myself only been able to think and write about prehistory and the mind by using two metaphors within this book: our past as a play and the mind as a cathedral.

It is perhaps fitting, therefore, that this last chapter has been largely written while staying in the Spanish city of Santiago de Compostela.

This was one of the great centres of pilgrimage in the medieval world. The town has a remarkable collection of religious buildings which were built, and constantly modified, during the Middle Ages. These range from the simplicity of small churches with no more than a single nave to the complexity of the cathedral. Built on the site of a small ninth-century church, the cathedral is one of the masterpieces of Romanesque architecture. It has a three-aisled nave and no fewer than 20 chapels, each of which is dedicated to a different saint. The original Romanesque design has been modified by Gothic and later additions. My guide book to this cathedral and the other churches of Santiago tells me that walking within and between them will be like walking through history. But for me, it has been like walking through the Prehistory of the Mind.

Epilogue: the origins of agriculture

AROUND 10,000 years ago, people changed from being hunter-gatherers to farmers in many different regions of the world. This transformation took place quite independently in parts of Southwest Asia, Equatorial Africa, the Southeast Asian mainland, Central America and in lowland and highland South America. The onset of farming is frequently invoked as *the* turning point of prehistory. Without agriculture we would not have had towns, cities and state society. It is these that have so fundamentally changed the contexts in which the minds of individuals develop today from those of our hunter-gatherer ancestors. So how did this change come about? In my Epilogue I will argue that the rise of agriculture was a direct consequence of the type of thinking that evolved with the emergence of cognitive fluidity. More specifically, I will propose that there were four aspects of the change in the nature of the mind which resulted in a reliance on domesticated plants and animals when environmental conditions abruptly altered 10,000 years ago. Before looking, however, at just what these changes in the mind might have been, we need to consider briefly some of the broader issues involved in the origins of agriculture.

The introduction of farming is viewed as one of the great mysteries of our past. Why did it happen? Certainly not because of the crossing of a threshold in accumulated knowledge about plants and animals, enabling people to domesticate them.[1] As I have argued in this book, hunter-gatherers – whether Early or Modern Humans – are and were expert natural historians. We can be confident that knowledge about how animals and plants reproduce, and the conditions they need for growth, had been acquired by human minds as soon as a fully developed natural history intelligence had evolved, at least 1.8 million years ago.

The knowledge prehistoric hunter-gatherers possessed about animals is readily apparent from the diversity of species we know they hunted, to judge by the bones found at their settlements. It is only quite recently, however, that archaeologists have been able to document a similar level of exploitation of plant foods by prehistoric hunter-gatherers. Consider, for instance, the 18,000-year-old sites in the Wadi Kubbaniya, which lies to the west of the Nile Valley. The charred plant remains discovered here indicate that a finely ground plant 'mush' had been used, probably to wean infants. A diverse array of roots and tubers had been exploited, possibly all the year round, from permanent settlements.[2] Similarly, at Tell Abu Hureyra in Syria, occupied by hunter-gatherers between 20,000 and 10,000 years ago, no fewer than 150 species of edible plants have been identified, even though roots, tubers and leafy plants were not preserved.[3] At both these locations we see the technology for pounding and grinding plant material – the same as that used by the first farmers (see Figure 34). In summary, these sites demonstrate that the origins of agriculture 10,000 years ago are not to be sought in a sudden breakthrough in technology, or the crossing of a threshold in botanical knowledge.

So why did people take up farming? An element of compulsion must have been involved. Despite what we might intuitively imagine, farming did not automatically liberate our Stone Age ancestors from a hand-to-mouth, catch-as-catch-can existence. Indeed quite the opposite. Living by agriculture comes a very poor second when compared with living by hunting and gathering. The need to look after a field of crops ties down some members of a community to a particular spot, creating problems of sanitation, social tensions and the depletion of resources such as firewood. Hunter-gatherers easily solve these problems by being mobile. As soon as their waste accumulates, or firewood is depleted, they move on to another campsite. If individuals or families have disagreements, they can move away to different camps. But as soon as crops need regular weeding, and labour has been invested in building storage facilities or irrigation canals which need maintaining, the option to move on is lost. It is no coincidence that the earliest agricultural communities of the Near East show substantially poorer states of health than their hunter-gatherer forebears, as we know from studies of their bones and teeth.[4]

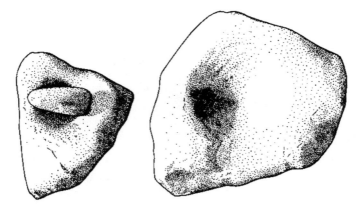

34 Mortar and pestle for processing plants from site E-78-4, Wadi Kubbaniya, c. 18,000 years old.

People therefore must have had some *incentive* to switch to farming. Moreover that incentive must have been on a worldwide scale 10,000 years ago, if we are to account for the fact that diverse methods of food production started independently in such a relatively short time period around the globe.[5] The crops being cultivated varied markedly, from wheat and barley in Southwest Asia, to yams in West Africa, to taro and coconuts in Southeast Asia.

Conventionally, two explanations are put forward for this near-simultaneous adoption of agriculture. The first is that at around 10,000 years ago population levels had gone beyond those that could be supported on wild food alone. The world had effectively become full up with hunter-gatherers and there were no new lands to colonize. As a result, new methods of subsistence were required to provide more food, even if they were labour intensive and came with an assortment of health and social problems.[6]

This idea of a global food crisis in prehistory is both implausible and not supported by the evidence. We know from studies of modern hunter-gatherers that they have many means available for controlling their population levels, such as infanticide. Mobility itself constrains the size of population due to the difficulties of carrying more than one child. Furthermore, we know that in some instances at least the health of the last hunter-gatherers in a region where agriculture was adopted appears to have been significantly better than that of the first farmers. This is evident from the study of pathologies on the bones of the last hunter-gatherers and the first farmers. Such evidence shows that the onset of agriculture brought with it a surge of infections, a decline in the overall quality of nutrition and a reduction in the average length of life.[7] The rise of farming was certainly not a solution to health and nutritional problems faced by prehistoric populations; in many cases it appears to have caused them. Nevertheless, although a global population crisis is implausible, the possibility remains that production of foodstuffs became necessary to feed relatively high local populations.

A second and partially more convincing explanation for the introduction of farming 10,000 years ago is that the whole world at that time was experiencing dramatic climatic changes associated with the end of the last ice age. There was a period of very rapid global warming – recent research indicating perhaps as much as an astonishing 7°C (over 12°F) in a few decades – that marked the end of the last glacial period.[8] This was preceded by a series of fluctuations 15,000–10,000 years ago, switching the globe from periods of warm/wet to cold/dry climate and back again. These climatic fluctuations were truly global affairs. The near-simultaneous adoption of farming in different parts of the world therefore appears to represent local responses, to the local environmental developments, caused by the global climatic changes immediately before and at 10,000 years ago as the last ice age came to an end. As we shall see, this cannot entirely account for the rise of farming, since Early Humans experienced similar climatic fluctuations without abandoning their hunting and gathering way of life. But first let us pause in our argument to consider one particular region, so as to understand better what really happened as farming took hold.

We can see the close relationship between changing methods of food procurement and late ice age climatic instabilities in Southwest Asia, where the origins of agriculture have been studied in most detail. Here we see the first farming communities of domesticated cereals (barley and wheat) and animals (sheep and goat) at sites such as Jericho and Gilgad at around 10,000 years ago. These settlements are found in precisely the area where the wild ancestors of these domesticated cereals had grown and had been exploited by the hunter-gatherers, such as those from Abu Hureyra.

Indeed the stratified sequence of plant remains at Abu Hureyra, as studied by the archaeobotanist Gordon Hillman and briefly referred to above, is very informative about the switch from a hunting and gathering to a farming lifestyle.[9] Between 19,000 and 11,000 years ago the environmental conditions in Southwest Asia improved, as the ice sheets of Europe retreated, leading to warmer and moister conditions, particularly during the growing season. This is likely to have been a period during which hunter-gatherer populations increased, since they were able to exploit ever more productive food plants, and gazelle herds moving along predictable routes.[10] At Abu Hureyra we find evidence in fact that a wide range of plants was being gathered. Between 11,000 and 10,000 years ago, however, there was a marked return to much drier environmental conditions, even drought.[11]

This drought had severe consequences for the hunter-gatherers of Abu Hureyra. In successive archaeological layers at the site we see the loss of tree fruits as a source of food – reflecting the loss of trees because of the drought – and then the loss of wild cereals, which were unable to survive the cold dry environments. To compensate we see a marked increase in small seeded legumes, plants which were more drought resistant but which also required careful detoxification to make them edible. At around 10,500 years ago Abu Hureyra was abandoned; when people returned there 500 years later, they came to live as farmers.

The significance of this drought, and possibly earlier climatic fluctuations, for the change in hunter-gatherer lifestyles is seen throughout Southwest Asia. In the region of the Levant, to the south and west of

Abu Hureyra, we can see that around 13,000–12,000 years ago hunter-gatherers changed from a mobile to a sedentary lifestyle probably in response to a short, abrupt climatic crisis of increased aridity which resulted in dwindling and less predictable food supplies.[12] Although people continued to live by hunting and gathering, the first permanent settlements with architecture and storage facilities were constructed.[13] This period of settlement is known as the 'Natufian', and lasted until 10,500 years ago when the first true farming settlements appear.

The Natufian culture marked a dramatic break with what went before.[14] Some of the new settlements were extensive. That at Mallaha involved digging underground storage pits and levelling slopes to create terraces for huts. The range of bone tools, art objects, jewellery and ground stone tools expanded markedly. Some of the Natufian flint blades have what is known as a 'sickle gloss', which suggests that stands of wild barley were being intensively exploited. But the people living in these settlements still supported themselves by wild resources alone. The critical importance of the Natufian for the origins of agriculture is that it constituted what has been described by the archaeologists Ofer Bar-Yosef and Anna Belfer-Cohen as 'a point of no return'.[15] Once that sedentary lifestyle had been put in place it was inevitable that the level of food production would need to increase, because the constraint on population growth imposed by a mobile lifestyle had been relaxed. Although it remains unclear quite why the sedentary lifestyle was chosen, it seems to have arisen out of decisions made by hunter-gatherers when faced with the short, abrupt climatic fluctuations at the very end of the last ice age.

It is likely that elsewhere in the world hunter-gatherers also reacted to the climatic fluctuations of the late Pleistocene in ways that involved either the direct cultivation of plants, or the adoption of a sedentary lifestyle which eventually committed them to a dependence on domesticated crops. But this cannot be the whole story of the origins of agriculture. As I have stressed at several places in this book, the Early Humans of Act 3 lived through successive ice ages. They too had been faced with marked climatic fluctuations, and experienced a dwindling of plant foods and the need for change in their hunting and gathering practices. But at no time did they develop sedentary lifestyles or begin to cultivate crops or domesticate animals. So why did so many groups of Modern Humans, when faced with similar environmental changes, independently develop an agricultural way of life?

The answer lies in the differences between the Early Human and the Modern Human mind. If my proposals for the evolution of the mind are correct, then Early Humans simply could not have entertained the idea of domesticating plants and animals, even when suffering severe economic stress, hypothetically surrounded by wild barley and wheat, and magically provided with pestles, mortars and grinding stones. The origins of agriculture lie as much in the new way in which the natural world was thought about by the modern mind, as in the particular sequence of environmental and economic developments at the end of the Pleistocene. There are four aspects of the change in the nature of the mind which were critical to the origins of agriculture.

1. The ability to develop tools which could be used intensively to harvest and process plant resources. This arose from an integration of technical and natural history intelligence. Little more needs to be said about this ability, for such technological developments were discussed in Chapter 9. We see the appropriate technology for the cultivation of plants in use at Wadi Kubbaniya and Abu Hureyra by 20,000 years ago.

2. The propensity to use animals and plants as the medium for acquiring social prestige and power. This arose from an integration of social and natural history intelligence. We can see several examples of this in the behaviour of hunter-gatherers after 40,000 years ago in Europe. Consider, for instance, the way in which the storage of meat and bone was used on the Central Russian Plain between 20,000 and 12,000 years ago, a period during which people constructed dwellings from mammoth bones and tusks (see Figure 35). The stored resources came from animals such as bison, reindeer and horse which were hunted on the tundra-like environments of the last ice age. Olga Soffer has described how during the course of this period access to stored resources came increasingly under the control of particular dwellings.[16] Individuals appear to have been using stored meat, bone and ivory not just as a source of raw material and food, but as a source of power.

We can see something similar in the hunter-gatherer communities of southern Scandinavia between 7,500 and 5,000 years ago. These people exploited game such as red deer, wild pig and roe deer in thick mixed-oak forests. By looking at the frequencies with which different species were hunted, and by studying the hunting patterns with computer simulation, we can deduce that they were focussing on red deer – even though this often left the hunters returning to their settlements empty-handed, because red deer were much scarcer and more difficult to kill than, say, the smaller and more abundant roe deer.[17] Why were they doing this? It is most likely that the preference for red deer arose from the larger size of the animal. More meat could be given away from a red deer carcass, pro-

35 *Mammoth-bone dwellings and storage pits on the Central Russian Plain, c. 12,000 years ago.*

viding greater social prestige and power. Day-to-day fluctuations in meat from hunting could be coped with by exploiting the rich plant, coastal and aquatic foods in the region, especially by using facilities such as fish traps that could be left unattended, some of which have been found almost perfectly preserved in waterlogged conditions. This idea is confirmed when we look at the burials of the hunter-gatherers. Antlers of red deer and necklaces made from their teeth are prominent in the grave goods.[18]

This use of animals, and no doubt plants, as the means for gaining social control and power within a society was absent from Early Humans. Their thought about social interaction and the natural world was undertaken within isolated cognitive domains and could not be brought together in the required fashion. This difference is critical to the origins of agriculture. While sedentary farming may represent a poorer quality of life for a community as a whole, when compared with a mobile hunting-gathering lifestyle, it provides particular individuals with opportunities to secure social control and power. And consequently, if we follow the proper Darwinian line of focussing on individuals rather than groups, we can indeed see agriculture as just another strategy whereby some individuals gain and maintain power.[19]

The archaeologist Brian Hayden favours this explanation for the origins of agriculture. In a 1990 article he argued that 'the advent of competition between individuals using food resources to wage their competitive battles provides the motives and the means for the development of food production'.[20] He used examples from various modern hunter-gatherer societies to show that when technological and environmental conditions allow it, individuals try to maximize their power and influence by accumulating desirable foods and goods, and by claiming ownership of land and resources.

When Hayden looked at the Natufian culture, he felt that the evidence for the long-distance trade of prestige items, and the abundance of jewellery, stone figurines and architecture were all clear signs of social inequality, reflecting the emergence of powerful individuals. Once that social structure had arisen, there was a need for the powerful individuals continually to introduce new types of prestige items and to generate economic surpluses to maintain their power base. Food production is an inevitable consequence – as long as there are suitable plants and animals in the environment for domestication. As Hayden notes, many of the first domesticates appear to be prestige items – such as dogs, gourds, chilli peppers and avocados – rather than resources which could feed a population grown too large to be supported by wild resources alone.

3. The propensity to develop 'social relationships' with plants and animals, structurally similar to those developed with people. This is a further consequence of an integration of social and natural history intelligence. In order to domesticate animals and plants, it was necessary for prehistoric minds to be able to think of them as beings with whom 'social' relationships could be established. As I have argued, Early Humans with their Swiss-army-knife mentality could not have entertained such ideas.

We can see evidence for the emergence of 'social relationships' between people and wild animals and plants among the prehistoric hunter-gatherers of Europe. For instance, in the Upper Palaeolithic cave sites of Trois-Frères and Isturitz in France reindeer bones have been found with fractures and injuries that would have seriously inhibited the animals' ability to move and feed. Nevertheless these reindeer survived for sufficient time to allow the fractures to start healing and it has been proposed that they were cared for by humans[21] – in much the same way as the crippled Neanderthal from Shanidar Cave referred to in Chapter 7 had been looked after.

There are also a few intriguing examples of horse depictions from Palaeolithic art which seem to show the animals wearing bridles – although it is difficult to tell, and the marks may simply identify changes in colour or bone structure (see Figure 36).[22] We know for sure, however, that dogs were domesticated shortly after the end of the ice age. Indeed in the hunter-gatherer cemeteries of southern Scandinavia dating to around 7,000 years ago, we find dogs which had received burial ritual and grave goods identical to those of humans. There is also a grave from the Natufian settlement of Mallaha which has a joint burial of a boy with a dog.[23]

The ability to enter into social relationships with animals and plants is indeed critical to the origins of agriculture. The psychologist Nicholas Humphrey drew attention to the fact that the relationships people have

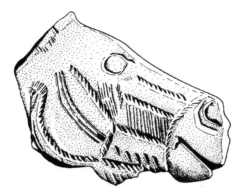

36 *Horse's head from St-Michael d'Arudy, Pyrénées-Atlantiques, France. Length 4.5 cm.*

with plants bear close structural similarities to those with other people. Let me quote him:

the care which a gardener gives to his plants (watering, fertilising, hoeing, pruning etc.) is attuned to the plants' emerging properties.... True, plants will not respond to ordinary social pressures (though men *do* talk to them), but the way in which they give to and receive from a gardener bears, I suggest, a close structural similarity to a simple social relationship. If ... [we] ... can speak of 'conversation' between a mother and her two month old baby, so too might we speak of a conversation between a gardener and his roses or a farmer and his corn.

As Humphrey goes on to note, 'many of mankind's most prized technological discoveries, from agriculture to chemistry, may have had their origin ... in the fortunate misapplication of social intelligence.'[24]

4. The propensity to manipulate plant and animals, arising from an integration of technical and natural history intelligence. We can think of this as the misapplication of technical intelligence, for just as Modern Humans appear to have begun treating animals and plants as if they were social beings, so too did they treat them as artifacts to be manipulated. Perhaps the best example of this is from the hunter-gatherers of Europe, who lived in the mixed-oak forests after the end of the last ice age. They were deliberately burning parts of the forest.[25] This is a form of environmental management/manipulation that acts to encourage new plant growth and attract game. It is a practice that has been well documented among the Aboriginal communities of Australia who undertook it perfectly aware that by doing so they were removing exhausted plant growth and returning nutrients to the soil to facilitate new growth. Indeed, by looking at the accounts of how the indigenous Australians exploited their environments we find evidence for many practices which are neither simple hunting and gathering, nor farming. For instance, in southwestern Australia, when yams were intensively collected, a piece of the root was always left in the ground to ensure future supplies.[26]

Modern Humans living as hunter-gatherers during prehistory probably developed relationships with plants and animals of a similar nature to those observed among recent hunter-gatherers. They are unlikely to have been simple predators, but engaged in the manipulation and management of their environments – although this fell short of domesticating resources. This was indeed recognized a quarter of a century ago by the Cambridge archaeologist Eric Higgs.[27] He encouraged a generation of research students to challenge the simple dualism between hunting-gathering and farming. We now know that these are just two poles on a continuum of relationships developed by prehistoric hunter-gatherers. But these relationships were only developed after 40,000 years ago, when ideas about animals and plants as beings to be manipulated at will or with whom 'social relationships' could be developed arose.

The four abilities and propensities I have outlined fundamentally altered the nature of human interaction with animals and plants. When people were faced with immense environmental changes at the end of the last ice age it was the cognitively fluid mind that made it possible for them to find a solution: the development of an agricultural lifestyle. In any one region there was a unique historical pathway to agriculture, in which some of these mental abilities and propensities may have been more important than others. But while the seeds for agriculture may have been first planted 10,000 years ago, they were first laid in the mind at the time of the Middle/Upper Palaeolithic transition. It is this key epoch and not the period of the birth of agriculture that lies at the root of the modern world. I have therefore treated the origins of agriculture as no more than an epilogue to my book. Nevertheless agriculture fundamentally changed the developmental contexts for young minds: for the vast majority of people alive today, the world of hunting and gathering, with its specialized cognitive domains of technical and natural history intelligence, have been left behind as no more than prehistory.

I have tried to demonstrate in this book the value of reconstructing that prehistory. For our minds today are as much a product of our evolutionary history as they are of the contexts in which we as individuals develop. Those stone tools, broken bones and carved figurines that archaeologists meticulously excavate and describe can tell us about the prehistory of the mind. And so, if you wish to know about the mind, do not ask only psychologists and philosophers: make sure you also ask an archaeologist.

Notes and further reading

Ch. 1. Why ask an archaeologist about the human mind? (pp. 9–16)

1 The evolution of the human mind's capacities for art and science is perhaps the key problem concerning the mind. The evolutionary linguist Steven Pinker describes this as a 'fundamental problem'. How could it have been possible, he asks, for evolution to 'have produced a brain capable of intricate specialized achievements like mathematics, science, and art, given the total absence of selective pressures for such abstract abilities at any point in history' (1989, 371).

2 Creationists in this context are not necessarily those who are anti-science or anti-evolution with regard to human anatomy. For instance Alfred Wallace Russell, the co-discoverer of the theory of natural selection, believed that human intelligence can only be explained by divine creation (Gould 1981, 39). In his 1989 book *The Evolution of the Brain*, the Nobel-prize-winning neurologist Sir John Eccles concludes that human consciousness derives from 'supernatural spiritual creation' (1989, 287).

3 I use the term 'ancestors' in a rather loose sense here as the evolutionary relationships between members of the australopithecines and *Homo* are highly contentious. Whether a species was a direct ancestor, or merely a relative, remains unclear in many cases, especially with *H. neanderthalensis* as will be discussed later in this book.

4 Merlin Donald's 1991 book *The Origins of the Modern Mind* was an excellent and very important attempt to integrate data and ideas from psychology, evolutionary biology and archaeology. He proposes that the mind has passed through three major stages: an 'episodic culture' associated with australopithecines, earliest *Homo* and living apes; a 'mimetic culture' associated with *H. erectus* and a 'mythic' culture associated with *H. sapiens*. The last of these involved the ability to construct conceptual models and was closely related to the evolution of language. He believes that with this third stage the 'mind' became extended in the sense of beginning to use external storage devices i.e. material symbols. Any readers of my book are highly recommended to read *The Origins of the Modern Mind* as an alternative interpretation of how data and ideas from psychology and archaeology can be integrated. The principal weakness in Donald's work is his use of archaeological data: the complexity and variability of this is often not appreciated, and certainly not exploited to its full extent. Lake (1992) makes numerous perceptive criticisms in this regard. Donald also appears to underestimate the cognitive capacities of living apes, as the type of intelligence he attributes to *H. erectus* is similar to that found in chimpanzees today (Byrne, personal communication). Donald (1994) provides a précis which is followed by a critical discussion of his book.

The psychologist Michael Corballis (1992) has also drawn on archaeological data, especially when exploring the evolution of language. He argues that the origin of language was gesture – speech only became the principal medium for language relatively late in human evolution, at the time of the Middle/Upper Palaeolithic transition (*c.* 40,000 years ago). He supports this idea by referring to the expansion in the range of technical behaviour at the time of the transition, in the sense of bone, antler and ivory working, the production of art and the use of prismatic blade cores for stone tools. These arose, he suggests, because the hands had become freed from being used as the medium of communication due to the evolution of speech. The major problem with this is that the lithic technology of the Middle Palaeolithic involved as much manual dexterity as the techniques of the Upper Palaeolithic, as explained in my Chapter 6. Nevertheless, as with Donald's (1991) work, this is a valuable attempt to integrate ideas and data from psychology and archaeology.

5 The most explicit call for a 'cognitive archaeology' came from Colin Renfrew (1983). Prior to that, however, Thomas Wynn (1979, 1981) and Alexander Marshack (1972a,b) had attempted to draw inferences about past cognition from specific types of artifacts. More recently, archaeologists have shifted their attention to the evolution of language (e.g. Davidson & Noble 1989; Whallon 1989; Mellars 1989a) but with little concern as to the relationship between language and other aspects of cognition. As far

as I know, no archaeologist has attempted to track the evolution of the mind throughout the course of prehistory.

6 Aiello (1996a).

7 As we will see in Chapter 3, this is in fact not a particularly new idea and one that does not necessarily require an explicit evolutionary argument for support.

Ch. 2. The drama of our past (pp. 17–32) Further reading

Human evolution

Jones et al (1992) contains a series of excellent chapters covering all aspects of human evolution, with descriptions of fossils and what can be learnt from living primates and human genetics. For a discussion of the methods of molecular taxonomy for reconstructing human and primate evolutionary relationships see Byrne (1995, Chapter 1). The most recent australopithecine discoveries are described by White et al (1994), WoldeGabriel et al (1994), Leakey et al (1995) and Brunet et al (1995), while Wood (1994) and Andrews (1995) discuss their significance. Susman (1991) discusses the anatomy of the australopithecine hand, with regard to their potential for making stone tools. Johanson & Eddy (1980) provide an account of the discovery of 'Lucy' and a discussion of her significance. A review of the earliest fossils of *Homo* is provided by Wood (1992), while Tobias (1991) is a comprehensive study of the hominid fossils from Olduvai Gorge.

The evolution of *H. erectus* is discussed by Rightmire (1990), while dates for the *H. erectus* fossils in Java are provided by Swisher *et al* (1994); and in China by Wanpo *et al* (1995). The significance of the new finds in China and the problems of their taxonomic identification are discussed by Wood & Turner (1995) and Culotta (1995). A detailed study of the *H. erectus* specimen known as KNM-WT 15000 is provided by Walker & Leakey (1993). The evolution of modern humans has been a matter of intense debate during the last decade, between those supporting multi-regional and those supporting out of Africa scenarios. Important papers regarding the contribution of molecular genetics include Cann *et al* (1987) and Templeton (1993), while summaries of the debating points regarding hominid fossils are found in Hublin (1992), Frayer *et al* (1993, 1994), Aiello (1993), Stringer & Bräuer

(1994) and Wolpoff (1989; Wolpoff *et al* 1984). The earliest fossils in Europe are described by Arsuaga *et al* (1993), Carbonell *et al* (1995) and Roberts *et al* (1994). Stringer (1993) provides a summary of differing interpretations. The evolution and nature of the Neanderthals are described in Stringer & Gamble (1993) and Trinkaus & Shipman (1993). A summary of the dating evidence for the earliest anatomically modern humans is given by Grün & Stringer (1991).

There are numerous edited volumes dealing with the origins of modern humans. The most notable are by Akazawa *et al* (1992), Mellars & Stringer (1989), Bräuer & Smith (1992) and Nitecki & Nitecki (1994).

Stone tool technology

General introductions to stone tool technology describing the different techniques and the periods in which they are found are provided by Bordes (1961a, 1968) and Inizan *et al* (1992).

The archaeology of Act 2

The earliest stone tools are described by Merrick & Merrick (1976), Chavaillon (1976), Roche (1989), Roche & Tiercelin (1977) and Kibunjia (1994; Kibunjia *et al* 1992). Harris & Capaldo (1993) provide a review of the earliest archaeological sites and their interpretation. The archaeology of Olduvai Gorge is described by Leakey (1971), while Hay (1976) provides the critical geological background. Good accounts of the Oldowan industry are provided by Toth (1985) and Schick & Toth (1993), while Potts (1988) summarizes the archaeology of Bed I. Isaac (1984) provides a summary of other site complexes in East Africa, such as Koobi Fora. With regards to the interpretation of animal bones associated with these stone tools see Binford (1981, 1985, 1986), Bunn (1981, 1983a, 1983b), Bunn & Kroll (1986), Potts (1988) and Potts & Shipman (1981). The collected papers of Glynn Isaac (B. Isaac 1989) are essential reading for an understanding of the archaeology of Act 2. Useful papers concerning the environmental context of early hominids are those by Cerling (1992) and Sikes (1994). Claims for 2-million-year-old stone tools in Pakistan have been made by Dennell *et al* (1988a,b).

The archaeology of Act 3

The earliest use of bifacial technology is described by Leakey (1971) while Asfaw *et al*

(1992) provide dates for the first handaxes. For a general review of the dispersal of early humans into Asia and Europe see Gamble (1993, 1994). Bar-Yosef (1994a) describes the site of Dmanisi, while the earliest sites in West Asia are described by Bar-Yosef (1980, 1989, 1994a), Bar-Yosef & Goren-Inbar (1993) and Goren-Inbar (1992). For the earliest sites in East Asia see Schick & Zhuan (1993), while Zhoukoudian is summarized by Wu & Lin (1983). The debate about the first colonization of Europe is discussed by Roebroeks & van Kolfschoten (1994), while the early dated artifacts from Atapuerca are briefly described by Parés & Pérez-González (1995). Claims for occupation prior to 1 million years ago are made by Bonifay & Vandermeersch (1991). The site of Boxgrove is described by Roberts (1986), and questions about its date are raised by Bowen & Sykes (1994).

The archaeology of Africa between 1.5 million and 200,000 years ago, the Lower Palaeolithic, is summarized by Isaac (1982) and Phillipson (1985). Particularly important sites are Olorgesailie in Kenya (Isaac 1977; Potts 1989, 1994); Isimila in Tanzania (Howell 1961); Gadeb in Ethiopia (Clark & Kurashina 1979a, 1979b) and Sterkfontein in South Africa (Kuman 1994). For sites in West Asia for this period see Bar-Yosef (1980, 1994a), in East Asia see Schick & Zhuan (1993), and in Southeast Asia see Ayers & Rhee (1984), Bartstra (1982), Sémah et al (1992), Pope (1985, 1989) and Yi & Clark (1985). Early sites in Europe are discussed by Roebroeks et al (1992) and Gamble (1986). Roe (1981) summarizes the sites in Britain while Villa (1983) does likewise for France, focusing on the site of Terra Amata. Other important sites are Pontnewydd Cave in Wales (Green 1984); High Lodge in England (Ashton et al 1992) and La Cotte on Jersey (Callow & Cornford 1986). Sites lacking handaxes are described by Svoboda (1987) and Vértes (1975).

For the period between 200,000 and 50,000 years ago, Clark (1982) outlines the archaeology of Africa, while Allsworth-Jones (1993) provides a useful review of the associations between human species and stone tool industries. Particularly important sites with stratified sequences of material are the Haua Fteah in North Africa (McBurney 1967), Muguruk in Kenya (McBrearty 1988), Kalambo Falls in Zaire (Clark 1969, 1974), Klasies River Mouth in South Africa

(Singer & Wymer 1982; Thackeray 1989) and Border Cave, also in South Africa (Beaumont et al 1978). Reviews for sites of this period in West Asia are provided by Bar-Yosef (1988, 1994b) and Jelenik (1982). Recent work in the important cave site of Kebara is described by Bar-Yosef et al (1992). For Europe, Gamble (1986) and Roebroeks et al (1992) provide a general review, while important studies are those of Laville et al (1980) of the rockshelters from Southwest France, Tuffreau (1992) for sites in North France, Kuhn (1995) for sites in Western Italy and Conrad (1990) for sites in the central Rhine Valley. The archaeology of East Asia for this time period is very poorly known. Schick & Zhuan (1993) and Zhonglong (1992) review the currently known, but often very poorly dated, sites.

The use of marine sediment cores to reconstruct the changing environments of this period is described by Dawson (1992), while important papers are those of Shackleton & Opdyke (1973) and Shackleton (1987). Initial results from the study of ice cores are described by Alley et al (1993), Johnsen et al (1992) and Taylor et al (1993).

The archaeology of Act 4

For the earliest use of red ochre in South Africa see Knight et al (1995), and for bone harpoons dating to earlier than 90,000 years ago see Yellen et al (1995). Roberts et al (1990, 1993, 1994) and Allen (1994) describe the earliest dated sites in Australia, while discussions of the colonization process are provided by Gamble (1993) and Bowdler (1992). Davidson & Noble (1992) discuss the implications of the colonization for cultural capacities, while Bahn (1994) provides dates for the earliest art in Australia. Bowdler (1992) and Brown (1981) examine the varying morphology of the modern humans in Australia while Flood (1983) describes the archaeology of the first Australians. For the colonization of North America see Hoffecker et al (1993), C. Haynes (1980), G. Haynes (1991), Gamble (1993) and Greenberg et al (1986). Larichev et al (1988, 1990, 1992) summarizes the evidence for occupation in northern Siberia. Important sites in the Americas regarding the earliest occupation include Meadowcroft Rockshelter (Adovasio et al 1990), Monte Verde in Chile (Dillehay 1989; Dillehay & Collins 1988) and Pedra Furada in Brazil (Guidon et al 1994; Meltzer et al 1994). Dillehay et al (1992) review the earliest archaeology of South America.

The changes in technology and behaviour at 40,000 years ago in Africa are discussed by Smith (1982), Parkington (1986) and Wadley (1993). The new technology in the Haua Fteah is summarized by Close (1986) while important cultural developments in the Wadi Kubbaniya, such as grinding stones, are described by Wendorf *et al* (1980). The first technological changes happening in West Asia are described by Bar-Yosef (1988, 1994b), Gilead (1991), Gilead & Bar-Yosef (1993) and Olszewski & Dibble (1994). With regard to East Asia, Bednarik & Yuzhu (1991) and Aikens & Higuchi (1982) describe the earliest pieces of art while Zhonglong (1992) and Reynolds & Barnes (1984) describe changes in stone tools. Anderson (1990) and Groube *et al* (1986) describe the first known archaeological sites in Southeast Asia.

Important summaries for the cultural changes in Europe after 40,000 years ago are provided by Mellars (1973, 1989a, 1989b, 1992), White (1982), Gamble (1986) and Allsworth-Jones (1986). Crucial dating evidence for the spread of modern humans is provided by Hedges *et al* (1994), Bischoff *et al* (1989) and Cabrera & Bischoff (1989). The earliest bone technology is considered by Knecht (1993a, 1993b) and bead technology by White (1989a, 1993a, 1993b). The earliest art is described by Delluc & Delluc (1978) and Hahn (1993), while claims for art in Act 3 are made by Bednarik (1992, 1995) and Marshack (1990). Interpretations of the relationship between Neanderthals and modern humans are considered by Harold (1989) and Mellars (1989a). The art of the last ice age from Europe is described by Bahn & Vertut (1988), while technological developments and adaptations to the last glacial maximum are described by Straus (1991), Jochim (1983) and Gamble & Soffer (1990). For later European prehistory see Barton *et al* (1992) and Cunliffe (1994).

Ch. 3. The architecture of the modern mind (pp. 33–60)

1 Whether or not there is a valid distinction to make here has troubled philosophers for many years; the mind-body problem being one of the major issues of philosophy. Dennett (1991) gives an entertaining introduction to this problem while MacDonald (1992) provides a review of mind-body identity theories. For body-mind concepts in the

ancient world see Hankoff (1980).

2 Our bodies are physiologically adapted to the diet of Pleistocene hunter-gatherers: wild game, nuts, fruit and fresh vegetables. The fact that our diet today (and for much of later prehistory) contrasts with this in terms of the consumption of dairy products, cereals, fatty meat, sugars, oils and alcohol has profound consequences for our health today: heart attacks, strokes, cancers and diabetes are all nutritionally related.

3 Tooby & Cosmides (1992) have reviewed the manner in which most social scientists (they claim) see the mind as a 'tabula rasa', a blank slate, waiting to be filled by the cultural context of development. For instance Clifford Geertz, perhaps the most influential social anthropologist of the 20th century, has written about how the mind is 'desperately dependent upon such extragenetic, outside-the-skin control mechanisms ... for the governing of behaviour' (Geertz 1973, 44). Closely allied with this is what might be interpreted as a denial of human nature: 'humanity is as various in its essence as in its expression' (ibid, 37).

4 The view of the brain as hardware and the mind as software has been expressed by the archaeologist, Colin Renfrew: 'The hardware (directly dependent upon the genetic base) may have changed little over the timespan [of the past 40,000 years] but it is in the software ("culture") that the radical transformations from the hunter-gatherer to the space age have to be understood' (Renfrew 1993, 249).

5 Whether or not computers can be truly creative has been discussed by the cognitive scientist Margaret Boden (1990), who is more sympathetic to the cause of creative computers than I am myself. As with making computers intelligent, it hinges on how the term 'creativity' is defined.

6 The need to reconstruct the cognition of our earliest ancestors was always implicit in Glynn Isaac's work (e.g. 1978, 1981) and was addressed directly in Isaac (1986). Other Palaeolithic archaeologists were more disparaging about both the need and our ability to make cognitive interpretations. For instance, Lewis Binford, perhaps the most influential Palaeolithic archaeologist of the 20th century, condemns attempts at 'palaeopsychology'. Similarly, but much more recently, another highly influential Palaeolithic archaeologist, Clive Gamble, has written that 'stone tools can tell us ... precious little about

intelligence or its potential' (1993, 170). Wynn (1979, 1981, 1989) thought precisely the opposite. In his early work Thomas Wynn clung onto the idea that intelligence is a single, generalized capacity. In his later work (e.g. Wynn 1991, 1993) he has become less ambitious with regard to inferring the mental capacities of early hominids by recognizing that intelligence may be a modular phenomenon. And consequently he now uses the morphological attributes of early stone tools to infer levels of spatial competence rather than overall intelligence.

7 The notion that 'ontogeny recapitulates phylogeny' was originally proposed by Haeckel in the 19th century, although the roots of this idea can be traced back to Aristotle. Gould (1977) is a seminal volume discussing the relationship between phylogeny and ontogeny, while Gould (1981) explains how the notion of recapitulation was used in the 19th and 20th centuries to justify racist and sexist attitudes. With regard to recent work, several psychologists have suggested that the ontogeny of language recapitulates its phylogeny, notably Parker & Gibson (1979). Although there continue to be major disagreements about recapitulation, ontogenetic perspectives are now commonplace in discussions of cognitive evolution. This is amply illustrated by papers in Gibson & Ingold (1993). I will return to the notion of recapitulation in Chapter 4.

8 Piaget published his ideas in a whole stream of books, and they showed a certain degree of development throughout his lifetime. A good starting place is his 1971 book *Biology and Knowledge*. He argued that there were just three 'programs' running in the mind which he referred to as 'assimilation', 'accommodation' and 'equilibration'. The first of these is the manner in which new knowledge becomes integrated with that already in the mind, while the second refers to how existing knowledge is changed to accommodate new knowledge. These are therefore reciprocal processes working in tandem. Equilibration was proposed as a term to describe the mental restructuring that occurs during development. Piaget proposed a stage model of development with mental restructuring marking the start of each new stage. In its simplest form Piaget proposed four stages: sensorimotor intelligence (birth–2 yrs), preoperational intelligence (2–6/7 yrs), concrete operational intelligence (6/7–11 yrs) and formal opera-

tional intelligence after the age of about 12 yrs. During the sensorimotor stage there is an absence of internalized, representational thought which only emerges with preoperational intelligence and allows the development of language. The two forms of operational intelligence involve a series of mental operations that allow, among other things, long-term planning of actions. Formal operational intelligence is particularly concerned with thinking about hypothetical objects and events.

9 Many more psychologists have adopted this Swiss-army-knife view of the mind than I am willing to discuss in my main text. For instance while Gardner (1983) has 'cut the cake' of intelligence into seven pieces, Robert Sternberg (1988) cut it into just three, which he named analytical, creative and practical intelligence. The neurophysiologist Michael Gazzaniga (1985; Gazzaniga & Lerdoux 1978) has argued that the mind is a coalition of bundles of semi-independent agencies, and Khalfa (1994) has written in the introduction to a book entitled *What is Intelligence?* that there are 'many types of intelligence and they cannot be easily compared, let alone rated on a common scale.' The cake of memory has also been sliced up in various ways during the last two decades. One slicing has created working, short-term and long-term memory. Endel Tulving (1983) has cut this cognitive cake into procedural and propositional memories, which approximates to a distinction between knowing about skills and knowing about knowledge. Propositional memory has then been cut again into episodic and semantic memories. The first is involved in the recording and subsequent retrieval of memories of personal happenings and doings, the second is concerned with knowledge of the world that is independent of a person's identity and past.

10 Fodor (1983). A summary and critical discussion of Fodor's book is provided in Fodor (1985).

11 This quote by Fodor is so good it is worth repeating: ' "But look," you might ask, "why do you care about modules so much? You've got tenure; why don't you take off and go sailing?" This is a perfectly reasonable question and one that I often ask myself.... But ... the idea that cognition saturates perception belongs with (and is, indeed, historically connected with) the idea in the philosophy of science that one's observations are comprehensively determined by one's theories; with the idea in anthropology that one's values are comprehensively determined by one's culture; with the idea in sociology that one's epistemic commitments, including especially one's science, are comprehensively determined by one's class affiliations; and with the idea in linguistics that one's metaphysics is comprehensively determined by one's syntax. All these ideas imply a kind of relativistic holism: because perception is saturated with cognition, observation by theory, values by culture, science by class, and metaphysics by language, rational criticism of scientific theories, ethical values, metaphysical worldviews, or whatever can take place only *within* the framework of assumptions that – as a matter of geographical, historical or sociological accident – the interlocutors happen to share. What you can't do is rationally criticize the framework.

The thing is: I hate relativism. I hate relativism more than I hate anything else, excepting, maybe, fibreglass powerboats. More to the point I think that relativism is very probably false. What it overlooks, to put it briefly and crudely, is the fixed structure of human nature.... Well, in cognitive psychology the claim that there is a fixed structure of human nature traditionally takes the form of an insistence on the heterogeneity of cognitive mechanisms and the rigidity of the cognitive architecture that effects their encapsulation. If there are faculties and modules, then not everything affects everything else; not everything is plastic. Whatever the All is, at least there is more than One of it.' (Fodor 1985, 5).

12 Fodor (1985, 4).

13 Fodor (1985, 4).

14 Fodor (1985, 4).

15 Gardner (1983). *Frames of Mind* was also published as a 10th-anniversary edition in 1993 and accompanied by a sequel *Multiple Intelligences: The Theory in Practice* (Gardner 1993).

16 Gardner (1983, 279).

17 Gardner (1983, 279).

18 This was suggested by Gallistel & Cheng (1985) when commenting on Fodor's ideas.

19 In addition to Cosmides and Tooby, other prominent evolutionary psychologists are Steven Pinker (1994) who focuses on the evolution of language and the psychologist David Buss (1994) who researches human mate selection using cross-cultural data.

20 My discussion of Cosmides and Tooby's work draws on Cosmides (1989), Cosmides & Tooby (1987, 1992, 1994) and Tooby & Cosmides (1989, 1992).

21 At the joint meeting of the Royal Society/British Academy entitled 'The evolution of social behaviour patterns in primates and man', London, 4–6 April 1995.

22 The notion of divine intervention is perhaps harder to resist when dealing with the mind than with other parts of the body and person. For instance when describing the evolution of the brain, the Nobel-prize-winning scientist Sir John Eccles decided that it was necessary to invoke supernatural spiritual creation for the qualities of the human mind (Eccles 1989).

23 At the meeting of the 'Human Behavior and Evolution Society', Santa Barbara, 28 June–1 July 1995, John Tooby argued that episodic memory, as defined by Tulving (1983), is fundamentally related to the 'theory of mind' module. Tooby wishes to cut the cake of memory into many thin slices, with each cognitive module having its own independent memory system.

24 Kaplan & Hill (1985) provide evidence for a relationship between hunting ability and reproductive success among modern hunter-gatherers.

25 Tooby & Cosmides (1992, 113).

26 Fodor (1987, 27).

27 For an account of Andrew Wiles' announcement of a proof see *New Scientist* 3 July 1993 and 5 November 1994.

28 Bird-David (1990).

29 Riddington (1982, 471). Also quoted in Ingold (1993, 440).

30 Morphy (1989b) provides a succinct discussion of how the landscape was created by the Ancestral Beings during the Dreamtime. As he describes, the Ancestral past is more appropriately thought of as a dimension of the present and consequently the landscape is not simply a record of past mythological events but plays an active role in creating those events.

31 Saladin D'Anglure (1990, 187). This work discusses the complex and often ambiguous conception of the polar bear by the Inuit. The Inuit draw parallels between humans and the polar bear due to similarities in behaviour: the bear stands on two legs, constructs winter shelters, travels across land and sea, and hunts seals using similar tactics to those of the hunters. The bear plays a central role in many of the rituals during the growing up of an Inuit boy and is associated

with masculine sexual powers. For instance killing one's first bear is a sign of adult virility and sterile women eat polar bear penises.

32 Willis (1990) provides a review of changing definitions and interpretations of totemism in the introduction to his edited volume about human meaning in the natural world. As he describes, Lévi-Strauss raised the whole level of the totemic debate to a level of generality about universal human thought processes by the publication in 1962 of his two major works, *Le Totémisme Aujourd'hui* and *La Pensée Sauvage* (The Savage Mind). Douglas (1990, 35) characterizes Lévi-Strauss' views as the practice of humanity brooding on itself and place in nature.

33 Ingold (1992, 42).

34 Gellner (1988, 45) emphasizes that the seemingly absurd associations that are made in the thought and language of non-Western traditional societies, reflect a complex and sophisticated cognition which serves to accomplish many ends at once. It is the 'single strandedness, the neat and logical division of labour, the separation of functions' that is characteristic of modern Western society which is the anomaly and which needs explaining. Ingold (1993) makes a very similar argument to Gellner, by suggesting that the cognitive separation between 'nature', 'society' and 'technology' is a product of Western thought. Modern hunter-gatherers make no such distinctions and exhibit unrestrained cognitive fluidity. The issue that neither Ingold nor Gellner addresses and which is central to this book is that this may not have been the case for pre-modern hunter-gatherers.

35 For instance, in the case of the polar bear and the Inuit referred to above, the bear is strongly associated with male strength. By associating themselves with the polar bear, the Inuit males use the bear as a potent ideological tool to consolidate their domination of women. Saladin D'Anglure (1990).

36 Whitelaw (1991) has made a detailed cross-cultural study of the use of space in hunter-gatherer camps, demonstrating how community layout maps kinship relations, and how space is an active medium for social interaction. To quote him: 'spatial organization is used by different individuals and in different cultures to generate, amplify, facilitate, manipulate and control social interaction and organization' (1991, 181).

37 To quote the social anthropologist Andrew Strathern: 'what people wear, and what they do to and with their bodies in general, forms an important part of the flow of information – establishing, modifying and commenting on major social categories, such as age, sex and status' (quoted in White 1992, 539–40). Similarly, Turner stated that 'the surface of the body ... becomes the symbolic stage upon which the drama of socialization is enacted, and bodily adornment ... becomes the language through which it is expressed' (quoted in White 1992, 539).

38 The tools of modern humans display very effective designs for their functional tasks (e.g. Oswalt 1976; Torrence 1983; Bleed 1986; Churchill 1993). But at the same time these tools are used in conducting social relationships. Polly Wiessner (1983) has documented this for the arrows of the Kalahari San. While these are very effective hunting weapons, the shapes of the arrow heads carry information about group affiliation. Their use in hunting the eland, an animal central to San mythology, results in the arrows also having considerable symbolic significance.

39 Whiten & Perner (1991). See also Gopnik & Wellman (1994), Whiten (1991) and Wellman (1991).

40 For the relationship between autism and the impairment of the theory of mind module see Leslie (1991, 1994), Frith (1989) and Baron-Cohen (1995). These works describe how other aspects of cognition may be left unaffected. Some autistic children appear to have prodigious talents in the fields of art, music or mathematics. For an account of these see Sacks (1995), particularly the essay within that volume entitled 'Prodigies'. A remarkable case of an *idiot savant* is described by Smith & Tsimpli (1995). This is a man known as Christopher who at the age of 35 has an IQ of between 40 and 70 (human average is 100) and who fails tests set for five year olds. He has to live in sheltered accommodation because he cannot look after himself. Yet Christopher can speak more than 15 languages in addition to his native English.

41 Humphrey (1976). His ideas have also been elaborated in Humphrey (1984, 1993).

42 Atran (1990, 1994).

43 Keil (1994) and Atran (1994).

44 Atran (1990).

45 Berlin (1992; Berlin *et al* 1973) and Atran (1994).

46 Sacks (1995, 269). Other examples are described in Atran (1990).

47 Mithen (1990, 52–88) reviews the methods by which modern hunter-gatherers gath-

er information from their environments, and how this information is used in decision making. Particularly useful ethnographic accounts, which include examples of the extensive and detailed natural history knowledge that hunter-gatherers rely upon, are as follows: !Kung (Lee 1976, 1979; Lee & DeVore 1976; Marshall 1976; Blurton-Jones & Konner 1976), G/Wi (Silberbauer 1981), Valley Bisa (Marks 1976), Ache (Hill & Hawkes 1983), Mistassini Cree (Tanner 1979; Winterhalder 1981), Koyukon (Nelson 1983), Kutchin (Nelson 1973), Ten'a (Sullivan 1942), Nuñamiut (Gubser 1965; Binford 1978), Groote Eylandt Islanders (Levitt 1981), Gidjingali (Meehan 1982), Tiwi (Goodale 1971) and Canadian Indians (Jennes 1977).
48 Spelke (1991; Spelke *et al* 1992). See also Pinker (1994, 423–24).
49 Atran (1990, 57).
50 Kennedy (1992) argues that people are prone to a compulsive anthropomorphizing. The idea that animals are conscious and have purpose appears to be built into us by nature. He does not discuss what appears to be a similar compulsiveness for children to attribute minds to inert physical objects.
51 Greenfield (1991). See also Lock (1993). There is, however, considerable disagreement on this issue and intuitive knowledge systems may be present and working in the mind from birth.
52 Karmiloff-Smith (1992). A summary of her book and a critical discussion of the ideas are found in Karmiloff-Smith (1994).
53 Karmiloff-Smith (1994, 695).
54 Geary (1995) uses the term 'primary biological abilities', rather than intuitive knowledge, to refer to those abilities which are hard-wired into the brain as a consequence of our evolutionary history. He argues that the kick start to the development of mathematical knowledge is a pan-human capacity for counting. This provides a set of 'skeletal principles' that guide counting behaviour before children have acquired the use of number words.
55 Karmiloff-Smith (1994, 701, 706). It is important to note that Karmiloff-Smith's model for mental development is not a simple stage model. She believes that there are two distinct parallel processes happening at the same time: 'one of progressive modularization, the other of progressive explicitness of knowledge representations' (1994, 733).
56 Carey & Spelke (1994, 184). The precise

similarities and differences between the ideas of Carey and Spelke and Karmiloff-Smith have yet to be explored. Carey and Spelke draw interesting comparisons between conceptual change in the history of science and during child development arguing for similarities in how children and scientists construct mappings across different knowledge domains.
57 Boden (1990). A summary and critical discussion of Boden's ideas are found in Boden (1994).
58 Koestler, quoted in Boden (1990).
59 Rozin (1976); Rozin & Schull (1988).
60 Rozin (1976, 262).
61 Sperber (1994).

Ch. 4. A new proposal for the mind's evolution (pp. 61–72)
1 The excavation and phasing of the South Church are described in Hodges & Mithen (1993).
2 Quoted in Gould (1977, 76).
3 Gould (1977, 116).
4 Gibson (editorial, p. 276 in Gibson & Ingold 1993).
5 Lock (1993).
6 As the psychologist Daniel Povinelli stated in 1993 regarding the evolution of a theory of mind, 'comparing the ontogeny of psychological capacities should allow evolutionary psychologists to reconstruct the order in which particular features of mental state attribution evolved' (Povinelli 1993, 506). This is precisely my aim in this chapter – although my intention is to do this with regard to the mind in general.
7 Gould (1981, 115).
8 Lock (1993) argues that the use of ontogenetic information for developing hypothetical scenarios for evolution to be tested by other data is an appropriate method of research.
9 I must stress here that Karmiloff-Smith does not separate progressive modularization of the mind and 'representational redescription' into two consecutive processes; she argues that these happen in parallel with each other. However, a time lag is implied between them as knowledge has to become part of a specialized module, before becoming explicitly represented and applicable between domains.
10 Natural selection is unlikely to have done all the shaping by itself. There were other evolutionary processes at work, such as genetic drift and founder effects, which may

have also played a significant role in the continual tinkering. The relative importance of natural selection is a matter of considerable debate among evolutionary biologists.

11 The significance of throwing for the evolution of the mind has been explored by Calvin (1983, 1993).

Ch. 5. Apes, monkeys and the mind of the missing link (pp. 73–94)

1 Examples of the use of the chimpanzee as an analogy for early human ancestors are McGrew (1992) and Falk (1992). Byrne (1995, 27–30) explains how a better approach is to reconstruct the behaviour and cognition of our ancestors by using the methods of cladistics.

2 Goodall's work is summarized in her two books (Goodall 1986, 1990).

3 Twenty years after Goodall first recognized tool use by chimpanzees Christophe and Hedwige Boesch in West Africa have been extending the observed repertoire of chimpanzee tool use by describing the use of anvils and hammerstone to crack nuts in the Tai forest (e.g. 1983, 1984a, 1984b, 1990, 1993). There have also been a large number of studies of chimpanzee technology undertaken by Bill McGrew and his colleagues, culminating in his book entitled *Chimpanzee Material Culture* published in 1992. Together with studies by other primatologists such as Sugiyama (1993) and Matsuzawa (1991) a very substantial database concerning chimpanzee tool use has been created, which, as McGrew argues, has considerable implications for human evolution – although quite what those implications are remains contentious.

4 McGrew (1992).

5 Boesch & Boesch (1993) explain that just seven types of actions are used for making the whole repertoire of chimpanzee tools: (1) detaching a leafy twig or branch from a plant to use as a stick; (2) cutting a stick to a specific length with teeth or hands; (3) removing the bark or leaves from a stick with teeth or hands; (4) sharpening the end of a stick using teeth; (5) modifying the length of a stick (after initial use) with teeth or hands; (6) breaking a branch or stone in two by hitting it on a hard surface to make a hammer; (7) breaking a branch in two by pulling while standing on it to make a hammer. There have been no observations of intentional flaking of stone. Among the Tai chimpanzees the first four actions are often used in succession

while 83% of the observed modifications to sticks involved the first three.

6 Matsuzawa (1991).

7 Nishida (1987), Boesch & Boesch (1990) and McGrew (1992).

8 The processes of social learning have been the subject of much discussion in recent literature about primates, e.g. Clayton (1978), Galef (1988, 1990), Whiten (1989), Visalberghi & Fragaszy (1990), Tomasello *et al* (1987, 1993), Tomasello (1990) and Byrne (1995). In addition to imitation, social learning might involve the processes of stimulus enhancement and response facilitation. Stimulus enhancement is the process in which an animal's interest in objects may be stimulated simply by the activities of another. The actual process of learning to use the objects as tools may follow on a trial-and-error basis. Another social learning process is response facilitation in which the presence of a conspecific performing an action increases the likelihood that another animal seeing it will do the same. A critical difference between this and imitation is that for the latter it is normally supposed that the action must be new to the animal, whereas response facilitation evokes actions that already existed in the animal's behavioural repertoire. Many primatologists now believe that monkeys never imitate, and some extend this to chimpanzees especially when they are in wild situations. Even if imitation is present among chimpanzees it seems to be at a markedly lower intensity than in modern humans. Yet these types of social learning are likely to be the primary processes by which tool use diffuses within chimpanzee populations.

9 For example, McGrew (1992, 186–7), Byrne (1995, 86–8).

10 Boesch (1991, 1993).

11 Wrangham (1977).

12 Menzel (1973, 1978).

13 Boesch & Boesch (1984a)

14 Katherine Milton has proposed that the greatest environmental challenges are faced by those primates which rely on fruit because this resource is the most widely dispersed in space and time (Milton 1988). Primates must solve the problem of remembering the location of fruit trees, and exploiting the fruit at the appropriate time in its ripening cycle. This, she argued, would have created a selective pressure for greater intelligence and she suggested that there is indeed a correlation between brain size and diet among the primates. Similarly Kathleen Gibson has stressed the selective pressures on cognition that 'omnivorous extractive foraging' would create (Gibson 1986, 1990). By this she refers to the practice of removing food from various types of matrices – kernels from nut shells, ants from mounds, eggs from shells. These foodstuffs, which come encased in an inedible layer, are typically high in energy and protein. They are often available during the dry season, when other resources may be scarce. They are, however, difficult to exploit, requiring either very specialized anatomical adaptations or the use of tools and an intelligence that can conceive of 'hidden' food sources.

Robin Dunbar has since shown that the correlations between brain size and foraging patterns are likely to be spurious (Dunbar 1992), while McGrew has dismissed the idea that there is a clear relationship between the use of tools and brain size (McGrew 1992). Moreover, Cheney and Seyfarth have pointed out that when we look at animals in general, rather than just primates, diet, foraging behaviour and brain size vary widely with no clear correlations (Cheney & Seyfarth 1990). In addition, they point to the difficulty in making a distinction between ecological and social pressures. Primates use social strategies to cope with environmental complexity. Patchy and irregular food supplies provide selective pressures for greater cooperation in foraging, abilities to detect cheaters in food sharing and for communication about resource distribution. Group size among primates, for instance, which is Dunbar's measure of social complexity, is strongly related to predator risk and food availability (Dunbar 1988).

15 Consider, for instance, the little bird known as Clark's nutcracker. This small bird has a brain weighing less than 10g, but each winter hides more than 30,000 seeds for winter stores. Not only does it hide them, but it regularly finds at least half of the hidden nuts. Laboratory studies have shown that this bird has a prodigious spatial memory, far greater than that of humans (Mackintosh 1994).

16 Boesch & Boesch (1989).

17 Cheney & Seyfarth (1990) undertook an extensive series of experiments to explore the types of clues from which vervet monkeys could infer information, focusing on clues which one would expect to be of significance for the monkeys. For instance one of the species feared by vervet monkeys are

humans, in the form of the local Maasai people who herd cattle and goats. The monkeys tend to give a human alarm call and then flee whenever Maasai appear. Can the monkeys use the approach of cows to infer the approach of the Maasai? Cheney and Seyfarth used hidden loud speakers to play the lowing of cows. They found a positive reaction. Although cows offer no threat to the monkeys, they reacted to the lowing as if they were hearing the Maasai themselves, indicating that they have a mental association between these two species. The monkeys' reacted in a similar fashion when the ringing of bells was played, another sound associated with approaching Maasai. Consequently the monkeys appeared adept at using such secondary auditory clues and mental associations to infer approaching danger.

Conversely however, when the secondary clues are visual rather than auditory the monkeys appear to be much less 'intelligent'. For instance they do not react to the distinctive dust clouds created by the approach of Maasai with their cows, and only flee when the cows and people emerge. The monkeys difficulty with visual clues was explored in a series of experiments using a stuffed gazelle carcass placed in a tree to mimic a leopard kill. Leopards are one of the major predators of the monkeys and normally remain in the close vicinity of their recent kills. The carcass was placed in a tree during the night so that it would be readily visible to the monkeys the next morning. Yet they ignored it and undertook their normal activities as if the carcass was simply not there.

Similarly the monkeys appear not to understand the implications of fresh python tracks. Pythons are another major predator of monkeys and they leave distinctive trails in the sand. Cheney and Seyfarth observed that when monkeys approach such tracks they show no increase in vigilance or any change of behaviour. Indeed, they watched monkeys follow such tracks to bushes and then become shocked when they stumbled upon a python!

18 It is likely that humans are the only primate able to draw inferences from visual clues which are displaced from their referent e.g. footprints (Davidson & Noble 1989; Hewes 1986, 1989).

19 Byrne & Whiten (1988).

20 Byrne & Whiten (1988, editorial p. 4).

21 de Waal (1982).

22 Byrne & Whiten (1991, 1992), Byrne

(1995, 124–40). Heyes (1993) provides an important critical review of studies such as those drawing on anecdotal data by Byrne and Whiten which purport to demonstrate a 'theory of mind' in non-human primates.

23 Premack & Woodruff (1978), Premack (1988).

24 Humphrey describes his ideas in two very readable short books (Humphrey 1984, 1993 (originally published 1986)). In his more recent work (Humphrey 1992) he deals with consciousness as raw sensation rather than what he describes as the second order mental faculties 'thoughts about feelings' and 'thoughts about thoughts'. It is this type of consciousness, however, that remains my interest when dealing with the evolution of the human mind.

25 Gardner *et al* (1989).

26 Premack & Premack (1972).

27 Savage-Rumbaugh & Rumbaugh (1993).

28 Terrace (1979), Terrace *et al* (1979).

29 Greenfield & Savage-Rumbaugh (1990), Savage-Rumbaugh & Rumbaugh (1993). Sue Savage Rumbaugh argues that the small size and other morphological traits of the bonobo make it a better model for the common pongid/hominid ancestor than the common chimpanzee. Kanzi was born in captivity in 1980 to Matata, who had been caught in the wild. Matata never performed well on language tasks, although her social skills were excellent.

30 Pinker (1994, 151).

31 Marler (1970).

32 The cerebral cortex is the outer layer of the cerebral hemispheres referred to as 'grey matter', comprising layers of nerve cells and their interconnections which are thrown into a series of folds and troughs. In contrast, the vocal calls of primates are controlled by neural processes in the brain stem (the part of the brain connecting the cerebral hemispheres to the spinal cord) and limbic systems (the nerve pathways and networks within the temporal lobes of the cerebral hemispheres) (Marler 1970).

33 Alex is an African Grey parrot who exhibits cognitive capacities that appear to be analogous (though not homologous) to those of primates and humans. Alex has been a good subject to explore inter-species cognitive similarities since he has learnt to speak and hence one of the major constraints on exploring primate minds can partly be overcome. Pepperberg (1990) provides a review of her studies of Alex and their implications.

34 Boesch & Boesch (1983).

35 Boesch & Boesch (1989).

36 This episode of Kate's tool use was described by Brewer & McGrew (1990). She first used a stout chisel and then a finer chisel to make an indentation in the nest. A sharp pointed stick was then used to puncture the nest wall and finally a longer, flexible stick was used to dip for honey. Overall, Kate appears to have sequentially used a set of tools each appropriate for a specific task. McGrew feels justified in describing these as a toolkit.

37 Boesch (1991, 1993).

38 Boesch & Boesch (1989).

39 Boesch & Boesch (1989, 569).

40 Byrne (1995).

41 Cheney & Seyfarth (1988, 1990).

42 While monkeys appear unable to recognize themselves in mirrors, they are able to learn to use mirrors, such as to see if another monkey is around the corner (Byrne 1995).

43 Byrne & Whiten (1992).

Ch. 6. The mind of the first stone toolmaker (pp. 95–114)

1 When discussing Oldowan technology, it is more appropriate to use the term 'artifact' than 'tool'. When archaeologists find these Oldowan flakes and cores it is not clear whether they are the pieces thrown away during manufacture (like the leaves from a twig when stripping it for a termite stick) or those pieces kept for some task or other. It is not even clear that the actors themselves had any idea of this division between 'waste' and 'tools'. So archaeologists, being cautious creatures, use a neutral term, artifacts. Potts (1988, table 8.6) provides data on frequency of raw material use by weight and number of artifacts at four sites from Bed I, Olduvai: DK, FLKNN-3, FLK 'Zinj' and FLK North-6. At FLK 'Zinj' 90.2% of artifacts are made from quartzite, although as these are small they constitute only 27.6% of the total weight of the assemblage. Artifacts made from vesicular basalt, on the other hand, compose only 4.7% of the total number of artifacts, but 44.7% of the total weight. DK is notable for having a relatively high frequency of nephelinite (a type of lava) in terms of artifact numbers (22.7%) and weight (12.6%). Chert, gneiss and feldspar never reach more than 0.2% of an assemblage by number or weight, except at FLK North-6 where 1.6% of the artifacts are made from chert.

2 Wynn & McGrew (1989).

3 Traces of 'polish' from woodworking have been found on the edges of 1.5-million-year-old artifacts from Koobi Fora (Keeley & Toth 1981). The possible functions of Oldowan artifacts have been discussed by Schick & Toth (1993, 150–86).

4 Schick & Toth (1993, 118–22) summarize the manufacturing techniques of Oldowan stone tools.

5 Toth *et al* (1993). The basic format of the experiment involved placing a desired object within a box with a transparent lid which could only be opened by cutting a cord. Kanzi was shown how stone flakes could be produced from nodules and used for this purpose. At first he was simply provided with flakes to cut the cord, but then he was given nodules and had to produce the flakes himself. During these experiments Kanzi employed two basic techniques for producing flakes: hard hammer percussion involving striking two rocks against each other; and throwing rocks so that they shattered. In both of these some degree of improvement could be observed, but the resulting artifacts consistently remained very different from those of the Oldowan. Toth & Schick (1993, 351) note that the argument that chimpanzees may be constrained from modifying stones in an Oldowan manner due to a lack of motor skills seems implausible, since they have shown abilities to tie shoelaces and unbutton shirts. Westergaard (1995) describes the stone-flaking abilities of capuchin monkeys. These appear similar to Kanzi's and significantly different to those of Oldowan hominids.

6 Lokalalei (GaJh 5) has an age slightly younger than 2.36 ± 0.04 million years ago and was excavated in 1991. The artifacts are in a fresh condition and made from a medium-grained lava which has good conchoidal fracture. These, together with the geological context of the site and faunal assemblage, are described by Kibunjia (1994).

7 Toth (1985) undertook thousands of replication experiments to explore this. He demonstrates how in the Koobi Fora region the variation in artifact form across the landscape can be explained by the variation in raw material characteristics and availability. See also Potts (1988, 235–37).

8 This can be seen at Sterkfontein where an introduction of new types of raw materials occurs with the Acheulian in a stratified sequence of assemblages (Kuman 1994).

9 Direct evidence for the use of stone tools in processing carcasses comes from cutmarks on animal bones (Bunn 1981; Potts & Shipman 1981) and wear patterns on stone tools (Keeley & Toth 1981). Indirect evidence comes from the regular association of stone artifacts and animal bones on archaeological sites, and the effectiveness of stone artifacts at processing carcasses in experimental work (Schick & Toth 1993).

10 The HAS site is found in 1.6-million-year-old sediments in the Koobi Fora region. Amongst the hippopotamus bones were 119 chipped stones and a pebble which had been used as a hammerstone (Isaac 1978).

11 Potts (1988) summarizes the archaeology at FLK 22, together with the other sites from Bed I at Olduvai Gorge.

12 Isaac was one of the most significant Palaeolithic archaeologists of the 20th century on the basis of his contributions to the discovery and excavation of new sites, analytical methods and theory. He tragically died in 1983 at the pinnacle of his career as a professor at Harvard. His contribution to the discipline can be appreciated from his collected papers, edited by his wife (B. Isaac 1989).

13 Isaac's home base model was most clearly set out in his 1978 paper in *Scientific American* entitled 'The food sharing behaviour of proto-human hominids'. Potts (1988) provides an excellent summary and critique of the model.

14 Binford (1981)

15 The debate concerning the prevalence of hunting, primary scavenging (i.e. scavenging from a recently killed carcass which provides an equivalent amount of meat to that of an animal which had been hunted) and marginal scavenging partly arose out of, and partly stimulated, a remarkable advance in the methods archaeologists use to interpret their materials, especially animal bones. These included microscopic analysis of gnawing, tooth and cutmarks on bones, the analysis of body part representation and inferences about the extent of bone weathering. All these advances were reliant upon programmes of ethnoarchaeological and actualistic studies concerning the processes of site formation. These debates were marred, however, by the failure of the participants even to agree on the contents of the archaeological record, let alone its interpretation. One theme was the implications of stone tool cutmarks on bones in terms of their temporal relationships to carnivore gnawmarks, their frequency and the type of butchery they implied. Body part representation was also intensely debated since this may provide a means to differentiate between marginal scavenging and hunting. Only with the latter would one expect to find the major meat-bearing bones on a site, although primary scavenging in which a hominid has access to a freshly killed carcass is likely to result in a similar body-part signature. Major papers in this dispute include: Binford (1984b, 1985, 1986, 1988), Binford *et al* (1988), Bunn (1981, 1983a, 1983b, 1994), Bunn & Kroll (1986), Isaac (1983a, 1983b), Kroll (1994), Kroll & Isaac (1984), Oliver (1994), Potts & Shipman (1981) and Shipman (1983, 1986).

16 This is most extensively described in Binford (1984a).

17 The 'stone cache' hypothesis is described in Potts (1988). Minimization of search time for sharp flakes to be used for entering/butchering the carcass would have been essential due to the high level of predator risk faced by the hominids. (See note 25.)

18 This was largely based on actualistic studies identifying the most feasible scavenging niche for early hominids (Blumenschine 1986, 1987; Blumenschine *et al* 1994).

19 Stern (1993, 1994) has stressed the difficulties of landscape archaeology in East Africa. She describes the inverse relationship between the area of an ancient landscape being sampled, the quantity of archaeological data available for study and the amount of time represented by that debris and the encasing sediments (1994, 89). As an example she uses the archaeological sites of the lower Okote member of Koobi Fora for which the finest time resolution is 65 ± 5 k.y.a. Consequently ethnographic scale observations of the interactions between individuals and their environment across the landscape can only be made by ignoring this time dimension of the data.

20 Potts (1988, 308). The likely diversity of hominid lifestyles has been noted by Potts (1994) and Blumenschine *et al* (1994). The latter suggest that variability in hominid ecology would have been largely due to variability in competition from carnivores for animal tissues.

21 A major difficulty with the interpretation of this material is that the exploitation of carcasses is practically the only evidence we have for hominid subsistence. We have little idea of the relative importance of meat in the hominid diet in relation to plant foods. Research on the likely contribution of plant foods to the hominid diet takes the form of actualistic studies in modern African environments which consider the availability of possible plant foods, and the costs and benefits of exploiting them (e.g. Hatley & Kappelman 1980; Sept 1994).

22 Aiello & Wheeler (1995). They find a correlation between gut size and brain size among primates in general. Organs such as the heart and liver cannot be reduced in size to compensate for the metabolic requirements, as they are physiologically constrained. The relatively large brains of australopithecines as compared to those of non-human primates suggest that they were consuming a range of high-quality plant foods, such as underground tubers.

23 See Blumenschine (1986). This has been explored using sophisticated computer simulation modelling by Lake (1995).

24 Several archaeologists have stressed the importance of stone transport. The identification of this at Olduvai was made possible by the geological studies of Hay (1976) which located the raw material sources. For Isaac (1978), stone transport was a further reason for building his home base hypothesis. Binford (1989) has argued that it was predominantly the core tools which were transported across the landscape, as these are not normally found with their manufacturing debris. Toth (1985) has devised a methodology for inferring artifact transport which relies on replicated assemblages and the frequencies of different artifact types in complete assemblages, as employed at FxJj50. The small spatial scale of such transport activity is indicated by the sites of FxJj and FeJj in East Turkana. These were occupied at *c*. 1.8 m.y.a. and are only 25 km apart. The lithic remains at each site are made only from the locally available raw material, lava at FxJj and quartz at FeJj (Rogers *et al* 1994, 151).

25 Richard Potts suggested that one reason for transporting stone nodules and artifacts was to create caches. Such caches would have allowed rapid access to stone artifacts/raw materials when they were needed to exploit a carcass. Using time efficiently may have been essential for survival in a predator-rich environment. This remains one of the most plausible explanations for the accumulations of artifacts, especially manuports (unmodified nodules) and faunal remains as specific points in the landscape. It remains unclear, however, whether hominids were intentionally creating such caches, or simply using those unintentionally created during previous carcass butchery. If they were being created, then this would provide further evidence for predicting and planning for future resource distributions. The stone cache hypothesis has been described in most detail in Potts (1988) where he demonstrates the functional benefit of creating caches with simple computer models. (See note 17.)

26 There are two examples of possible evidence for movement out of Africa by a hominid prior to *Homo erectus*. First, claimed artifacts from Riwat in Pakistan dating to 2 m.y.a. (Dennell *et al* 1988a, 1988b). I suspect these are natural 'artifacts', although Dennell provides a challenging defence that they were produced by early *Homo*. Second, hominid dental fragments from Longgupo Cave, China (Wanpo *et al* 1995). These have been dated to 1.9 m.y.a. and possibly belong to early *H. erectus*. However, they appear to possess some primitive features and the possibility remains that they are *H. ergaster* (a species I am including within the broad category of *H. habilis* and which is most likely directly ancestral to *H. erectus*). If so, this implies that *H. ergaster* may have dispersed out of Africa, and *H. erectus* evolved within Asia, to then return to Europe and Africa. But there is no consensus on the taxonomic identification of these hominid remains; indeed some even doubt that they are hominid at all. The range of different interpretations are discussed in Wood & Turner (1995) and Culotta (1995).

27 An attempt systematically to compare landuse before and after 1.6 m.y.a. has been made by Jack Harris and colleagues for the East Lake Turkana region (Rogers, Harris & Feibel 1994). They compared the distribution of settlement at three successive time intervals, 2.3 m.y.a., 1.9–1.8 m.y.a. and 1.7–1.5 m.y.a. and attribute the more diverse location of archaeological sites in the third of these to the wider ranging behaviour of *H. erectus*. They concluded that only after this date were more diverse types of environmental settings used and activities detached for the first time from landscape features, such as raw material sources and shade trees. In the period before 1.6 m.y.a. archaeological sites were 'tied' to the edges of permanent water sources where cobbles were available

in gravels. After this date, sites were found in floodplain locations, some distance from both permanent water and raw materials. The early hominids appear to have been more constrained than the early humans by the distribution of natural resources. A similar conclusion was reached by Richard Potts (1994) when he compared the archaeology of Bed I at Olduvai (1.8–1.7 m.y.a.) and Member I at Olorgesailie dating to 0.9 m.y.a.

28 See Leakey (1971) and Potts (1988, 1994). For instance the MNK main occupation in Bed II at Olduvai has six main archaeological layers in 1.5 m (5 ft) of sediment. Binford (1987a) has argued that sites such as these are in fact no different in terms of past behaviour than the dense concentration of artifacts and bone fragments found at discrete vertical levels, such as FLK 'Zinj'. The contrast simply reflects the rate at which sediments are accumulating, and consequently whether one ends up with a palimpsest or a vertically diffuse artifact distribution. Even when we do not have this stacking of sites through deep sedimentary layers, the evidence from bone weathering indicates that the 'living floor' assemblages accumulated over several years (Potts 1986; Behrensmeyer 1978).

29 This was the basic feature of the faunal assemblages that led Isaac to develop his home base hypothesis, for it implies the transport of animal body parts between micro-environments. Plummer & Bishop (1994) have suggested that the morphological variability in bovid metapoidals from Olduvai Bed I sites indicates that the Olduvai hominids were utilizing habitats ranging from open to closed, perhaps the full range in the lake margin zone. Blumenschine (1986, 1987) suggested that river-side woodland provided the optimal scavenging region. Sikes (1994) has used the stable isotope composition of paleosols from early hominid sites to estimate the original proportion of grasses (C_4) to woody (C_3) vegetation, finding the latter to be dominant. She concluded that Plio-Pleistocene hominids in East Africa may have preferred relatively closed, woodland habitats that may have offered shade, food and predator refuge. More generally Cerling (1992) has argued that open grasslands with >90% C_4 biomass did not become established in East Africa until around 1.0 m.y.a. Nevertheless, the diversity of animal species in faunal assemblages indicates that early *Homo* was foraging in a variety of environments, including open savannah conditions.

30 Testing for a relationship between brain size and measures of social complexity is by no means easy. The difficulty is that brain size is itself extremely difficult to measure in a meaningful fashion for inter-species comparison (e.g. see Jerison 1973; Clutton-Brock & Harvey 1980; Deacon 1990; Dunbar 1992). While larger animals have larger brains to cope with increased sensory and motor demands, brain size does not increase in a simple linear fashion with body size. One must also take into account differences in diet. A primate that is dependent upon eating leaves requires a larger gut and consequently has a larger body size, although no expansion in brain capacity is needed. In contrast primates who live on fruit tend to have a smaller body size as only a short gut is required. These complexities have led to various different measures of brain size being used in comparative studies. These rely on measures of allometric scaling which take into account body size effects and produce linear correlations between brain and body size. When such correlations are produced for either primates or mammals in general, one can inspect the residuals from the regression line for each species. Large positive residuals mark species out as having a relatively larger brain than one would expect for an animal of that size. For primates, the strepsirhines (lemurs) have the sort of brain sizes one would expect for their body size, while monkeys and apes have brain sizes almost twice as large as expected. The brain size of humans is very substantially larger than expected.

Of the brain size measures that have been used, that of the ratio of neocortex volume to the rest of the brain has been one of the most robust in face of the critical discussion surrounding this area. Robin Dunbar explored the correlation between neocortex ratio and factors that relate to the foraging and mobility behaviour of non-human primates, notably range area, day journey length and the amount of fruit in the diet (Dunbar 1992). A correlation here would suggest that the selective pressure for brain enlargement (used as a proxy measure for intelligence) was environmental complexity. Yet no correlations were found. In contrast, the neocortex ratio was correlated with mean group size of primates. Group size may be a reflection of social complexity as it reflects the number of animals an individual needs to

monitor and take account of when making behaviour decisions. This has been, therefore, an explicit test of the Machiavellian hypothesis, with a positive result.

31 As his measure of social complexity Byrne used the extent of tactical deception. By drawing on the reports of tactical deception in a range of primate species, he also found a strong positive correlation between its frequency and neocortex ratio. This supports the idea that the selective pressure for brain enlargement during hominoid evolution has been the social environment (Byrne 1995; see also Byrne & Whiten 1985, 1991, 1992).

32 For studies of group size see Clutton-Brock & Harvey (1977), van Schaik (1983), Foley (1987), Wrangham (1987), Dunbar (1988), Chapman (1990) and Isbell et al (1991). There have been very few explicit tests of the relative importance of predator risk and resource patchiness to group size because of the inherent problems of measuring such variables (Wrangham 1987). Any particular group size is likely to derive from a range of ecological, evolutionary and historical factors (Wrangham 1987; Dunbar 1988). Moreover, the idea that 'group size' is a useful social variable can be questioned. More profitable research is likely to derive from considering specific types of groups, such as feeding or reproductive groups, and taking account of the different social strategies employed by each sex (Cheney et al 1987). Yet due to the resolution of the archaeological record, prehistorians appear to be forced to consider group size as a coarse-grained social variable.

33 For instance, the cranium from Swartkrans known as SK54 of an australopithecine child has two holes which were probably caused by the lower canines of a leopard as it grasped the child within its jaws (Brain 1981). Brain suggests that early hominids would have been preyed on by a range of large carnivores. It has also been suggested that the juvenile australopithecine represented by the skull from Taung had once been the prey of an eagle which had swooped down to steal it from its mother, as they are observed to do today with monkeys (*New Scientist* 9 September 1995, p. 7).

34 Jones et al (1992).

35 Lake (1995).

36 Dennett (1988).

37 Dennett (1988, 185–86).

38 Dibble (1989) reviews the various attempts to make inferences about linguistic capacities from stone artifacts.

39 The significance of Broca's and Wernicke's area for language have been discussed in several recent publications concerned with the evolution of the brain and language (e.g. Corballis 1991, 1992; Donald 1991; Falk 1983, 1990, 1992; Pinker 1994), but there remains some confusion about their function. After a lengthy description of the possible roles of Broca's and Wernicke's area for language, Steven Pinker recently concluded that 'to be honest no one really knows what either Broca's or Wernicke's area is for' (1994, 311).

40 These are referred to as endocasts. Some are created naturally as brain cases become filled with fine-grained sediment that turns to stone as the brain case decays, leaving a copy of the contours of the inside of the brain case. Others are made artificially by using a latex mould.

41 Tobias (1987, 741), Falk (1983).

42 Deacon's (1992) work was based on trying to understand how evolution could move from the vocal communications of apes to the language of modern humans when these appear to be produced by different parts of the brain. Primate calls have their source in subcortical areas, whereas human language depends on activity within the neocortex (see Chapter 5, note 32). Deacon argues that rather than language requiring completely new circuits, it may be accounted for by shifts in the relative proportions of circuits in different parts of the brain as these enlarge by different amounts during encephalization.

43 Aiello & Dunbar (1993), Dunbar (1991, 1992, 1993).

44 Aiello (1996a).

Ch. 7. The multiple intelligences of the Early Human mind (pp. 115–146)

1 Charles Caleb Colton, *Lacon* (1820), vol i, No. 408.

2 Gowlett (1984). At Boxgrove the debris from making ovate handaxes has been excavated in undisturbed contexts and refitted so that each strike of the knapper's hammer can be reconstructed. Here the fine, shallow finishing flakes across the artifacts indicate that the knappers used at least two different types of hammers – hard hammers of stone and soft hammers of bone. Indeed these bone hammers have recently been found at Boxgrove with minute flint flakes still embedded in the striking ends (Bergman & Roberts 1988; Roberts 1994).

3 Pelegrin (1993). Following rules in a rote fashion enable many non-human animals, particularly social insects, to create 'artifacts' of considerable complexity and symmetry, epitomized by a honeycomb. Such 'artifacts' have been compared with handaxes to suggest that Early Humans were not so clever after all. But this comparison is flawed since knapping is a process of reduction, rather than construction, and one must continually modify one's plans due to the unpredictability of fracture.

4 There are many groups of handaxes which contain artifacts of great similarity. One of the most impressive collections in this regard is that from the Wolvercote Channel near Oxford (Tyldesley 1986). These show near perfect symmetry, partly accomplished by the removal of tiny finishing flakes which would appear to have limited, if any, functional value. Many of these artifacts are almost exact replicas of each other in both size and shape.

5 Our understanding of the Levallois method has advanced considerably during the last few years by extensive refitting of Levallois debitage and replication experiments (e.g. Boëda 1988, 1990; Roebroeks 1988). Inizan *et al* (1992) suggest that it may be the most technically demanding knapping method.

6 Hayden (1993, 118).

7 The definition of a Levallois point is an artifact produced by the Levallois method which has a 'symmetrical morphology, a clearly pointed distal end with the overturned "Y" dorsal scar pattern obtained by three or at most four removals regardless of their direction' (Bar-Yosef & Meignen 1992, 175).

8 Schlanger (1996). Maastricht-Belvédère has several discrete clusters of knapping debris. 'Marjories core' consists of 41 refitted flakes out of 145 which are thought to have derived from the same core. None of the refitted flakes have been retouched or used, and nine of them have been classified as Levallois flakes. The core appears to have been brought to the site in a partially worked condition since there are no flakes from the outside part of the flint nodule.

9 The technical intelligence of Early Humans can also be appreciated from artifact types and production methods which are not widespread throughout the Old World. For instance, archaic *H. sapiens* in sub-Saharan Africa made long bifacial implements, which are described as Lumpeban bifaces. These are often impressive due to their size, symmetry and the fact that some specimens are made from very intractable rocks. One specimen from Muguruk in western Kenya is 267mm (10 1/2 inches) long, with a maximum thickness of only 35mm(1 2/5 inches). Such artifacts were made by bifacial knapping, with the use of both hard and soft hammers (McBrearty 1988). We should also note here that in a few rare instances Early Humans engaged in a blade technology of a type very similar to that of the Upper Palaeolithic, at the start of Act 4. Assemblages made by Early Humans which include blades are described by Ronen (1992) who characterizes them as 'PUP' for Pre-Upper Palaeolithic. Conrad (1990) discusses blade assemblages made by Neanderthals during the last interglacial of North West Europe. In the latter case at least, however, there is a marked difference between the type of blades being produced in these assemblages, and those of the Upper Palaeolithic. For instance, the Early Humans were not making prismatic blade cores but removing blades from a variety of directions on a core.

In one industry, the Howieson's Poort of South Africa dating to after 75,000 years ago, blades were turned into small crescent-shaped artifacts, described as microliths. Parkington (1990) reviews the dating of the Howieson's Poort. He draws together evidence from numerous sites in South Africa to argue that some Howieson's Poort assemblages could by as young as 40,000 years old. This view has been supported by electron spin resonance (ESR) dates which suggest that the Howieson's Poort artifacts from Klasies River Mouth are between 40,000 and 60,000 years old and those from Border Cave between 45,000 and 75,000 years old. One of the problems is that the Howieson's Poort industry may not be a unitary phenomenon, and it may have appeared at different times in different sites between 100,000 and 40,000 years ago. Parkington notes that only at three sites in South Africa are Howieson's Poort artifacts overlain by Middle Stone Age (MSA) flake/blade assemblages. In others, it is overlain by assemblages which are transitional to the Late Stone Age (LSA) with increasing numbers of bladelet cores. Other than in this industry – which may in fact belong to Act 4 – microliths are confined to the toolkits of Modern Humans which begin to appear towards the end of the last ice age,

many thousands of years after the start of Act 4.

10 Kuman (1994). See also Clarke (1988).

11 For instance, during the Middle Stone Age in Africa a range of relatively intractable materials were worked, contrasting substantially to earlier periods (Clark 1982).

12 Goren-Inbar (1992), Belfer-Cohen & Goren-Inbar (1994) and Villa (1983).

13 The handbones of Neanderthals imply a somewhat less precise grip than that of Modern Humans between the thumb and forefinger (Jones et al 1992). Dennell (1983, 81–3) suggests that Early Humans lacked the motor abilities to work bone, antler and ivory. This seems unlikely in light of the need for these actions to make the few wooden artifacts of the archaeological record, and the diversity of motor actions used in tasks such as animal butchery and plant processing.

14 Knecht (1993a) has demonstrated the effectiveness of organic materials as projectiles in a series of experimental studies, while Straus (1990a) compares the suitability of lithic and organic materials used for projectiles in the context of the Later Upper Palaeolithic. Wooden artifacts made by Early Humans are described by Oakley et al (1977) and Belitzky et al (1991).

15 Unfortunately there are rather few microwear studies of early prehistoric artifacts, largely due to the unsuitability of their raw material for such studies. Microwear studies on African handaxes, demonstrating that they were general-purpose tools, have been undertaken by Keeley & Toth (1981), and studies of Acheulian and Clactonian artifacts from England gave similar results (Keeley 1980). Experimental use of replicated artifacts (e.g. Jones 1980, 1981) also supports the notion that early artifacts were general-purpose rather than dedicated tools. Anderson-Gerfund (1990) and Béyries (1988) have found similar results with Mousterian artifacts.

16 Kuhn (1993) discusses the narrow range of variability in Mousterian points, while relationships between Upper Palaeolithic weapons and specific types of game are demonstrated by Peterkin (1993) and Clark et al (1986). Straus (1990a, 1993) examines weapon specialization during the Upper Palaeolithic, which is considered in Chapter 9.

17 Shea (1988, 1989; Lieberman & Shea 1994) has demonstrated breakage patterns,

microfracturing debitage and abrasive wear on pointed artifacts. Wear analysis has also been undertaken on Mousterian artifacts from western Europe, but with no clear evidence for their use as spear points (Anderson-Gerfund 1990; Béyries 1988).

18 Binford (1989, 28).

19 One study has shown that when more than 1000 handaxes from 17 sites in Europe, Africa, India and the Near East were statistically compared, only those from one of these regions appeared to show any distinctive shape (Wynn & Tierson 1990). As this sample includes sites from high to low latitudes, in which different types of animals were exploited, and plant foods probably had different degrees of importance in the Early Human diet, the only conclusion is that handaxe morphology bears very little relation to variability in the natural environment and subsistence behaviour.

20 Klein (1989).

21 Gamble (1993).

22 Many of the faunal assemblages from the Middle Pleistocene, such as the elephant dominated assemblage from Torralba in Spain, the assemblages from Zhoukoudian in China and those from Olorgesailie in Africa, were originally interpreted as reflecting big-game hunting (e.g. Howell 1965; Isaac 1978; Shipman *et al* 1981). Binford reinterpreted many of these during the 1980s as the product of hominid scavenging (Binford 1985, 1987b; Binford & Ho 1985; Binford & Stone 1986; Binford & Todd 1982). However, many of these faunal assemblages may be simply too disturbed and poorly preserved to extract any inferences about past behaviour (Villa 1983, 1990, 1991; Stopp 1988).

23 See summaries in Gamble (1986) and Stringer & Gamble (1993). For more detailed studies of Pleistocene fauna see Stuart (1982). High degrees of species diversity are generally thought to reflect a true difference between the animal communities of the Pleistocene and the modern world. But we must remember that Pleistocene faunal assemblages often have a very poor chronological resolution and are invariably palimpsests. The recent data from ice cores tell us that there were many short-lived, but quite marked, environmental fluctuations, during which certain species may temporarily have extended their range. Consequently the idea that such diverse communities (as opposed to assemblages) were a typical feature of the Pleistocene may be unfounded.

24 A further environmental feature which may have challenged the Neanderthals was that Pleistocene vegetation showed a markedly lower degree of zonation than is found today, with plant communities having a patchwork or plaid distribution. Today we find distinctive types of vegetation, such as woodland, grassland and tundra, coming in broad bands, within which a typical range of animal species will be found. But prior to the end of the last ice age at 10,000 years ago vegetation types appear to have been much more inter-mingled with each other (Guthrie 1984, 1990). Evidence for this comes both from pollen and, more importantly, the remarkable diversity of game found in Pleistocene landscapes. Guthrie explains this contrast in vegetation pattern by the richer soils, longer growing season and the greater degree of variability between growing seasons. This would have reduced the predictability of game species making their exploitation even more difficult than that in high latitude environments today.

Adding to the Neanderthal difficulties was the fact that in these fluctuating and unpredictable environments they would have been competing with carnivores for both food and shelter. This competition is apparent from the mixture of human and carnivore activity often represented within the same faunal assemblages (Straus 1982). Gamble (1986, 1989) attempts to monitor the variation in competitive pressure between carnivores and humans across Pleistocene Europe, and suggests that this may partly account for the variation in the extent to which Neanderthal skeletons and burials survive.

25 For information concerning Inuit technology see Oswalt (1973) and for modern hunter-gatherers in general see Oswalt (1976). Torrence (1983) has demonstrated that technological complexity is related to latitude and she interprets this as reflecting time stress. Hence groups such as the Inuit have to ensure that attempted kills are successful due to the limited opportunities of a second chance. In addition, it is likely that the exploitation of aquatic mammals requires particularly complex technology since the animal must be retrieved as well as killed. A very useful discussion of weapon technology and hunting methods among modern hunter-gatherers is provided by Churchill (1993).

26 Soffer (1989b) reviews the different storage technologies available to hunter-

gatherers. For permanent storage these include the use of various types of pits, storehouses and other devices, while for portable storage the drying of meat is useful, but labour intensive. Social storage is also possible in terms of building up reciprocal obligations and is likely to include the use of artifacts to symbolize debts. Finally, one form of storage Neanderthals are likely to have used was storage in the self by building up fat reserves.

27 Trinkaus (1995) provides a comprehensive study of Neanderthal mortality patterns. Two factors may question the apparent high levels of mortality. First, the sample is drawn from across the Old World and combines Neanderthals from many tens of thousands of years. Consequently it may not reflect any true population. Secondly, the sample is inevitably composed of individuals from cave situations. If individuals of different ages died in different parts of the landscape, sampling just one type of context may lead to very biased conclusions. A comparison between the injuries of Neanderthals and rodeo riders is made by Berger (*National Geographic* 1996, 189, p. 27).

28 A review of Middle Palaeolithic faunal assemblages is provided by Chase (1986). Part of the problem with the interpretation of these cave faunas is that the products of human activity are often mixed together with that of hyenas, bears and other carnivores. It is often difficult to distinguish between the two. Most of the debate about their interpretation has been stimulated by Binford (1985) who suggested that Neanderthals were essentially scavengers. Mellars (1989a) and Stringer & Gamble (1993) review interpretations of the relevant faunal assemblages.

29 Chase (1986, 1989). The patterns of body part representation at the site (predominantly meat-bearing bones) and the presence of cutmarks at those locations on the skeleton where fillets would be removed, are the exact opposite of what would be expected from opportunistic scavenging near the bottom of the predator hierarchy. Bovid and horse remains have relatively high frequencies of less utilitarian carcass parts (as might be left at kill sites by carnivores), although butchery marks on limb bones are still present (Chase 1986). Levine (1983) has shown that horse remains have a catastrophic mortality profile (i.e. animals of different ages are represented in the same proportions as in a living herd) which is more likely a product of hunting rather than scavenging.

30 The fauna from Grotta di Sant'Agostino has been analyzed by Mary Stiner (Stiner & Kuhn 1992).

31 Evidence for Neanderthal hunting has also come from open sites, as opposed to cave occupations. At both Mauran in the Pyrenees and La Borde in the Lot valley the substantial faunal assemblages are dominated by bovids. At Mauran there are the remains of at least 108 bovids, constituting over 90% of the assemblage. The site is at the base of a steep riverside escarpment and may reflect 'cliff-fall' hunting (Girard & David 1982; Mellars 1989a). There are no absolute dates for the site and Straus (1990b) has questioned the dating of the site to the Middle Palaeolithic, noting that this is essentially done by circular reasoning and that the lithic assemblage does not preclude an early Upper Palaeolithic date. He also notes that the faunal assemblage is likely to have formed over a long period of time and consequently there may not have been the mass slaughter of bovids that cliff-fall hunting implies. La Borde is apparently well dated at 120,000 BP (Stringer & Gamble 1993, 163). Had Neanderthals been opportunistic scavengers we would expect such sites to have a more even distribution of game species. Another possible case of cliff-fall hunting is La Cotte on Jersey, a cave site at the base of a cliff dated to 180,000 years ago (Scott 1980; Callow & Cornford 1986). Mellars (1989a) argues that sites such as La Cotte imply that Neanderthals were practising cliff-fall hunting of an equivalent nature to the massive bison-jump kill sites created by Palaeo-Indians of North America. Gamble (Stringer & Gamble 1993, 162) also interprets La Cotte as reflecting specialist hunting but has suggested that it might reflect 'dangerous driving by desperate people' rather than carefully controlled and planned hunting. Piles of mammoth and rhino bones within this cave have been interpreted as parts of carcasses dragged into the cave after animals were forced off the cliff above to fall to their death.

32 Stiner (1991).

33 Gamble (1987).

34 As we move into lower latitudes the environmental challenges faced by Early Humans may have been reduced, but nevertheless remained substantial. The faunal assemblages from the caves of the Levant indicate that diverse animal faunas were a common feature of the Pleistocene, as was the competition for prey and shelters between humans and carnivores. The Neanderthals using Kebara Cave appear to have had the upper hand in this competition as the gnawmarks on the fauna generally postdate the human cutmarks (Bar-Yosef *et al* 1992).

Both the Neanderthals and anatomically Modern Humans in the Near East made Mousterian industries, and both appear to have been competent hunters. The Levallois points from both Kebara and Qafzeh caves, associated with Neanderthals and Modern Humans respectively, have wear traces and fracture patterns that indicate they had been hafted and used as spear tips (Shea 1988, 1989).

These spear tips were used for hunting a range of game species including gazelle, fallow deer and roe deer. The first of these appears to have been the major prey item, constituting over 75% of the faunal remains from Kebara. While both Neanderthals and anatomically Modern Humans were hunting such animals, the precise patterns of their hunting behaviour appear to have differed (Lieberman & Shea 1994), with Neanderthals practising a less mobile strategy that nevertheless required a higher daily expenditure of effort than the anatomically Modern Humans. This agrees with the skeletal evidence indicating high degrees of physical activity by the muscular anatomy and high frequencies of stress fractures (Trinkaus 1995). As in Europe, the long-term success and effective hunting strategies of these Early Humans in the Levant imply a sophisticated natural history intelligence. An understanding of animal behaviour and the ability to 'read' visual cues are both implied by the long-term success of Early Humans in the Levant. The knowledge bases of Early Humans in Europe and western Asia are bound to have been different, however, not only because of the different range of game, but also because of the greater availability of plant foods in lower latitudes. We have archaeological evidence for their exploitation, such as the fruits of *Celtis* sp. from Doura Cave and wild peas in the hearths at Kebara (Bar-Yosef 1994b; Bar-Yosef *et al* 1992). But such evidence still remains sparse.

The subsistence behaviour of the Early Humans of the Middle Stone Age (MSA) in South Africa shares many similarities to that in the Levant and Europe. There are also similar disputes concerning interpretation of the faunal remains following Binford's (1984a) controversial volume on Klasies River Mouth. Klein (1989) provides the most reasonable interpretation of MSA subsistence patterns and how they differ to those of the Late Stone Age (LSA). The faunal remains from Klasies River Mouth indicate that eland were hunted, while the larger bovids such as cape buffalo were likely to have been scavenged. The MSA Early Humans also exploited seals and gathered shellfish, demonstrating the application of an advanced natural history intelligence to the exploitation of coastal resources. As with the Neanderthals of Europe, the Early Humans of South Africa do not appear to have actively gone fishing and fowling.

35 Trinkaus (1987, 1995). Neanderthals have a high frequency of traumatic injuries and developmental stress indicators. Their low survival rate may also reflect frequent population crashes, perhaps from seasonal shortages of food which may have been induced by environmental fluctuations or hunting failure.

36 This is a feature they share with other Early Humans except for the early anatomically Modern Humans (Trinkaus 1987).

37 Some very fine bone needles come from the site of Combe Saunière in southwest France dated to 18,000 years ago (Geneste & Plisson 1993).

38 Gamble (1994).

39 The evidence for the ability of Early Humans to exploit interglacial environments has been discussed by Gamble (1986, 1992) and Roebroeks *et al* (1992). The absence of any archaeological traces from the Ipswichian of Britain (i.e. the last interglacial, *c.* 125, 000 BP – stage 5e, see Box p. 32) when there was abundant game but relatively thick forest cover may well indicate that the technologically-challenged Neanderthals could not exploit such environments. Alternatively, if the Neanderthals were living in small groups, their archaeological record may simply be extremely sparse, or their absence due to their failure to colonize Britain before it was cut off by rising sea levels after the preceding glacial maximum.

40 Villa (1983), see also Stepanchuk (1993).

41 Oswalt (1973, 1976).

42 The manner in which climate influenced the toolmaking of Neanderthals in France has been discussed by Nicholas Rolland and Harold Dibble (1990; Dibble & Rolland

1992). (See also Turq (1992) for an explanation of how the Quina Mousterian variant is a reflection of time-stressed activities during harsh climatic conditions.) They have shown that when the climate was relatively mild, artifacts were produced which had a relatively low degree of reduction – i.e. they were relatively large and were infrequently resharpened. In contrast, when climatic conditions were severely cold, artifacts were more frequently resharpened and toolmakers were more conservative with their raw material. To explain this, they argue that the long winters of these cold phases would have forced groups to minimize journeys and reduced access to raw materials. During milder conditions Neanderthals would have changed their habitation sites more often. This would have allowed more frequent replenishment of raw materials, resulting in less intensively reduced assemblages.

Mary Stiner and Steven Kuhn have explored the connection between variability in stone tool technology and collections of animal bones from four cave sites in west-central Italy, each of which had been occupied by Neanderthals (Grotta Breuil, Grotta Guattari, Grotta dei Moscerini and Grotta di Sant'Agostino). The character of the animal bones prior to *c*. 55,000 years ago suggested that animal carcasses were acquired by scavenging. The tools and flakes associated with these bones are relatively large and exhibit evidence of prolonged use and relatively high frequencies of transport between sites. After 55,000 years ago Neanderthals appear primarily to have been hunting animals such as deer and horse. And their stone artifacts had changed. They were now dominated by production techniques that yielded relatively large numbers of small flakes, and the artifacts were neither worked intensively nor transported over long distances.

While there is a clear association between the variation in stone tool technology and the manner in which meat was acquired, there is no direct or obvious functional link between them. The stone tools from either pre- or post-55,000 years ago are mainly sidescrapers. Stone points remain at about the same low frequency in both collections. Stiner & Kuhn (1992) argue that differences in the Neanderthals' patterns of movements across the landscape, as they engaged in either carcass scavenging or hunting, provided different opportunities to replenish their raw materials for toolmaking. Scavenging and gathering imply relatively wide-ranging search patterns, and the production of large flakes by centripetal core reduction techniques would be advantageous because such blanks would be suitable when gathering/scavenging in areas where raw materials were scarce. Similarly, the persistent resharpening made possible by such blanks is a way of coping with the uncertainty about when and where raw materials for manufacturing new tools will be available. After 55,000 years ago, hunting is likely to have involved targeting concentrated food patches, reducing the ranging area of the hominids, increasing the duration of occupations within caves and reducing uncertainties about raw material availability. As a consequence, greater numbers of light tools were made using a platform core reduction technique producing blanks which could be used unmodified, or after light retouching, for processing animal tissue. This case study illustrates once again how the variation in Early Human toolmaking at a regional level is essentially a passive reflection of mobility and the distribution of raw materials. It did not structure mobility and hunting patterns in the way that toolmaking does among modern hunter-gatherers. Additional studies of artifact transport and mobility by Early Humans are provided by Roebroeks *et al* (1988) and Féblot-Augustins (1993). For earlier interpretations of Middle Palaeolithic technology see Binford & Binford (1969), Binford (1973) and Bordes (1961b, 1972).

43 Similar passive reflections of environmental variability and the making of simple cost/benefit decisions are apparent in several other regions. In the Aquitaine area, Geneste (1985) has recognized that the 'utilization' index (UI) of raw materials progressively increases with the distance from the sources at which they were procured – the UI is a measure of the intensity of use of a raw material once it has been procured. In a 5-km radius, the UI is only 5%; for sources between 5–20 km from the sites the UI was 10–20%; while for exotic materials 50–80 km away the UI was 75–100%. Moreover the form in which the raw material entered the sites systematically varied, with prepared blocks only for the 5–20-km distant sources, and pieces at the final stage of the reduction sequence for those materials from exotic sources.

Otte (1992) has explained how at the site of Sclayn, where occupation is dated to

130,000 BP, Early Humans made simple denticulates from local chert, the quartz from a slightly more distant origin was used to make becs and perforators, flint from about 30 km away was used to make heavily retouched sidescrapers, while Levallois flakes made of a fine sandstone had been transported into the site from a distant source.

Callow (Callow & Cornford 1986) attributes a substantial amount of the technological variability at La Cotte to changes in raw material availability. When the sea levels were high and raw material access difficult, artifacts were small and made of thick flakes with an inverse or bifacial retouch. When the sea level was lower, and raw materials more readily available, these traits diminished.

44 Dunbar (1992) explores this using various different measures of brain size, all of which shows some degree of correlation with mean group size. The strongest correlation is when brain size is estimated by the ratio of the neocortex to the rest of the brain.

45 Aiello & Dunbar (1993). These are mean figures taken from data provided in their table 1.

46 Dunbar (1993). A figure of 147.8 is given for Modern Humans. All these estimates have wide 95% confidence limits, that for Modern Humans ranging between 100.2 and 231.1. The extrapolation beyond the range of X-variable values is rather poorly justified on the basis that the study is exploratory rather than explanatory. A range of methodological issues are discussed in the commentary following Dunbar's article. He suggests that the predicted group size for Modern Humans fits well with the size of intermediate-level grouping among hunter-gatherers, lying between the group that lives together on a day-to-day basis (30–50 individuals) and the population unit (500–2000 individuals). The intermediate-level groups range in size between 100 and 200, with a mean not significantly different to that of his predicted figure of 147.8. Dunbar also suggests that there are many groupings within prehistoric farming and modern societies (such as in armies) of around 150 individuals and these support the idea that Modern Humans are cognitively constrained to maintaining personal contact with this size of group; a rather tenuous argument, to say the least.

47 Neanderthal remains from Grotta Guattari and Krapina have been substantially chewed by carnivores (Trinkaus 1985, White & Toth 1991). It is not clear whether the Neanderthals were already dead before the carnivores chewed them. This is perhaps the most likely story, although there is clear evidence that early hominids were hunted and killed by carnivores (e.g. Brain 1981).

48 A nice example of this from Africa is the elephant butchery site of Mwanganda's Village (Clark & Haynes 1970). Dennell (1983) notes the consequences of megafaunal food packages for group size.

49 Even among modern hunter-gatherers with firearms the rate of hunting success is often very low. For instance Marks (1976) describes the rarity of the Valley Bisa actually succeeding in killing an animal, even though they used shotguns.

50 Wrangham (1987) discusses the competition for food as a disincentive to group living. The frequency of aggressive encounters in groups of non-human primates appears to be directly correlated to group size and the degree to which food is clumped (Dunbar 1988, 113–15). This is likely to be a major cause of the fusion–fission pattern frequently noted among large primate groups (Beauchamp & Cabana 1990).

51 Stringer & Gamble (1993), Trinkaus (1983).

52 For example, see Naroll (1962), Yellen (1977). O'Connell (1987) provides one of the most useful studies demonstrating how the spatial area of artifact distributions is influenced by both the number of people occupying a site, and the duration of occupation.

53 Binford (1989, 33).

54 Mellars (1989a, 358).

55 White (1993a, 352).

56 Soffer (1994, 113).

57 This is a widely held view (see Mellars 1989a and for a specific example of apparent lack of spatial structure in butchery sites, Farizy & David 1992). This is not a function of preservation, for, as Clive Gamble (1994; Stringer & Gamble 1993) stresses, we have several well-preserved and extensive undisturbed occupation areas from the Early Human sites of Hoxne and Boxgrove in England, Biache-St-Vaast in Northern France and Maastricht-Belvédère in the Netherlands. None of these have pits, post-holes, hearths or stone structures of the type that are used to structure social interaction among Modern Humans. Precisely the same phenomenon has been found in the 0.99-million-year-old sediments at Olorgesailie. As Richard Potts has described, even though the archaeological sediments of these sites have preserved footprint trails and animal burrows, there are no signs of hearths, shelters or 'traces of distinctive social units' (Potts 1994, 18). Hayden (1993) has challenged this view, suggesting that there are numerous Middle Palaeolithic sites with spatial structure in artifact distributions and indeed features such as post-holes and wall constructions indicating a social use of space. Few, if any, of his examples, however, stand up to scrutiny and cannot be explained in more parsimonious terms.

58 Stringer & Gamble (1993, 154–58), Gamble (1994, 24–6).

59 A recent review of this data by Knight *et al* (1995) concludes that there are no more than 12 such pieces from the whole of the period prior to the start of the Upper Palaeolithic, all of which date to after 250,000 years ago. Nevertheless, they believe that these lumps of red ochre indicate that Early Humans were engaging in body painting. They argue that ochre was used as a symbol of menstrual blood and construct an intriguing, but unconvincing, argument for the origins of ritual and symbolic behaviour, building on the previous work of Knight (1991).

60 Gargett (1989) reviews the evidence for Neanderthal burial (for Kebara, see Bar-Yosef *et al* 1992). With regard to Shanidar (Solecki 1971), he suggests that it is more likely that the pollen was deposited in the cave by wind, while Gamble (1989) notes the possibility that flower pollen had been introduced into the cave by workmen during the excavation. Gamble (1989) highlights that the distribution of Neanderthal burials appears to be inversely correlated with the intensity of carnivore activity. Akazawa *et al* (1995) have described what they claim is a burial of a Neanderthal child from Dederiyeh Cave in Syria. From the brief report they provide there seems to be no evidence for a pit, but the excellent preservation may well indicate a burial. They claim that a piece of flint was intentionally placed over the heart of the child, but they provide insufficient data to support such an assertion.

61 These are described for Inuit groups by Birket-Smith (1936) and Weyer (1932) while Knight (1991) draws numerous accounts together from all over the world.

62 Mithen (1994) discusses this in detail with regard to the Acheulian and Clactonian from southeast England (Wymer 1974, Ashton *et*

al 1994), drawing on Wymer's (1988) tentative correlation of assemblages with past environments. Gamble (1992, table 2) correlates Early Palaeolithic sites lacking handaxes from northwest Europe with interglacial stages, while Valoch (1984) and Svoboda (1992) have also argued that pebble/flake industries come from wooded environments. See also McNabb & Ashton (1995) and Mithen (1995).

The chain of consequences from wooded environments, to small group size, to a predominance of trial-and-error individual learning over social learning, resulting in a stone technology displaying a low level of technical skill (see Mithen 1996, figure 7.2), may also explain the stone tools from the site of Gran Dolina, one of many caverns in the limestone hill of Atapuerca in Spain. These stone tools may well be the earliest artifacts found in Europe, as they come from a deposit which has been dated to at least 780,000 years ago. This deposit also contains many fossil remains of animals and those of at least four Early Humans, which have been tentatively assigned to *H. heidelbergensis*. The tools exhibit a very low level of technical skill and are comparable to those of the Oldowan. What is significant is that the types of animals that are represented by the fossils are those of wooded environments, such as beaver, wild boar, red deer and fallow deer. These Early Humans appear to have been living in wooded environments and hence would have lacked the social structure to maintain a high level of technical skill within the group. The date for the deposits at Gran Dolina must remain provisional until it is confirmed by additional methods of dating. The hominids and stone tools from this site are described in Carbonell *et al* (1995) and the dating method in Parés & Pérez-González (1995).

John Shea (personal communication 20 June 1994) suggests that a relationship between industry and environment may also be seen at Ubeidiya in Israel. This site had a long (but probably intermittant) occupation between *c.* 1.4 and 0.85 m.y.a. Many of the artifacts in the lower levels of this site are similar to those of the Oldowan industry and reflect limited technical skill. The environment in which they were made, as reconstructed from pollen in associated sediments, appears to have been thick woodland. This would suggest small social groups, which in turn imply low degrees of social learning.

Higher up in the Ùbeidiya formation, hand-axes were being made. These appear to be associated with steppe/savannah environments, in which larger group sizes, and therefore more social learning, are expected. The result would be an increase in technical skill and cultural tradition – as are indeed reflected in the production of the technically more demanding handaxes.

63 Holloway (1985) attributes the degree of Neanderthal brain enlargement over that of Modern Humans as due to a metabolic adaptation to cold environments.

64 Aiello & Dunbar (1993), Dunbar (1993). Dunbar suggests that language is a considerably more efficient means of transmitting social information than grooming for two reasons: first it can be undertaken at the same time as other activities; and secondly one can speak to many people at once, whereas grooming is restricted to one person alone.

65 Aiello (1996a).

66 Begun & Walker (1993).

67 Holloway (1981a, 1981b, 1985), Holloway & de la Coste-Lareymondie (1982). Similarly, LeMay (1975, 1976) has argued that Neanderthal endocasts imply an essentially modern neural structure.

68 A very influential reconstruction of a Neanderthal vocal tract was presented by Phillip Lieberman and Ed Crelin in 1971. They suggested that Neanderthal crania show significant similarities to the morphology of a new born rather than an adult Modern Human, and on that basis reconstructed the vocal tract. The size and shape of this was found to be only capable of producing a limited range of vowel sounds, when compared with Modern Humans. As a result, while they claimed that Neanderthals had language and speech, this was very restricted in its vocal range. Fremlen (1975) showed that this restricted range of vowels would have had little consequence for the nature of language in the following manner: '... et seems emprebeble thet ther speech wes enedeqwete bekes ef the leck ef the three vewels seggested. the kemplexete ef speech depends en the kensenents, net en the vewels, es ken be seen frem the generel kemprehensebelete ef thes letter.' Perhaps rather surprisingly, by using the same method as before Lieberman and Crelin found that archaic *H. sapiens*, in contrast to Neanderthals, were capable of fully modern speech. A similar conclusion was reached by Jeffrey Laitman and his colleagues who

reconstructed the vocal tract by using the shape of the base of the cranium, which they argued was correlated with the positioning of soft tissues (Laitman *et al* 1979, 1991, 1993). By measuring this on a range of Neanderthal and archaic *H. sapiens* fossils they reached the same conclusion as Lieberman and Crelin: Neanderthals, unlike archaic *H. sapiens*, were unlikely to have had the full range of modern vocalizations. Both of these studies have received severe criticisms, summarized in Schepartz (1993). See also Frayer (1992) and Houghton (1993). One of the most important of the criticisms is that the reconstructions of the Neanderthal skulls used by Lieberman and others, notably that from the site of Chapelle-aux-Saints, are inaccurate.

69 Arensburg *et al* (1989). There has been marked disagreements over the implications of this tiny ancient bone (Arensburg *et al* 1990; Laitman *et al* 1990; Lieberman 1993).

70 Lieberman (1984).

71 Aiello (1996b).

Ch. 8. Trying to think like a Neanderthal (pp. 147–150)

1 Block (1995) discusses different types of consciousness.

2 Dennett (1991, 137).

3 Dennett (1991, 308).

4 The consequences of 'petit mal' seizures are described in Penfield (1975) and summarized in Block (1995).

5 Nagel (1974).

6 Wynn (1995, 21).

Ch. 9. The big bang of human culture: the origins of art and religion (pp. 151–184)

1 The idea that the Middle/Upper Palaeolithic transition marks a dramatic break in human behaviour is the most widely accepted position and is particularly favoured by Mellars (e.g. 1973, 1989a,b) and White (e.g. 1982, 1993a,b). Marshack (1990) however argues that the capacity for visual symbolism evolved gradually during the Pleistocene, while Lindly and Clark (1990) suggest that the changes in behaviour at *c.* 20,000 BP are of much greater significance than those at 40,000–35,000 BP. They seem to forget about the sudden appearance and abundance of items of personal ornamentation at *c.* 40,000 BP when coming to this conclusion. Bednarik (1994) has suggested that the current chronological and spatial patterning in 'art objects' is purely a reflection of preservation and discovery and has no bearing on patterns of past behaviour. This extremely bleak view is also extremely wrong. For instance the taphonomic contrasts between later Middle Palaeolithic and early Upper Palaeolithic assemblages in southwest Europe cannot account for the different quantities of art. There are a vast number of organic objects surviving from many thousands of years of Neanderthal activity in the form of the bones of the animals they were hunting. But not one of these has evidence for the carving or engraving of images with symbolic meanings. Also, while the Early Palaeolithic record as a whole may be relatively poorly preserved, we nevertheless do have some almost perfectly preserved sites, such as Boxgrove, and, as discussed in Chapter 7, these give no indication of activities with symbolic meaning.

2 White (1982, 176) has written of the 'total restructuring of social relations across the Middle/Upper Palaeolithic boundary' and of the 'transformation from internally un- or weakly-differentiated social systems' (1993a, 352). Soffer (1994) provides a social scenario for the transition in which the sexual division of labour and biparental provisioning of young were absent in the Middle Palaeolithic. In this regard she sees the origin of the home base/food sharing model, that Isaac (1978) had proposed, occurring at 2 million years ago, at the start of the Upper Palaeolithic. Her evidence for this is slim, to say the least, and the social intelligence and likely social complexity of Early Humans, as discussed in Chapter 6, suggest that the proposals of Soffer and White regarding a simple form of social organization in the Middle Palaeolithic are wide of the mark.

3 Orquera (1984) suggests that the transition can be accounted for by an increase in specialized hunting technology. Hayden (1993) believes that the contrast between Middle and Upper Palaeolithic communities in Europe is equivalent to that between generalized and complex hunter-gatherers, as documented in the ethnographic record. The latter are characterized by food storage, private ownership and social differentiation, while generalized hunter-gatherer communities are small in size and highly mobile. The problem with this idea is that the Middle Palaeolithic populations in Europe were living in precisely those environments and under the type of adaptive stress in which we would expect the attributes of complex hunter-gatherer societies to develop. But they didn't. This implies that there were cognitive constraints preventing Neanderthals from making technical and economic innovations. Hayden perhaps acknowledges this when he suggests there may 'have been some changes in mental capacity and composition from Neanderthal to fully modern human forms' (1993, 137), although he goes on to suggest these would not appear to have been significant changes.

4 Bar-Yosef (1994b) has made an explicit comparison between the origin of the Upper Palaeolithic and that of agriculture. He suggests that archaeologists should adopt a similar research strategy to the Middle/Upper Palaeolithic transition, as has been undertaken for the origins of agriculture. This would include trying to identify the 'core area' where critical technical developments occurred and then the process by which these spread, either by migration or technological diffusion. A problem with this comparison is that the changes at the Middle/Upper Palaeolithic transition appear to be much more diverse and profound than those at 10,000 years ago without just one 'big idea' (such as domesticating plants), and appear to have occurred in many regions of the world in a very short space of time.

5 The language interpretation varies, some arguing that the transition marked the switch from gestural to spoken language (e.g. Corballis 1992), others that this switch was from a proto-language lacking a full range of tenses to fully modern language (Whallon 1989). Mellars suggests that the 'emergence of complex, highly structured language' could 'potentially, have revolutionized the whole spectrum of human culture' (Mellars 1989a, 364), without specifying quite what is meant by 'complex' and 'highly structured', nor how the revolution would have taken place. Gamble and Stringer (1993) refer to the lack of symbolic capacities in the Middle Palaeolithic, but it is not clear whether they are including linguistic and visual symbolism in the same capacity.

6 Fodor (1985, 4), Gardner (1983, 279), Rozin (1976, 262), Sperber (1994, 61), Karmiloff-Smith (1994, 706), Carey & Spelke (1994, 184) and Boden (1994, 522).

7 White (1992) suggests that the difficulty in defining art has been a serious hindrance to explaining the origin of 'art'. Conkey (1983,

1987) has discussed how the adoption by archaeologists of the modern concept of art as a universal category is a handicap to explaining the cultural developments at the start of the Upper Palaeolithic.

8 Bednarik (1995) makes extravagant claims about such artifacts. He describes pieces of bone with simple scratches on as having 'concept mediated' markings, with no explanation of what he means by this term. Simple sets of juxtaposed lines are claimed to be 'structured sets', 'identically angled', having an 'extraordinary straightness' and being 'intentional', with no attempt to justify such claims. His discussion of these illustrates the type of uncritical, subjective interpretation of archaeological data that severely constrains our progress towards understanding the pattern of cognitive evolution.

9 Marshack (1990, 457–98).

10 Aurignacian figurative art in Central Europe is restricted to four sites: Vogelherd, Hohlenstein-Stadel, Geißenklösterle, all in Germany, and Stratzing/Krems-Rehberg in Austria. The largest single collection of ten statuettes comes from Vogelherd Cave, consisting of 2 mammoths, 1 horse, 2–3 felids or other indeterminable animals, a half relief mammoth head on a retoucher, a half relief lion, a fully sculptured bison, a lion's head and an anthropomorph (Hahn 1972, 1984, 1993). Marshack (1990) describes how the microscopic examination of the Vogelherd figurines revealed that the animal figures were often marked and over marked, as if in periodic ritual.

11 Delluc & Delluc (1978).

12 White (1989, 1992, 1993a,b) has made a detailed study of the production and distribution of these items throughout Europe, indicating their considerable complexity and their abundance in southwest Europe. Of the many important aspects of his studies, we might note that the beads form a distinct time horizon at *c.* 40,000 BP and that in southwest Europe they are not from burial contexts but occupation layers. White stresses that we should view these beads as objects of art, rather than trivializing them by simply calling them decorative items.

13 Bahn & Vertut (1989) and Clottes (1990) review the problems of dating rock art. Our knowledge of the chronology of Palaeolithic art is being dramatically changed by the use of AMS radiocarbon dating (e.g. Valladas *et al* 1992), which hopefully will become widely used.

14 The art in Chauvet Cave is described in Chauvet, Deschamps & Hillaire (1996). In addition to its early date, 10,000 years earlier than many experts were expecting, the cave is also notable for the dominance of rhinoceroses and carnivores in the art. In other caves these tend to be rather infrequent, outnumbered by paintings of horses and bison. In addition, all the other 'classic' painted caves have been found in the Perigord/Quercy and Pyrenees regions of France or in Cantabria, Spain. The discovery of Chauvet Cave has fundamentally changed our knowledge of Palaeolithic cave painting.

15 Bahn (1991, 1994) reviews Pleistocene art outside Europe. There are numerous Australian sites with Pleistocene dates. At Sandy Creek in Queensland, engravings have been dated to 32,000 BP by the sediments which cover them, and red paint has been directly dated to 26,000 BP. AMS dating of organic material in varnish covering petroglyphs in south Australia has provided dates of 42,700 BP for an oval figure at Wharton Hill and 43,140 ± 3000 BP for a curved line at Panaramitec North. These very early dates are controversial and should not be accepted without confirmation. Items of art of Pleistocene age are now also claimed to come from China and South America.

16 Mithen (1989, 1990) argues that the combination of severe climatic conditions and the intensification of hunting led to fluctuations in the principal prey items, which in turn created the conditions in which Palaeolithic art flourished. More generally Jochim (1983) has emphasized the role of southwest Europe as a population refugia during the time of the last glacial maximum, resulting in the cave art and associated rituals which served to mark territories and cope with the resulting social stress of high population densities. See also Soffer (1987).

17 Chase (1991) provides a useful discussion of the complex terminology surrounding symbol and style in archaeology, and different ways in which the word 'arbitrary' is used. He distinguishes between 'icons', which point to something by resembling it (such as a portrait), 'indexes', which point to something by being associated with it (such as smoke from a fire) and 'symbols', which have an entirely arbitrary relationship with their referent that has to be learnt.

18 This is perhaps the critical difference

between an artifact that has symbolic as opposed to stylistic attributes (Chase 1991). Sackett (1982) distinguishes between 'active style', in which there is an intention to communicate, and 'passive style', in which an artifact adopts certain attributes distinctive to an individual or group, although there was no intention to communicate such identity by the artisan. Something with active style will act as a symbol (Wobst 1977). Halverson (1987) suggests that Palaeolithic cave art may have no meaning (and consequently was created with no intention of communication) – 'no religious, mythic or metaphysical reference' (1987, 63). This seems extremely unlikely in light of the very narrow range of subject matter that Palaeolithic artists chose to depict.

19 Layton (1994) provides an excellent synthesis of our current understanding of Aboriginal art.

20 Faulstich (1992) discusses the use of abstraction and naturalism in Walpiri art. He describes how abstractions usually have various levels of meaning, while a naturalistic image will have a single referent, although that referent in itself may have multiple meanings.

21 Tacon (1989) provides an account of the representation of fish in the art of western Arnhem Land, explaining their economic and symbolic importance. With regard to the latter he describes how among the Kunwinjku of central Arnhem Land fish are such a potent symbol of fertility, sexual relations and rebirth that coitus is often described as a 'women netting a fish' in everyday speech. This refers to a similarity between the role of nets to catch fish and legs to catch a penis, and points to a symbolic link between fish and penises as the sources of human life. Fish are also good to paint and to think about due to their anatomy. In paintings, their bones – symbols of the transformation from life to death – can be well displayed. They are also good to paint and think about due to their colour because, more than any other animal, they exhibit the quality of 'rainbowness', which is associated with the essence of Ancestral Beings. Fascinating discussions of the multivalency of images in Aboriginal art are given by Taylor (1989) for the Kunwinjku of western Arnhem Land, and by Morphy (1989b) for the Yolngu of eastern Arnhem Land.

22 Lewis-Williams (1982, 1983, 1987, 1995) has made particularly detailed studies of the rock art of South Africa exposing its complex symbolic meanings. He has stressed the presence of 'entoptic' phenomena in this art's images generated by the nervous system when under states of altered consciousness (Lewis-Williams & Dowson 1988; Lewis-Williams 1991). Similar images, he argues, are found in many rock art traditions including Palaeolithic art. A good example of multivalency from San rock art is the image of a nested series of U-shaped curves from Natal Drakensberg which are surrounded by tiny flying insects (Lewis-Williams 1995). In one respect this is a painting of a beehive, probably reflecting the great love of honey found among all hunter-gatherers. But Lewis-Williams also explains how this image is likely to have entoptic significance and also reflect the work of shamans.

23 Morris (1962) contains many splendid paintings by chimpanzees.

24 There are numerous artifacts from the Early Palaeolithic which have been claimed to be 'art' or have symbolic meanings due to the presence of engraved lines (see note 8). These have been reviewed in a favourable light by Marshack (1990) and Bednarik (1992, 1995). However, the majority of these can be explained as artifacts which have become unintentionally marked, whether by human activities (such as cutting grass on a bone support), by carnivores or during the physical processes of site formation (Chase & Dibble 1987, 1992; Davidson 1990, 1991, 1992; Pelcin 1994). The few remaining artifacts exist in isolation from each other in terms of space or time and there is no reason to believe that the marks upon them constituted part of a symbolic code.

25 Knight et al (1995).

26 This is very different to the attribution of meaning to the behaviour of another individual by inferring the contents of his/her mind, at which Early Humans are likely to have excelled. In this type of meaning attribution, the signified (the cognitive state) is spatially and temporally close to the signifier (observed behaviour). This is a central feature of social intelligence and one that non-human primates show varying degrees of competence in. As we saw in Chapter 4, non-human primates appear unable to attribute meaning to inanimate marks or objects displaced from their referents.

27 This has also been independently noted by White (1992, 558) and Hewes (1989, 145). Hewes states that 'I see no perceptual difference between the decoding of animal tracks, not produced deliberately, and the decoding of man-made "depictions", although the effective reading of hoofprints may demand greater cognitive ability'.

28 Bégouen & Clottes (1991) suggest that some of the engravings on bone from the cave of Enlène in the Pyrenees may have been the work of novice artists, as they show considerably less skill than the engravings on the walls of the adjacent caves of Tuc d'Audoubert and Trois-Frères. However, they are reluctant to return to the rather simplistic idea of Capitan and Bouyssonie, put forward in 1924, that Enlène represents a workshop where apprentices worked under the supervision of master artists. More generally, while the technically accomplished and realistic animal images are most frequently depicted in books, Palaeolithic art contains numerous images of disproportioned animals which may have been made by an untrained hand (Bahn & Vertut 1989).

29 Morphy (1989a) provides a collection of papers illustrating the diverse and complex ways in which animals are used in art. Particularly good examples of anthropomorphism can be seen in the ceramic art of the Ilama potters, an Amerindian group flourishing during the first millennium BC in Colombia (pp. 87–97), and the art of the Solomon Islands (pp. 318–42). Anthropomorphic images are also described within the rock art of Kenya, the Aboriginal art of Australia, and the art of the Hopi and Zuni Pueblo groups of Arizona and New Mexico.

30 Anthropomorphic imagery in Palaeolithic art is reviewed by Bahn & Vertut (1989, p. 144 for the description of the Trois-Frères sorcerer), while Lorblanchet (1989) discusses the continuity between images of humans and animals. The splendid figure from Grimaldi is 47.2 mm (1 9/10 inches) high and made from green serpentine. The female and animal are connected at the back of the heads, the shoulders and the feet. This is one of a group of figurines from Grimaldi which were 'rediscovered' in Montreal in 1991, after having been dug up in Grimaldi some time between 1883 and 1895 (Bisson & Bolduc 1994). Human figurines from the Palaeolithic are described by Delporte (1979, 1993) and Gvozdover (1989) and interpreted by Gamble (1982, 1993), Duhard (1993) and Rice (1981).

31 Srejovic (1972).

32 Kennedy (1992) provides an overview of anthropomorphic thinking, particularly its pervasiveness in ethology, which he suggests has resulted in many mistaken interpretations of animal behaviour. He describes how even those scientists who attempt to avoid anthropomorphizing animals unwittingly slip into it from time to time. He suggests that people are prone to compulsive anthropomorphizing because the idea that animals are conscious and have purpose appears to be built into us by nature and nurture.

33 Willis (1990) provides a review of changing definitions and interpretations of totemism in the introduction to his edited volume about human meaning in the natural world.

34 Willis (1990, 4).

35 In the cemetery of Oleneostrovski Mogilnik in Karelia, dating to *c.* 7800 BP, the graves are distributed into a northern and southern cluster. In the northern one effigies of elk were present in the graves, while in the southern one effigies of snakes and humans were present. This has been interpreted as reflecting two groups divided on a totemic basis (O'Shea & Zvelebil 1984).

36 Morphy (1989b, 145). As the Ancestral Beings are continually being created anew through the performance of ceremonies, the Ancestral past is more appropriately conceived of as a dimension of the present, and consequently the landscape is not simply a record of past mythological events but plays an active role in creating those events.

37 Carmichael *et al* (1994) contains a set of papers which suggests that humans universally assign symbolic meanings to topographic features such as caves, odd-shaped rocks and rivers.

38 Ingold (1992, 42).

39 The hunting tactics of the early Upper Palaeolithic appear to have been based on the stalking and killing of individual animals rather than the mass slaughter of herds, and in this regard they are more typical of the Middle Palaeolithic. Enloe (1993), for instance, has demonstrated this for Level V at Abri du Flageolet (25,700 ± 700 BP) and it conforms to the Aurignacian reindeer-hunting pattern that Spiess (1979) inferred at Abri Pataud, and those of red deer that Pike-Tay (1991, 1993) has reconstructed for Roc de Combe and La Ferrassie. Pike-Tay argues that during the Upper Perigordian hunting was not organized in such a logistic manner as during the later Upper Palaeolithic.

Mellars (1989a, 357–38) however refers to the reindeer-dominated assemblages of Abri Pataud, Roc de Combe, La Gravette and Le Piage, all of which date to between 32,000 and 34,000 BP, in which 95–99% of the faunal remains are reindeer. The dominance of these early Upper Palaeolithic assemblages by a single species remains a significant contrast to the Middle Palaeolithic assemblages from the same region. Only the Middle Palaeolithic site of Mauran appears to have an equivalent level of dominance by a single species, in that case bovids. Specialized reindeer hunting during the later Upper Palaeolithic is described by Audouze (1987), Audouze & Enloe (1992), Bokelmann (1992), Bratlund (1992) and Grønnow (1987).

40 White (1989); Mithen (1990).

41 Straus (1992, 84). Specialized ibex hunting is a feature of late Upper Palaeolithic subsistence throughout mountainous regions of southern Europe (Straus 1987b). Sites such as Bolinkoba and Rascaño in Cantabrian Spain, however, in steep cliff side locations, also have early Upper Palaeolithic levels.

42 Soffer (1989a, 714–42).

43 Klein (1989, 540–41).

44 Silberbauer (1981) provides a particularly detailed description of the anthropomorphic models used by the G/Wi. In this case human attributes are imposed on mammals in particular, and to a lesser extent on birds, reptiles and amphibians. Silberbauer explains how attributing such animals with human personalities and characteristics serves to predict their behaviour both before and after they are shot (and while being tracked when wounded). Marks (1976) highlights a similar point regarding the Valley Bisa, as does Gubser (1965) for the Nunamiut. Blurton-Jones & Konner (1976) have recognized how the !Kung knowledge of animal behaviour, based on anthropomorphic models, is as good as that of Western scientists.

45 Douglas (1990, 33). Her argument was developed with specific regard to the Lele people of Zaire. These have numerous prohibitions about eating spotted animals, which appear to relate to their interest in skin diseases including smallpox. She suggests that they 'are not using animals for drawing elaborate pictures of themselves, nor are they necessarily using them for posing and answering profound metaphysical problems. The argument is that they have practical reasons for trying to understand and predict the animals' ways, reasons to do with health, hygiene and sickness. The principles of seniority, marriage exchange, territory and political hegemony they use for explaining their own behaviour they also use for prediction about animal behaviour'.

46 Knecht (1993a,b, 1994) has made extensive experimental studies in the manufacture and use of early Upper Palaeolithic organic hunting weapons. She has also explicitly compared the utility of stone and antler as raw materials for hunting weapons, noting that while the former may have greater penetrating and cutting ability and are quicker to work, tools made from organic material are more durable and easier to repair. Pike-Tay (1993) discusses how her faunal studies and Knecht's technological studies imply that Upper Perigordian foragers were skilled hunters. She interprets the organic weapons from the early Upper Palaeolithic as being made to hunt a variety of game, rather than being dedicated to specific types.

47 For instance, Clark *et al* (1986) have undertaken a multivariate statistical analysis of the lithic and faunal assemblages from La Riera and showed a persistent association between Solutrean points and ibex. Using similar methods, Peterkin (1993) demonstrates a positive association between the haft length of lithic artifacts and the proportion of bovines within assemblages from the Upper Palaeolithic in southwest France, indicating the use of durable hafting technology for the procurement of bovines. See Bergman (1993) for development of bow technology.

48 This can be recognized by using the criteria that Bleed (1986) put forward regarding the optimal design of hunting weapons (see also Torrence 1983). He contrasted two different design alternatives: reliable and maintainable tools, each appropriate for different circumstances. When food resources are predictable, but available in very short time periods (a situation that Torrence (1983) would describe as 'time-stressed') one would expect tools to be reliable. As such they would be 'over-designed', having redundant parts, and be dedicated to specific resources and produced by specialists. When food resources are more evenly distributed in time and relatively unpredictable, the optimal tools would have a maintainable design. These are tools which can be repaired and maintained during use, often having multiple standardized components. At a very broad scale of analysis we do indeed find reliable tools being manufactured in the time-stressed environments of the last glacial maximum, as we should expect, and a switch to a maintainable technology in the forested environments of the Holocene in which game was more dispersed and less predictable. Straus (1991) and Geneste & Plisson (1993) describe the specialized hunting technology in southwest Europe at the height of the last glacial maximum, while Zvelebil (1984) contrasts this with the microlithic and maintainable technology of the Mesolithic. He provides an excellent description of how Mesolithic technology was very well suited to hunting in forested environments (Zvelebil 1986). The contrast between reliable and maintainable tools can also be seen at a finer scale of analysis. For instance, Pike-Tay & Bricker (1993) note that while Gravettian artifact assemblages in southwest France are dominated by lithic artifacts from tools they believe to be easily maintainable hunting weapons for red deer and reindeer exploitation, the Gravettian assemblage from Abri Pataud Layer 4 is dominated by organic weapons. This layer is also characterized by a tight seasonal period of hunting, the spring and fall only, which appears to have resulted in the production of reliable organic tools, just as Bleed's theory would suggest.

49 Straus (1990a) uses this phrase to characterize the interplay between microlithic technology, organic harpoons and large projectile points during the Solutrean and Magdalenian. But it is probably also appropriate as a general description of technological developments among Modern Humans.

50 Wendorf *et al* (1980).

51 The most impressive evidence for storage from the Upper Palaeolithic comes from the Russian Plain, where Soffer (1985) has described storage pits on many sites which had been used to cache frozen meat supplies. In the Late Pleistocene/Early Holocene, the communities in Japan (Jomon) and the Near East (Natufian) were building storage facilities for plant material (Soffer 1989b). It is widely accepted that Mesolithic groups were routinely storing foods, although the archaeological evidence remains rare.

52 This is a piece of bone from the Grotte de Taï (Drôme, France), dating to the Magdalenian, which has 1020 incisions on one side and 90 on the other, all of which are arranged in parallel lines following the axis of the bone. Marshack (1991) provides a very

detailed description, and interprets the piece as representing a system of notation, and more specifically a lunar calendar.

53 The interpretations of these artifacts have included the following: hunting tallies, lunar calendars, a 'mathematical conception of the cosmos', the 'knowledge of a numbering or calculating system', and 'a rhythmical support for traditional recitation ... or musical instruments' (D'Errico & Cacho 1994, 185).

54 Both Marshack (1972a, 1972b, 1991) and D'Errico (1991; D'Errico & Cacho 1994) have used microscopic examination of the marks to try and ascertain the manner and order in which they have been made. While Marshack innovated this research, D'Errico has introduced a much higher degree of objective evaluation of the marks, partly by using experimentally produced artifacts to establish the criteria to be used in drawing inferences concerning the direction, type and changes of tool. Perhaps not surprisingly, there has been some disagreement between them, with D'Errico sceptical of many of Marshack's methods and interpretations (D'Errico 1989a, 1989b, 1991, 1992; Marshack 1989). The most robust cases for inferring systems of notation from these artifacts are D'Errico & Cacho's (1994) study of the Upper Palaeolithic engraved artifact from Tossal de la Roca, Spain, and D'Errico's (1995) study of the engraved antler from La Marche, France. Robinson (1992) provides a perceptive critique of Marshack's work.

55 Good ethnographic examples are the calendar stick from North America described by Marshack (1985) and the Siberian Yakut calenders made from fossil ivory strips (Marshack 1991).

56 Pfeiffer (1982).

57 Mithen (1988, 1990).

58 These carvings from Mal'ta, and many other pieces of Palaeolithic art, are beautifully illustrated in the *National Geographic*, Vol 174, no. 4 (October 1988).

59 The trophy arrays of the Wopkaimin of central New Guinea are described and interpreted as mental maps by Hyndman (1990). He emphasizes their role as a trigger in recalling the characteristics of specific places and areas of their environment. The arrangement of bones in the trophy array of the Bakonabip men's house is as follows: 'Ancestral relics (*menamen*) are stored in string bags centrally at eye level on the trophy level. These belong to the *ahip* [inner circle of hamlets] realm in the relatively long-term hamlet sites ... placed centrally in the homeland. Domestic pigs are fostered to select families residing a short distance from the hamlets, and mandibles from these animals are displayed below the ancestral relics.... Wild pig bones are placed lower than domestic ones; they come from *gipsak*, the lowest zone of rainforest encircling the inner garden and hamlet zones.... Marsupial mandibles are displayed highest off the floor, they primarily come from the mid to highest rainforests. Cassowary pelvis and thigh bones are placed in association with the wild pigs and the marsupials representing the coexistence of these animals in the outer rainforests' (Hyndman 1990, 72).

60 Leroi-Gourhan (1968) suggests that there is deliberate patterning in the layout of figures within painted caves, with animals such as carnivores being found in deep recesses, and bison being found in central areas. This proposal has never been formally tested, partly due to the difficulty of identifying original entrances, and where entrance, central and rear parts of the caves begin and end. Sieveking (1984) believes that the patterning Leroi-Gourhan claims to identify could be related to the ecological characteristics of the animals which were regularly associated together, in much the same manner as these are encoded in the trophy arrays of the Wopkaimin.

61 Eastham & Eastham (1991).

62 See White (1989b, 1992, 1993a, 1993b) for the early Upper Palaeolithic items of personal adornment, and Soffer (1985) for those manufactured on the Russian Plain during the later Upper Palaeolithic.

63 This is likely to explain the discrete spatial and temporal distributions of points which have very specific forms and have been given their own special name by archaeologists such as the 'Font Robert points' from western Europe and 'Emireh points' from the Near East. These artifacts, so useful to archaeologists as they can be used as chronological markers when other dating information is absent, were probably carrying social information about group membership, intentionally invested on the tool at the time of manufacture. Other aspects of variability between tools, such as markings on harpoons, may have been used to communicate individual ownership. The belief that these typologically distinct artifacts of the Upper Palaeolithic were carrying social information is widely held by archaeologists (e.g. Mellars 1989b). An excellent ethnographic study which illustrates how artifacts are invested with social information is by Wiessner (1983). She explores which items of material culture among the Kalahari San carry social information, and finds that projectile points are very well suited for carrying information about groups and boundaries because of their widespread social, economic, political and symbolic importance. She refers to this type of information as 'emblemic' style and contrasts it with 'assertive' style, which is information about individual ownership. With regard to the Palaeolithic we should perhaps expect assertive style to be present on organic artifacts, such as harpoons and arrow shafts, which may involve greater investment of time to produce than chipped stone points. In addition, the very process of manufacture had acquired new significance. Sinclair (1995, 50) argues that 'the symbolic aspects of [Upper Palaeolithic] technology is not restricted to the external form of tools.... Symbolism pervades the entire process of manufacture, through the use of a salient set of skills and desires which are common to both technology and other practices within societies'.

64 Gellner (1988, 45).

65 Morphy (1989b) provides a summary of the characteristics of the Ancestral Beings.

66 Gamble (1993).

67 The Skhūl burial was described by McCown (1937) and that at Qafzeh by Vandermeersch (1970). Lindly & Clark (1990) have questioned whether the animal parts were deliberately included with the anatomically Modern Humans at the time of burial. But due to the very close association between animal and human bones, there appears little doubt that parts of animal carcasses were intentionally placed in graves.

68 Lieberman & Shea (1994). The inferences regarding seasonality are made by using the cementum layers on gazelle teeth, while those concerning the intensity of hunting are made by the frequency of points within the artifact assemblages and the character of impact fractures. Evidence for a greater expenditure of energy by the Neanderthals comes from the character of their post-cranial skeleton (Trinkaus 1992).

69 Grün *et al* (1990), Grün & Stringer (1991), Stringer & Bräuer (1994).

70 Singer & Wymer (1982). A summary of the archaeological sequence at Klasies River

Mouth is provided by Thackeray (1989).

71 The evidence for the use of red ochre in the Middle Stone Age has been summarized by Knight *et al* (1995).

72 Knight *et al* (1995), Knight (1991).

73 This site was excavated in 1941 and the true date of the grave, if indeed it is a grave, remains unclear. Unfortunately the bone material itself cannot be dated (Grün & Stringer 1991).

74 Parkington (1990) draws together the dating evidence for the Howieson's Poort industry, and shows that some of these assemblages could be as young as 40,000 years old. He suggests that this industry is unlikely to be a unitary phenomenon, and that it appeared at various times between 100,000 and 40,000 years ago.

75 Yellen *et al* (1995).

76 I am here choosing just one of the possible scenarios for the origin and distribution of Modern Humans throughout the world. The major opposing view is that of multiregional evolution (see Mellars & Stringer 1989, Nitecki & Nitecki 1994 for debates about the origins of Modern Humans). The strongest argument supporting the multiregional hypothesis of evolution is the continuity in morphological features of fossils in different parts of the world, especially Southeast Asia/Australasia and China. I suspect that this continuity can be explained by the emergence of a similar set of adaptive features and by some degree of hybridization between incoming and resident populations.

77 Jones & Rouhani (1986), Jones *et al* (1992).

78 We should expect to find in the period between 100,000 and 60,000–30,000 years ago archaeological sites created by Early Modern Humans that do indeed look a bit like those of Early Humans, and a bit like those of fully Modern Humans. One such site is likely to be Prolom II in the Crimea which has stone tools typical of those made by Neanderthals, but also a large number of bones, some of which are pierced, engraved or chipped (Stepanchuk 1993). The site is as yet undated and there are no human skeletal remains associated with it. My guess is that it will prove to be an archaeological site of Early Modern Humans who had a glimmer of cognitive fluidity.

Ch. 10. So how did it happen? (pp. 185–194)

1 Dunbar makes this point in the following terms: 'ecologically related information exchange might be a subsequent development that capitalized on a window of opportunity created by the availability of a computer with a substantial information-processing capacity' (1993, 689).

2 Talmy (1988).

3 Pinker (1989).

4 Sperber (1994, 61).

5 Intriguingly, the philosopher Daniel Dennett suggests a similar scenario to that provided by Sperber for the evolution of the mind when playing one of his 'thought experiments' in his 1991 book *Consciousness Explained*. In his case, however, he emphasizes the importance not of talking to other people but of talking to oneself. He describes this as 'autostimulation' and the consequences he proposes are what I have been describing as 'cognitive fluidity'. Let me quote Dennett (1991, 195–96): 'the practice of asking oneself questions could arise as a natural side-effect of asking questions of others, and its utility would be similar: it would be a behaviour that could be recognized to enhance one's prospects by better informed action-guidance.... Suppose ... that although the right information is already in the brain, it is in the hands of the wrong specialist; the subsystem in the brain that needs the information cannot obtain it directly from the specialist – because evolution simply has not got around to providing such a "wire". Provoking the specialist to "broadcast" the information into the environment, however, and then relying on an existing pair of ears (and an auditory system) to pick it up, would be a way of building a "virtual wire" between the relevant subsystems. Such an act of autostimulation could blaze a valuable new trail between one's internal components.' Replace Dennett's terms of 'specialist' with 'specialized intelligence', and 'virtual wire' with 'cognitive fluidity' and his argument conforms to the one I have proposed, except that he suggests that any 'specialist' could 'broadcast' information, whereas I argue that this is likely to have been restricted to social intelligence.

6 Rozin (1976, 246).

7 Pigeot (1990), Fischer (1990).

8 It is significant to note here that although Modern Humans do have a capacity for verbal instruction, specialized craftspeople often acquire their technical skills not by explicit

teaching but by observation and trial-and-error learning: Wynn (1991) describes this for several modern groups, acquiring skills ranging from those of trawler fishing to those of toolmaking in traditional societies. Such a learning method may ensure that technical knowledge is built up within a specialized intelligence, as opposed to simply becoming part of what Sperber (1994) calls the meta-representational module, where knowledge acquired by language is placed. Psychologists refer to the type of knowledge that can only be expressed by demonstration as 'procedural' memory. They contrast this with 'propositional memory' which is divided into two types: episodic and semantic. This distinction has been proposed and explored in detail by the psychologist Endel Tulving (1983). While these types of memory share many features, they differ in that episodic memory refers to memories of personal happenings and doings, while semantic memory refers to knowledge of the world that is independent of a person's identity and past. With regard to the evolutionary scenario I have proposed, episodic memory is likely to be the original form of memory within social intelligence, and would have been possessed by Early Humans – just as they would have possessed forms of procedural memory within natural history and technical intelligences. Semantic memory, however, might be a unique possession of the Modern Human mind. If the principal difference between this and episodic memory is the type of information they deal with – and Tulving emphasizes that the critical differences between these two types of memory remain unclear – then semantic memory may have arisen from the invasion of social intelligence by non-social information. This information became available to those mental modules which had previously been dedicated to creating memories concerning only personal events within social intelligence, just as it became available for reflexive consciousness.

9 Schacter (1989, 360).

10 Searle (1992, 108–9).

11 Aiello (1996a), Wills (1994).

12 Wills (1994).

13 Knight *et al* (1995).

14 Smith *et al* (1995).

15 Stringer & Gamble (1993), Dean *et al* (1986), Zollikofer *et al* (1995). See also Smith *et al* 1993.

16 Akazawa *et al* (1995).

Ch. 11. The evolution of the mind (pp. 195–216)

1 The following brief summary of primate evolution draws on Martin (1990) and Simons (1992).

2 McFarland (1987).

3 Simons (1992).

4 Milton (1988).

5 Aiello & Wheeler (1995).

6 Whiten (1990, 367).

7 Humphrey (1984, 22).

8 The phylogenetic relationships between Eurasian fossil primates found between 15 and 4.5 m.y.a. and hominids remains unclear. The best represented of these fossils is *Dryopithecus*, with remains found in Hungary, southern France and Spain. A particularly well-preserved specimen of *D. laietanus* was recently found in the Valle Penedes region of Spain. This shows the dryopithecines swung from branches and moved on four legs, in a similar manner to orang-utans today (Moyà-Solà & Köhler 1996). Andrews & Pilbeam (1996) comment on the phylogenetic reconstruction of this period.

9 Aiello (1996a).

10 Wheeler (1984, 1988, 1991, 1994).

11 deMenocal (1995).

12 Falk (1990).

13 Falk (1990, 334).

14 Aiello & Wheeler (1995).

15 Humphrey (1984, 23).

16 Aiello (1996a, 1996b).

17 Aiello & Dunbar (1993). Aiello (1996b) draws on recent work by Robert Foley to suggest that a very gradual increase at an exponential rate in human population, beginning with *H. erectus* 1.8 million years ago, might lead to a seeming population explosion, forcing people to live within large groups.

18 The most notable of these are bifacially worked artifacts similar to handaxes which are found in the very final Mousterian assemblages from sites such as Combe Grenal. Clive Gamble (1993, 1994; Stringer & Gamble 1993) has suggested that one can see further features in Neanderthal behaviour after 60,000 years ago which foreshadow the behavioural developments of the Upper Palaeolithic, such as a greater amount of spatial structure on archaeological sites. He refers to this period as a 'pioneer phase'. But the evidence for any cognitive fluidity remains very slight, and there is nothing that approaches a capacity for symbolism.

19 Lake suggests: 'It seems plausible that evolution by natural selection typically occurs by repeatedly isolating, honing and then re-integrating parts. Natural selection is most efficacious when genotypic variability and fitness are closely correlated; it is impossible when they are completely uncorrelated. The degree of correlation is likely to be weakest in generalized systems since fitness will be subject to a larger number of selective pressures which require conflicting adaptive responses. For this reason natural selection might be expected to operate most successfully on specialized systems. However, such systems are often brittle in the sense that there is simply no way of adapting them to cope with a radical change in selective conditions. Thus it would appear that the long-term persistence of a type of system (or lineage) requires that it possess the contradictory properties of predictability and flexibility. I suggest that natural selection has frequently solved this conundrum by decomposing systems into weakly coupled parts. In this way it can respond to small changes in selective conditions by adapting the relevant subsystem without radically affecting the rest of the system. Equally, however, the possibility of rearranging the links between the subsystems provides the flexibility required to cope with radically altered selective conditions' (personal communication 16 November 1995).

20 Dawkins (1986).

21 The problem of trying to define quite what science is can be seen by contrasting two very different viewpoints. The first view is that held by the philosophers and historians of science. They have discussed the nature of science ever since Francis Bacon published his works at the start of the 17th century arguing that science must involve empirical observation of the world and experiment. Following Bacon's work, various other definitions of science have been proposed. Karl Popper challenged the view that science is the process of generalization from a mass of observations, by arguing that the essence of science is the ability to falsify one's hypotheses. Thomas Kuhn introduced the notion that science is deeply embedded in a social matrix and proceeds in sudden jumps ('paradigm changes') rather than a gradual accumulation of knowledge. More recently the whole notion that there is such as thing as a scientific method at all has been challenged by philosophers such as Paul Feyerbend.

There are many books that provide reviews of these changing ideas of science (e.g. Gillies 1993) and others that describe the development of scientific thought, perhaps most notably the seminal 1957 work of Herbert Butterworth, *The Origins of Modern Science 1300–1800*. As can be seen from that title, such histories of science almost invariably begin at the end of the Medieval period and focus on the work of figures such as Galileo, Copernicus, Newton and Einstein. Indeed, in such works there is an assumption that although the intellectual foundations for these scientists may be found in the work of Classical and Islamic scholars, science is a product of Western civilization. One recent review article in the *British Journal for the History of Science*, concluded that science is no more than 250 years old and confined to western Europe and America (Cunningham & Williams 1993).

Now let us look at a radically different view of science, one that has come from a scientist himself. In his 1995 book, *The Trouble with Science*, Robin Dunbar – whose views about the evolution of language we have considered – argues that science is 'a method for finding out about the world based on the generation of hypotheses and the testing of predictions derived from those hypotheses.' As such this is a fairly conventional position. But Dunbar takes a radical stance by questioning the assumption that this is unique to modern Western culture.

In his book, Dunbar argues that not only can the technological inventions of the Chinese during the 1st millennium BC, such as printing, silk and gunpowder, be described as arising from science, but so too can the knowledge that Aristotle acquired about the natural world in the 4th century BC and the developments in mathematics and physics made by Islamic scholars during the 9th to 12th centuries AD. This much is no doubt acceptable to the majority of his readers. But he goes on to argue that science is rife in traditional non-Western societies. According to Dunbar, 'science' is the method used to acquire the prodigious and accurate knowledge about the natural world possessed by hunter-gatherers, pastoralists and farmers. As if this was not enough, Dunbar proceeds to argue that many non-human animals also engage in science, because hypothesis testing appears to be one of the means by which they acquire their knowledge of the world. He concludes that 'science is a genuine universal, characteristic of all advanced life forms' (p. 75).

22 D'Errico (1995). Donald (1991) similarly emphasizes the importance of these which he describes as 'external storage devices'.

23 Dennett (1991).

24 In his book *The Trouble with Science* (1995) Robin Dunbar argues that the use of metaphors appears most commonly in physics and evolutionary biology, as these subjects involve ideas which are alien to our everyday experience. To understand these, scientists are prone not only to use metaphors, but to choose those which draw on the social world of humans. For instance the geneticist Steve Jones (1993) uses the metaphor of the genetic code as possessing a language; as Pinker (1994) describes, the use of a linguistic metaphor in genetics has been widely adopted. Dunbar provides examples of many other metaphors used in biological thought, such as the intriguing 'Kamikaze Sperm' hypothesis.

25 Gould (1990, 229).

26 Kuhn (1979).

27 Dennett (1991, 455).

Epilogue. The origins of agriculture (pp. 217–226)

1 Hole (1992) provides a brief overview of ideas concerning the origins of agriculture.

2 Wendorf *et al* (1990) describe the archaeology of Wadi Kubbaniya, while Hillman (1989) summarizes the Late Palaeolithic food remains.

3 Hillman *et al* (1989).

4 Cohen & Armelagos (1984).

5 Hole (1992).

6 This argument was forwarded in most detail by Nathan Cohen in a 1977 book entitled *The Food Crisis in Prehistory*.

7 Cohen & Armelagos (1984).

8 Dansgaard, White & Johnsen (1989).

9 The following summary follows Moore & Hillman (1992).

10 Legge & Rowley-Conwy (1987).

11 This is the period of the Younger Dryas, a global environmental event which saw the re-advance of the ice sheets in Europe. It was a short, sharp cold interval that was followed by the very rapid global warming which marked the true end of the last ice age.

12 Bar-Yosef & Belfer-Cohen (1989).

13 The architecture itself is not necessarily indicative of sedentism; mobile hunter-gatherers do in some circumstances build substantial dwellings and facilities which are returned to on a regular basis. Bar-Yosef & Belfer-Cohen (1989) suggest that the best evidence for sedentism comes from the appearance of house sparrows, mice and rats in the fauna from these sites.

14 For a summary of Natufian settlement and economy see Byrd (1989) and Bar-Yosef & Belfer-Cohen (1989).

15 Bar-Yosef & Belfer-Cohen (1989, 490).

16 This is evident from the spatial relationships between storage pits and dwellings. At Radomyshl' we see several dwellings surrounding a central storage pit, implying 'open, visible and equal access to stored resources for all inhabitants of the site'. At the slightly later site of Dobranichevka we see similar numbers of similar-sized storage pits distributed around each dwelling, implying that the residents of each dwelling now owned their own stored resources, although the distribution of resources remained equitable. At later sites, such as Mezin, Gontsy and Eliseevichi, the storage pits are preferentially distributed around one single dwelling. For instance at Mezin there appears to have been 5 dwellings, but 6 out of the 7 (or 8) storage pits there were located adjacent to just one of these dwellings. The residents of this dwelling, therefore, appear to have controlled access to stored resources (Soffer 1985, 459–63).

17 Mithen (1990).

18 See Albrethsen & Petersen (1976), Larsson (1983) and Clark & Neeley (1987).

19 For differing views on how a Darwinian perspective should be used when looking at prehistoric behaviour see Clark (1992) and Mithen (1993).

20 Hayden (1990, 35).

21 Bahn (1978). This evidence has been critically assessed by White (1989b).

22 Bahn (1978).

23 For burial of dogs in southern Scandinavia see Larsson (1983); for the Natufian see Byrd (1989).

24 Humphrey (1984, 26–7)

25 Evidence for the management and manipulation of plants resources in the European Mesolithic has been summarized by Zvelebil (1994).

26 Yen (1989) and Hallam (1989) summarize evidence for the 'domestication' of the environment by indigenous Australians. See also Chase (1989) and Jones & Meehan (1989).

27 See Higgs & Jarman (1969), Higgs (1972).

Bibliography

Adovasio, J.M., Donahue, J. & Stuckenrath, R.
1990. The Meadowcroft Rockshelter
radiocarbon chronology. *American Antiquity* 55,
348–54.

Aiello, L. 1993. The fossil evidence for modern
human origins in Africa: a revised view.
American Anthropologist 95, 73–96.

Aiello, L. 1996a. Terrestriality, bipedalism and
the origin of language. In *The Evolution of Social
Behaviour Patterns in Primates and Man*, ed., J.
Maynard-Smith. London: Proceedings of the
British Academy (in press).

Aiello, L. 1996b. Hominine preadaptations for
language and cognition. In *Modelling the Early
Human Mind*, eds., P. Mellars & K. Gibson.
Cambridge: McDonald Institute Monograph
Series.

Aiello, L. & Dunbar, R.I.M. 1993. Neocortex
size, group size and the evolution of language.
Current Anthropology 34, 184–93.

Aiello, L. & Wheeler, P. 1995. The expensive-
tissue hypothesis. *Current Anthropology* 36,
199–221.

Aikens, C.M. & Higuchi, T. 1982. *Prehistory of
Japan*. New York: Academic Press.

Akazawa, T., Aoki, K. & Kimura,T. 1992. *The
Evolution and Dispersal of Modern Humans in
Asia*. Tokyo: Hokusen-Sha.

Akazawa, T., Muhesen, M., Dodo, Y., Kondo, O.
& Mizoguchi, Y. 1995. Neanderthal infant
burial. *Nature* 377, 585–86.

Albrethsen, S.E. & Petersen, E.B. 1976.
Excavation of a Mesolithic cemetery at Vedbaek,
Denmark. *Acta Archaeologica* 47, 1–28.

Allen, J. 1994. Radiocarbon determinations,
luminescence dates and Australian archaeology.
Antiquity 68, 339–43.

Alley, R.B., Meese, D.A., Shuman, C.A., Gow,
A.J., Taylor, K.C., Gorrtes, P.M., Whitell,
J.W.C., Ram, M., Waddington, E.D.,
Mayewski, P.A. & Zielinski, G.A. 1993. Abrupt
increase in Greenland snow accumulation at the
end of the Younger Dryas event. *Nature* 362,
527–29.

Allsworth-Jones, P. 1986. *The Szeletian and the
Transition from the Middle to Upper Palaeolithic
in Central Europe*. Oxford: Clarendon Press.

Allsworth-Jones, P. 1993. The archaeology of
archaic and early modern *Homo sapiens*: an
African perspective. *Cambridge Archaeological
Journal* 3, 21–39.

Anderson, D.D. 1990. *Lang Rongrien Rockshelter:
A Pleistocene-Early Holocene Archaeological Site
from Krabi, Southwestern Thailand*. Philadelphia:
The University Museum, University of
Pennsylvania.

Anderson. J. R. 1980. *Cognitive Psychology and its
Implications* (2nd edition). New York: W.H.
Freeman.

Anderson-Gerfund, P. 1990. Aspects of
behaviour in the Middle Palaeolithic: functional
analysis of stone tools from southwest France. In
The Emergence of Modern Humans, ed., P.
Mellars, pp. 389–418. Edinburgh: Edinburgh
University Press.

Andrews, P. 1995. Ecological apes and ancestors.
Nature 376, 555–56.

Andrews, P. & Pilbeam, D. 1996. The nature of
the evidence. *Nature* 379, 123–24.

Arensburg, B., Tillier, A-M., Vandermeersch, B.,
Duday, H., Schepartz, L.A. & Rak, Y. 1989. A
Middle Palaeolithic hyoid bone. *Nature* 338,
758–60.

Arensburg, B., Schepartz, L.A., Tillier, A-M.,
Vandermeersch, B. & Rak, Y. 1990. A
reappraisal of the anatomical basis for speech in
Middle Palaeolithic hominids. *American Journal
of Physical Anthropology* 83, 137–46.

Arsuaga, J-L., Martinez, I., Gracia, A., Carretero,
J-M. & Carbonell, E. 1993. Three new human
skulls from the Sima de los Huesos Middle
Pleistocene site in Sierra de Atapuerca, Spain.
Nature 362, 534–37.

Ashton, N.M., Cook, J., Lewis, S.G. & Rose, J.
(eds.) 1992. *High Lodge: Excavations by G. de G.
Sieveking 1962–68 & J. Cook 1988*. London:
British Museum Press.

Ashton, N.M. & McNabb, J. 1992. The
interpretation and context of the High Lodge
flint industries. In *High Lodge: Excavations by G.
de G. Sieveking 1962–68 & J. Cook 1988*, eds.,
N.M. Ashton, J. Cook, S.G. Lewis & J. Rose,
pp. 164–68. London: British Museum Press.

Ashton, N.M., McNabb, J., Irving, B., Lewes, S.
& Parfitt, S. 1994. Contemporaneity of
Clactonian and Acheulian flint industries at
Barnham, Suffolk. *Antiquity* 68, 585–89.

Asfaw, B., Beyene, Y., Suwa, G., Walter, R.C.,
White, T., WoldeGabriel, G. & Yemane, T.
1992. The earliest Acheulean from Konso-
Gardula. *Nature* 360, 732–35.

Atran, S. 1990. *Cognitive Foundations of Natural
History: Towards an Anthropology of Science*.
Cambridge: Cambridge University Press.

Atran, S. 1994. Core domains versus scientific
theories: evidence from systematics and Itza-
Maya folkbiology. In *Mapping the Mind: Domain
Specificity in Cognition and Culture*, eds., L.A.
Hirschfeld & S.A. Gelman, pp. 316–40.
Cambridge: Cambridge University Press.

Audouze, F. 1987. The Paris Basin in
Magdalenian times. In *The Pleistocene Old
World*, ed., O. Soffer, pp. 183–200. New York:
Plenum Press.

Audouze, F. & Enloe, J. 1992. Subsistence
strategies and economy in the Magdalenian of

the Paris Basin. In *The Late Glacial in North-West Europe: Human Adaptation and Environmental Change at the End of the Pleistocene*, eds., N. Barton, A.J. Roberts & D.A. Roe, pp. 63–71. London: Council for British Archaeology Research Report No. 17.

Ayers, W.S. & Rhee, S.N. 1984. The Acheulian in Asia? A review of research on the Korean Palaeolithic culture. *Proceedings of the Prehistoric Society* 50, 35–48.

Bahn, P.G. 1978. On the unacceptable face of the West European Upper Palaeolithic. *Antiquity* 52, 183–92.

Bahn, P.G. 1991. Pleistocene images outside of Europe. *Proceedings of the Prehistoric Society* 57 (i), 99–102.

Bahn, P.G. 1994. New advances in the field of Ice Age art. In *Origins of Anatomically Modern Humans*, eds., M.H. Nitecki & D.V. Nitecki, pp. 121–32. New York: Plenum Press.

Bahn, P.G. & Vertut, J. 1988. *Images of the Ice Age*. London: Windward.

Bar-Yosef, O. 1980. Prehistory of the Levant. *Annual Review of Anthropology* 9, 101–33.

Bar-Yosef, O. 1989. Geochronology of the Levantine Middle Palaeolithic. In *The Human Revolution*, eds., P. Mellars & C. Stringer, pp. 589–610. Edinburgh: Edinburgh University Press.

Bar-Yosef, O. 1994a. The Lower Palaeolithic of the Near East. *Journal of World Prehistory* 8, 211–65.

Bar-Yosef, O. 1994b. The contributions of southwest Asia to the study of the origin of modern humans. In *Origins of Anatomically Modern Humans*, eds., M.H. Nitecki & D.V. Nitecki, pp. 23–66. New York: Plenum Press.

Bar-Yosef, O. & Belfer-Cohen, A. 1989. The origins of sedentism and farming communities in the Levant. *Journal of World Prehistory* 3, 447–97.

Bar-Yosef, O. & Goren-Inbar, N. 1993. *The Lithic Assemblages of the Site of Úbeidiya, Jordan Valley*. Jerusalem: Qedem 34.

Bar-Yosef, O. & Meignen, L. 1992. Insights into Levantine Middle Palaeolithic cultural variability. In *The Middle Palaeolithic: Adaptation, Behaviour and Variability*, eds., H.L. Dibble & P. Mellars, pp. 163–82. Philadelphia: The University Museum, University of Pennsylvania.

Bar-Yosef, O., Vandermeersch, B., Arensburg, B., Belfer-Cohen, A., Goldberg, P., Laville, H., Meignen, L., Rak, Y., Speth, J.D., Tchernov, E., Tillier, A-M. & Weiner, S. 1992. The excavations in Kebara Cave, Mt. Carmel. *Current Anthropology* 33, 497–551.

Baron-Cohen, S. 1995. *Mindblindness*. Cambridge MA: MIT Press.

Barkow, J.H., Cosmides, L. & Tooby, J. 1992. *The Adapted Mind: Evolutionary Psychology and the Generation of Culture*. Oxford: Oxford University Press.

Barton, N., Roberts, A.J. & Roe, D.A. (eds.) 1992.

The Late Glacial in North-West Europe: Human Adaptation and Environmental Change at the End of the Pleistocene. London: Council for British Archaeology Research Report No. 77.

Bartstra, G. 1982. *Homo erectus erectus:* the search for his artifacts. *Current Anthropology* 23, 318–20.

Beauchamp, G. & Cabana, G. 1990. Group size and variability in primates. *Primates* 31, 171–82.

Beaumont, P.B., Villers, D. & Vogel, J.C. 1978. Modern man in sub-Saharan Africa prior to 49,000 BP: a review and evaluation with particular reference to Border Cave. *South African Journal of Science* 74, 409–19.

Bednarik, R.G. 1992. Palaeoart and archaeological myths. *Cambridge Archaeological Journal* 2, 27–57.

Bednarik, R.G. 1994. A taphonomy of palaeoart. *Antiquity* 68, 68–74.

Bednarik, R.G. 1995. Concept-mediated marking in the Lower Palaeolithic. *Current Anthropology* 36, 605–34.

Bednarik, R.G. & Yuzhu, Y. 1991. Palaeolithic art in China. *Rock Art Research* 8, 119–23.

Bégouen, R. & Clottes, J. 1991. Portable and wall art in the Volp caves, Montesquieu-Avantès (Ariège). *Proceedings of the Prehistoric Society* 57 (i), 65–80.

Begun, D. & Walker, D. 1993. The endocast. In *The Nariokotome Homo erectus Skeleton*, eds., D. Walker & R. Leakey, pp. 26–358. Berlin: Springer Verlag.

Behrensmeyer, A.K. 1978. Taphonomic and ecologic information from bone weathering. *Palaeobiology* 2, 150–62.

Belfer-Cohen, A. & Goren-Inbar, N. 1994. Cognition and communication in the Levantine Lower Palaeolithic. *World Archaeology* 26, 144–57.

Belitzky, S., Goren-Inbar, N. & Werker, E. 1991. A Middle Pleistocene wooden plank with man-made polish. *Journal of Human Evolution* 20, 349–53.

Bergman, C.A. 1993. The development of the bow in western Europe: a technological and functional perspective. In *Hunting and Animal Exploitation in the Later Palaeolithic and Mesolithic of Eurasia*, eds., G.L. Peterkin, H.M. Bricker & P. Mellars, pp. 95–105. Archaeological Papers of the American Anthropological Association, No. 4.

Bergman, C.A. & Roberts, M.B. 1988. Flaking technology at the Acheulian site of Boxgrove, West Sussex (England). *Revue Archéologique de Picardie* 1–2, 105–13.

Berlin, B. 1992. *Ethnobiological Classification: Principles of Categorization of Plants and Animals in Traditional Societies*. Princeton: Princeton University Press.

Berlin, B., Breedlove, D. & Raven, P. 1973. General principles of classification and nomenclature in folk biology. *American Anthropologist* 87, 298–315.

Béyries, S. 1988. Functional variability of lithic

sets in the Middle Paleolithic. In *Upper Pleistocene Prehistory of Western Eurasia*, eds., H.L. Dibble & A. Montet-White, pp. 213–23. Philadelphia: The University Museum, University of Pennsylvania.

Binford, L.R. 1973. Interassemblage variability – the Mousterian and the functional argument. In *The Explanation of Culture Change*, ed., C. Renfrew, pp. 227–54. London: Duckworth.

Binford, L.R. 1978. *Nunamiut Ethnoarchaeology*. New York: Academic Press.

Binford, L.R. 1981. *Bones: Ancient Men and Modern Myths*. New York: Academic Press.

Binford, L.R. 1984a. *Faunal Remains from Klasies River Mouth*. Orlando: Academic Press.

Binford, L.R. 1984b. Butchering, sharing and the archaeological record. *Journal of Anthropological Archaeology* 3, 235–57.

Binford, L.R. 1985. Human ancestors: changing views of their behavior. *Journal of Anthropological Archaeology* 4, 292–327.

Binford, L.R. 1986. Comment on 'Systematic butchery by Plio/Pleistocene hominids at Olduvai Gorge' by H.T. Bunn & E.M. Kroll. *Current Anthropology* 27, 444–46.

Binford, L.R. 1987a. Searching for camps and missing the evidence? Another look at the Lower Palaeolithic. In *The Pleistocene Old World: Regional Perspectives*, ed., O. Soffer, pp. 17–31. New York: Plenum Press.

Binford, L.R. 1987b. Were there elephant hunters at Torralba? In *The Evolution of Human Hunting*, eds., M.H. Nitecki & D.V. Nitecki, pp. 47–105. New York: Plenum Press.

Binford, L.R. 1988. Fact and fiction about the Zinjanthropus floor: data, arguments and interpretations. *Current Anthropology* 29, 123–35.

Binford, L.R. 1989. Isolating the transition to cultural adaptations: an organizational approach. In *The Emergence of Modern Humans: Biocultural Adaptations in the Later Pleistocene*, ed., E. Trinkaus, pp. 18–41. Cambridge: Cambridge University Press.

Binford, L.R. & Binford S.R. 1969. Stone tools and human behavior. *Scientific American* 220, 70–84.

Binford, L.R. & Chuan Kun Ho 1985. Taphonomy at a distance: Zhoukoudian, 'the cave home of Beijing Man'. *Current Anthropology* 26, 413–42.

Binford, L.R. & Stone, N.M. 1986. Zhoukoudian: a closer look. *Current Anthropology* 27, 453–75.

Binford, L.R., Mills, M.G.L. & Stone, N.M. 1988. Hyena scavenging behavior and its implications for the interpretation of faunal assemblages from FLK 22 (the Zinj floor) at Olduvai Gorge. *Journal of Anthropological Archaeology* 7, 99–135.

Binford, L.R. & Todd, L. 1982. On arguments for the 'butchering' of giant geladas. *Current Anthropology* 23, 108–10.

Birket-Smith, K. 1936. *The Eskimos*. London: Methuen.

Bird-David, N. 1990. The 'giving environment': another perspective on the economic system of gatherer-hunters. *Current Anthropology* 31, 189–96.

Bischoff, J.L., Soler, N., Maroto, J. & Julia, R. 1989. Abrupt Mousterian/Aurignacian boundary at *c.* 40 ka bp: accelerator 14C dates from L'Arbreda cave. *Journal of Archaeological Science* 16, 563–76.

Bisson, M.S. & Bolduc. P. 1994. Previously undescribed figurines from the Grimaldi Caves. *Current Anthropology* 35, 458–68.

Bleed, P. 1986. The optimal design of hunting weapons. *American Antiquity* 51, 737–47.

Block, N. 1995. On a confusion about the function of consciousness. *Behavioral and Brain Sciences* 18, 227–87.

Blurton-Jones, H. & Konner, M.J. 1976. !Kung knowledge of animal behavior. In *Kalahari Hunter-Gatherers*, eds., R. Lee & I. DeVore. Cambridge MA: Harvard University Press.

Blumenschine, R.J. 1986. *Early Hominid Scavenging Opportunities*. Oxford: British Archaeological Reports, International Series 283.

Blumenschine, R.J. 1987. Characteristics of an early hominid scavenging niche. *Current Anthropology* 28, 383–407.

Blumenschine, R.J., Cavallo, J.A. & Capaldo, S.D. 1994. Competition for carcasses and early hominid behavioural ecology: a case study and conceptual framework. *Journal of Human Evolution* 27, 17–213.

Boden, M. 1990. *The Creative Mind: Myths and Mechanisms*. London: Weidenfeld and Nicolson.

Boden, M. 1994. Précis of 'The Creative Mind: Myths and Mechanisms'. *Behavioral and Brain Sciences* 17, 519–70.

Boëda, E. 1988. Le concept laminaire: rupture et filiation avec le concept Levallois. In *L'Homme Neanderthal, Vol. 8, La Mutation*, ed., J. Kozlowski, pp. 41–60. Liège, Belgium: ERAUL.

Boëda, E. 1990. De la surface au volume, analyse des conceptions des débitages Levallois et laminaires. *Mémoires du Musée de Préhistoire*. 3, 63–8.

Boesch, C. 1991. Teaching among wild chimpanzees. *Animal Behavior* 41, 530–32.

Boesch, C. 1993. Aspects of transmission of tool-use in wild chimpanzees. In *Tools, Language and Cognition in Human Evolution*, eds., K.G. Gibson & T. Ingold, pp. 171–83. Cambridge: Cambridge University Press.

Boesch, C. & Boesch, H. 1983. Optimization of nut-cracking with natural hammers by wild chimpanzees. *Behaviour* 83, 265–86.

Boesch, C. & Boesch, H. 1984a. Mental maps in wild chimpanzees: an analysis of hammer transports for nut cracking. *Primates* 25, 160–70.

Boesch, C. & Boesch, H. 1984b. Possible causes of sex differences in the use of natural hammers by wild chimpanzees. *Journal of Human Evolution* 13, 415–40.

Boesch, C. & Boesch, H. 1989. Hunting behavior of wild chimpanzees in the Taï National Park.

American Journal of Physical Anthropology 78, 547–73.

Boesch, C. & Boesch, H. 1990. Tool-use and tool-making in wild chimpanzees. *Folia Primatologica* 54, 86–99.

Boesch, C. & Boesch, H. 1993. Diversity of tool-use and tool-making in wild chimpanzees. In *The Use of Tools by Human and Non-human Primates*, eds., A. Berthelet & J. Chavaillon, pp. 158–74. Oxford: Clarendon Press.

Bokelmann, K. 1992. Some new thoughts on old data on humans and reindeer in the Arhensburgian tunnel valley in Schleswig-Holstein, Germany. In *The Late Glacial in North-West Europe: Human Adaptation and Environmental Change at the End of the Pleistocene*, eds., N. Barton, A.J. Roberts & D.A. Roe, pp. 72–81. London: Council for British Archaeology Research Report No. 17.

Bonifay, E. & Vandermeersch, B. (eds.) 1991. *Les Premiers Européens*. Paris: Editions du C.T.H.S.

Bordes, F. 1961a. *Typologie du Paléolithique Ancien et Moyen*. Publications de l'Institut de Préhistoire de l'Université de Bordeaux, Memoiré No 1, 2 Vols.

Bordes, F. 1961b. Mousterian cultures in France. *Science* 134, 803–10.

Bordes, F. 1968. *Tools of the Old Stone Age*. London: Weidenfeld & Nicolson.

Bordes, F. 1972. *A Tale of Two Caves*. New York: Harper and Row.

Bowdler, S. 1992. *Homo sapiens* in Southeast Asia and the Antipodes: archaeological versus biological interpretations. In *The Evolution and Dispersal of Modern Humans in Asia*, eds., T. Akazawa, K. Aoki & T. Kimura, pp. 559–89. Tokyo: Hokusen-Sha.

Bowen, D.Q. & Sykes, G.A. 1994. How old is Boxgrove Man? *Nature* 371, 751.

Boyer, P. 1990. *Tradition as Truth and Communication*. New York: Cambridge University Press.

Boyer, P. 1994a. *The Naturalness of Religious Ideas. A Cognitive Theory of Religion*. Berkeley: University of California Press.

Boyer, P. 1994b. Cognitive constraints on cultural representations: natural ontologies and religious ideas. In *Mapping the Mind: Domain Specificity in Cognition and Culture*, eds. L.A. Hirschfeld & S.A. Gelman, pp. 391–411. Cambridge: Cambridge University Press.

Brain, C.K. 1981. *The Hunters or the Hunted?* Chicago: University of Chicago Press.

Bräuer, G. & Smith, F.H. (eds.) 1992. *Continuity or Replacement? Controversies in Homo sapiens Evolution*. Rotterdam: Balkema.

Bratlund, B. 1992. A study of hunting lesions containing flint fragments on reindeer bones at Stellmoor, Schleswig-Holstein, Germany. In *The Late Glacial in North-West Europe: Human Adaptation and Environmental Change at the End of the Pleistocene*, eds., N. Barton, A.J. Roberts & D.A. Roe, pp. 193–207. London: Council for British Archaeology Research Report No. 17.

Breuil, H. 1952. *Four Hundred Centuries of Cave Art*. Montignac: Centre d'Etudes et de Documentation Préhistoriques.

Brewer, S.M. & McGrew, W.C. 1990. Chimpanzee use of a tool-set to get honey. *Folia Primatologica* 54, 100–04.

Brothwell, D. 1986. *The Bogman and the Archaeology of People*. London: British Museum Press.

Brown, P. 1981. Artificial cranial deformations as a component in the variation in Pleistocene Australian crania. *Archaeology in Oceania* 16, 156–67.

Brunet, M., Beauvilain, A., Coppens, Y., Heintz, E., Moutaye, A.H.E. & Pilbeam, D. 1995. The first australopithecine 2,500 kilometres west of the Rift Valley (Chad). *Nature* 378, 273–74.

Bunn, H.T. 1981. Archaeological evidence for meat eating by Plio-Pleistocene hominids from Koobi Fora and Olduvai Gorge. *Nature* 291, 574–77.

Bunn, H.T. 1983a. Evidence on the diet and subsistence patterns of Plio-Pleistocene hominids at Koobi Fora, Kenya and Olduvai Gorge, Tanzania. In *Animals and Archaeology: 1. Hunters and their Prey*, eds., J. Clutton-Brock and C. Grigson, pp. 21–30. Oxford: British Archaeological Reports, International Series 163.

Bunn, H.T. 1983b. Comparative analysis of modern bone assemblages from a San hunter-gatherer camp in the Kalahari Desert, Botswana, and from a spotted hyena den near Nairobi, Kenya. In *Animals and Archaeology: 1. Hunters and their Prey*, eds., J. Clutton-Brock and C. Grigson, pp. 143–48. Oxford: British Archaeological Reports, International Series 163.

Bunn, H.T. 1994. Early Pleistocene hominid foraging strategies along the ancestral Omo River at Koobi Fora, Kenya. *Journal of Human Evolution* 27, 247–66.

Bunn, H.T. & Kroll, E.M. 1986. Systematic butchery by Plio-Pleistocene hominids at Olduvai Gorge, Tanzania. *Current Anthropology* 27, 431–52.

Buss, D. 1994. *The Evolution of Desire: Strategies of Human Mating*. New York: Basic Books.

Byrd, B.F. 1989. The Natufian: settlement, variability and economic adaptations in the Levant at the end of the Pleistocene. *Journal of World Prehistory* 3, 159–97.

Byrne, R.W. 1995. *The Thinking Ape: Evolutionary Origins of Intelligence*. Oxford: Oxford University Press.

Byrne, R.W. & Whiten, A. 1985. Tactical deception of familiar individuals in baboons (*Papio ursinus*). *Animal Behavior* 33, 669–73.

Byrne R.W. & Whiten, A. (eds.) 1988. *Machiavellian Intelligence: Social Expertise and the Evolution of Intellect in Monkeys, Apes and Humans*. Oxford: Clarendon Press.

Byrne, R.W. & Whiten, A. 1991. Computation and mindreading in primate tactical deception. In *Natural Theories of Mind*, ed., A. Whiten, pp. 127–41. Oxford: Blackwell.

Byrne, R.W. & Whiten, A. 1992. Cognitive evolution in primates: evidence from tactical deception. *Man (N.S.)* 27, 609–27.

Cabrera, V. & Bischoff, J. 1989. Accelerator 14C dates for Early Upper Palaeolithic at El Castillo Cave. *Journal of Archaeological Science* 16, 577–84.

Callow, P. & Cornford, J.M. (eds.) 1986. *La Cotte de St Brelade 1961–1978: Excavations by C.B.M. McBurney*. Norwich: GeoBooks.

Calvin, W.H. 1983. A stone's throw and its launch window: timing, precision and its implications for language and hominid brains. *Journal of Theoretical Biology* 104, 121–35.

Calvin, W.H. 1993. The unitary hypothesis: a common neural circuitry for novel manipulations, language, plan-ahead and throwing. In *Tools, Language and Cognition in Human Evolution*, eds., K.R. Gibson & T. Ingold, pp. 230–250. Cambridge: Cambridge University Press.

Cann, R.L., Stoneking, M. & Wilson, A. 1987. Mitochondrial DNA and human evolution. *Nature* 325, 32–6.

Carbonell, E., Bermúdez de Castro, J.M., Arsuaga, J.C., Diez, J.C., Rosas, A., Cuenca-Bercós, G., Sala, R., Mosquera, M. & Rodriguez, X.P. 1995. Lower Pleistocene hominids and artifacts from Atapuerca-TD6 (Spain). *Science* 269, 826–30.

Carey, S. & Spelke, E. 1994. Domain-specific knowledge and conceptual change. In *Mapping the Mind: Domain Specificity in Cognition and Culture*, eds., L.A. Hirschfeld and S.A. Gelman pp. 169–200. Cambridge: Cambridge University Press.

Carmichael, D.L., Hubert, J., Reeves, B. & Schanche, A. 1994. *Sacred Sites, Sacred Places*. London: Routledge.

Cerling, T.E. 1992. The development of grasslands and savanna in East Africa during the Neogene. *Palaeogeography, Palaeoclimateology and Palaeoecology* 97, 241–47.

Chapman, C. 1990. Ecological constraints on group size in three species of neotropical primates. *Folia Primatologica* 55, 1–9.

Chase, A.K. 1989. Domestication and domiculture in northern Australia: a social perspective. In *Foraging and Farming: The Evolution of Plant Exploitation*, eds., D.R. Harris & G.C. Hillman, pp. 42–78. London: Unwin Hyman.

Chase, P. 1986. *The Hunters of Combe Grenal: Approaches to Middle Palaeolithic Subsistence in Europe*. Oxford: British Archaeological Reports, International Series, S286.

Chase, P. 1989. How different was Middle Palaeolithic subsistence? A zooarchaeological perspective on the Middle to Upper Palaeolithic transition. In *The Human Revolution*, eds., P. Mellars & C. Stringer, pp. 321–37. Edinburgh: Edinburgh University Press.

Chase, P. 1991. Symbols and palaeolithic artifacts: style, standardization and the imposition of arbitrary form. *Journal of Anthropological Archaeology* 10, 193–214.

Chase, P. & Dibble, H. 1987. Middle Palaeolithic symbolism: a review of current evidence and interpretations. *Journal of Anthropological Archaeology*, 6, 263–93.

Chase, P. & Dibble, H. 1992. Scientific archaeology and the origins of symbolism: a reply to Bednarik. *Cambridge Archaeological Journal* 2, 43–51.

Chauvet, J-M., Deschamps, E.B. & Hillaire, C. 1996. *Chauvet Cave: The Discovery of the World's Oldest Paintings*. London: Thames and Hudson; New York: Abrams.

Chavaillon, J. 1976. Evidence for the technical practices of early Pleistocene hominids. In *Earliest Man and Environments in the Lake Rudolf Basin: Stratigraphy, Paleoecology and Evolution*, eds., Y. Coppens, F.C. Howell, G. Isaac & R.E.F. Leakey, pp. 565–73. Chicago: Chicago University Press.

Cheney, D.L. & Seyfarth, R.S. 1988. Social and non-social knowledge in vervet monkeys. In *Machiavellian Intelligence: Social Expertise and the Evolution of Intellect in Monkeys, Apes and Humans*, eds., R.W. Byrne & A. Whiten, pp. 255–70. Oxford: Clarendon Press.

Cheney, D.L. & Seyfarth, R.S. 1990. *How Monkeys See the World*. Chicago: Chicago University Press.

Cheney, D.L., Seyfarth, R.S., Smuts, B.B. & Wrangham, R.W. 1987. The future of primate research. In *Primate Societies*, eds., B.B. Smuts, D.L. Cheney, R.M. Seyfarth, R.W. Wrangham & T.T. Struhsaker, pp. 491–96. Chicago: Chicago University Press.

Churchill, S. 1993. Weapon technology, prey size selection and hunting methods in modern hunter-gatherers: implications for hunting in the Palaeolithic and Mesolithic. In *Hunting and Animal Exploitation in the Later Palaeolithic and Mesolithic of Eurasia*, eds., G.L. Peterkin, H.M. Bricker & P. Mellars, pp. 11–24. Archaeological Papers of the American Anthropological Association, No. 4.

Clark, G.A. 1992. A comment on Mithen's ecological interpretation of Palaeolithic art. *Proceedings of the Prehistoric Society* 58, 107–09.

Clark, G.A. & Neeley, M. 1987. Social differentiation in European Mesolithic burial data. In *Mesolithic Northwest Europe: Recent Trends*, eds., P.A. Rowley-Conwy, M. Zvelebil & H.P. Blankholm, pp. 121–27. Sheffield: Department of Archaeology and Prehistory.

Clark, G.A., Young, D., Straus, L.G. & Jewett, R. 1986. Multivariate analysis of La Riera industries and fauna. In *La Riera Cave*, eds., L.G. Straus & G.A. Clark, pp. 325–50. Anthropological Research Papers 36, Tempe: Arizona State University.

Clark, J.D. 1969. *The Kalambo Falls Prehistoric Site, Vol I*. Cambridge: Cambridge University Press.

Clark, J.D. 1974. *The Kalambo Falls Prehistoric*

Site, Vol II. Cambridge: Cambridge University Press.

Clark, J.D. 1982. The cultures of the Middle Palaeolithic/Middle Stone Age. In *The Cambridge History of Africa, Volume 1, From the Earliest Times to c. 500 BC*, ed., J.D. Clark, pp. 248–341. Cambridge: Cambridge University Press.

Clark, J.D. & Haynes, C.V. 1970. An elephant butchery site at Mwanganda's Village, Karonga, Malawi. *World Archaeology* 1, 390–411.

Clark, J.D. & Kurashina, H. 1979a. An analysis of earlier stone age bifaces from Gadeb (Locality 8E), Northern Bale Highlands, Ethiopia. *South African Archaeological Bulletin* 34, 93–109.

Clark, J.D. & Kurashina, H. 1979b. Hominid occupation of the east-central highlands of Ethiopia in the Plio-Pleistocene. *Nature* 282, 33–9.

Clarke, R.J. 1988. Habiline handaxes and Paranthropine pedigree at Sterkfontein. *World Archaeology* 20, 1–12.

Clayton, D. 1978. Socially facilitated behaviour. *Quarterly Review of Biology* 53, 373–91.

Close, A. 1986. The place of the Haua Fteah in the late Palaeolithic of North Africa. In *Stone Age Prehistory*, eds., G.N. Bailey & P. Callow, pp. 169–80. Cambridge: Cambridge University Press.

Clottes, J. 1990. The parietal art of the Late Magdalenian. *Antiquity* 64, 527–48.

Clutton-Brock, T.H. & Harvey, P. 1977. Primate ecology and social organisation. *Journal of the Zoological Society of London* 183, 1–39.

Clutton-Brock, T.H. & Harvey, P. 1980. Primates, brains and ecology. *Journal of the Zoological Society of London* 190, 309–23.

Cohen, M.N. 1977. *The Food Crisis in Prehistory*. New Haven CT: Yale University Press.

Cohen, M.N. & Armelagos, G.J. 1984. *Paleopathology at the Origins of Agriculture*. New York: Academic Press.

Conkey, M. 1980. The identification of prehistoric hunter-gatherer aggregation: the case of Altamira. *Current Anthropology* 21, 609–30.

Conkey, M. 1983. On the origins of Palaeolithic art: a review and some critical thoughts. In *The Mousterian Legacy: Human Biocultural Change in the Upper Pleistocene*, ed., E. Trinkaus, pp. 201–27. Oxford: British Archaeological Reports 164.

Conkey, M. 1987. New approaches in the search for meaning? A review of research in 'Palaeolithic art'. *Journal of Field Archaeology* 14, 413–30.

Conrad, N. 1990. Laminar lithic assemblages from the last interglacial complex in Northwest Europe. *Journal of Anthropological Research* 46, 243–62.

Cook, J. 1992. Preliminary report on marked human bones from the 1986–1987 excavations at Gough's Cave, Somerset, England. In *The Late Glacial in North-West Europe: Human Adaptation and Environmental Change at the End*

of the Pleistocene, eds., N. Barton, A.J. Roberts & D.A. Roe, pp. 160–78. London: Council for British Archaeology Research Report No. 17.

Cook, J. & Welté, A.C. 1992. A newly discovered female engraving from Courbet (Penne-Tarn), France. *Proceedings of the Prehistoric Society* 58, 29–35.

Corballis, M.C. 1991. *The Lopsided Ape*. Oxford: Oxford University Press.

Corballis, M.C. 1992. On the evolution of language and generativity. *Cognition* 44, 197–226.

Cosmides, L. 1989. The logic of social exchange: has natural selection shaped how humans reason? Studies with the Wason selection task. *Cognition* 31, 187–276.

Cosmides, L. & Tooby, J. 1987. From evolution to behaviour: evolutionary psychology as the missing link. In *The Latest on the Best: Essays on Evolution and Optimality*, ed., J. Dupré, pp. 277–306. Cambridge: Cambridge University Press.

Cosmides, L. & Tooby, J. 1992. Cognitive adaptations for social exchange. In *The Adapted Mind*, eds., J.H. Barkow, L. Cosmides & J. Tooby, pp. 163–228. New York: Oxford University Press.

Cosmides, L. & Tooby, J. 1994. Origins of domain specificity: the evolution of functional organization, In *Mapping the Mind: Domain Specificity in Cognition and Culture*, eds., L.A. Hirschfeld & S.A. Gelman, pp. 85–116. Cambridge: Cambridge University Press.

Culotta, E. 1995. Asian hominids grow older. *Science* 270, 1116–17.

Cunliffe, B. (ed.) 1994. *The Oxford Illustrated Prehistory of Europe*. Oxford: Oxford University Press.

Cunningham, A. & Williams, P. 1993. De-centering the 'big' picture: the origins of modern science and the modern origins of science. *British Journal of the History of Science* 26, 407–32.

Currant, A.P., Jacobi, R.M. & Stringer, C.B. 1989. Excavations at Gough's Cave, Somerset 1986–7. *Antiquity* 63, 131–36.

Dansgaard, W., White, J.W.C. & Johnsen, S.J. 1989. The abrupt termination of the Younger Dryas climate event. *Nature* 339, 532–34.

Darwin, C. 1859. *The Origin of Species*. London: John Murray.

Darwin, C. 1913 [1871]. *The Descent of Man*. London: John Murray.

Davidson, I. 1990. Bilzingsleben and early marking. *Rock Art Research* 7, 52–6.

Davidson, I. 1991. The archaeology of language origins: a review. *Antiquity* 65, 39–48.

Davidson, I. 1992. There's no art – To find the mind's construction – In offence (reply to R. Bednarik). *Cambridge Archaeological Journal* 2, 52–7.

Davidson, I. & Noble, W. 1989. The archaeology of perception: traces of depiction and language. *Current Anthropology* 30, 125–55.

Davidson, I. & Noble, W. 1992. Why the first

colonisation of the Australian region is the earliest evidence of modern human behaviour. *Archaeology in Oceania* 27, 113–19.

Dawkins, R. 1976. *The Selfish Gene*. Oxford: Oxford University Press.

Dawkins, R. 1986. *The Blind Watchmaker*. Harmondsworth: Penguin Books.

Dawkins, R. 1995. *River Out of Eden*. London & New York: Weidenfeld & Nicolson.

Dawson, A.G. 1992. *Ice Age Earth: Late Quaternary Geology and Climate*. London: Routledge.

Deacon, T.W. 1990. Fallacies of progression in theories of brain-size evolution. *International Journal of Primatology* 11, 193–236.

Deacon, T.W. 1992. The neural circuitry underlying primate calls and human language. In *Language Origin: A Multidisciplinary Approach*, eds., J. Wind, B. Chiarelli, B. Bichakhian & A. Nocentini, pp. 121–62. Dordrecht: Kluwer Academic Publishing.

Dean, M.C., Stringer, C.B. & Bromgate, T.G. 1986. Age at death of the Neanderthal child from Devil's Tower Gibraltar and the implications for studies of general growth and development in Neanderthals. *American Journal of Physical Anthropology* 70, 301–09.

Delluc, B. & Delluc, G. 1978. Les manifestations graphiques aurignaciennes sur support rocheux des environs des Eyzies (Dordogne). *Gallia Préhistoire* 21, 213–438.

Delporte, H. 1979. *L'Image de la Femme dans l'Art Préhistorique*. Paris: Picard.

Delporte, H. 1993. Gravettian female figurines: a regional survey. In *Before Lascaux: The Complex Record of the Early Upper Palaeolithic*, eds., H. Knecht, A. Pike-Tay & R. White, pp. 243–57. Boca Raton: CRC Press.

deMenocal, P.B. 1995. Plio–Pleistocene African Climate. *Science* 270, 53–9.

Dennell, R. W. 1983. *European Economic Prehistory*. London: Academic Press.

Dennell, R.W. & Rendell, H. 1991. De Terra and Paterson and the Soan flake industry: a new perspective from the Soan valley, North Pakistan. *Man and Environment* XVI, 91–9.

Dennell, R.W., Rendell, H. & Hailwood, E. 1988a. Early tool making in Asia: two million year old artifacts in Pakistan. *Antiquity* 62, 98–106.

Dennell, R.W., Rendell, H. & Hailwood, E. 1988b. Late Pliocene artifacts from North Pakistan. *Current Anthropology*, 29, 495–98.

Dennett, D. 1988 The intentional stance in theory and practice. In *Machiavellian Intelligence: Social Expertise and the Evolution of Intellect in Monkeys, Apes and Humans*, eds., R.W. Byrne & A. Whiten, pp. 180–202. Oxford: Clarendon Press.

Dennett, D. 1991. *Consciousness Explained*. New York: Little, Brown & Company.

Dibble, H.L. 1987. The interpretation of Middle Palaeolithic scraper morphology. *American Antiquity* 52, 109–17.

Dibble, H.L. 1989. The implications of stone tool types for the presence of language during the Lower and Middle Palaeolithic. In *The Human Revolution*, eds., P. Mellars & C. Stringer, pp. 415–32 Edinburgh: Edinburgh University Press.

Dibble, H.L. & Rolland, N. 1992. On assemblage variability in the Middle Palaeolithic of western Europe: history, perspectives and a new interpretation. In *The Middle Palaeolithic: Adaptation, Behaviour and Variability*, eds., H.L. Dibble & P. Mellars, pp. 1–28. Philadelphia: The University Museum, University of Pennsylvania.

Dillehay, T.D. 1989. *Monte Verde: A Late Pleistocene Settlement in Chile*. Washington DC: Smithsonian Institute.

Dillehay, T.D. & Collins, M.B. 1988. Early cultural evidence from Monte Verde in Chile. *Nature* 332, 150–52.

Dillehay, T.D., Calderón, C.A., Politis, G. & Beltrao, M.C.M.C. 1992. The earliest hunter-gatherers of South America. *Journal of World Prehistory* 6, 145–203.

Donald, M. 1991. *Origins of the Modern Mind*. Cambridge MA: Harvard University Press.

Donald, M. 1994. Précis of 'Origins of the Modern Mind'. *Behavioral and Brain Sciences* 16, 737–91.

Douglas, M. 1990. The pangolin revisited: a new approach to animal symbolism. In *Signifying Animals: Human Meaning in the Natural World*, ed., R.G. Willis, pp. 25–42. London: Unwin Hyman.

Duhard, J-P. 1993. Upper Palaeolithic figures as a reflection of human morphology and social organization. *Antiquity* 67, 83–91.

Dunbar, R.I.M. 1988. *Primate Societies*. London: Chapman & Hall.

Dunbar, R.I.M. 1991. Functional significance of social grooming in primates. *Folia Primatologica* 57, 121–31.

Dunbar, R.I.M. 1992. Neocortex size as a constraint on group size in primates. *Journal of Human Evolution* 20, 469–93.

Dunbar, R.I.M. 1993. Coevolution of neocortical size, group size and language in humans. *Behavioral and Brain Sciences* 16, 681–735.

Dunbar, R.I.M. 1995. *The Trouble with Science*. London: Faber & Faber.

Eastham, M. & Eastham, A. 1991. Palaeolithic parietal art and its topographic context. *Proceedings of the Prehistoric Society* 51 (i), 115–28.

Eccles, J. 1989. *Evolution of the Brain: Creation of the Self*. London: Routledge.

Eisenberg, J. 1981. *The Mammalian Radiations: An Analysis of Trends in Evolution, Adaptation and Behaviour*. London: Athlone Press.

Enloe, J.G. 1993. Subsistence organization in the Early Upper Palaeolithic: reindeer hunters of the Abri du Flageolet, Couche V. In *Before Lascaux: The Complex Record of the Early Upper Palaeolithic*, eds., H. Knecht, A. Pike-Tay & R. White, pp. 101–15. Boca Raton: CRC Press.

D'Errico, F. 1989a. Palaeolithic lunar calendars: a case of wishful thinking. *Current Anthropology* 30, 117–18.

D'Errico, F. 1989b. A reply to Alexander Marshack. *Current Anthropology* 30, 495–500.

D'Errico, F. 1991. Microscopic and statistical criteria for the identification of prehistoric systems of notation. *Rock Art Research* 8, 83–93.

D'Errico, F. 1992. A reply to Alexander Marshack. *Rock Art Research* 9, 59–64.

D'Errico, F. 1995. A new model and its implications for the origin of writing: the La Marche antler revisited. *Cambridge Archaeological Journal* 5, 163–206.

D'Errico, F. & Cacho, C. 1994. Notation versus decoration in the Upper Palaeolithic: a case study from Tossal de la Roca, Alicante, Spain. *Journal of Archaeological Science* 21, 185–200.

Falk, D. 1983. Cerebral cortices of East African early hominids. *Science* 221, 1072–74.

Falk, D. 1990. Brain evolution in *Homo*. The 'radiator theory'. *Behavioral and Brain Sciences* 13, 333–81.

Falk, D. 1992. *Braindance: New Discoveries about Human Brain Evolution*. New York: Henry Holt.

Farizy, C. 1990. The transition from the Middle to Upper Palaeolithic at Arcy-sur-Cure (Yonne, France): technological, economic and social aspects. In *The Emergence of Modern Humans*, ed., P. Mellars, pp. 303–26. Edinburgh: Edinburgh University Press.

Farizy, C. & David, F. 1992. Subsistence and behavioral patterns of some Middle Palaeolithic local groups. In *The Middle Palaeolithic, Adaptation, Behaviour and Variability*, eds., H.L. Dibble & P. Mellars, pp. 87–96. Philadelphia: The University Museum, University of Pennsylvania.

Faulstich, P. 1992. Of earth and dreaming: abstraction and naturalism in Walpiri art. In *Rock Art and Ethnography*, eds., M.J. Morwood & D.R. Hobbs, pp. 19–23. Melbourne: Occasional AURA Publication No. 5.

Féblot-Augustins, J. 1993. Mobility strategies in the late Middle Palaeolithic of Central Europe and Western Europe: elements of stability and variability. *Journal of Anthropological Archaeology* 12, 211–65.

Fischer, A. 1990. On being a pupil of a flintknapper of 11,000 years ago. A preliminary analysis of settlement organization and flint technology based on conjoined flint artifacts from the Trollesgave site. In *The Big Puzzle: International Symposium on Refitting Stone Artifacts*, eds., E. Cziesla, S. Eickhoff, N. Arts & D. Winter, pp. 447–64. Bonn: Holos.

Flood, J. 1983. *Archaeology of the Dreamtime*. London: Collins.

Fodor, J. 1983. *The Modularity of Mind*. Cambridge MA: MIT Press.

Fodor, J. 1985. Précis of 'The Modularity of Mind'. *The Behavioral and Brain Sciences* 8, 1–42.

Fodor, J. 1987. Modules, frames and fridgeons, sleeping dogs and the music of the spheres. In *Modularity in Knowledge Representation and Natural Language Understanding*, ed., J.L. Garfield, pp. 25–36. Cambridge MA: MIT Press.

Foley, R. 1987. *Another Unique Species*. Harlow: Longman.

Frayer, D.W. 1992. Cranial base flattening in Europe: Neanderthals and recent *Homo sapiens*. *American Journal of Physical Anthropology* (supplement) 14, 77.

Frayer, D.W., Wolpoff, M.H., Thorne, A.G., Smith, F.H. & Pope, G. 1993. Theories of modern human origins: the paleontological test. *American Anthropologist* 95, 14–50.

Frayer, D.W., Wolpoff, M.H., Thorne, A.G., Smith, F.H. & Pope, G. 1994. Getting it straight. *American Anthropologist* 96, 424–38.

Fremlen, J. 1975. Letter to the editor. *Science* 187, 600.

Frith, U. 1989. *Autism: Explaining the Enigma*. Oxford: Blackwell.

Gallistel, C.R. & Cheng, K. 1985. A modular sense of place? *The Behavioral and Brain Sciences* 8, 11–12.

Galef, B.G. 1988. Imitation in animals: history, definition and interpretation of data from the psychological laboratory. In *Social Learning: A Comparative Approach*, eds., T.R. Zentall & B.G. Galef pp. 3–28. Hillsdale NJ: Erlbaum.

Galef, B.G. 1990. Tradition in animals: field observations and laboratory analysis. In *Methods, Inferences, Interpretations and Explanations in the Study of Behavior*, eds., M. Bekoff & D. Jamieson pp. 74–95. Boulder: Westview Press.

Gamble, C. 1982. Interaction and alliance in Palaeolithic society. *Man* 17, 92–107.

Gamble, C. 1986. *The Palaeolithic Settlement of Europe*. Cambridge: Cambridge University Press.

Gamble, C. 1987. Man the shoveler: alternative models for Middle Pleistocene colonization and occupation in northern latitudes. In *The Pleistocene Old World*, ed., O. Soffer, pp. 81–98. New York: Plenum Press.

Gamble, C. 1989. Comment on 'Grave shortcomings: the evidence for Neanderthal burial by R. Gargett', *Current Anthropology* 30, 181–82.

Gamble, C. 1991. The social context for European Palaeolithic art. *Proceedings of the Prehistoric Society* 57 (i), 3–15.

Gamble, C. 1992. Comment on 'Dense forests, cold steppes, and the Palaeolithic settlement of Northern Europe' by W. Roebroeks, N.J. Conrad & T. van Kolfschoten. *Current Anthropology* 33, 569–72.

Gamble, C. 1993. *Timewalkers: The Prehistory of Global Colonization*. Stroud: Alan Sutton.

Gamble, C. 1994. The peopling of Europe, 700,000–40,000 years before the present. In *The Oxford Illustrated Prehistory of Europe*, ed., B. Cunliffe, pp. 5–41. Oxford: Oxford University Press.

Gamble, C. & Soffer, O. 1990. *The World at 18,000 B.P.* (2 vols). London: Unwin Hyman.

Gannon, P.J. & Laitman, J.T. 1993. Can we see language areas on hominid brain endocasts? *American Journal of Physical Anthropology* (supplement) 16, 91.

Gardner, R.A., Garner, B.T. & van Cantfort, T.E. 1989. *Teaching Sign Language to Chimpanzees.* New York: State University of New York Press.

Gardner, H. 1983. *Frames of Mind: The Theory of Multiple Intelligences.* New York: Basic Books.

Gardner, H. 1993. *Multiple Intelligences: The Theory in Practice.* New York: Basic Books.

Gargett, R. 1989. Grave shortcomings: the evidence for Neanderthal burial. *Current Anthropology* 30, 157–90.

Gazzaniga, M. 1985. *The Social Brain: Discovering the Networks of the Mind.* New York: Basic Books.

Gazzaniga, M. & Ledoux, J. 1978. *The Interpreted Mind.* New York: Plenum Press.

Geary, D.C. 1995. Reflections of evolution and culture in children's cognition: implications for mathematical development and instruction. *American Psychologist* 50, 24–37.

Geertz, C. 1973. *The Interpretation of Cultures.* New York: Basic Books.

Gellner, E. 1988. *Plough, Sword and Book: The Structure of Human History.* London: Collins Harvill.

Geneste, J-M. 1985. *Analyse lithique d'Industries Moustériennes du Perigord: une approche technologique du comportement des groupes humaines au Paléolithique moyen.* Thèse Univérsite Bordeaux I.

Geneste, J-M. & Plisson, H. 1993. Hunting technologies and human behavior: lithic analysis of Solutrean shouldered points. In *Before Lascaux: The Complex Record of the Early Upper Palaeolithic,* eds., H. Knecht, A. Pike-Tay & R. White, pp. 117–35. Boca Raton: CRC Press.

Gibson, K.R. 1986. Cognition, brain size and the extraction of embedded food resources. In *Primate Ontogeny, Cognition and Social Behaviour,* eds., J.G. Else & P.C. Lee, pp. 93–103. Cambridge: Cambridge University Press.

Gibson, K.R. 1990. New perspectives on instincts and intelligence: brain size and the emergence of hierarchical construction skills. In *'Language' and Intelligence in Monkeys and Apes: Comparative Developmental Perspectives,* eds., S.T. Parker & K.R. Gibson, pp. 97–128. Cambridge: Cambridge University Press.

Gibson, K.R. & Ingold, T. (eds.) 1993. *Tools, Language and Cognition in Human Evolution.* Cambridge: Cambridge University Press.

Gilead, I. 1991. The Upper Palaeolithic period in the Levant. *Journal of World Prehistory* 5, 105–54.

Gilead, I. & Bar-Yosef, O. 1993. Early Upper Palaeolithic sites on the Qadesh Barnea area, N.E. Sinai. *Journal of Field Archaeology* 20,

265–80.

Gillies, D. 1993. *Philosophy in the Twentieth Century: Four Central Themes.* Oxford: Blackwell.

Girard, C. & David, F. 1982. A propos de la chase spécialisée au Paléolithique moyen: l'exemple de Mauran (Haute-Garonne). *Bulletin de la Société Préhistorique Française* 79, 11–12.

Goodale, J.C. 1971. *Tiwi Wives: A Study of the Women of Melville Island, North Australia.* Seattle: University of Washington Press.

Goodall, J. 1986. *The Chimpanzees of Gombe.* Cambridge MA: Harvard University Press.

Goodall, J. 1990. *Through a Window: Thirty Years with the Chimpanzees of Gombe.* London: Weidenfeld & Nicolson.

Gopnik, A. & Wellman, H.M. 1994. The theory theory. In *Mapping the Mind: Domain Specificity in Cognition and Culture,* eds., L.A. Hirschfeld & S.A. Gelman, pp. 257–93. Cambridge: Cambridge University Press.

Goren-Inbar, N. 1992. The Acheulian site of Gesher Benot Ya'aqov: an African or Asian entity. In *The Evolution and Dispersal of Modern Humans in Asia,* eds., T. Akazawa, K. Aoki & T. Kimura, pp. 67–82. Tokyo: Hokusen-Sha.

Gould, S. J. 1977. *Ontogeny and Phylogeny.* Cambridge MA: Harvard University Press.

Gould, S. J. 1981. *The Mismeasure of Man.* New York: W.W. Norton.

Gould, S. J. 1990. *Wonderful Life.* London: Hutchinson Radius.

Gould, S.J. & Lewontin, R.C. 1979. The spandrels of San Marco and the Panglossian paradigm: a critique of the adaptationist programme. *Proceedings of the Royal Society of London B* 205, 581–98.

Gowlett, J. 1984. Mental abilities of early man: a look at some hard evidence. In *Hominid Evolution and Community Ecology,* ed., R. Foley, pp. 167–92. London: Academic Press.

Green, H.S. (ed.) 1984. *Pontnewydd Cave: A Lower Palaeolithic Hominid Site in Wales. The First Report.* Cardiff: National Museum of Wales.

Greenberg, J.H., Turner, C.G. II. & Zegura, S.L. 1986. The settlement of the Americas: a comparative study of the linguistic, dental and genetic evidence. *Current Anthropology* 27, 477–97.

Greenfield, P.M. 1991. Language, tools and brain: the ontogeny and phylogeny of hierarchically organized sequential behavior. *Behavioral and Brain Sciences* 14, 531–95.

Greenfield, P.M. & Savage-Rumbaugh, E.S. 1990. Grammatical combination in *Pan paniscus*: processes of learning and invention in the evolution and development of language. In *'Language' and Intelligence in Monkeys and Apes: Comparative Developmental Perspectives,* eds., S.T. Parker & K.R. Gibson, pp. 540–74. Cambridge: Cambridge University Press.

Grønnow, R. 1987. Meiendorf and Stellmoor revisited: an analysis of Late Palaeolithic reindeer exploitation. *Acta Archaeologica* 56, 131–66.

Groube, L., Chappell, J., Muke, J. & Price, D. 1986. A 40,000-year-old human occupation site at Huon Peninsula, Papua New Guinea. *Nature* 324, 453–55.

Grün, R., Beaumont, P. & Stringer, C. 1990. ESR dating evidence for early modern humans at Border Cave in South Africa. *Nature* 344, 537–39.

Grün, R. & Stringer, C. 1991. Electron spin resonance dating and the evolution of modern humans. *Archaeometry* 33, 153–99.

Gubser, N.J. 1965. *The Nunamiut Eskimos: Hunters of Caribou*. New Haven: Yale University Press.

Guidon, N., Parenti, F., Da Luz, M., Guérin, C. & Faure, M. 1994. Le plus ancien peuplement de l'Amérique: le Paléolithique du Nordeste Brésilien. *Bulletin de la Société Prehistorique Française* 91, 246–50.

Guthrie, D. 1984. Mosaics, allelochemicals and nutrients: an ecological theory of late Pleistocene extinctions. In *Quaternary Extinctions: A Prehistoric Revolution*, eds., P.S. Martin & R.G. Klein, pp. 259–98. Tucson: University of Arizona Press.

Guthrie, R.D. 1990. *Frozen Fauna of the Mammoth Steppe*. Chicago: Chicago University Press.

Gvozdover, M.D. 1989. The typology of female figurines of the Kostenki Palaeolithic culture. *Soviet Anthropology and Archaeology* 27, 32–94.

Hallam, S.J. 1989. Plant usage and management in Southwest Australian Aboriginal societies. In *Foraging and Farming: The Evolution of Plant Exploitation*, eds., D.R. Harris & G.C. Hillman, pp. 136–51. London: Unwin Hyman.

Halverson, J. 1987. Art for art's sake in the Palaeolithic. *Current Anthropology* 28, 65–89.

Hahn, J. 1972. Aurignacian signs, pendants, and art objects in Central and Eastern Europe. *World Archaeology* 3, 252–66.

Hahn, J. 1984. Recherches sur l'art Paléolithique depuis 1976. In *Aurignacian et Gravettien en Europe*, Vol. 1, eds., J.K. Kozlowski & B. Klima, pp. 157–71. Etudes et Recherches Archéologiques de l'Universite de Liège.

Hahn, J. 1993. Aurignacian art in Central Europe. In *Before Lascaux: The Complex Record of the Early Upper Palaeolithic*, eds., H. Knecht, A. Pike-Tay & R. White, pp. 229–41. Boca Raton: CRC Press.

Hankoff, L.D. 1980. Body-mind concepts in the Ancient Near East: a comparison of Egypt and Israel in the second millennium B.C. In *Body and Mind, Past, Present and Future*, ed., R.W. Rieber, pp. 3–31. New York: Academic Press.

Hatley, T. & Kappelman, J. 1980. Bears, pigs and Plio-Pleistocene hominids: a case for the exploitation of below-ground food resources. *Human Ecology* 8, 371–87.

Harris, J.W.K. & Capaldo, S.D. 1993. The earliest stone tools: their implications for an understanding of the activities and behaviour of late Pliocene hominids. In *The Use of Tools by Human and Non-human Primates*, eds., A. Berthelet & J. Chavaillon, pp. 196–220. Oxford: Clarendon Press.

Harrold, F. 1989. Mousterian, Chatelperronian and early Aurignacian in western Europe: continuity or discontinuity? In *The Human Revolution*, eds., P. Mellars & C. Stringer, pp. 677–713. Edinburgh: Edinburgh University Press.

Hay, R. 1976. *Geology of Olduvai Gorge*. Berkeley: University of California Press.

Hayden, B. 1990. Nimrods, piscators, pluckers and planters: the emergence of food production. *Journal of Anthropological Archaeology* 9, 31–69.

Hayden, B. 1993. The cultural capacities of Neanderthals: a review and re-evaluation. *Journal of Human Evolution* 24, 113–46.

Haynes, C.V. 1980. The Clovis culture. *Canadian Journal of Anthropology* 1, 115–21.

Haynes, G. 1991. *Mammoths, Mastodents and Elephants: Biology, Behaviour and the Fossil Record*. Cambridge: Cambridge University Press.

Hedges, R.E.M., Housley, R.A., Bronk Ramsey, C. & Van Klinken, G.J. 1994. Radiocarbon dates from the Oxford AMS system: archaeometry datelist 18. *Archaeometry* 36, 337–74.

Hewes, G. 1986. Comment on 'The origins of image making, by W. Davis'. *Current Anthropology* 27, 193–215.

Hewes, G. 1989. Comment on 'The archaeology of perception. Traces of depiction and language, by I. Davidson & W. Noble'. *Current Anthropology* 30, 145–46.

Heyes, C.M. 1993. Anecdotes, training and triangulating: do animals attribute mental states? *Animal Behavior* 46, 177–88.

Higgs, E. (ed.) 1972. *Papers in Economic Prehistory*. Cambridge: Cambridge University Press.

Higgs, E. & Jarman M.R. 1969. The origins of agriculture: a reconsideration. *Antiquity* 43, 31–41.

Hill, A. 1994. Early hominid behavioural ecology: a personal postscript. *Journal of Human Ecology* 27, 321–28.

Hill, K. & Hawkes, K. 1983. Neotropical hunting among the Ache of Eastern Paraguay. In *Adaptive Responses of Native American Indians*, eds., R. Hames & W. Vickers, pp. 139–88. New York: Academic Press.

Hillman, G.C. 1989. Late Palaeolithic plant foods from Wadi Kubbaniya in Upper Egypt: dietary diversity, infant weaning and seasonality in a riverine environment. In *Foraging and Farming: The Evolution of Plant Exploitation*, eds., D.R. Harris & G.C. Hillman, pp. 207–39. London: Unwin Hyman.

Hillman, G.C., Colledge, S.M. & Harris, D.R. 1989. Plant food economy during the Epipalaeolithic period at Tell Abu Hureya, Syria: dietary diversity, seasonality and modes of exploitation. In *Foraging and Farming: The Evolution of Plant Exploitation*, eds., D.R. Harris & G.C. Hillman, pp. 240–68. London: Unwin Hyman.

Hirschfeld, L.A. 1995. Do children have a theory of race? *Cognition* 54, 209–52.

Hodder, I. 1985. *Symbols in Action*. Cambridge: Cambridge University Press.

Hodder, I. 1991. *Reading the Past* (2nd edition). Cambridge: Cambridge University Press.

Hodges, R. & Mithen, S. 1993. The 'South Church': a late Roman funerary church (San Vincenzo Minore) and hall for distinguished guests (with contributions by Shiela Gibson and John Mitchell). In *San Vincenzo al Volturno I*, ed., R. Hodges, pp. 123–90. London: British School at Rome.

Hoffecker, J.F., Powers, W.R. & Goebel, T. 1993. The colonization of Beringia and the peopling of the New World. *Science* 259, 46–53.

Hole, F. 1992. Origins of agriculture. In *The Cambridge Encyclopedia of Human Evolution*, eds., S, Jones, R. Martin & D. Pilbeam, pp. 373–79. Cambridge: Cambridge University Press.

Holloway, R.L. 1969. Culture, a human domain. *Current Anthropology* 20, 395–412.

Holloway, R.L. 1981a. Culture, symbols and human brain evolution. *Dialectical Anthropology* 5, 287–303.

Holloway, R.L. 1981b. Volumetric and asymmetry determinations on recent hominid endocasts: Spy I and II, Djebel Irhoud I, and Sale *Homo erectus* specimens, with some notes on Neanderthal brain size. *American Journal of Physical Anthropology* 55, 385–93.

Holloway, R.L. 1985. The poor brain of *Homo sapiens neanderthalensis*: see what you please. In *Ancestors: The Hard Evidence*, ed., E. Delson, pp. 319–24. New York: Alan R. Liss.

Holloway, R.L. & de La Coste-Lareymondie, M.C. 1982. Brain endocast assymetry in pongids and hominids: some preliminary findings on the paleontology of cerebral dominance. *American Journal of Physical Anthropology* 58, 101–10.

Houghton, P. 1993. Neanderthal supralaryngeal vocal tract. *American Journal of Physical Anthropology* 90, 139–46.

Howell, F.C. 1961. Isimila: a Palaeolithic site in Africa. *Scientific American* 205, 118–29.

Howell, F.C. 1965. *Early Man*. New York: Time-Life Books.

Hublin, J.J. 1992. Recent human evolution in northwestern Africa. *Philosophical Transactions of the Royal Society*, Series 13, 337, 185–91.

Humphrey, N. 1976. The social function of intellect. In *Growing Points in Ethology*, eds., P.P.G. Bateson & R.A. Hinde, pp. 303–17. Cambridge: Cambridge University Press.

Humphrey, N. 1984. *Consciousness Regained*. Oxford: Oxford University Press.

Humphrey, N. 1992. *A History of the Mind*. London: Chatto & Windus.

Humphrey, N. 1993. *The Inner Eye*. London:

Vintage (first published by Faber & Faber in 1986).

Hyndman, D. 1990. Back to the future: trophy arrays as mental maps in the Wopkaimin's culture of place. In *Signifying Animals: Human Meaning in the Natural World*, ed., R.G. Willis, pp. 63–73. London: Unwin Hyman.

Ingold, T. 1992. Comment on 'Beyond the original affluent society' by N. Bird-David. *Current Anthropology* 33, 34–47.

Ingold, T. 1993. Tool-use, sociality and intelligence. In *Tools, Language and Cognition in Human Evolution*, eds., K.R. Gibson & T. Ingold, pp. 429–45. Cambridge: Cambridge University Press.

Inizan, M-L., Roche, H. & Tixier, J. 1992. *Technology of Knapped Stone*. Paris: Cercle de Recherches et d'Etudes Préhistorique, CNRS.

Isaac, B. 1989. *The Archaeology of Human Origins: Papers by Glynn Isaac*. Cambridge: Cambridge University Press.

Isaac, G. 1977. *Olorgesailie*. Chicago: University of Chicago Press.

Isaac, G. 1978. The food-sharing behaviour of proto-human hominids. *Scientific American* 238 (April), 90–108.

Isaac, G. 1981. Stone age visiting cards: approaches to the study of early land-use patterns. In *Pattern of the Past*, eds., I. Hodder, G. Isaac & N. Hammond, pp. 131–55. Cambridge: Cambridge University Press.

Isaac, G. 1982. The earliest archaeological traces. In *The Cambridge History of Africa, Volume 1, From the Earliest Times to c. 500 BC*, ed., J.D. Clark, pp. 157–247. Cambridge: Cambridge University Press.

Isaac, G. 1983a. Bones in contention: competing explanations for the juxtaposition of Early Pleistocene artifacts and faunal remains. In *Animals and Archaeology: Hunters and their Prey*, eds., J. Clutton-Brock & C. Grigson, pp. 3–19. Oxford: British Archaeological Reports, International Series 163.

Isaac, G. 1983b. Review of bones: ancient men and modern myths. *American Antiquity* 48, 416–19.

Isaac, G. 1984. The archaeology of human origins: studies of the Lower Pleistocene in East Africa 1971–1981. *Advances in World Archaeology* 3, 1–87.

Isaac, G. 1986. Foundation stones: early artifacts as indicators of activities and abilities. In *Stone Age Prehistory*, eds., G.N. Bailey & P. Callow, pp. 221–41. Cambridge: Cambridge University Press.

Isbell, L.A., Cheney, D.L. & Seyfarth, R.M. 1991 Group fusions and minimum group sizes in Vervet monkeys (*Cercopithecus aethiops*). *American Journal of Primatology* 25, 57–65.

Jelenik, A. 1982. The Tabūn cave and Palaeolithic man in the Levant. *Science* 216, 1369–75.

Jennes, D. 1977. *The Indians of Canada* (7th edition). Ottawa: University of Toronto Press.

Jerison, H.J. 1973. *Evolution of Brain and*

Intelligence. New York: Academic Press.

Jochim, M. 1983. Palaeolithic cave art in ecological perspective. In *Hunter-Gatherer Economy in Prehistory*, ed., G.N. Bailey, pp. 212–19. Cambridge: Cambridge University Press.

Johanson, D.C. & Eddy, M.A. 1980. *Lucy: The Beginnings of Human Kind*. New York: Simon & Schuster.

Johnsen, S.J., Clausen, H.B., Dansgaard, W., Fuhrer, K., Gundestrup, N., Hammer, C.U., Iversen, P., Jouzel, J., Stauffer, B. & Steffensen, J.P. 1992. Irregular glacial interstadials recorded in a new Greenland ice core. *Nature* 359, 311–13.

Jones, J.S. 1993 *The Language of the Genes*. London: HarperCollins.

Jones, J.S., Martin, R. & Pilbeam, D. (eds.) 1992. *The Cambridge Encyclopedia of Human Evolution*. Cambridge: Cambridge University Press.

Jones, J.S. & Rouhani, S. 1986. How small was the bottleneck? *Nature* 319, 449–50.

Jones, P. 1980. Experimental butchery with modern stone tools and its relevance for Palaeolithic archaeology. *World Archaeology* 12, 153–65.

Jones, P. 1981. Experimental implement manufacture and use: a case study from Olduvai Gorge. *Philosophical Transactions of the Royal Society of London* B 292, 189–95.

Jones, R. & Meehan, B. 1989. Plant foods of the Gidjingali: ethnographic and archaeological perspectives from northern Australia on tuber and seed exploitation. In *Foraging and Farming: The Evolution of Plant Exploitation*, eds., D.R. Harris & G.C. Hillman, pp. 120–35. London: Unwin Hyman.

Kaplan, H. & Hill, K. 1985. Hunting ability and reproductive success among male Ache foragers: preliminary results. *Current Anthropology* 26, 131–33.

Karmiloff-Smith, A. 1992. *Beyond Modularity: A Developmental Perspective on Cognitive Science*. Cambridge MA: MIT Press.

Karmiloff-Smith, A. 1994. Précis of 'Beyond Modularity: A Developmental Perspective on Cognitive Science'. *Behavioral and Brain Sciences* 17, 693–745.

Keeley, L. 1980. *Experimental Determination of Stone Tool Uses: A Microwear Analysis*. Chicago: Chicago University Press.

Keeley, L. & Toth, N. 1981. Microwear polishes on early stone tools from Koobi Fora, Kenya. *Nature* 203, 464–65.

Keil, F.C. 1994. The birth and nurturance of concepts by domains: the origins of concepts of living things. In *Mapping the Mind: Domain Specificity in Cognition and Culture*, eds., L.A. Hirschfeld & S.A. Gelman, pp. 234–54. Cambridge: Cambridge University Press.

Kennedy, J.S. 1992. *The New Anthropomorphism*. Cambridge: Cambridge University Press.

Khalfa, J. (ed.) 1994. *What is Intelligence?* Cambridge: Cambridge University Press.

Kibunjia, M. 1994. Pliocene archaeological occurrences in the Lake Turkana basin. *Journal of Human Evolution* 27, 159–71.

Kibunjia, M., Roche, H., Bown, F.H. & Leakey, R.E. 1992. Pliocene and Pleistocene archaeological sites west of Lake Turkana, Kenya. *Journal of Human Evolution* 23, 431–38.

Kilma, B. 1988. A triple burial from the Upper Palaeolithic of Dolni Vestonice, Czechoslovakia. *Journal of Human Evolution* 16, 831–35.

Klein, R.G. 1989. Biological and behavioural perspectives on modern human origins in Southern Africa. In *The Human Revolution*, eds., P. Mellars & C. Stringer, pp. 530–46. Edinburgh: Edinburgh University Press.

Knecht, H. 1993a. Early Upper Paleolithic approaches to bone and antler projectile technology. In *Hunting and Animal Exploitation in the Later Palaeolithic and Mesolithic of Eurasia*, eds., G.L. Peterkin, H.M. Bricker & P. Mellars, pp. 33–47. Archaeological Papers of the American Anthropological Association, No. 4.

Knecht, H. 1993b. Splits and wedges: the techniques and technology of Early Aurignacian antler working. In *Before Lascaux: The Complex Record of the Early Upper Palaeolithic*, eds., H. Knecht, A. Pike-Tay & R. White, pp. 137–61. Boca Raton: CRC Press.

Knecht, H. 1994. Projectile points of bone, antler and stone: experimental explorations of manufacture and function. Paper presented at the 59th annual meeting of the Society for American Archaeology, Anaheim, California.

Knight, C. 1991. *Blood Relations: Menstruation and the Origins of Culture*. New Haven: Yale University Press.

Knight, C., Powers, C. & Watts, I. 1995. The human symbolic revolution: a Darwinian account. *Cambridge Archaeological Journal* 5, 75–114.

Koestler, A. 1975. *The Act of Creation*. London: Picador.

Kozlowski, J.K. (ed.) 1982. *Excavation in the Bacho Kiro Cave, Bulgaria (Final Report)*. Warsaw: Paristwowe Wydarunictwo, Naukowe.

Kroll, E.M. 1994. Behavioral implications of Plio-Pleistocene archaeological site structure. *Journal of Human Ecology* 27, 107–38.

Kroll, E.M. & Isaac, G.I. 1984. Configurations of artifacts and bones at early Pleistocene sites in East Africa. In *Intrasite Spatial Analysis in Archaeology*, ed., H.J. Hietela, pp. 4–31. Cambridge: Cambridge University Press.

Kuhn, S. 1993. Mousterian technology as adaptive response. In *Hunting and Animal Exploitation in the Later Palaeolithic and Mesolithic of Eurasia*, eds., G.L. Peterkin, H.M. Bricker & P. Mellars, pp. 25–31. Archaeological Papers of the American Anthropological Association, No. 4.

Kuhn, S. 1995. *Mousterian Lithic Technology*. Princeton: Princeton University Press.

Kuhn, T. 1979. Metaphor in science. In *Metaphor and Thought*, ed., A. Ortony, pp. 409–19.

Cambridge: Cambridge University Press.

Kuman, K. 1994. The archaeology of Sterkfontein: preliminary findings on site formation and cultural change. *South African Journal of Science* 90, 215–19.

Laitman, J.T. & Heimbuch, R.C. 1982. The basicranium of Plio-Pleistocene hominids as an indicator of their upper respiratory system. *American Journal of Physical Anthropology* 59, 323–44.

Laitman, J.T., Heimbuch, R.C. & Crelin, E.C. 1979. The basicranium of fossil hominids as an indicator of their upper respiratory systems. *American Journal of Physical Anthropology* 51, 15–34.

Laitman, J.T., Reidenberg, J.S., Gannon, P.J., Johanson, B., Landahl, K. & Lieberman, P. 1990. The Kebara hyoid: what can it tell us about the evolution of the hominid vocal tract? *American Journal of Physical Anthropology* 18, 254.

Laitman, J.T., Reidenberg, J.S., Friedland, D.R. & Gannon, P.J. 1991. What sayeth thou Neanderthal? A look at the evolution of their vocal tract and speech. *American Journal of Physical Anthropology* (supplement) 12, 109.

Laitman, J.T., Reidenberg, J.S., Friedland, D.R., Reidenberg, B.E. & Gannon, P.J. 1993. Neanderthal upper respiratory specializations and their effect upon respiration and speech. *American Journal of Physical Anthropology* (supplement) 16, 129.

Lake, M. 1992. Evolving thought (review of M. Donald's 'Origin of the Modern Mind'). *Cambridge Archaeological Journal* 2, 267–70.

Lake, M. 1995. Computer simulation of Early Hominid subsistence activities. Unpublished Ph.D. thesis, University of Cambridge.

Larichev, V., Khol'ushkin, V. & Laricheva, I. 1988. The Upper Palaeolithic of Northern Asia: achievements, problems and perspectives. I: Western Siberia. *Journal of World Prehistory* 2, 359–97.

Larichev, V., Khol'ushkin, V. & Laricheva, I. 1990. The Upper Palaeolithic of Northern Asia: achievements, problems and perspectives. II: Central and Eastern Siberia. *Journal of World Prehistory* 4, 347–85.

Larichev, V., Khol'ushkin, V. & Laricheva, I. 1992. The Upper Palaeolithic of Northern Asia: achievements, problems and perspectives. III: Northeastern Siberia and the Russian far east. *Journal of World Prehistory* 6, 441–76.

Larsson, L. 1983. The Skateholm Project – A Late Mesolithic Settlement and Cemetery complex at a southern Swedish bay. *Meddelånden från Lunds Universitets Historiska Museum* 1983–84, 4–38.

Laville, H., Rigaud, J-P. & Sackett, J.R. 1980. *Rockshelters of the Périgord*. New York: Academic Press.

Layton, R. 1985. The cultural context of hunter-gatherer rock art. *Man* (N.S.) 20, 434–53.

Layton, R. 1994. *Australian Rock Art: A New*

Synthesis. Cambridge: Cambridge University Press.

Leakey, M. 1971. *Olduvai Gorge. Volume 3. Excavations in Beds I and II, 1960–1963*. Cambridge: Cambridge University Press.

Leakey, M., Feibel, C.S., McDougall, I. & Walker, A. 1995. New four million-year-old hominid species from Kanapoi and Allia Bay, Kenya. *Nature* 376, 565–71.

Leakey, R.E. & Walker, A. 1976. Australopithecines, *H. erectus* and the single species hypothesis. *Nature* 222, 1132–38.

Lee, R.B. 1976. !Kung spatial organisation. In *Kalahari Hunter-Gatherers: Studies of the !Kung San and their Neighbors*, eds., R.B. Lee & I. DeVore, pp. 73–98. Cambridge MA: Harvard University Press.

Lee, R.B. 1979. *The !Kung San: Men, Women and Work in a Foraging Society*. Cambridge: Cambridge University Press.

Lee, R.B. & DeVore, I. (eds.) 1976. *Kalahari Hunter-Gatherers: Studies of the !Kung San and their Neighbours*. Cambridge MA: Harvard University Press.

Legge, A.J. & Rowley-Conwy, P. 1987. Gazelle killing in Stone Age Syria. *Scientific American* 255, 88–95.

LeMay, M. 1975. The language capability of Neanderthal man. *American Journal of Physical Anthropology* 49, 9–14.

LeMay, M. 1976. Morphological cerebral asymmetries of modern man, fossil man and nonhuman primates. In *Origins and Evolution of Language and Speech*, eds., S.R. Harnard, H.D. Steklis & J. Lancaster, pp. 349–66. New York: Annals of the New York Academy of Sciences, Vol. 280.

Leroi-Gourhan, A. 1968. *The Art of Prehistoric Man in Western Europe*. London: Thames & Hudson.

Leslie, A. 1991. The theory of mind impairment in autism: evidence for a modular mechanism of development. In *Natural Theories of Mind: Evolution, Development and Simulation of Everyday Mindreading*, ed., A. Whiten, pp. 63–78. Oxford: Blackwell.

Leslie, A. 1994. ToMM, ToBY, and agency: core architecture and domain specificity. In *Mapping the Mind: Domain Specificity in Cognition and Culture*, eds., L.A. Hirschfield & S. Gellman, pp. 119–48. Cambridge: Cambridge University Press.

Levine, M. 1983. Mortality models and interpretation of horse population structure. In *Hunter-Gatherer Economy in Prehistory: A European Perspective*, ed., G.N. Bailey, pp. 23–46. Cambridge: Cambridge University Press.

Levitt, D. 1981. *Plants and People: Aboriginal Uses of Plants on Groote Eylandt*. Canberra: Australian Institute of Aboriginal Studies.

Lewis-Williams, J.D. 1982. The economic and social context of southern San rock art. *Current Anthropology* 23, 429–49.

Lewis-Williams, J.D. 1983. *The Rock Art of*

Southern Africa. Cambridge: Cambridge University Press.

Lewis-Williams, J.D. 1987. A dream of eland: an unexplored component of San shamanism and rock art. *World Archaeology* 19, 165–77.

Lewis-Williams, J.D. 1991. Wrestling with analogy: a methodological dilemma in Upper Palaeolithic art research. *Proceedings of the Prehistoric Society* 57 (i), 149–62.

Lewis-Williams, J.D. 1995. Seeing and construing: the making and meaning of a southern African rock art motif. *Cambridge Archaeological Journal* (in press).

Lewis-Williams, J.D. & Dowson, T.A. 1988. The signs of all times: entoptic phenomena in Upper Palaeolithic art. *Current Anthropology* 24, 201–45.

Lieberman, P. 1984. *The Biology and Evolution of Language*. Cambridge MA: Harvard University Press.

Lieberman, P. 1993. On the Kebara KMH 2 hyoid and Neanderthal speech. *Current Anthropology* 34, 172–75.

Lieberman, P. & Crelin, E.S. 1971. On the speech of Neanderthal man. *Linguistic Enquiry* 2, 203–22.

Lieberman, D.E. & Shea, J.J. 1994. Behavioral differences between Archaic and Modern Humans in the Levantine Mousterian. *American Anthropologist* 96, 330–32.

Lindly, J. & Clark, G. 1990. Symbolism and modern human origins. *Current Anthropology* 31, 233–61.

Lock, A. 1993. Human language development and object manipulation: their relation in ontogeny and its possible relevance for phylogenetic questions. In *Tools, Language and Cognition in Human Evolution*, eds., K.R. Gibson & T. Ingold, pp. 279–99. Cambridge: Cambridge University Press.

Lockhart, R.S. 1989. Consciousness and the function of remembered episodes: comments on the fourth section. In *Varieties of Memory and Consciousness: Essays in Honour of Endel Tulving*, eds., H.L. Roedinger & F.I.M. Craik, pp. 423–29. Hillsdale NJ: Erlbaum.

Lorblanchet, M. 1989. From man to animal and sign in Palaeolithic art. In *Animals into Art*, ed., H. Morphy, pp. 109–43. London: Unwin Hyman.

MacDonald, C. 1991. *Mind-Body Identity Theories*. London: Routledge.

Mackintosh, N. 1983. *Conditioning and Associative Learning*. Oxford: Oxford University Press.

Mackintosh, N. 1994. Intelligence in evolution. In *What is Intelligence?*, ed., J. Khalfa, pp. 27–48. Cambridge: Cambridge University Press.

Marks, S.A. 1976. *Large Mammals and a Brave People: Subsistence Hunters in Zambia*. Seattle: University of Washington Press.

Marler, P. 1970. Birdsong and human speech: can there be parallels? *American Scientist* 58, 669–74.

Marshack, A. 1972a. *The Roots of Civilization*. London: McGraw Hill.

Marshack, A. 1972b. Upper Palaeolithic notation and symbol. *Science* 178, 817–28.

Marshack, A. 1985. A lunar solar year calendar stick from North America. *American Antiquity* 50, 27–51.

Marshack, A. 1989. On wishful thinking and lunar 'calendars'. A reply to Francesco d'Errico. *Current Anthropology* 30, 491–95.

Marshack, A. 1990. Early hominid symbolism and the evolution of human capacity. In *The Emergence of Modern Humans*, ed., P. Mellars, pp. 457–98. Edinburgh: Edinburgh University Press.

Marshack, A. 1991. The Täi plaque and calendrical notation in the Upper Palaeolithic. *Cambridge Archaeological Journal* 1, 25–61.

Marshall, L. 1976. *The !Kung of Nyae Nyae*. Cambridge MA: Harvard University Press.

Martin, R.S. 1981. Relative brain size and basal metabolic rates in terrestrial vertebrates. *Nature* 293, 57–60.

Martin, R.S. 1990. *Primate Origins and Evolution*. London: Chapman & Hall.

Martin, P.S. & Klein, R.C. (eds.) 1984. *Quaternary Extinctions: A Prehistoric Revolution*. Tucson: University of Arizona Press.

Matsuzawa, T. 1991. Nesting cups and metatools in chimpanzees. *Behavioral and Brain Sciences* 14, 570–71.

McBrearty, S. 1988. The Sangoan-Lupemban and Middle Stone Age sequence at the Muguruk Site, Western Kenya. *World Archaeology* 19, 388–420.

McBurney, C.B.M. 1967. *The Haua Fteah (Cyrenaica)*. Cambridge: Cambridge University Press.

McCown, T. 1937. Mugharet es-Skhūl: description and excavation. In *The Stone Age of Mount Carmel*, eds., D. Garrod & D. Bate, pp. 91–107. Oxford: Clarendon Press.

McFarland, D. (ed.) 1987. *The Oxford Companion to Animal Behaviour*. Oxford: Oxford University Press.

McGrew, W.C. 1987. Tools to get food: the subsistants of Tasmanian Aborigines and Tanzanian chimpanzees compared. *Journal of Anthropological Research* 43, 247–58.

McNabb, J. & Ashton, N. 1995. Thoughtful flakers. *Cambridge Archaeological Journal* 5, 289–301.

McGrew, W.C. 1992. *Chimpanzee Material Culture*. Cambridge: Cambridge University Press.

Meehan, B. 1982. *From Shell Bed to Shell Midden*. Canberra: Australian Institute of Australian Studies.

Mellars, P. 1973. The character of the Middle-Upper transition in southwest France. In *The Explanation of Culture Change*, ed., C. Renfrew, pp. 255–76. London: Duckworth.

Mellars, P. 1989a. Major issues in the emergence of modern humans. *Current Anthropology* 30, 349–85.

Mellars, P. 1989b. Technological changes at the

Middle–Upper Palaeolithic transition: economic, social and cognitive perspectives. In *The Human Revolution*, eds., P. Mellars & C. Stringer, pp. 338–65. Edinburgh: Edinburgh University Press.

Mellars, P. 1992. Technological change in the Mousterian of southwest France. In *The Middle Palaeolithic: Adaptation, Behaviour and Variability*, eds., H.L. Dibble & P. Mellars, pp. 29–44. Philadelphia: The University Museum, University of Pennsylvania.

Mellars, P. & Stringer, C. (eds.) 1989. *The Human Revolution: Behavioural and Biological Perspectives in the Origins of Modern Humans*. Edinburgh: Edinburgh University Press.

Meltzer, D., Adovasio, J.M. & Dillehay, T. 1994. On a Pleistocene human occupation at Pedra Furada, Brazil. *Antiquity* 68, 695–714.

Menzel, E. 1973. Chimpanzee spatial memory organization. *Science* 182, 943–45.

Menzel, E. 1978. Cognitive mapping in chimpanzees. In *Cognitive Processes in Animal Behavior*, eds., S. Hulse, H. Fowler & W. Honig, pp. 375–422. Hillsdale NJ: Erlbaum.

Merrick, H.V. & Merrick J.P.S. 1976. Archaeological occurrences of earlier Pleistocene age from the Shungura Formation. In *Earliest Man and Environments in the Lake Rudolf Basin: Stratigraphy, Paleoecology and Evolution*, eds., Y. Coppens, F.C. Howell, G. Isaac & R.E.F. Leakey, pp. 574–84. Chicago: Chicago University Press.

Milton, K. 1988. Foraging behaviour and the evolution of primate intelligence. In *Machiavellian Intelligence: Social Expertise and the Evolution of Intellect in Monkeys, Apes and Humans*, eds., R.W. Byrne & A. Whiten, pp. 285–305. Oxford: Clarendon Press.

Mithen, S. 1988. Looking and learning: Upper Palaeolithic art and information gathering. *World Archaeology* 19, 297–327.

Mithen, S. 1989. To hunt or to paint? Animals and art in the Upper Palaeolithic. *Man* 23, 671–95.

Mithen, S. 1990. *Thoughtful Foragers: A Study of Prehistoric Decision Making*. Cambridge: Cambridge University Press.

Mithen, S. 1993. Individuals, groups and the Palaeolithic record: a reply to Clark. *Proceedings of the Prehistoric Society* 59, 393–98.

Mithen, S. 1994. Technology and society during the Middle Pleistocene. *Cambridge Archaeological Journal* 4 (1), 3–33.

Mithen, S. 1995. Reply to Ashton & McNabb. *Cambridge Archaeological Journal* 5, 298–302.

Mithen, S. 1996. Social learning and cultural traditions: interpreting Early Palaeolithic technology. In *The Archaeology of Human Ancestry: Power, Sex and Tradition*, eds., J. Steele & S. Shennon, pp. 207–29. London: Routledge.

Moore, A.M.T. & Hillman, G.C. 1992. The Pleistocene-Holocene transition and human economy in southwest Asia: the impact of the Younger Dryas. *American Antiquity* 57, 482–94.

Morphy, H. (ed.) 1989a. *Animals into Art*, London: Unwin Hyman.

Morphy, H. 1989b. On representing Ancestral Beings. In *Animals into Art*, ed., H. Morphy, pp. 144–60. London: Unwin Hyman.

Morris, D. 1962. *The Biology of Art*. London: Methuen.

Mosiman, J.E. & Martin, P.S. 1976. Simulating overkill by Paleoindians. *American Scientist* 63, 304–13.

Movius, H. 1950. A wooden spear of third interglacial age from Lower Saxony. *Southwestern Journal of Anthropology* 6, 139–42.

Moyà-Solà, S. & Köhler, M. 1996. A *Dryopithecus* skeleton and the origins of great ape locomotion. *Nature* 379, 156–59.

Nagel, T. 1974. What is it like to be a bat? *Philosophical Review* 83, 435–50.

Naroll, R.S. 1962. Floor area and settlement population. *American Antiquity* 27, 587–89.

Nelson, R.K. 1973. *Hunters of the Northern Forest: Designs for Survival among the Alaskan Kutchin*. Chicago: University of Chicago Press.

Nelson, R.K. 1983. *Make Prayers to the Raven: A Koyukon View of the Northern Forest*. Chicago: Chicago University Press.

Nishida, T. 1987. Local traditions and cultural transmission. In *Primate Societies*, eds., B.B. Smuts, R.W. Wrangham & T.T. Struhsaker, pp. 462–74. Chicago: Chicago University Press.

Nitecki, M.H. & Nitecki, D.V. (eds.) 1994. *Origins of Anatomically Modern Humans*. New York: Plenum Press.

Oakley, K.P., Andrews, P., Keeley, L.H. & Clark, J.D. 1977. A reappraisal of the Clacton spear point. *Proceedings of the Prehistoric Society* 43, 13–30.

O'Connell, J. 1987. Alyawara site structure and its archaeological implications. *American Antiquity* 52, 74–108.

Oliver, J.S. 1994. Estimates of hominid and carnivore involvement in the FLK Zinjanthropus fossil assemblages: some sociological implications. *Journal of Human Evolution* 27, 267–94.

Olszewski, D.I. & Dibble, H.L. 1994. The Zagros Aurignacian. *Current Anthropology* 35, 68–75.

Oring, E. 1992. *Jokes and their Relations*. Lexington: University of Kentucky Press.

Orquera, L.A. 1984. Specialization and the Middle/Upper Palaeolithic transition. *Current Anthropology* 25, 73–98.

O'Shea, J. & Zvelebil, M. 1984. Oleneostrovski Mogilnik: reconstructing the social and economic organisation of prehistoric foragers in northern Russia. *Journal of Anthropological Archaeology* 3, 1–40.

Oswalt, W.H. 1973. *Habitat and Technology*. New York: Holt, Rinehart & Winston.

Oswalt, W.H. 1976. *An Anthropological Analysis of Food-Getting Technology*. New York: John Wiley.

Otte, M. 1992. The significance of variability in the European Mousterian. In *The Middle*

Palaeolithic, Adaptation, Behaviour and Variability, eds., H. Dibble & P. Mellars, pp. 45–52. Philadelphia: The University Museum, University of Pennsylvania.

Parés, J.M. & Pérez-González, A. 1995. Paleomagnetic age for hominid fossils of Atapuerca archaeological site, Spain. *Science* 269, 830–32.

Parker, S.T. & Gibson, K.R. 1979. A developmental model for the evolution of language and intelligence in early hominids. *Behavioral and Brain Sciences* 3, 367–408.

Parker, S.T. & Gibson, K.R. (eds.) 1990. *'Language' and Intelligence in Monkeys and Apes.* Cambridge: Cambridge University Press.

Parkin, R.A., Rowley-Conwy, P. & Serjeantson, D. 1986. Late Palaeolithic exploitation of horse and red deer at Gough's Cave, Cheddar, Somerset. *Proceedings of the University of Bristol Speleological Society* 17, 311–30.

Parkington, J.E. 1986. Stone tool assemblages, raw material distributions and prehistoric subsistence activities: the Late Stone Age of South Africa. In *Stone Age Prehistory*, eds., G.N. Bailey & P. Callow, pp. 181–94. Cambridge: Cambridge University Press.

Parkington, J.E. 1990. A critique of the consensus view on the age of Howieson's Poort assemblages in South Africa. In *The Emergence of Modern Humans*, ed., P. Mellars, pp. 34–55. Edinburgh: Edinburgh University Press.

Pelcin, A. 1994. A geological explanation for the Berekhat Ram figurine. *Current Anthropology* 35, 674–75.

Pelegrin, J. 1993. A framework for analysing prehistoric stone tool manufacture and a tentative application to some early stone industries. In *The Use of Tools by Human and Non-human Primates*, eds., A. Berthelet & J. Chavaillon, pp. 302–14. Oxford: Clarendon Press.

Penfield, W. 1975. *The Mystery of the Mind: A Critical Study of Consciousness and the Human Brain.* Princeton: Princeton University Press.

Pepperberg, I. 1990. Conceptual abilities of some non-primate species, with an emphasis on an African Grey parrot. In *'Language' and Intelligence in Monkeys and Apes*, eds., S.T. Parker & K.R. Gibson, pp. 469–507. Cambridge: Cambridge University Press.

Peterkin, G.L. 1993. Lithic and organic hunting technology in the French Upper Palaeolithic. In *Hunting and Animal Exploitation in the Later Palaeolithic and Mesolithic of Eurasia*, eds., G.L. Peterkin, H.M. Bricker & P. Mellars, pp. 49–67. Archaeological Papers of the American Anthropological Association, No. 4.

Pfeiffer, J. 1982. *The Creative Explosion.* New York: Harper & Row.

Phillipson. D.W. 1985. *African Archaeology.* Cambridge: Cambridge University Press.

Piaget, J. 1971. *Biology and Knowledge.* Edinburgh: Edinburgh University Press.

Piette, E. 1906. Le chevêtre et la semi-domestication des animaux aux temps pléistocènes. *L'Anthropologie* 17, 27–53.

Pigeot, N. 1990. Technical and social actors: flint knapping specialists and apprentices at Magdalenian Etiolles. *Archaeological Review from Cambridge* 9, 126–41.

Pike-Tay, A. 1991. *Red Deer Hunting in the Upper Palaeolithic of Southwest France.* Oxford: British Archaeological Reports, International Series 569.

Pike-Tay, A. 1993. Hunting in the Upper Périgordian: a matter of strategy or expediency. In *Before Lascaux: The Complex Record of the Early Upper Palaeolithic*, eds., H. Knecht, A. Pike-Tay & R. White, pp. 85–99. Boca Raton: CRC Press.

Pike-Tay, A. & Bricker, H.M. 1993. Hunting in the Gravettian: an examination of the evidence from southwestern France. In *Hunting and Animal Exploitation in the Later Palaeolithic and Mesolithic of Eurasia*, eds. G.L. Peterkin, H.M. Bricker & P. Mellars, pp. 127–43. Archaeological Papers of the American Anthropological Association, No. 4.

Pinker, S. 1989. *Learnability and Cognition.* Cambridge MA: MIT Press.

Pinker, S. 1994. *The Language Instinct.* New York: William Morrow.

Plummer, T.W. & Bishop, L.C. 1994. Hominid paleoecology at Olduvai Gorge, Tanzania as indicated by antelope remains. *Journal of Human Evolution* 27, 47–75.

Pope, G. 1985. Taxonomy, dating and palaeoenvironments: the Palaeoecology of early far eastern hominids. *Modern Quaternary Research in Southeast Asia* 5, 65–80.

Pope, G. 1989. Bamboo and human evolution. *Natural History* 10, 49–56.

Potts, R. 1986. Temporal span of bone accumulations at Olduvai Gorge and implications for early hominid foraging behavior. *Paleobiology* 12, 25–31.

Potts, R. 1988. *Early Hominid Activities at Olduvai Gorge.* New York: Aldine de Gruyter.

Potts, R. 1989. Olorgesailie: new excavations and findings in Early and Middle Pleistocene contexts, southern Kenya rift valley. *Journal of Human Evolution* 18, 269–76.

Potts, R. 1994. Variables versus models of early Pleistocene hominid land use. *Journal of Human Evolution* 27, 7–24.

Potts, R. & Shipman, P. 1981. Cutmarks made by stone tools on bones from Olduvai Gorge, Tanzania. *Nature* 29, 577–80.

Povenelli, D.J. 1993. Reconstructing the evolution of the mind. *American Psychologist* 48, 493–509.

Premack, A.J. & Premack, D. 1972. Teaching language to an ape. *Scientific American* 227, 92–9.

Premack, D. 1988. 'Does the chimpanzee have a theory of mind?' revisited. In *Machiavellian Intelligence: Social Expertise and the Evolution of Intellect in Monkeys, Apes and Humans*, eds., R.W. Byrne & A. Whiten, pp. 160–79. Oxford: Clarendon Press.

Premack, D. & Woodruff, G. 1978. Does the

chimpanzee have a theory of mind? *The Behavioral and Brain Sciences* 1, 515–26.

Pulliam, H.R. & Dunford, C. 1980. *Programmed to Learn: An Essay on the Evolution of Culture.* New York: Basic Books.

Rae, A. 1986. *Quantum Physics: Illusion or Reality?* Cambridge: Cambridge University Press.

Renfrew, C. 1983. *Towards an Archaeology of Mind.* Cambridge: Cambridge University Press.

Renfrew, C. 1993. What is cognitive archaeology? *Cambridge Archaeological Journal* 3 (2), 248–50.

Reynolds, T.D. & Barnes, G. 1984. The Japanese Palaeolithic: a review. *Proceedings of the Prehistoric Society* 50, 49–62.

Riddington, R. 1982. Technology, world view and adaptive strategy in a northern hunting society. *Canadian Review of Sociology and Anthropology* 19, 469–81.

Rightmire, G.P. 1990. *The Evolution of H. erectus: Comparative Anatomical Studies of an Extinct Species.* Cambridge: Cambridge University Press.

Rice, P. 1981. Prehistoric venuses: symbols of motherhood or womenhood? *Journal of Anthropological Research* 37, 402–14.

Roberts, M.B. 1986. Excavation of the Lower Palaeolithic site at Amey's Eartham Pit, Boxgrove, West Sussex: a preliminary report. *Proceedings of the Prehistoric Society* 52, 215–46.

Roberts, M.B. 1994. Paper presented at Conference on the English Lower Palaeolithic, London, October 1994.

Roberts, M.B., Stringer, C.B. & Parfitt, S.A. 1994. A hominid tibia from Middle Pleistocene sediments at Boxgrove, UK. *Nature* 369, 311–13.

Roberts, R.G., Jones, R. & Smith, M.A. 1990. Thermoluminescence dating of a 50,000-year-old human occupation site in northern Australia. *Nature* 345, 153–56.

Roberts, R.G., Jones, R. & Smith, M.A. 1993. Optical dating at Deaf Adder Gorge, Northern Territory, indicates human occupation between 53,000 and 60,000 years ago. *Australian Archaeology* 37, 58–9.

Roberts, R.G., Jones, R. & Smith, M.A. 1994. Beyond the radiocarbon barrier in Australian prehistory. *Antiquity* 68, 611–16.

Robinson, J. 1992. Not counting on Marshack: a reassessment of the work of Alexander Marshack on notation in the Upper Palaeolithic. *Journal of Mediterranean Studies* 2, 1–16.

Roche, H. 1989. Technological evolution in the early hominids. *OSSA, International Journal of Skeletal Research* 14, 97–8.

Roche, H. & Tiercelin, J.J. 1977. Découverte d'une industrie lithique ancienne in situ dans la formation d'Hadar, Afar central, Ethiopia. *Competes Rendus de l'Académie des Sciences* 284-D, 1871–74.

Roe, D. 1981. *The Lower and Middle Palaeolithic Periods in Britain.* London: Routledge & Kegan Paul.

Roebroeks, W. 1988. From flint scatters to early hominid behaviour: a study of Middle Palaeolithic riverside settlements at Maastrict-Belvedere. *Analecta Praehistorica Leidensai* 1988.

Roebroeks, W., Conrad, N.J. & van Kolfschoten, T. 1992. Dense forests, cold steppes, and the Palaeolithic settlement of Northern Europe. *Current Anthropology* 33, 551–86.

Roebroeks, W., Kolen, J. & Rensink, E. 1988. Planning depth, anticipation and the organization of Middle Palaeolithic technology: the 'archaic natives' meet Eve's descendants. *Helinium* 28, 17–34.

Roebroeks, W. & van Kolfschoten, T. 1994. The earliest occupation of Europe: a short chronology. *Antiquity* 68, 489–503.

Rogers, M.J., Harris, J.W.K. & Feibel, C.S. 1994. Changing patterns of land use by Plio-Pleistocene hominids in the Lake Turkana Basin. *Journal of Human Evolution* 27, 139–58.

Rolland, N. & Dibble, H.L. 1990. A new synthesis of Middle Palaeolithic variability. *American Antiquity* 55, 480–99.

Ronen, A. 1992. The emergence of blade technology: cultural affinities. In *The Evolution and Dispersal of Modern Humans in Asia*, eds., T. Akazawa, K. Aoki & T. Kimura, pp. 217–28. Tokyo: Hokusen-Sha.

Rozin, P. 1976. The evolution of intelligence and access to the cognitive unconscious. In *Progress in Psychobiology and Physiological Psychology*, eds., J.M. Sprague & A.N. Epstein, pp. 245–77. New York: Academic Press.

Rozin, P. & Schull, J. 1988. The adaptive-evolutionary point of view in experimental psychology. In *Steven's Handbook of Experimental Psychology, Vol 1: Perception and Motivation*, eds., R.C. Atkinson, R.J. Hernstein, G. Lindzey & R.D. Luce, pp. 503–46. New York: John Wiley & Sons.

Sackett, J.R. 1981. From de Mortillet to Bordes: a century of French Palaeolithic research. In *Towards a History of Archaeology*, ed., G. Daniel, pp. 85–99. London: Thames & Hudson.

Sackett, J. 1982. Approaches to style in lithic archaeology. *Journal of Anthropological Archaeology* 1, 59–112.

Sacks, O. 1995. *An Anthropologist on Mars.* New York: Knopf.

Saladin D'Anglure, B. 1990. Nanook, super-male: the polar bear in the imaginary space and social time of the Inuit of the Canadian Arctic. In *Signifying Animals: Human Meaning in the Natural World*, ed., R.G. Willis, pp. 173–95. London: Unwin Hyman.

Santonja, M. & Villa, P. 1990. The Lower Palaeolithic of Spain and Portugal. *Journal of World Prehistory* 4, 45–94.

Savage-Rumbaugh, E.S. & Rumbaugh, D.M. 1993. The emergence of language. In *Tools, Language and Cognition in Human Evolution*, eds., K.R. Gibson & T. Ingold, pp. 86–108. Cambridge: Cambridge University Press.

Schacter, D. 1989. On the relation between memory and consciousness: dissociable interactions and conscious experience. In *Varieties of Memory and Consciousness: Essays in Honour of Endel Tulving*, eds., H.L. Roedinger & F.I.M. Craik, pp. 355–90. Hillsdale NJ: Erlbaum.

Schepartz, L.A. 1993. Language and modern human origins. *Yearbook of Physical Anthropology* 36, 91–126.

Schick, K. & Toth, N. 1993. *Making Silent Stones Speak: Human Evolution and the Dawn of Technology*. New York: Simon & Schuster.

Schick, K. & Zhuan, D. 1993. Early Paleolithic of China and Eastern Asia. *Evolutionary Anthropology* 2, 22–35.

Schlanger, N. 1996. Understanding levallois: lithic technology and cognitive archaeology. *Cambridge Archaeological Journal* 6 (in press).

Scott, K. 1980. Two hunting episodes of Middle Palaeolithic age at La Cotte de Saint-Brelade, Jersey (Channel Islands). *World Archaeology* 12, 137–52.

Searle, J. 1990. Consciousness, explanatory inversion and cognitive science. *Behavioral and Brain Sciences* 13, 585–95.

Searle, J. 1992. *The Rediscovery of the Mind*. Cambridge MA: MIT Press.

Sémah, F., Sémah, A-H., Djubiantono, T. & Simanjuntak, H.T. 1992. Did they also make stone tools? *Journal of Human Evolution* 23, 439–46.

Sept, J.M. 1994. Beyond bones: archaeological sites, early hominid subsistence, and the costs and benefits of exploiting wild plant foods in east African riverine landscapes. *Journal of Human Evolution* 27, 295–320.

Shackleton, N.J. 1987. Oxygen isotopes, ice volume and sea level. *Quaternary Science Reviews* 6, 183–90.

Shackleton, N.J. & Opdyke, N.D. 1973. Oxygen isotope and palaeomagnetic stratigraphy of equatorial Pacific core V28-238. *Quaternary Research* 3, 39–55.

Shea, J.J. 1988. Spear points from the Middle Palaeolithic of the Levant. *Journal of Field Archaeology* 15, 441–50.

Shea, J.J. 1989. A functional study of the lithic industries associated with hominid fossils in the Kebara and Qafzeh caves, Israel. In *The Human Revolution*, eds., P. Mellars & C. Stringer, pp. 611–25. Edinburgh: Edinburgh University Press.

Shipman, P. 1983. Early hominid lifestyle: hunting and gathering or foraging and scavenging? In *Animals and Archaeology: 1. Hunters and their Prey*, eds., J. Clutton-Brock and C. Grigson, pp. 31–49. Oxford: British Archaeological Reports, International Series 163.

Shipman, P. 1986. Scavenging or hunting in the early hominids. Theoretical framework and tests. *American Anthropologist* 88, 27–43.

Shipman, P., Bosler, W. & Davis, K.L. 1981. Butchering of giant geladas at an Acheulian site. *Current Anthropology* 22, 257–68.

Shipman, P., Bosler, W. & Davis, K.L. 1982.

Reply to Binford & Todd 'On arguments for the butchering of giant geladas'. *Current Anthropology* 23, 110–11.

Sieveking, A. 1984. Palaeolithic art and animal behaviour. In *La Contribution de la Zoologie et de l'ethologie à l'Interprétation de l'Art des Peuples Chasseurs Préhistoriques*, eds., H. Bandi *et al*, pp. 99–109. Fribourg: Editions Universitaires.

Sikes, N.E. 1994. Early hominid habitat preferences in East Africa: paleosol carbon isotopic evidence. *Journal of Human Evolution* 27, 25–45.

Silberbauer, G. 1981. *Hunter and Habitat in the Central Kalahari Desert*. Cambridge: Cambridge University Press.

Simons, E. 1992. The fossil history of primates. In *The Cambridge Encyclopedia of Human Evolution*, eds., J.S. Jones, R. Martin & D. Pilbeam, pp. 373–79. Cambridge: Cambridge University Press.

Sinclair, A. 1995. The technique as symbol in late glacial Europe. *World Archaeology* 27, 50–62.

Singer, R. & Wymer, J. 1982. *The Middle Stone Age at Klasies River Mouth in South Africa*. Chicago: Chicago University Press.

Smith, B.H. 1993. The physiological age of KNM-WT 15000. In *The Nariokotome Homo erectus Skeleton*, eds., A. Walker & R. Leakey, pp. 195–220. Berlin: Springer Verlag.

Smith, N. & Tsimpli, I-M. 1995. *The Mind of a Savant: Language Learning and Modularity*. Oxford: Clarendon Press.

Smith, P.E. 1982. The Late Palaeolithic and Epi-Palaeolithic of northern Africa. In *The Cambridge History of Africa, Volume 1, From the Earliest Times to c. 500 BC*, ed., J.D. Clark, pp. 342–409. Cambridge: Cambridge University Press.

Smith, R.J., Gannon, P.J. & Smith, B.H. 1995. Ontogeny of australopithecines and early *Homo*: evidence from cranial capacity and dental eruption. *Journal of Human Evolution* 29, 155–68.

Soffer, O. 1985. *The Upper Palaeolithic of the Central Russian Plain*. New York: Academic Press.

Soffer, O. 1987. Upper Palaeolithic connubia, refugia and the archaeological record from Eastern Europe. In *The Pleistocene Old World: Regional Perspectives*, ed., O. Soffer, pp. 333–48. New York: Plenum Press.

Soffer, O. 1989a. The Middle to Upper Palaeolithic transition on the Russian Plain. In *The Human Revolution*, eds., P. Mellars & C. Stringer, pp. 714–42. Edinburgh: Edinburgh University Press.

Soffer, O. 1989b. Storage, sedentism and the Eurasian Palaeolithic record. *Antiquity* 63, 719–32.

Soffer, O. 1994. Ancestral lifeways in Eurasia – The Middle and Upper Palaeolithic records. In *Origins of Anatomically Modern Humans*, eds., M.H. Nitecki & D.V. Nitecki, pp. 101–20. New York: Plenum Press.

Solecki, R. 1971. *Shanidar: The First Flower*

People. New York: Knopf.

Spelke, E.S. 1991. Physical knowledge in infancy: reflections on Piaget's theory. In *Epigenesis of Mind: Studies in Biology and Culture*, eds., S. Carey & R. Gelman, pp. 133–69. Hillsdale NJ: Erlbaum.

Spelke, E.S., Breinlinger, K., Macomber, J. & Jacobsen, K. 1992. Origins of knowledge. *Psychological Review*, 99, 605–32.

Sperber, D. 1994. The modularity of thought and the epidemiology of representations. In *Mapping the Mind: Domain Specificity in Cognition and Culture*, eds., L.A. Hirschfeld & S.A. Gelman, pp. 39–67. Cambridge: Cambridge University Press.

Spiess, A. E. 1979. *Reindeer and Caribou Hunters.* New York: Academic Press.

Srejovic, D. 1972. *Lepenski Vir.* London: Thames & Hudson.

Stepanchuk, V.N. 1993. Prolom II, a Middle Palaeolithic cave site in the eastern Crimea with non-utilitarian bone artifacts. *Proceedings of the Prehistoric Society* 59, 17–37.

Stern, N. 1993. The structure of the Lower Pleistocene archaeological record: a case study from the Koobi Fora formation. *Current Anthropology* 34, 201–25.

Stern, N. 1994. The implications of time averaging for reconstructing the land-use patterns of early tool-using hominids. *Journal of Human Evolution* 27, 89–105.

Sternberg, R. 1988. *The Triarchic Mind: A New Theory of Human Intelligence.* New York: Viking Press.

Stiles, D.N. 1991. Early hominid behaviour and culture tradition: raw material studies in Bed II, Olduvai Gorge. *The African Archaeological Review* 9, 1–19.

Stiles, D.N., Hay, R.L. & O'Neil, J.R. 1974. The MNK chert factory site, Olduvai Gorge, Tanzania. *World Archaeology* 5, 285–308.

Stiner, M. 1991. A taphonomic perspective on the origins of the faunal remains of Grotta Guattari (Latium, Italy). *Current Anthropology* 32, 103–17.

Stiner, M. & Kuhn, S. 1992. Subsistence, technology and adaptive variation in Middle Palaeolithic Italy. *American Anthropologist* 94, 12–46.

Stopp, M. 1988. A taphonomic analysis of the Hoxne site faunal assemblages. Unpublished M.Phil thesis, University of Cambridge.

Straus, L.G. 1982. Carnivores and cave sites in Cantabrian Spain. *Journal of Anthropological Research* 38, 75–96.

Straus, L.G. 1987b. Upper Palaeolithic ibex hunting is SW Europe. *Journal of Archaeological Science* 14, 149–63.

Straus, L.G. 1990a. The original arms race: Iberian perspectives on the Solutrean phenomenon. In *Feuilles de Pierre: Les Industries Foliacées du Paléolithique Supérieur Européen*, ed., J. Kozlowski, pp. 425–47. Liège, Belgium: ERAUL 42.

Straus, L.G. 1990b. On the emergence of modern humans. *Current Anthropology* 31, 63–4.

Straus, L.G. 1991. Southwestern Europe at the last glacial maximum. *Current Anthropology* 32, 189–99.

Straus, L.G. 1992. *Iberia Before the Iberians.* Albuquerque: University of New Mexico Press.

Straus, L.G. 1993. Upper Palaeolithic hunting tactics and weapons in western Europe. In *Hunting and Animal Exploitation in the Later Palaeolithic and Mesolithic of Eurasia*, eds., G.L. Peterkin, H.M. Bricker & P. Mellars, pp. 83–93. Archaeological Papers of the American Anthropological Association, No. 4.

Stringer, C. 1993. Secrets of the pit of the bones. *Nature* 362, 501–02.

Stringer, C. & Bräuer, G. 1994. Methods, misreading and bias. *American Anthropologist* 96, 416–24.

Stringer, C. & Gamble, C. 1993. *In Search of the Neanderthals.* London & New York: Thames & Hudson.

Stuart, A.J. 1982. *Pleistocene Vertebrates in the British Isles.* New York: Longman.

Sugiyama, Y. 1993. Local variation of tools and tool use among wild chimpanzee populations. In *The Use of Tools by Human and Non-human Primates*, eds., A. Berthelet & J. Chavaillon, pp. 175–90. Oxford: Clarendon Press.

Sullivan, R.J. 1942. *The Ten'a Food Quest.* Washington: The Catholic University of America Press.

Susman, R.L. 1991. Who made the Oldowan tools? Fossil evidence for tool behaviour in Plio-Pleistocene hominids. *Journal of Anthropological Research* 47, 129–51.

Svoboda, J. 1987. Lithic industries of the Arago, Vértesszöllös and Bilzingsleben hominids: comparisons and evolutionary interpretations. *Current Anthropology* 28, 219–27.

Svoboda, J. 1988. A new male burial from Dolni Vestonice. *Journal of Human Evolution* 16, 827–30.

Svoboda, J. 1992. Comment on 'Dense forests, cold steppes, and the Palaeolithic settlement of Northern Europe by W. Roebroeks, N.J. Conrad & T. van Kolfschoten'. *Current Anthropology* 33, 569–72.

Swisher, C.C. III., Curtis, G.H., Jacob, T., Getty, A.G., Suprijo, A. & Widiasmoro. 1994. Age of the earliest known hominids in Java, Indonesia. *Science* 263, 1118–21.

Tacon, P.S.C. 1989. Art and the essence of being: symbolic and economic aspects of fish among the peoples of western Arnhem Land, Australia. In *Animals into Art*, ed., H. Morphy, pp. 236–50. London: Unwin Hyman.

Talmy, L. 1988. Force dynamics in language and cognition. *Cognitive Science* 12, 49–100.

Tanner, A. 1979. *Bringing Home Animals: Religious Ideology and Mode of Production of the Mistassini Cree Hunters.* London: C. Hurst.

Tatton-Brown, T. 1989. *Great Cathedrals of Britain.* London: BBC Books.

Taylor, K.C., Lamorey, G.W., Doyle, G.A., Alley, R.B., Grootes, P.M., Mayewski, P.A., White, J.W.C. & Barlow, L.K. 1993. The 'flickering switch' of late Pleistocene climate change. *Nature* 361, 432–35.

Taylor, L. 1989. Seeing the 'inside': Kunwinjku paintings and the symbol of the divided body. In *Animals into Art*, ed., H. Morphy, pp. 371–89. London: Unwin Hyman.

Templeton, A.R. 1993. The 'Eve' hypothesis: a genetic critique and reanalysis. *American Anthropologist* 95, 51–72.

Terrace, H.S. 1979. *Nim*. New York: Knopf.

Terrace, H.S., Pettito, L.A., Saunders, R.J. & Bever, T.G. 1979. Can an ape create a sentence? *Science* 206, 891–902.

Thackeray, A.I. 1989. Changing fashions in the Middle Stone Age: the stone artefact sequence from Klasies River main site, South Africa. *African Archaeological Review* 7, 33–57.

Tobias, P.V. 1987. The brain of *Homo habilis*: a new level of organisation in cerebral evolution. *Journal of Human Evolution* 16, 741–61.

Tobias, P.V. 1991. *Olduvai Gorge, Volume 4*. Cambridge: Cambridge University Press.

Tomasello, M. 1990. Cultural transmission in the tool use and communicatory signaling of chimpanzees? In *'Language' and Intelligence in Monkeys and Apes: Comparative Developmental Perspectives*, eds., S.T. Parker & K.R. Gibson, pp. 274–311. Cambridge: Cambridge University Press.

Tomasello, M., Davis-Dasilva, M., Camak, L. & Bard, K. 1987. Observational learning of tool use by young chimpanzees. *Human Evolution* 2, 175–83.

Tomasello, M., Kruger, A.C. & Ratner, H.H. 1993. Cultural learning. *Behavioral and Brain Sciences* 16, 495–552.

Tooby, J. & Cosmides, L. 1989. Evolutionary psychology and the generation of culture, part I. Theoretical considerations. *Ethology and Sociobiology* 10, 29–49.

Tooby, J. & Cosmides, L. 1992. The psychological foundations of culture. In *The Adapted Mind*, eds., J.H. Barkow, L. Cosmides & J. Tooby, pp. 19–136. New York: Oxford University Press.

Torrence, R. 1983. Time budgeting and hunter-gatherer technology. In *Hunter-Gatherer Economy in Prehistory*, ed., G.N.B. Bailey, pp. 11–22. Cambridge: Cambridge University Press.

Toth, N. 1985. The Oldowan reassessed: a close look at early stone artifacts. *Journal of Archaeological Science* 12, 101–20.

Toth, N. & Schick, K.D. 1993. Early stone industries and inferences regarding language and cognition. In *Tools, Language and Cognition in Human Evolution*, eds., K.R. Gibson & T. Ingold, pp. 346–62. Cambridge: Cambridge University Press.

Toth, N., Schick, K.D., Savage-Rumbaugh, E.S., Sevcik, R.A. & Rumbaugh, D.M. 1993. *Pan* the tool-maker: investigations into the stone tool-making and tool-using capabilities of a bonobo (*Pan paniscus*). *Journal of Archaeological Science* 20, 81–91.

Torrence, R. 1983. Time budgeting and hunter-gatherer technology. In *Hunter-Gatherer Economy in Prehistory*, ed., G.N.B. Bailey, pp. 57–66. Cambridge: Cambridge University Press.

Trinkaus, E. 1983. *The Shanidar Neandertals*. New York: Academic Press.

Trinkaus, E. 1985. Pathology and posture of the La Chapelle-aux-Saints Neandertal. *American Journal of Physical Anthropology* 67, 19–41.

Trinkaus, E. 1985. Cannibalism and burial at Krapina. *Journal of Human Evolution* 14, 203–16.

Trinkaus, E. 1987. Bodies, brawn, brains and noses: human ancestors and human predation. In *The Evolution of Human Hunting*, eds., M.H. Nitecki & D.V. Nitecki, pp. 107–45. New York: Plenum Press.

Trinkaus, E. 1992. Morphological contrasts between the Near Eastern Qafzeh-Skhūl and Late Archaic human samples: grounds for a behavioral difference. In *The Evolution and Dispersal of Modern Humans in Asia*, eds., T. Akazawa, K. Aoki & T. Kimura, pp. 277–94. Tokyo: Hokusen-Sha.

Trinkaus, E. 1995. Neandertal mortality patterns. *Journal of Archaeological Science* 22, 121–42.

Trinkaus, E. & Shipman, P. 1992. *The Neandertals*. New York: Knopf.

Tuffreau, A. 1992. Middle Palaeolithic settlement in Northern France. In *The Middle Palaeolithic: Adaptation, Behaviour and Variability*, eds., H.L. Dibble & P. Mellars, pp. 59–73. Philadelphia: The University Museum, University of Pennsylvania.

Tulving, E. 1983. *Elements of Episodic Memory*. Oxford: Clarendon Press.

Turq, A. 1992. Raw material and technological studies of the Quina Mousterian in Perigord. In *The Middle Palaeolithic: Adaptation, Behaviour and Variability*, eds., H.L. Dibble & P. Mellars, pp. 75–85. Philadelphia: The University Museum, University of Pennsylvania.

Tuttle, R.H. 1987. Kinesiological inferences and evolutionary implications from Laetoli bipedal trails G-1, G-2/3 and A. In *Laetoli, a Pliocene Site in Northern Tanzania*, eds., M.D. Leakey & J.M. Harris, pp. 503–23. Oxford: Clarendon Press.

Tyldesley, J. 1986. *The Wolvercote Channel Handaxe Assemblage: A Comparative Study*. Oxford: British Archaeological Reports, British Series 152.

Valladas, H., Cachier, H., Maurice, P., Bernaldo de Quiros, F., Clottes, J., Cabrera Valdés, V., Uzquiano, P. & Arnold, M. 1992. Direct radiocarbon dates for prehistoric paintings at the Altamira, El Castillo and Niaux caves. *Nature* 357, 68–70.

Valoch, K. 1984. Le Taubachien, sa géochronologie, paléoécologie et sa paléoethnologie. *L'Anthropologie* 88, 193–208.

Vandermeersch, B. 1970. Une sépulture moustérienne avec offrandes découverte dans la grotte de Qafzeh. *Comptes Rendus Hebdomadaires des Séances de l'Académie des Sciences* 270, 298–301.

Vandermeersch, B. 1989. The evolution of modern humans, recent evidence from Southwest Asia. In *The Human Revolution*, eds., P. Mellars & C. Stringer, pp. 155–63. Edinburgh: Edinburgh University Press.

van Schaik, C.P. 1983. Why are diurnal primates living in large groups? *Behaviour* 87, 120–44.

Vértes, L. 1975. The Lower Palaeolithic site of Vértesszöllös, Hungary. In *Recent Archaeological Excavations in Europe*, ed., R. Bruce-Mitford, pp. 287–301. London: Routledge and Kegan Paul.

Villa, P. 1983. *Terra Amata and the Middle Pleistocene Archaeological Record from Southern France*. Berkeley: University of California Press.

Villa, P. 1990. Torralba and Aridos: elephant exploitation in Middle Pleistocene Spain. *Journal of Human Evolution* 19, 299–309.

Villa, P. 1991. Middle Pleistocene prehistory in southwestern Europe: the state of our knowledge and ignorance. *Journal of Anthropological Research* 47, 193–217.

Visalberghi, E. & Fragaszy, D.M. 1990. Do monkeys ape? In *'Language' and Intelligence in Monkeys and Apes: Comparative Developmental Perspectives*, eds., S.T. Parker & K.R. Gibson, pp. 247–73. Cambridge: Cambridge University Press.

de Waal, F. 1982. *Chimpanzee Politics: Power and Sex among Apes*. London: Jonathan Cape.

Wadley, L. 1993. The Pleistocene Late Stone Age south of the Limpopo River. *Journal of World Prehistory* 7, 243–96.

Walker, A. & Leakey, R. (eds.) 1993. *The Nariokotome Homo erectus Skeleton*. Berlin: Springer Verlag.

Wanpo, H., Ciochon, R., Yumin, G., Larick, R., Qiren, F., Schwarcz, H., Yonge, C., de Vos, J. & Rink, W. 1995. Early *Homo* and associated artifacts from China. *Nature* 378, 275–78.

Wellman, H.M. 1991. From desires to beliefs: acquisition of a theory of mind. In *Natural Theories of Mind: Evolution, Development and Simulation of Everyday Mindreading*, ed., A. Whiten, pp. 19–38. Oxford: Blackwell.

Wendorf, F., Schild, R. & Close, A. (eds.) 1980. *Loaves and Fishes: The Prehistory of Wadi Kubbaniya*. Dallas: Southern Methodist University Press.

Westergaard, G.C. 1995. The stone tool technology of capuchin monkeys: possible implications for the evolution of symbolic communication in hominids. *World Archaeology* 27, 1–24.

Weyer, E.M. 1932. *The Eskimos*. New Haven: York University Press.

Whallon, R. 1989. Elements of culture change in the Later Palaeolithic. In *The Human Revolution*, eds., P. Mellars & C. Stringer, pp. 433–54.

Edinburgh: Edinburgh University Press.

Wheeler, P. 1984. The evolution of bipedality and the loss of functional body hair in hominids. *Journal of Human Evolution* 13, 91–8.

Wheeler, P. 1988. Stand tall and stay cool. *New Scientist* 12, 60–5.

Wheeler, P. 1991. The influence of bipedalism on the energy and water budgets of early hominids. *Journal of Human Evolution* 21, 107–36.

Wheeler, P. 1994. The thermoregulatory advantages of heat storage and shade seeking behaviour to hominids foraging in equatorial savannah environments. *Journal of Human Evolution* 26, 339–50.

White, R. 1982. Rethinking the Middle/Upper Paleolithic transition. *Current Anthropology* 23, 169–92.

White, R. 1989a. Production complexity and standardization in early Aurignacian bead and pendant manufacture: evolutionary implications. In *The Human Revolution*, eds., P. Mellars & C. Stringer, pp. 366–90. Edinburgh: Edinburgh University Press.

White, R. 1989b. Husbandry and herd control in the Upper Palaeolithic. *Current Anthropology* 30, 609–31.

White, R. 1992. Beyond art: toward an understanding of the origins of material representation in Europe. *Annual Review of Anthropology* 21, 537–64.

White, R. 1993a. A social and technological view of Aurignacian and Castelperronian personal ornaments in S.W. Europe. in *El Origin del Hombre Moderno en el Suroeste de Europa*, ed., V. Cabrera Valdés, pp. 327–57. Madrid: Ministerio des Educacion y Ciencia.

White, R. 1993b. Technological and social dimensions of 'Aurignacian-Age' body ornaments across Europe. In *Before Lascaux: The Complex Record of the Early Upper Palaeolithic*, eds., H. Knecht, A. Pike-Tay & R. White, pp. 247–99. Boca Raton: CRC Press.

White, T.D., Suwa, G. & Asfaw, B. 1994. *Australopithecus ramidus*, a new species of early hominid from Aramis, Ethiopia. *Nature* 371, 306–12.

White, T.D. & Toth, N. 1991. The question of ritual cannibalism at Grotta Guattari. *Current Anthropology* 32, 118–38.

Whitelaw, T. 1991. Some dimensions of variability in the social organisation of community space among foragers. In *Ethnoarchaeological Approaches to Mobile Campsites*, eds., C. Gamble & W. Boismier, pp. 139–88. Ann Arbor: International Monographs in Prehistory.

Whiten, A. 1989. Transmission mechanisms in primate cultural evolution. *Trends in Ecology and Evolution* 4, 61–2.

Whiten, A. 1990. Causes and consequences in the evolution of hominid brain size. *Behavioral and Brain Sciences* 13, 367.

Whiten, A. (ed.) 1991. *Natural Theories of Mind: Evolution, Development and Simulation of*

Everyday Mindreading. Oxford: Blackwell.

Whiten, A. & Perner, J. 1991. Fundamental issues in the multidisciplinary study of mindreading. In *Natural Theories of Mind: Evolution, Development and Simulation of Everyday Mindreading*, ed., A. Whiten, pp. 1–18. Oxford: Blackwell.

Wiessner, P. 1983. Style and social information in Kalahari San projectile points. *American Antiquity* 48, 253–57.

Willis, R.G. (ed.) 1990. *Signifying Animals: Human Meaning in the Natural World*. London: Unwin Hyman.

Wills, C. 1994. *The Runaway Brain*. London: HarperCollins.

Winterhalder, B. 1981. Foraging strategies in the boreal environment: an analysis of Cree hunting and gathering. In *Hunter-Gatherer Foraging Strategies: Ethnographic and Archaeological Analyses*, eds., B. Winterhalder & B. Smith, pp. 66–98. Chicago: Chicago University Press.

Wobst, H.M. 1977. Stylistic behavior and information exchange. In *Papers for the Director: Research Essays in Honour of James B. Griffin*, ed., C.E. Cleland, pp. 317–42. Anthropological Papers no. 61, Museum of Anthropology, University of Michigan.

WoldeGabriel, G., White, T.D., Suwa, G., Renne, P., de Heinzelin, J., Hart, W.K. & Heiken, G. 1994. Ecological and temporal placement of early Pliocene hominids at Aramis, Ethiopia. *Nature* 371, 330–33.

Wolpoff, M.H. 1989. The place of Neanderthals in human evolution. In *The Emergence of Modern Humans*, ed., E. Trinkaus, pp. 97–141. Cambridge: Cambridge University Press.

Wolpoff, M.H., Wu, Xinzhi & Thorne, A.G. 1984. Modern *Homo sapien* origins: a general theory of hominid evolution involving the fossil evidence from East Asia. In *Origins of Modern Humans: A World Survey of the Fossil Evidence*, eds., F.H. Smith & F. Spencer, pp. 411–83. New York: Alan R. Liss.

Wood, B. 1992. Origin and evolution of the genus *Homo*. *Nature* 355, 783–90.

Wood, B. 1994. The oldest hominid yet. *Nature* 371, 280–81.

Wood, B. & Turner, A. 1995. Out of Africa and into Asia. *Nature* 378, 239–40.

Wrangham, R.W. 1977. Feeding behaviour of chimpanzees in Gombe National Park, Tanzania. In *Primate Ecology: Studies of Feedings and Ranging Behaviour in Lemurs, Monkeys and Apes*, ed., T.H. Clutton-Brock, pp. 503–78. London: Academic Press.

Wrangham, R.W. 1987. Evolution of social structure. In *Primate Societies*, eds., B.B. Smuts, D.L. Cheney, R.M. Seyfarth, R.W. Wrangham & T.T. Struhsaker. Chicago: Chicago University Press, pp. 342–57.

Wu, Rukang & Lin, Shenglong 1983. Peking Man. *Scientific American* 248, 86–94.

Wymer, J. 1974. Clactonian and Acheulian industries from Britain: their character and significance. *Proceedings of the Geological Association* 85, 391–421.

Wymer, J. 1988. Palaeolithic archaeology and the British Quaternary sequence. *Quaternary Science Reviews* 7, 79–98.

Wynn, T. 1979. The intelligence of later Acheulian hominids. *Man* 14, 371–91.

Wynn, T. 1981. The intelligence of Oldowan hominids. *Journal of Human Evolution* 10, 529–41.

Wynn, T. 1989. *The Evolution of Spatial Competence*. Urbana: University of Illinois Press.

Wynn, T. 1991. Tools, grammar and the archaeology of cognition. *Cambridge Archaeological Journal* 1, 191–206.

Wynn, T. 1993. Two developments in the mind of early *Homo*. *Journal of Anthropological Archaeology* 12, 299–322.

Wynn, T. 1995. Handaxe enigmas. *World Archaeology* 27, 10–23.

Wynn, T. & McGrew, W.C. 1989. An ape's view of the Oldowan. *Man* 24, 383–98.

Wynn, T. & Tierson, F. 1990. Regional comparison of the shapes of later Acheulean handaxes. *American Anthropologist* 92, 73–84.

Yellen, J.E. 1977. *Archaeological Approaches to the Present*. New York: Academic Press.

Yellen, J.E., Brooks, A.S., Cornelissen, E., Mehlman, M.J. & Steward, K. 1995. A Middle Stone Age worked bone industry from Katanda, Upper Semliki Valley, Zaire. *Science* 268, 553–56.

Yen, D.E. 1989. The domestication of the environment. In *Foraging and Farming: The Evolution of Plant Exploitation*, eds., D.R. Harris & G.C. Hillman, pp. 55–78. London: Unwin Hyman.

Yi, S. & Clark, G. 1983. Observations on the Lower Palaeolithic of Northeast Asia. *Current Anthropology* 24, 181–203.

Yost, J.A. & Kelley, P.M. 1983. Shotguns, blowguns and spears: the analysis of technological efficiency. In *Adaptive Responses of Native Amazonians*, eds., R. Hames & W. Vickers, pp. 189–224. New York: Academic Press.

Zhonglong, Q. 1992. The stone industries of *H. sapiens* from China. In *The Evolution and Dispersal of Modern Humans in Asia*, eds., T. Akazawa, K. Aoki & T. Kimura, pp. 363–72. Tokyo: Hokusen-Sha.

Zollikofer, C.P.E., Ponce de Leon, M.S., Martin, R.D. & Stucki, P. 1995. Neanderthal computer skulls. *Nature* 375, 283–84.

Zvelebil, M. 1984. Clues to recent human evolution from specialised technology. *Nature* 307, 314–15.

Zvelebil, M. 1986. Postglacial foraging in the forests of Europe. *Scientific American* (May), 86–93.

Zvelebil, M. 1994. Plant use in the Mesolithic and the transition to farming. *Proceedings of the Prehistoric Society* 60, 35–74.

Illustration credits

Figures

1. Illustration by Steven Mithen using data from Aiello & Dunbar (1993); upper figure modified from Aiello (1996b).
2. Drawing by Margaret Mathews, after Saladin D'Angular (1990).
3. Drawing by Margaret Mathews, after McGrew (1992).
4. Illustration by Margaret Mathews and Steven Mithen.
5. Drawing by Margaret Mathews, modified from Schick & Toth (1993).
6. Illustration by Steven Mithen.
7. Drawing by Aaron Watson.
8. Drawing by Aaron Watson.
9. Drawing by Margaret Mathews, after Jones *et al* (1992).
10. Illustration by Margaret Mathews and Steven Mithen.
11. Drawing by Margaret Mathews.
12. Drawing by Margaret Mathews.
13. Drawing by Aaron Watson.
14. Drawing by Aaron Watson.
15. Illustration by Margaret Mathews and Steven Mithen.
16. Illustration by Margaret Mathews and Steven Mithen.
17. Illustration by Margaret Mathews and Steven Mithen.
18. Drawing by Margaret Mathews, based on a photograph by A. Marshack in *National Geographic* 174 (1988).
19. Drawing by Margaret Mathews, after Delluc & Delluc (1978).
20. Drawing by Margaret Mathews, after Mania, D. & Mania, U. (1988). Deliberate engravings on bone artefacts by *Homo erectus*, *Rock Art Research* 5: 91–107.
21. Drawing by Margaret Mathews, after Breuil (1952).
22. Drawing by Simon S. S. Driver, in Fagan, B. (1990) *Journey from Eden* (London & New York: Thames and Hudson).
23. Drawing by Margaret Mathews, after Bahn & Vertut (1989).
24. Drawing by Margaret Mathews, after Marshack (1991).
25. Illustration by Margaret Mathews and Steven Mithen.
26. Illustration by Margaret Mathews and Steven Mithen.
27. Illustration by Margaret Mathews and Steven Mithen.
28. Drawing by Margaret Mathews, modified from Schick & Toth (1993).
29. Drawing by Margaret Mathews, after Jones *et al* (1992).
30. Drawing by Margaret Mathews, after Jones *et al* (1992).
31. Drawing by Margaret Mathews, after Jones *et al* (1992).
32. Drawing by Margaret Mathews, after Jones *et al* (1992).
33. Illustration by Margaret Mathews and Steven Mithen.
34. Drawing by Margaret Mathews, after Wendorf *et al* (1980).
35. Drawing by Aaron Watson.
36. Drawing by Margaret Mathews, after Piette (1906).

Boxes

p. 14. Illustration by Steven Mithen.
pp. 24–5. Drawings by Margaret Mathews, after Jones *et al* (1992).
pp. 26–7. Drawings by Margaret Mathews, (from top to bottom) quartz flake, after Merrick & Merrick (1976); chopper, after Bordes (1968); pointed handaxe, after Roe (1981); Levallois flake and core, after Bordes (1968); the Clacton-on-Sea 'Spear', after Oakley, K. (1949) *Man the Tool-maker* (London: Trustees of the British Museum (Natural History)); blade core, after Bordes (1968); bone harpoon, after Bordes (1968); the 'Willendorf Venus', after Marshack (1991).
p. 28. Drawing by Margaret Mathews.
p. 29. Drawing by Margaret Mathews.
p. 30. Drawing by Margaret Mathews.
p. 31. Illustration by Steven Mithen, modified from Wood (1993).
p. 32. Illustration by Steven Mithen, after Stringer & Gamble (1993).
p. 67. Illustration by Steven Mithen.
p. 127. Drawings by Margaret Mathews, after Shea (1988) and Oswalt (1973).
p. 158. Drawings by Margaret Mathews, after Morphy (1989) and Leroi-Gourhan (1968).
p. 163. Illustration by Steven Mithen.
p. 166. Illustration by Steven Mithen.
p. 175. Drawing by Margaret Mathews, after Cunliffe (1994).
Box pp. 196–97. Illustration by Steven Mithen.
Box p 198. Illustration by Steven Mithen.

Index

Numerals in italics refer to pages with illustrations

Aborigines, Australian 47; art of 157–59, 232; *158*; attitude to landscape 48, 166, 188–89; Dreamtime of 176; environmental manipulation by 225–26; *see also* Ancestral Beings
Abri Pataud 254, 256
Abu Hureyra 218, 220, 222
Aegyptopithecus 202; *199*
agriculture, origins of 10, 11, 16, 210, 216–26
Aiello, Leslie 12, 103, 111, 133, 140, 144, 206, 208
Altamira 156
Americas, colonization of 23, 30, 178; *30*
analogy 39, 41, 70; role in science 214–15
Ancestral Beings 159, 232, 253, 254; intuitive knowledge 176
animal tracks 80, 104, 236, 253–54; in cave art 172; as natural symbols 161–62
anthropomorphism 48, 50; as predictor of animal behaviour 180, 255; compulsion for 234, 252; in art 164–67, 252, 254; *164, 166*
Apollo Cave 156
archaic *Homo sapiens* 20, 22, 25, 31, 116, 137, 242; *31*
art 11, 27, 154–63; *27*; Australian 157–59, 232; *158*; and climate 157, 252; definition of 154–59; Early Human 155, 161, 163, 253; *155, 156*; and information storage 170, 172–174; *172, 173*; origins of 159–163, 252; *163*
Atapuerca 25, 29, 249; *29*
Atran, Scott 52–3, 57, 196
Australia, Aboriginal rock art 157–59, 232; colonization of, 22, 30, 152, 178; *30*; Pleistocene rock art 252; *see also* Aborigines
australopithecines 31, 203–04; *199*
Australopithecus afarensis 19, 24, 31, 95, 203–05; *31, 205*
Australopithecus africanus 24, 19, 31; *31*
Australopithecus anamensis 19, 24, 31, 95; *31*
Australopithecus ramidus 10, 19, 24, 31, 95; *31*
autism 51–2, 54, 233

Babbage, Charles 27, 35
Bar-Yosef, Ofer, 221, 251
behavioural flexibility 103
Belfer-Cohen, Anna 221
belief-desire psychology, *see* intuitive psychology
Benedict, Ruth 197
Berlin, Brent 53
Bilzingsleben 26, 155, 160, 161; engraved rib from 155, 160–61; *161*
Binford, Lewis 101, 123, 134, 230, 245; *102*
bipedalism 24; and childbirth 192; consequences for language 208; evolution of

204–06
bird song 87
Bird-David, Nurit 47
blade technology 22, 27, 119, 152, 169; *27, 171*; pre-Upper Palaeolithic 243
Blumenschine, Robert 103
Boden, Margaret 58, 70, 154, 230
body decoration 22–3, 27; absence among chimpanzees 90; absence among Early Humans 135, 139; appearance of 156, 173; and red ochre 182; and social information 175, 233
Boesch, Christophe & Hedwige 74, 77, 79, 81, 89–91, 235
bone artifacts 21, 22, 27; *27, 173*; appearance of 169–70, 183; lack of Early Human 121–22, 130–31
Border Cave 25, 27, 182, 243
bottleneck (in human evolution) 183
Boxgrove 25, 26, 29, 118, 242, 248, 251; *29*
Boyer, Pascal 174–77, 196
brain size 11–12, 144; *12*; of chimpanzee 73; and diet 103; of Early Human children 193; and group size 106–07, 132–33; and language 110, 140; growth rate 192; and foraging 235, 236; and social complexity 241
brain structure 87, 109, 110, 141; *109*
Broca's area 109, 141, 242; *109*
burial 22; *175*; of Early Humans 135–36, 249; of *H. sapiens sapiens* 180, 182–83, 257; of dogs 229, 261
butchery, by chimpanzees 91; by *H. habilis* 99; by Neanderthals 126–28; by *H. sapiens sapiens* 137
Byrne, Richard 81, 83, 93, 106, 202, 237, 241

cartoons 50
cave art 23, 135; *see also* Chauvet Cave
Central Russian Plain 135, 168, 222, 261; dwellings on 27, 222; *223*
Chase, Phillip 126
Chauvet Cave 156, 161, 163, 164, 252
Cheney, Dorothy 93, 236
childbirth 192
chimpanzees 10, 73; *199*; foraging 78–81; hunting 79–81; 'language' 84–8, 92; mind of 89; *89*; tool making and use 74–8, 88–91, 92, 96, 235, 237; *74*; traditions 91, 76–7
Chomsky, Noam 44
Clacton-on-Sea 27, 121
Clactonian industry 139, 140, 243, 249
climate change 23, 32, 116, 125, 169, 219
cognitive archaeology 11, 13, 227
cognitive fluidity 70, 136; and anthropomorphism 166; *166*; and agriculture 222–26; and art 165; *163, 179*; and consciousness 190–92; and Early Modern Humans 178–83; and humour 195; *198*; and

language *189*; and Middle/Upper Palaeolithic transition 179; and racism 196–97; *197*; and religion 177–78; and science 213–15
Colton, Charles 115
Combe Grenal 121, 126–28, 167, 257, 259
common ancestor 10, 14, 17, 18, 106, 203; *31*
consciousness 9; of chimpanzees 91; and Early Human mind 147–50, 186; *113*; evolution of 52, 84, 190–92
Corballis, Michael 227
cortex, of brain 110, 237
Cosmides, Leda 14, 42–5, 47, 50, 203
Cotte, La 245, 248
creationists 10, 16, 215, 227, 232
creativity 39, 58–9, 81, 191, 230

D'Errico, Francesco 170, 214, 256
Dawkins, Richard 212, 214
de Waal, Franz 82, 110
Deacon, Terrance 110, 242
deception 81, 83, 106
Dederiyeh Cave 193, 249
Dennett, Daniel 108, 147, 148, 149, 215, 258
development, cognitive 51–8, 193–94; Early Human 25, 193–94; and Piaget 231
Devil's Tower 193
Dmanisi 25, 29; *29*
domestication of animals 224; *225*
Donald, Merlin 10, 227
Douglas, Mary 168–69, 255
Dry Creek 30; *30*
Dryopithecus 259
Dunbar, Robin 106, 110–11, 133, 135, 140, 142, 185, 187, 208, 236, 241, 248, 258, 260–61

Early Humans 15, 221; *138*; defined 116; mind of 115–50; *113*; *see also* Neanderthals; *H. erectus*; archaic *H. sapiens*; *H. heidelbergensis*
Early Modern Humans 151, 180, 183–84, 192–93, 209, 258; mind of 176, 180, 182–83, 194; *181*
Eastham, Michael and Anne 173
entoptics 253
endocasts 242
evolutionary psychology 13, 42, 45, 58, 59; *14*
evolution of human intelligence *211*

Falk, Dean 110, 204, 205
feasting 137
Fermat's last theorem 46–7
Ferrassie, La 136, 254
Flageolet, Abri du 254
FLK North I, Olduvai Gorge 105
FLK 22 Zinj, Olduvai Gorge 99, 240
Fodor, Jerry 37–9, 40, 41–2, 43, 45, 69, 153, 215, 231–32
food sharing 137; *100*, *102*; by chimpanzees 91, 114; *see also* provisioning
FxJj50, Koobi Fora 239

G/Wi 168, 255
Gamble, Clive 126, 128, 134, 135, 178, 230–31
Gardner, Beatrice 84

Gardner, Howard 39–42, 45, 57–8, 154
Geary, David 57, 234
Gelada baboons 111
Gellner, Ernest 49, 174, 233
Gesher Benot 27, 121
Gibson, Kathleen 62, 63, 235–36
Goodall, Jane 74, 196
gossip 187
Gough's Cave 196
Gould, Stephen Jay 62, 64
Greenfield, Patricia 56
Grimaldi 164
grooming 110–11, 140, 250
group size, and brain size 106–07, 133, 248; and environment 133–34, 241, 246; and grooming 111
Guthrie, Dale 244
Guattari, Grotta 128, 247, 248

Hadar 24, 28; *28*
Haeckel, Ernest 62, 231
hafting 122–23
handaxes 21, 26, 116, 150; *26*; function of 122, 243; manufacture of 36, 117–19, 160; *118*; variation in 123, 139–40, 242, 244
HAS site, Koobi Fora 99, 238
Haua Fteah 27
Hayden, Brian 223–24
Hillman, Gordon 220
Hohlenstein-Stadel, lion/man statuette from 155; *155*
Holocene 23
home bases 99, 101, 129, 238; *101*, *102*
Homo erectus 10, 15, 20, 25, 29, 31, 36, 105, 116, 117, 124, 132, 141, 144–45, 206, 207, 240; *25*, *31*, *145*
Homo ergaster 19, 24, 31, 240; *31*
Homo habilis 10, 15, 19–20, 24, 28, 31, 95–115, 148, 240; *31*, *113*
Homo heidelbergensis 20, 25, 116, 207, 249; *25*, *31*
Homo neanderthalensis see Neanderthals
Homo rudolfensis 19, 24, 31; *31*
Homo sapiens sapiens 10, 11, 13, 15, 17, 22, 25, 30, 31, 115, 151; *25*, *31*, *138*, *153*
Howieson's Poort industry 242, 258
human evolution *31*, *199*
humour 198
Humphrey, Nicholas 51–2, 81, 84, 147, 149–50, 190, 203, 206, 224–25, 237
hypothesis testing 84, 104, 214

imagination 35, 38
imitation 77; *see also* learning, social
Ingold, Tim 48–9, 167, 233
intelligence, general 46, 56, 64, 66, 69, 74, 78, 88, 91, 92, 97, 112, 131, 132, 137, 139, 185–86, 191, 200–01; linguistic 40, 69; *see also* language; Machiavellian 81, 82, 90; *see also* social intelligence; multiple 39–41, 64; natural history 68, 78, 81, 99, 105, 123–130, 206; social 68, 81, 88, 92–4, 106–08, 113, 130–42, 147, 187, 202–03; specialized 13–14, 66–9; technical 68, 78, 92, 96–8, 117–21, 160–61,

206, 242
intentionality, orders of 108; in marking 161; in tool manufacture 98, 117–19; *see also* handaxes; Levallois flakes/points
intuitive knowledge 50; and biology 52–4; and physics 54–5, 77; and psychology 51–2
Inuit 47; and polar bear 48, 188, 232–33; *48*; technology 126–27, 131, 244; *127*
IQ test 34
Isaac, Glynn 21, 99–102, 123, 230, 238; *100, 102*

Java 25, 29

Kada Gona 26
Kalahari Bushmen 47, 168
Kanapoi 24
Kanzi 86–7, 97, 237, 238
Karmiloff-Smith, Annette 56–9, 60, 64, 69, 70, 154, 188, 193, 234
Katanda 27, 183
Kebara 25, 26, 119, 136, 141, 178, 246
Keil, Frank 52
Kesem-Kebana 26
Klasies River Mouth 182, 243, 246, 258
Klein, Richard 123, 163
knapping experiments 118–19
Knecht, Heidi 255
Knight, Chris 182, 192, 249
KNM-ER 1470 24, 110, 113; *113*; *see also H. habilis*
KNM-WT 15000 25, 144, 145; *145*; *see also H. erectus*
Koestler, Arthur 58
Konso-Gardula 26
Koobi Fora 24, 26, 28, 239; *28*
Kuhn, Steve 247
Kuhn, Thomas 215, 260
!Kung 168
Kunwinjku 253

Laetoli 204; *28*
Lake, Mark 107, 212, 260
language 40, 56, 69, 86–8, 149; and brain structure 108–11; and cognitive fluidity 185–87; *189*; of Early Humans 140–42, 250; evolution of 208–09; and Middle/Upper Palaeolithic transition 227, 251; *see also* chimpanzee 'language'
Lascaux 156, 164
Leakey, Mary 26
learning 34, 44, 46, 77; laboratory tests of 197, 200; social learning 114, 235; *see also* imitation
Lehringen 121
Lepenski Vir 165
Leroi-Gourhan, Andre 257
Levallois flakes/points 21, 26, 116, 152, 160; *26*; manufacture of 119–21, 144; *120*; refitting and replication 242; use for hunting 122, 246, 257
Levi-Strauss, Claude 165
Lewis-Williams, David 253
Lokalalei 26, 238

Longgupu Cave 27, 29, 240; *29*
Lower Palaeolithic 21
Lucy, *see Australopithecus afarensis*

Maastricht-Belvédère 120, 242, 248
Makapansgat 28; *28*
Malakunanja 30; *30*
Mal'ta 30, 173, 256; *30*
Marler, Peter 87
Marshack, Alexander 170, 253, 256
Mas d'Azil, spearthrower from 170, 172; *172*
mathematics 46, 57, 234
Mauer 25
Mauran 245
Mbuti 47
McGrew, Bill 74, 75, 76, 97
Meadowcroft 30, 229; *30*
meat eating, and brain size 206, 207; by *H. habilis* 99–105; *100, 102*; and language 208
Mellars, Paul 134
memory 79, 259, 231, 236
mental maps, of chimpanzees 79, 81; of *H. habilis* 105; of Neanderthals 129; triggered by art 173
Mesolithic 256, 261
metaphor 41, 70; in science 214–15, 261
metarepresentation, module of (MMR) 59–60, 142, 188
Middle Awash 24, 28; *28*
Middle/Upper Palaeolithic transition 151, 152, 153, 154, 177, 178, 182, 184, 194, 250–51
Milton, Katherine 201, 235–36
mind, as a cathedral 61, 65–72, 92, 112, 114, 146, 147, 151; *67*; as a computer 13, 34–5, 43, 212–13, 230; as a sponge 34–5, 43; as a Swiss army knife 14, 37, 38, 40, 42–5, 49, 50, 55, 57, 58, 59, 60, 79, 148, 150, 231; as a 'tabula-rasa' 14, 230
mind-body problem 9, 230
mind reading 68; *see also* theory of mind
missing link *see* common ancestor
MNK Main-II, Olduvai Gorge 105, 240
modules, mental 13, 37–9; of chimpanzees 88, 93–4; development of 56–7, 88; evolution of 42–5; *see also* intuitive knowledge; intelligence; mind
Mojokerto 29; *29*
Monte Verde 30, 229; *30*

Nagel, Thomas 150
Nariokotome boy, *see* KNM-WT 15000
Natufian 221, 223
natural selection 42, 65, 187, 207, 212, 234–35
Neanderthals 10, 11, 15, 21, 22, 23, 25, 31, 116, 117 132, 137; anatomy and demography 25, 126, 141, 243, 245, 246; *25, 31*; burial 135–36, 180, 249; child development 193–94; consciousness 147–50; foraging 125–30, 180; hunting 128, 129–30, 245, 246; language 140–142; manual dexterity 243; mind 143; *143*; technology 119–23, 126–27, 242–48; *127*; vocal tract 141, 250
needles 22, 27, 129

neotany 63
Nihewan 29; *29*
Notharctus 200, 202; *201*
Nunamiut 168

Oldowan industry 20, 26, 96–8, 113, 117, 120, 237–38; raw materials for 237
Olduvai Gorge 24, 26, 28, 96, 103, 105, 237, 240; *28*
Oleneostrovski Mogilnik 166, 254
Olorgesailie 26, 240, 244, 248–49
Omo 26, 28; *28*
Omo industry 26, 98
Oring, Eliot 198
Oswalt, Wendell 127
Oxygen isotope stages 32; *32*

Paranthropus 24, 31; *24, 31*
Pelegrin, Jacques 118
'petit mal' seizure 149, 191
Pfeiffer, John 166, 172
Piaget, Jean 36–7, 62, 231
Pinker, Steven 86, 87, 227, 242
Pleistocene 20, 34, 43, 47; fauna 125, 244; vegetation 244
plesiadapiforms 196, 200
Plesiadapis 196; *199*
Pontnewydd Cave 25, 26, 124, 207
Potts, Richard 101, 239, 249
Powers, Camilla 182
Premack, David 83, 85
Proconsul 202; *199, 202*
Prolom II 258
provisioning 209, 192–93
Purgatorius 195–96

Qafzeh 25, 178, 180, 181, 246, 257

racism 196–97
recapitulation 36, 56, 62–4, 231
red ochre 22, 27, 135, 160, 182, 192, 249
representational redescription 57–8, 59, 64
religion 174–78
Riera, La 255
Riwat 29, 240
Roc de Combe 254
Rozin, Paul 59, 154, 190

Sacks, Oliver 53–4
Saint Césaire 25
Sangiran 29; *29*
San Vincenzo 61, 71
Sant'Agostino, Grotta di 128
Savage-Rumbaugh, Sue 85–6
scavenging 20, 103, 126, 129, 137, 240, 244, 247; marginal 101; identifying 238–39; *102*
Schacter, Daniel 191
Schlanger, Nathan 120
science 213–15; definition of 260–61
Sclayn 248
Searle, John 191
sedentism 221, 261
Seyfarth, Robert 93, 236

Shanidar 134, 136, 143, 224, 249
Shea, John 249
Skhūl 25, 178, 180, 257
Soffer, Olga 135, 168, 222, 244–45, 256
Spelke, Elizabeth 54–5, 57, 58, 64, 70, 154
Sperber, Dan 59, 60, 70, 142, 154, 188, 190
Sterkfontein 28, 120, 238; *28*
Stiner, Mary 247
stone cache hypothesis 101–02, 239
storage 245, 256
Straus, Lawrence 168, 169, 255, 256
style 252–53
Sungir 174, 175, 196; *175*
Swartkrans 28, 241; *28*
symbolism 209; in tool making 257

Tabūn 25, 26, 121, 178
Taï plaque 170, 173, 256; *173*
Tata 160
Taung 241; *28*
teaching 90, 190, 259
technounits 75
Terra Amata 121
Terrace, Herbert 85
Teshik Tash 136
thematic relations hypothesis 187
theory of mind 51, 84, 132, 233, 234, 237; *see also* autism; intelligence, social
Tooby, John 42–5, 47, 203
totemism 48, 164–67; *166*
Toth, Nicholas 97, 98
transport, of artifacts 104–05, 239, 247; of foodstuffs 101; of hammerstones 79; of raw materials 239, 247
Trinkaus, Erik 245, 246
Trois-Frères, Les 164, 176, 224, 254; sorcerer from 164, 176; *164*

Ùbeidiya 26, 29, 249–50; *29*
Upper Palaeolithic 22, 119, 132; hunting 167–70, 254–55
Upper Swan River 30; *30*

Valley Bisa 168, 248
vervet monkeys 236
Villa, Paola 130
vocal tract, reconstruction of, *see* Neanderthal
Vogelherd 252

Wadi Kubbaniya 217, 222, 261; plant processing at 218; *218*
Walpiri 157, 253
Washoe 84–5
Wernicke's area 109, 242; *109*
Wheeler, Peter 103, 204, 206
White, Randall 134, 251
Whiten, Andrew 51, 81, 83, 93, 202, 203
Wiles, Andrew 46–7
Wopkaimin 173, 256–57
Wrangham, Richard 78
Wynn, Thomas 36–7, 62, 97, 150, 231

Zhoukoudian 25, 27, 244